Vicky Davis received her PhD from the School of Slavonic and East European Studies, University College London (UCL) and currently works as a freelance educational consultant and researcher. Davis has worked with a number of leading academics in her role as a researcher, including Roger Moorhouse on *The Devils' Alliance: Hitler's Pact with Stalin, 1939–1941* (2014) and for Polly Jones, Associate Professor of Russian Literature at the University of Oxford, on several Soviet history projects. She has also published and presented in peer-reviewed journals, edited collections and at international conferences. There is a section dedicated to her research on myth and war memory at the State Historical Museum in Novorossiisk, Russia.

'Using the example of Malaia zemlia, Davis deftly dissects the Soviet Union's wartime myth making, laying bare the processes by which myths were propagated and maintained. Thoughtful and thought-provoking, this is a profound and significant study.'

Roger Moorhouse, author of *The Devils' Alliance: Hitler's Pact with Stalin, 1939–1941*

'In his ghost-written memoirs that describe his participation in the Great Patriotic War, Leonid Brezhnev describes the area around Novorossiisk as "great", for these "little lands (Malaia zemlia in Russian)" became "soaked with the blood of heroes devoted to their cause". These "little lands" have been bound up ever since in Brezhnev's myth making attempts, seen as a sideshow to the real war fought elsewhere and dismissed as part of the bombastic war cult Brezhnev helped to construct during his years in power. In this outstanding new history, Vicky Davis takes us beyond these notions. She examines Novorossiisk as a case study in how a war myth develops and how it evolves across time. In doing so, Davis expands our understanding of the Great Patriotic War in memory and provides a much-needed local story of how the war myth functioned outside of the capitals. Davis listens to locals in Novorossiisk, allowing their voices to be heard in this story. *Myth Making in the Soviet Union and Modern Russia* traces the emergence of a local, multivalent memory culture of the campaign that predated Brezhnev's memoir and that has had remarkable staying power in the city itself.'

Stephen M. Norris, Professor of History, Miami University

'The World War II campaign in Russia is little known to the Western reader, but became the inspiration for this British historian's reflections on the interrelationship of historic myth, cultural values, politics and ideology. Through the prism of local history, Vicky Davis not only offers an original perspective on postwar and modern Russia but also touches upon the acute methodological problems of studying historic memory. The book gives strong impetus to think about the interrelation of sincere human feelings and politics. For the Russian reader, to whom the Great Patriotic War remains sacred, some of the comments may seem controversial, but without doubt, this book will be of interest to both specialists and the general reader.'

Irina Lapshina, Professor of Modern and Contemporary History and Head of the World History Department, Vladimir State University

'Vicky Davis's book is a fascinating insight into the way different stakeholders attempt to shape the memory of historic events, and the continuing importance of World War II in Russian identity. Through painstaking research in archives and on the ground, including many interviews, Davis's study reminds us that commemoration and remembrance create competing, overlapping and conflicting narratives, and although a dominant version of the past may emerge, it never achieves total acceptance and legitimacy. Her study is of value to both specialists in Russia and the Slavonic world, and those interested in war memory and commemoration.'

Mark Connelly, Professor of Modern British History, University of Kent

Library of Modern Russia

Building on I.B.Tauris' established record publishing Russian studies titles for both academic and general readers, the Library of Modern Russia will showcase the work of emerging and established writers who are setting new agendas in the field.

At a time when potentially dangerous misconceptions and misunderstandings about Russia abound, titles in the series will shed fresh light and nuance on Russian history. Volumes will take the idea of 'Russia' in its broadest, cultural sense and cover the entirety of the multi-ethnic lands that made up imperial Russia and the Soviet Union. Ranging in chronological scope from the Romanovs to the present day, the books will foster a community of scholars and readers devoted to a sharper understanding of the Russian experience, past and present.

New and forthcoming

Building Stalinism: The Moscow Canal and the Creation of Soviet Space, Cynthia Ruder
Criminal Subculture in the Gulag: Prisoner Society in the Stalinist Labour Camps, Mark Vincent
Dissident Histories in the Soviet Union: From De-Stalinization to Perestroika, Barbara Martin
Fascism in Manchuria: The Soviet–China Encounter in the 1930s, Susanne Hohler
Ideology and the Arts in the Soviet Union: The Establishment of Censorship and Control, Steven Richmond
Myth Making in the Soviet Union and Modern Russia: Remembering World War II in Brezhnev's Hero City, Vicky Davis
Nomads and Soviet Rule: Central Asia under Lenin and Stalin, Alun Thomas
Power and Conflict in Russia's Borderlands: The Post-Soviet Geopolitics of Dispute Resolution, Helena Rytövuori-Apunen
Power and Politics in Modern Chechnya: Ramzan Kadyrov and the New Digital Authoritarianism, Karena Avedissian
Russia in the Time of Cholera: Disease under Romanovs and Soviets, John P. Davis
Russian Pilgrimage to the Holy Land: Piety and Travel from the Middle Ages to the Revolution, Nikolaos Chrissidis
Science City, Siberia: Akademgorodok and the Late Soviet Politics of Expertise, Ksenia Tartachenko
Soviet Americana: The Cultural History of Russian and Ukrainian Americanists, Sergei Zhuk
Stalin's Economic Advisors: The Varga Institute and the Making of Soviet Foreign Policy, Kyung Deok Roh
The Communist Party in the Russian Civil War: A Political History, Gayle Lonergan
The Idea of Russia: The Life and Work of Dmitry Likhachev, Vladislav Zubok
The Politics of Football in Soviet Russia: Sport and Society after Stalin, Manfred Zeller
The Russian State and the People: Power, Corruption and the Individual in Putin's Russia, Geir Hønneland *et al.* (eds)
The Tsar's Armenians: A Minority in Late Imperial Russia, Onur Önol

MYTH MAKING IN THE SOVIET UNION AND MODERN RUSSIA

Remembering World War II in Brezhnev's Hero City

VICKY DAVIS

I.B. TAURIS
LONDON · NEW YORK

To the people of Novorossiisk

Published in 2018 by
I.B.Tauris & Co. Ltd
London • New York
www.ibtauris.com

Library of Modern Russia 4

ISBN: 978 1 78453 948 1
eISBN: 978 1 78672 273 7
ePDF: 978 1 78673 273 6

A full CIP record for this book is available from the British Library
A full CIP record is available from the Library of Congress

Library of Congress Catalog Card Number: available

Typeset in Garamond Three by OKS Prepress Services, Chennai, India
Printed and bound by CPI Group (UK) Ltd, Croydon, CR0 4YY

MIX
Paper from responsible sources
FSC® C013604
www.fsc.org

CONTENTS

LIST OF ILLUSTRATIONS

Maps

Figures

Graphs

Table

PREFACE

On my very first morning in Novorossiisk in 1999 I was taken to the huge Malaia zemlia memorial complex on the shore of the Black Sea, where I heard the story of the 1943 landings. Over the years I gradually became familiar with other monuments around the town as my visits evolved from purely professional to social. My desire to understand the language and culture of the country prompted me to become a (very) mature student, enrolling for an undergraduate degree in Russian Studies at the School of Slavonic and East European Studies, University College London. Developing a growing interest in Russian monumental remembrance, I started to explore the sociological aspects of commemorative rituals with the help of my Russian colleagues who had, over the years, become close friends.

My epiphany moment came after a few glasses together at a vineyard in Myskhako, a small village just outside Novorossiisk known for its robust red wine. We were touring the modest wine-making premises when I found myself in an old wine cellar that had, apparently, been used by Colonel Leonid Brezhnev during the war – not for the purposes of storing wine, but as his military headquarters. Until that moment I had been confident that I understood the Malaia zemlia campaign enough to appreciate the significance of the many monuments in the town, but this discovery nine years after my first visit was totally unexpected. After all, Brezhnev was one of the few Soviet politicians familiar to people in the West, so why didn't I know about Brezhnev's involvement with the war here, despite my known interest in the town's past? And if I hadn't been told, perhaps there was a deeper reason why he remained a hidden secret in the history of this hero city. Here, tucked away under the former Soviet collective vineyard on the outskirts of Novorossiisk, I discovered a ready-made research project for the postgraduate programme I was following, which stimulated my academic interest so much that it has been impossible to put aside.

Over the last nine years my journey of intellectual curiosity has evolved from how society remembers the war to the political history of why war memory is so prevalent in Novorossiisk, resulting in a quest to explore the impact of their local history on the population today.

This book was researched during several trips to Novorossiisk between 2010 and 2016, supported by an AHRC award and a field research grant from BASEES. Early visits confirmed that this was going to develop into a multidisciplinary project, with historical, cultural, geopolitical and sociological dimensions. From archival work on war correspondence and war memoirs, my research moved on to a sustained overview of the press in Novorossiisk from 1943 to the present. I have been moved when attending many rituals of commemoration from year to year, and have become familiar with battle sites and monuments, museums and libraries, large and small. Perhaps the most interesting aspect of my research for this book has been the weeks spent in schools over the years and the privilege of conducting extended personal interviews with well over a hundred inhabitants of Novorossiisk, very many of whom I have come to know well.

Throughout this academic journey I have been aided by a wonderful and ever-expanding network of generous friends, who have housed and fed me, guided me to outlying places, rescued me from libraries, introduced me to key people and provided premises for meetings and interviews. They even brought valuable resource materials to England, crammed into suitcases already full of Russian chocolates (for stamina) and caviar (for inspiration). I am delighted to acknowledge the friendship of Anna Danilova, Irina Nikitina, El'vina Settarova, Sergei Krasnolobov and Irina Rashkovetskaia (and their families), without whose unstinting help this work would not have come to fruition. I would like to thank my supervisors at SSEES over the years for their support and sound advice: Kristin Roth-Ey, Polly Jones and Sarah Young; and all those who have kindly read and commented constructively on my work, especially my editor Tom Stottor. Finally I am deeply grateful to my family for their encouragement and for living this project with me for longer than we all care to remember.

NOTES ON THE TEXT

Compared with most major hero cities, Novorossiisk remains a provincial town in character with a current population of just over 240,000 citizens.[1] I have chosen throughout the book to call Novorossiisk a town rather than a city, as its official title may suggest. The Russian word is the same in both cases (*gorod*), but Novorossiisk still does not possess the characteristics nor the population of a large, impersonal city. Society is relatively closed, based around communities in various areas of the town and several outlying villages.

All translations from the Russian are mine, unless quoted from other sources in English. Transliteration is according to the *Slavonic and East European Review* system, based on a modified Library of Congress convention. The only exceptions are the pseudonyms of interview subjects, where I have tried to render names more accessible for the Anglophone reader.

Short sections of Part II and an earlier version of Chapter 10 have previously been published and are reproduced here with permission.[2]

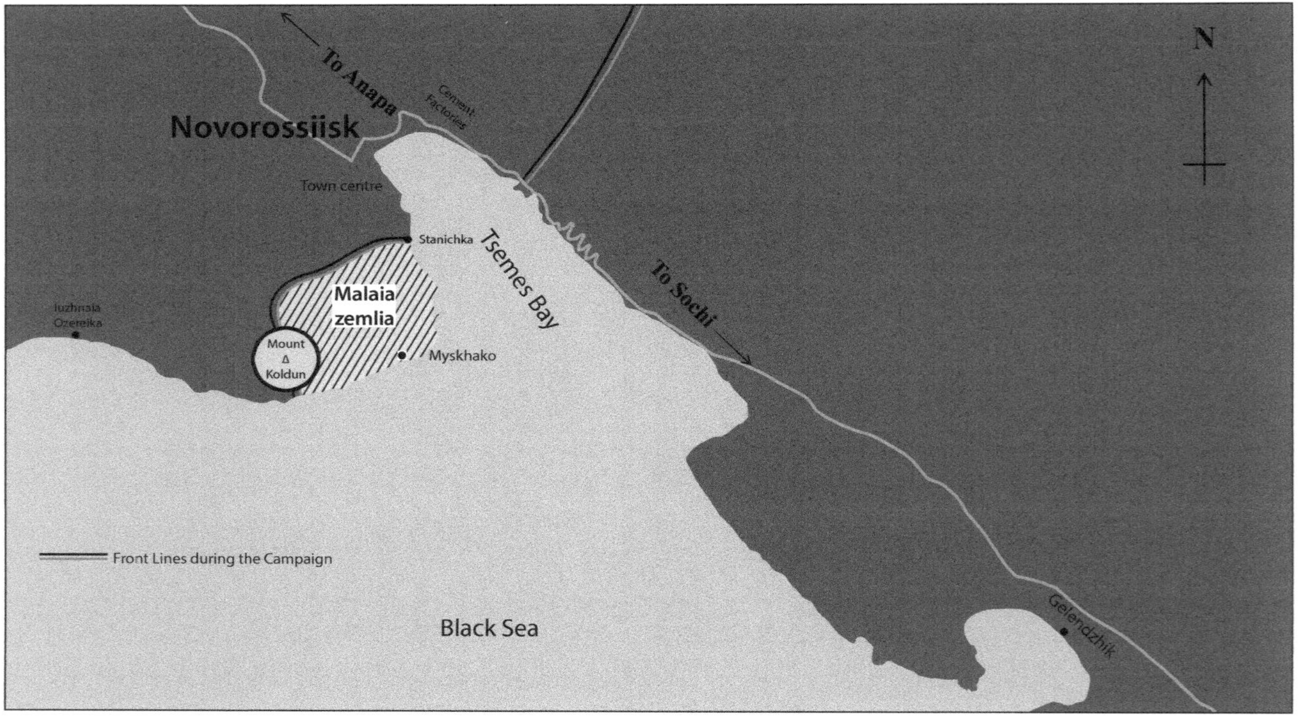

Map 1 The Novorossiisk area of the Krasnodar Region

INTRODUCTION

THE MYTH OF MALAIA ZEMLIA

Возложите на море венки.
Есть такой человечий обычай –
в память воинов, в море погибших,
возлагают на море венки.

Возложите на море венки
под свирель, барабан и сирены.
Из жасмина, из роз, из сирени
возложите на море венки.

Возложите на Время венки,
в этом вечном огне мы сгорели.
Из жасмина, из белой сирени
на огонь возложите венки.[1]

In the wintry early hours of 4 February 1943 a modest fleet of small craft escorted by two motor torpedo boats approached the shore of Tsemes Bay under cover of darkness and a thick smoke-screen. Before daybreak 630 Red Army marine infantry troops led by Major Tsezar' Kunikov had landed on the beach at Stanichka just outside the occupied Soviet Black Sea port of Novorossiisk.[2]

The Soviet Union had officially entered World War II, which it called the Great Patriotic War, in June 1941, suffering a series of humiliating losses for much of the first year as German forces pushed eastwards into the country. The strategic port of Novorossiisk, with a prewar population of 109,000,[3] was occupied by German and Romanian troops striking towards the oil-fields of the northern Caucasus in September 1942. However, it was not until the invaders had been defeated at Stalingrad early in 1943 that a turning point was reached and the battle to re-take Novorossiisk could begin in earnest. The main Soviet attack was directed at a spot further west along the coast, at Iuzhnaia Ozereika. However, this operation failed under heavy enemy fire and, ironically, it was the minor, diversionary landings at Stanichka which were successful. For seven months a defensive Soviet campaign by the North Caucasian 18th Army was fought against superior enemy forces from the small beach-head in the area behind Stanichka and the village of Myskhako that became known as Malaia zemlia (the 'Small Land'). Novorossiisk was finally liberated on 16 September 1943 following a brief concerted attack by Soviet land, sea and air forces.

The heroes of this localised campaign are still remembered today through an amalgam of memoirs, monuments and ritual. This

Map 2 The Novorossiisk Landings, 4 February 1943. Reproduced with the permission of Novorossiiskii istoricheskii muzei-zapovednik

commemoration is rendered particularly paradoxical by the discrepancy between the relative insignificance of the campaign at the time and the importance attributed to it retrospectively, largely because a certain Colonel Leonid Il'ich Brezhnev visited Malaia zemlia occasionally as leader of the 18th Army's political section. In 1964, 21 years after the Malaia zemlia campaign, Brezhnev became general secretary of the Communist Party of the Soviet Union and the de facto leader of the country. Once Brezhnev was in power, Novorossiisk became increasingly prominent on the political map of the country. It appears to have been honoured as a Hero City of the Soviet Union in 1973 largely due to Brezhnev's political influence and the town found further dubious fame in 1978 after the publication of his slim volume of war memoirs, *Malaia zemlia*. The longstanding and complex cultural heritage of remembrance which has been constructed around the war myth that eventually built up is the subject of this book.

The relevance of the war myth in Novorossiisk is not only confined to one provincial town in southern Russia, however. This book has far wider political and social connotations, linking individual citizens with evolving state policy in the Soviet Union and modern Russia since the war. Through the prism of this minor hero city I reveal the complexity of myth and memory, bringing new evidence to bear on a myth that most Russians consider dead, along with Brezhnev and the Soviet Union.

There is a substantial difference between the understanding of Malaia zemlia nationally and locally and a continuing inconsistency between the self-projected image of the hero city and the perception of Novorossiisk held by Russians elsewhere in the country. Rather than consigning this Soviet myth to the past, I trace the complex trajectory of its associated memoirs, monuments and memorial practices into the present and beyond, as I explore the meaning of the myth of Malaia zemlia for today's Novorossiisk. War memory in the states of the former Soviet Union is increasingly relevant for today's political agenda and is therefore becoming an important area for scholarly study.[4] This work is particularly timely, coming just as the Great Patriotic War in Russia is on the cusp of transition from living memory to history.

I examine how a local war myth was constructed and propagated in an authoritarian national context, largely thanks to the overriding influence of Brezhnev and his regime. The war myth of Malaia zemlia is unique, in view of the strategic insignificance of the campaign in comparison with other major and prolonged actions within the Soviet Union, such as the Battles of Stalingrad and Moscow, or the sieges of Leningrad and Sevastopol'. Despite this, Malaia zemlia became an overpowering mythical construct to the extent that it was for decades politically impossible to establish the historical facts behind the popular narrative. Previous Western historians and Soviet dissident scholars have dismissed Brezhnev's promotion of Malaia zemlia with more than a hint of ridicule, regarding the myth as at best an exercise in over-inflated self-promotion and at worst a fabricated work of fiction, as do many older citizens of other parts of Russia.[5] In contrast, this book focuses on how Malaia zemlia is regarded by Novorossiisk residents of all ages, for whom the myth is based on living memory and remains an integral part of the town's identity. The more positive attitude of the local community to the myth is just as valid as the dismissive top-down perspective, adding much-needed texture to existing oversimplified views about the national myth of the Great Patriotic War.

Much has been written of the wartime history of major hero cities of the Soviet Union.[6] Provincial Novorossiisk, though, was an afterthought in the honours list, and, as such, stands out through its overt political links to Brezhnev during his 18 years as leader of the Soviet Union. And those links survive even today. Which other town in modern Russia would erect a statue to Brezhnev in the twenty-first century – a complete mystery to puzzled Russians elsewhere in the country – and then keep it hidden from Western visitors? This book therefore offers an alternative perspective on Brezhnev through his close connection with Novorossiisk. It furthers the existing political science of the Brezhnev era by addressing his regime's war cult from a local perspective to give a more balanced picture of the mechanism and dynamics of myth making, showing how ideology interacted with and affected the ordinary, provincial citizen.

It is also an analysis of the personal influence of Brezhnev, the ultimate representative of the communist ideology of the collective, on the town where he saw war service. Just as there is a tension between the understanding of Western and dissident historians on the one hand, and the residents of Novorossiisk on the other, as to the significance of Malaia zemlia, there is also a polarity in the judgment of Brezhnev himself.

I challenge the latent assumption in the West of a monolithic Soviet state, showing that the dynamics of the myth-making process are not clear-cut, but more complicated and interesting than previously assumed. Brezhnev's memoirs, written from the point of view of the country's leader, were not the only account of the Malaia zemlia campaign. Local war memoirs published before and after Brezhnev's seminal work offer an intriguing insight into state influence on the form and content of memoir literature in the Soviet period. This is a genre rarely deemed significant enough for in-depth study, and yet, in this case, it offers an important complementary view of the war in the Soviet Union through its focus on the ordinary front-line soldier or sailor in action.

Even in a top-down remembrance environment, there was still scope for local groups and individuals to make an impact on commemorative ceremonies in the Soviet era. The close involvement of residents in decisions regarding the monumental landscape continues to this day, sometimes challenging the authorities and forcing changes of direction. And myth making is by no means just a phenomenon of the past. The interaction of the local war myth with the war cult which has emerged under President Vladimir Putin in the twenty-first century reveals how commemorative rituals continue to take on distinctly local forms, even if sometimes reflecting modes of remembrance found elsewhere in the world.

Brezhnev is not the only leader to have used war memory as a political tool. The war cults of two different eras have helped to shape the local war myth in Novorossiisk. By contextualising the current war cult in terms of the Soviet past, I make a necessary contribution to the wider political science of both the Brezhnev and the Putin regimes. The official view of the past in the Putinist present is key to the propagation of memory to a younger generation increasingly distanced from the war years. Understanding how Russians perceive and teach their history gives a valuable insight into political propaganda in action. I expose the complex dynamics of intergenerational transmission of the war myth, demonstrating the different ways in which the young people of today's Novorossiisk are introduced to the myth of Malaia zemlia from their very first days at school. I have found that a style of 'genetic' propagation is endemic in both Novorossiisk and even nationally, while the phenomenon of 'reverse propagation' from younger citizens to their parents and grandparents helps to cement the myth as part of the town's cultural heritage.

This analysis of the key modes of intergenerational transmission links the mechanism of myth making today with the maintenance and further development of a unique local identity to which most, if not all, residents of Novorossiisk subscribe. There comes a point, however, where a simplistic generalisation is not sufficient to convey the complexity of the war myth. Military personnel were not the only people killed in the war, but the fate of civilians is barely recognised in the local narrative. I demonstrate a polarity between the centralised celebration of the Soviet troops and the apparent collective amnesia on the outskirts relating to civilians, especially Jewish residents. Furthermore, I show that today's society is divided over its respect for fallen German soldiers and also displays an ambivalent attitude to the role of Cossacks in remembrance. Here, the case of Novorossiisk has much to bring to memorial situations elsewhere in the world, especially in once-occupied territories, where it is important to recognise the often silent voices sometimes smothered by an overwhelming public narrative. It is in the exceptions to the myth and the people still working on the periphery of official memory that the individual impact and intricacy of the myth of Malaia zemlia is to be found.

Sources and Methodology

The material I present in the following chapters was researched during several trips to Novorossiisk between 2010 and 2016, taking in archival and library work on war correspondence and memoirs, weeks of observation in schools, visits to monuments and battle sites and attendance at many rituals of commemoration from year to year.

I also conducted a close study of the local press in Novorossiisk dating from the war years to today. It is particularly challenging to interpret reports in Soviet newspapers, which were subject to the political control of the Communist Party. Newspapers may offer valuable evidence of the official state line at the time of publication, but it is difficult to measure the influence of newspaper propaganda on the ordinary Soviet citizen, whose attitude to key events was subject to ideological pressure and shaped by the pervading war cult. How was anybody to believe what was recorded in the press; and how can its impact on the individual citizen then be gauged today? Contemporaneous newspaper articles provide a testimony of past circumstances, subject to ideological manipulation by the state, past or present. It is not necessary for those today to *believe* what has been written in the past, merely to understand that it is this material that shaped the attitude of the people at that time. It may therefore be interpreted as a social construct of its time, the tangible product of propaganda in the Soviet Union and even modern Russia.

It is at the intersection of private memories and the collective, of the official and the unofficial, that I have uncovered a finely balanced equilibrium in the memorial relationship between the state, the local community and the individual. Much needed texture to my understanding of the impact of the local war myth was added by a series of extended personal interviews. These dynamic oral interviews complement the static information derived from the dry bones of dusty newspapers and long-standing monuments in shaping my understanding of individual remembrance and identity formation. Personal interviews help the researcher to get close to the individual within the collective and to establish areas of commonality or difference. They were largely intended as a valuable insight into current opinion and attitudes to remembrance of World War II on the personal level to inform the second half of this work. However, they produced much more than anticipated, revealing also historical perspectives on wartime Novorossiisk and Brezhnev's relationship with the town in the 1970s.

Interviews were conducted with two types of person: the ordinary Novorossiisk citizen and the specialist. In all, I spent time with 124 residents of Novorossiisk ranging in age from 18 to 93, and email exchanges over several years were conducted with ten respondents. Subjects had a wide range of backgrounds, including teachers and lecturers, students in higher education, military personnel, historians, librarians, architects, seamen, town councillors, journalists, divers, lawyers, shopkeepers, business people, housewives and pensioners. No jobseekers of working age or persons under the age of 18 were interviewed. My sample included slightly more females than males, largely because fewer men of working age were available for interview during working hours. This also reflects both natural demographics and the premature death of men who saw wartime service. Of the 124 interviewees, 55 were male and 69 were female, a ratio of 4:5, with males comprising 44 per cent of the total sample compared with 56 per cent for females. Details of the socio-economic class and approximate age distribution of these subjects are to be found in Appendix II, although it was sometimes necessary to make an informed estimate of the subject's age. In addition to these local interviews,

I interviewed briefly and on an ad hoc basis 35 subjects from places in Russia far removed from Novorossiisk in order to compare their understanding of Malaia zemlia with the attitude in Novorossiisk.

Although most interviewees seemed genuinely enthusiastic to talk to me, I was equally concerned to protect them and guarantee their anonymity. For this reason, pseudonyms are used throughout the book, except in the case of public figures and those experts who agreed to waive the right to anonymity. Some agreed to their name being mentioned if they were speaking in an official capacity, but asked that they remain anonymous in connection with any personal opinion expressed during the interview, a request which points to some possible tension between official and private opinion. Results were analysed with respect to gender, age cohort and occasionally to background.

I obtained access to a wide range of interviewees of various ages and ethnicities through the good offices of the Bekar School through which I invited parents and grandparents of pupils to a series of private meetings. A further large tranche of interviewees was introduced by key trusted colleagues. Access to expert interviewees and significant post-holders in the town was gained thanks to my professional network. Finally, many elderly interviewees were accessed thanks to the Veterans' Council in Myskhako. All interviewees were offered the chance to have a friend alongside them, which was usually not accepted, although in the case of older, potentially vulnerable volunteers, I insisted that a friend or relation was present.

In all interviews it is essential to build up a personal but professional relationship with the respondent. This is easier said than done when the subject is interviewed by a stranger, a foreigner to boot, from a different cultural and linguistic background. It is more comfortable to disclose potentially sensitive thoughts when in familiar surroundings, so all respondents were interviewed either at work, in their own home, at the Veterans' Council or in a public place of their choice. Those connected to the Bekar School were interviewed in an empty classroom there and one elderly lady chose the museum foyer for our meeting, perhaps subconsciously locating her memories of the past in a place where she felt they belonged.

Unlike the study of newspapers or monuments, live interviews demand attention to interpersonal dynamics. The ice was broken in many ways. English tea and light refreshments were offered to all those attending my classroom in the Bekar School, and I was invariably offered hospitality in the homes or offices of interviewees, which helped the conversation to flow more naturally. In a search for a common frame of reference, I often mentioned my family, especially my father who fought in the war on the same side as the Soviet Union, if in a different sphere of action. Photographs of where I lived helped bridge any geographical distance between us, although many subjects expressed surprise that somebody from as far away as England could be interested in the local history of a provincial Russian town. Many subjects referred positively to the fact that my results, obtained from an outsider's perspective, may render them more objective.

All interviews were conducted in Russian. However, such enormous cultural and linguistic barriers are not to be taken lightly and it is possible that I may have missed certain nuances in accounts. Would a Russian interviewer have been quicker to grasp these inferences? Were some subjects trying to put a positive spin on remembrance out of nationalistic pride? Elderly Marta initially accused me of being a spy, indicative not of a wartime alliance between our two countries, but rather of a Cold War hostility, only to agree after two hours of conversation that I was, after all, 'one of ours'. Similar suspicion was shown by one expert who only agreed to talk to me 'on the record' for brief periods of time. The rest of our conversation was not to be quoted, she ruled, displaying a tendency to restrict information and a lack of transparency common in the Soviet Union. Old habits die hard. It is evident, therefore, that care has to be taken with the interpretation of oral interviews. Cases where much reflection has been necessary are detailed in the text.

Discussions lasted from 30 minutes to three hours. Subjects were interviewed for an average of an hour: some very extensive, in-depth meetings with experts were balanced by a few shorter interviews with less forthcoming subjects. In practice I found that women were more than happy to talk to a female interviewer without any self-consciousness, whilst four men, who were rather hesitant about the experience at first, soon overcame their initial lack of confidence. 'We'll give it a try', offered Lev tentatively as we embarked on what turned out to be quite a lengthy conversation. More positively, several helpful subjects, both men and women, returned to me days after our initial meeting with further information and materials that they thought would be relevant.

My gradual integration into this parochial community improved as I was able to seek out and interview again many respondents over the years and build up a meaningful and trusting relationship with them.

No juveniles were interviewed for ethical reasons and precautions were taken to protect older subjects from potentially distressing memories. It was always stressed at the beginning of the interview that respondents were able to stop if they found the conversation difficult. In only one case did I terminate the interview prematurely when Diana, a relatively young lecturer, became distressed at the thought that young people today may fail to respect the memory of the war dead: she felt that this would be an indication of disrespect to her grandfather's generation.

In all cases I was interested in the respondent's own subjective discourse on remembrance. A few open-ended questions were used as the basis for extended discussions and to allow for the free flow of conversation. In general, subjects had the flexibility to speak in their own words and the time to develop their thoughts. My emphasis was on listening and observing the respondent, guiding the conversation a little if it lacked momentum. There was little real silence on the part of the respondents, although there was some pause for thought. I made no assumptions at the start of each interview and asked for explanations, even if I was already aware of the issues. In this way I was able to uncover new information, although it is important to bear in mind the fact that interviewees told me what they wanted me to hear and, possibly, what they thought I wanted to hear. In contrast, in the case of experts, questions were tailored in order to obtain more specific information.

After initial introductions and courtesies, discussions were mainly about remembrance of the war. In view of the consistency of attitude of many respondents and their use of vocabulary employed with respect to World War II, it was possible to judge how substantially citizens have assimilated the values of the current war cult as disseminated by President Putin and through media hype. The various 'frames of remembrance' acting around each individual are analysed in detail in the final part of this work,[7] and some salient observations from my interviewees are outlined in Appendix I. It was interesting also to identify examples of the 'post-memory' theorised by Marianne Hirsch, and Alison Landberg's 'prosthetic memory' on the part of younger generations who did not experience the war.[8] These are discussed in more detail in Chapters 7 and 13 respectively.

I was surprised to find that some of my interviewees remembered Brezhnev's visit to Novorossiisk in 1974. And it was a privilege to speak to a few veterans who had actually been alive during the war – and old enough at the time to recount some of their unsolicited memories to me. The results of these interviews are also examined in Chapters 7 and 13. It is this type of evidence, though, which needs to be considered carefully, rather than being taken simply at face value.[9] Discussions with subjects who were living in Novorossiisk in the 1970s produced testimony which may not reflect accurately what actually happened in the past by virtue not only of the influence of propaganda at the time, but also the prevailing mnemonic environment around the war and Brezhnev himself. The not inconsiderable problems, both psychological and physical, associated with retrospective demands on memory are numerous and largely beyond the scope of this work.[10] Suffice it to say that, in addition to the external pressure of the state propaganda machine, malleable individual memories of the past are also potentially subject to distortion by forgetfulness, blocking, bias or even misattribution. It is therefore impossible to accept without interrogation statements made today as either factual evidence or representative of attitudes pertaining in the past. I have attempted in relevant cases to ascertain if there is any evidence for such so-called memories, if they can be corroborated and if the accounts are consistent over time. Even today, citizens of Novorossiisk have their attitude to remembrance largely informed by the mass media, although most views expressed in research interviews I conducted may be accepted in the main as reflections of current opinion on the war myth.

It is important to recognise the emotional and moral impulses behind recalls of memory. When recounting their narratives, interviewees travel in their minds between past and present. It is their experience of the past which has built up their present identity, and rationalising their personal history within the overall history of the twentieth century often results in a positive representation of circumstances and events that may at the time have been particularly difficult.[11] Many older subjects tended to employ Soviet terms when describing ceremonies of remembrance, indicating how deeply they had absorbed the war myth and the social norms of the Brezhnev-era war cult in their personal memory construction. Shaped by the memorial environment then and now, their attitude to remembrance depended on the main tenets of the war myth – a victorious ending to the war and the need to thank those who died for their sacrifice.

But how does an interviewer know if something is omitted from the narrative, if something remains unspoken? Why are some details perhaps left out and others emphasised? Is it deliberate, or an unconscious strategy to protect an individual from shameful or traumatic memories? These questions have always dogged oral historians.[12] Although the emphasis of my research was on the current attitude of respondents rather than the testimony of war veterans, I was heartened by the relative openness with which older subjects spoke of issues such as rape or primitive living conditions without any evident taboo, although I will never know the full, raw story of these people's wartime experiences. It was the younger respondents, I found, who displayed more sensitivity to such delicate matters. It took a build-up of trust with my interviewees over the years before just a handful of them, all middle-aged respondents, began to mention some of the current issues circulating almost beneath the radar in Novorossiisk. These relatively hidden areas, spoken about quietly, if at all, serve to complicate with various shades of grey what seems superficially to be a black and white war myth.

Structure

Subsequent parts analyse the evolution of the myth of Malaia zemlia broadly chronologically, with each part also exploring a specific aspect of remembrance.

Part I examines the mechanism of construction of the war myth by war correspondence and memoir literature from 1943 to 1985. Following a consideration of Brezhnev's memoirs in Part I, Part II analyses the political place of Brezhnev in the myth and the difference between national and local attitudes to the general secretary and his links with the Malaia zemlia campaign. Moving to the current war cult, an analysis of recent visits by Presidents Putin and Medvedev to Novorossiisk demonstrates how the local myth is currently positioned politically.

Part III analyses the cultural dynamics of the propagation of the myth through monuments and ritual, notably the traditional 'Beskozyrka' ceremony, unique to Novorossiisk. Part IV brings us up to date by addressing the mechanism and agency of the intergenerational propagation of the myth today through an in-depth analysis of the overlapping roles played by the family, the school and local society in Novorossiisk.

From the domestic kitchen table in Myskhako to the town centre of Novorossiisk, from outlying communal graves to the huge Malaia zemlia memorial complex, from Heroes' Square in Novorossiisk to Moscow's Red Square, we will follow a complex route, linking individuals, families, civic society and the state. The lens pans from the local to the national and back again as I trace the myth of Malaia zemlia across more than 70 years within the meta-narrative of the national myth of the Great Patriotic War.

CHAPTER 1

WHAT IS A WAR MYTH?

> However intently you study a map of our Motherland, you will not find this name on the Black Sea coast. It was marked on wartime maps and remains only on the granite stone of monuments, in the yellowed triangular letters from the field, and in the memories of heroes.[1]

In 2015 I travelled across Russia by train from one coast to another. Starting in Novorossiisk on the Black Sea, I finished four weeks and 11,000 kilometres later in Vladivostok on the Pacific Ocean. Over the following few months I carefully revisited the thousands of photographs taken during this journey, selecting the best while discarding those that were less than perfect often where a bridge strut had suddenly come into view just as the shutter opened, spoiling the image of an otherwise picturesque river. Gradually, I whittled down my cumbersome collection to a manageable number, which I arranged chronologically and thematically into a photograph album of the trip. Finally, I prepared a presentation to deliver to various audiences about the experience.

The talks that I have given since then have presented this adventure as a mythologised expedition into the unknown, a condensed and sanitised version of the actual journey suitable for relatively quick oral narration. My images and the narrative around them were selected for the impression I wished to transmit of a coherent journey, omitting all the duds and misfits and those that were tangential to the main story-line. In this fashion, my talks spin an organised tale of a journey across an idealised Russia, situating my experience – based on fact but retrospectively ordered into a logical account – in the context of the already mythologised expanse of Siberia. In time, I suspect that I will only remember the journey thanks to the mediation of that concise photograph album, as many smaller details are forgotten and only the overview, a modern myth cooked up over a few months, passes into family folklore.

Classical war myths take much longer to mature, but go through basically the same process of simplification and sanitisation. A well-known example from the culture of ancient Greece is the tale of the Trojan War, which, according to archaeologists, could have taken place as early as the twelfth century BC.[2] Awash with powerful gods and fearless heroes, myths and legends grew up around the protracted siege of Troy by the Greeks, enduring to the present day. Modern war myths may superficially have something in common with the legends of antiquity: just like the Greeks, the Malaia zemlia campaign had its own small fleet and tenacious heroes. The classical legends were traditional narratives representing a people's shared system of morality and common heritage. Oral propagation was the norm until Homer's epic poem, the *Iliad*, brought together various existing versions of the siege of Troy and other exploits, many hundreds of years after the events. In Russian culture the tradition of epic poetry is much more modern than in ancient Greece: the process of oral myth making is described by Mikhail Lermontov in his poem about the legendary Battle of Borodino against Napoleon in 1812.[3]

An oral relationship with the past is not uncommon in traditional societies, where literacy is perhaps less established than in developed countries. The relationship between historical time and memorial time is key to an understanding of the mechanism of the propagation of any myth – not just in the Soviet Union or modern Russia. In the West the emphasis has long been on the objective, analytical discipline of history, where time conventionally flows in a linear fashion. In contrast, we have only to read Gabriel García Márquez's novel *One Hundred Years of Solitude* to recognise the circular temporality involved in the flow of mythical time in a traditional culture. Here, the gap between past and present is bridged and the temporal distance between generations is decreased, allowing for a greater empathy between contemporary citizens and their antecedents. The subjects of myth lived many years ago, but remain almost ahistorical – very much a part of the present and a constant reminder of the past even today, at the forefront of popular consciousness and fed by a string of anniversaries and related events.

From the point of view of the speed and scope of propagation of myths about ancient Greece or the Napoleonic wars, it is impossible to compare classical myths and legends with their modern counterparts. Malaia zemlia became a myth almost before its time, featuring in written accounts even as the campaign was being waged, rather like the aerial Battle of Britain in 1940. Nevertheless, all war myths present a narrative about a significant event in the past, often at a turning point in history, a coherent message disseminated down the generations, which tells the audience about the characteristics of the participants and helps to forge the identity of their descendants. This narrative represents public memory of the event, distilled and simplified from possibly disparate original accounts for effective transmission and ease of remembering.

Some scholars use the expression 'collective memory' or 'social memory' when speaking about the agreed popular narrative about a shared event in the past.[4] Both of these terms have their problems, as many would argue that memory resides in the minds of individuals rather than in a country, society or community. Jay Winter has suggested that the term 'collective remembrance' may be more suitable, emphasising the communal practices involved in the propagation of a publicly agreed narrative.[5] For the purposes of this book, I will try where possible to avoid the use of ambiguous expressions in favour of the term 'war myth' – a designation which can cause its own problems of interpretation and needs to be carefully defined.

The current understanding of the term 'myth' is clearly expressed in relation to memory of World War II in Britain by John Ramsden:

> Historians [. . .] use 'myth' to denote the way in which memories of the past have been selectively organised, an agreed version of the past that explains how a people came to be what they believe themselves to be in the present.[6]

The communal aspect of the term is emphasised by Lisa Kirschenbaum, writing of the myth of the siege of Leningrad: 'the shared narratives that give form and meaning to the recall of past experience'.[7] Similarly, Malcolm Smith uses the word in the context of the myth of 1940 in Britain to mean 'a widely held view of the past which has helped to shape and to explain the present'.[8] These three definitions show that, in order to survive, a myth must have utility in the present, normally for the ruling elite and often for the people themselves. The narrative is usually the property of victors, proud of their courageous ancestors, with the implication that their heroic characteristics are transmitted across the generations to their descendants today. A story that portrayed a people in a negative light would have no future: it is the positivity inherent in war myths that ensures their continuing popularity.

My definition explains this inherent popularity of a war myth thus:

> A war myth is a shared and simplified narrative of the past with utility in the present thanks to its enduring emotional and moral appeal.

This says nothing about how the myth is propagated, but acknowledges that it helps to support a community's memory of the past and keep it alive for future generations, as both the product and the process of remembrance. In essence, a myth is a narrative developed to portray a people in its best light, often depicting characters overcoming huge odds to win in the end. As such, a war myth may be exploited by a ruling elite to boost the morale of the population, often giving meaning and order to a difficult and chaotic period. For example, the martyrdom in wartime evident in the ancient legend of the siege of Masada was revived in the 1920s by Zionist intellectuals and is still invoked today in modern Israel.[9] A national war myth can help to unify a country, but would not last long unless it had some utility in the present for a nation's leaders or people.

Memory studies which concentrate on the manipulation of history by a dominant sector for current political utility employ a so-called 'presentist' paradigm, which is superficially applicable to studies of the Soviet and post-Soviet cults of war memory. Those in power are credited with re-interpreting a malleable past, picking and choosing its more useful aspects in order to render the whole more effective for current use. Aiming to unify the people and legitimise the prevailing institutions, the leaders may manipulate what is selected and what is deliberately omitted from the narrative they create, while promoting a contrived or agreed forgetting of any past events that may once have threatened national unity.

Traditional Russian communities have always been particularly fond of their canon of myths, legends and folk-tales. If the tsar once held the whole Russian Empire together by virtue of dynastic right, myths could be extremely useful tools in bonding its successor, the Union of Soviet Socialist Republics (USSR). This huge area spanning several time and geographical zones, with regional variations in race and ethnicity, language and religion, was not a strong candidate for nationhood in its own right. Only a strong interaction between myth and nation would be capable of bonding the people through a shared cultural heritage underpinning a new common ideology.

In this way, the first leaders of the new Soviet Union started to disseminate their ideology through the myths of the October Revolution of 1917 and the subsequent civil war (1917–22). In much the same way as Brezhnev's service on Malaia zemlia was warped and exaggerated in his memoirs, the life trajectories of individual revolutionary leaders were sometimes artificially created, such that, through them, the state acquired its own heroic identity as a nation prepared to fight for its new ideology. Gradually much of the population came to identify with the myth, in some cases re-inventing their own back-stories as incipient revolutionaries, either consciously due to coercion or unconsciously thanks to the ubiquity of the myth, to fit in with the official meta-narrative as it became assimilated into popular consciousness.[10] During the 1920s the myth of the revolution evolved quickly and pervasively. Portrayed retrospectively as the natural conclusion to the popular people's struggle, the revolution became the legitimate starting point for further conflicts, including the Great Patriotic War, in what appeared to be a coherent narrative of an organised and meaningful series of events.[11]

Soviet ideology, based on Marxism-Leninism, was disseminated to the masses through a distinctive use of language. The early leaders of the Soviet Union implemented a programme of literacy amongst the population and regulated the material available to read and to hear such that the people were exposed to a flow of ideological discourse via the press, posters, radio and key speeches. Language became the defining framework for ideology and heroes part of the official discourse of the times.

There is clearly an overlap in interpretation of the term 'ideology' and the means through which this ideology is disseminated: the belief system itself and the narrative discourse it employs.[12] The manipulation of the people by the elite through the use of propaganda served to legitimise the early Communist Party and persuade the population into conformity. By the time war broke out in 1941, people had got used to these conventions of discourse and often appropriated them themselves either unconsciously or in order to appear politically correct. A shared ideological discourse, with its own formulaic figures of speech and linguistic conventions, became a fact of everyday life. Public social conventions and behaviour were remodelled around ideological practices, for example educational meetings of party members after work. Labels were simplistic, allowing for little nuance of interpretation. Ideas and people were portrayed as black or white – communism or capitalism, bourgeois or peasant, enemy or friend. The war myth that developed contained many characteristics of a traditional fairy tale, as the 'fascist occupier' replaced the 'wicked witch' fighting a range of heroes of the Soviet Union in the starring roles.[13]

The myth was further promoted by the introduction of official public ceremonies and films mediated by the state to convince the population of the supremacy of the Bolshevik cause and to include them in its values. Aspects of the narrative of the revolution are common to most examples of mythology, including Malaia zemlia: its own symbolism (the hammer and sickle) and a language with its own loaded terminology and specialised vocabulary (for example, bourgeoisie or proletariat).

Twenty years after World War II the founding myth of the Soviet Union was supplemented by a cogent and unifying war myth which effectively glued the population together as it re-invoked heroic values to which virtually everybody could subscribe. In this way people could make sense of the war as a further step in the ongoing revolutionary process, with the added advantage that most citizens had at least some experience of the war, while not all had seen the revolution at first hand. During the Brezhnev era the war myth finally became embedded in schools and other institutions as official history in a mechanism similar to that whereby the myth of the October revolution had taken root. As the war myth evolved, the myth of the Bolshevik Revolution gradually became less prominent, especially after its fiftieth anniversary in 1967.[14]

Many of the strategies employed by the communist elite of the early Soviet Union, including the appropriation of history, are still in use today. The new Russian elite, in search of usable aspects of the Soviet past in the construction of a politically useful national identity, have revived the myth of the Great Patriotic War, which has now effectively displaced that of the Bolshevik Revolution. War memory is stated by President Putin to be 'an excellent cement, uniting people of different nationalities, different ethnicities and different religions into one indivisible Russian nation'.[15] The war myth is now so culturally ingrained in modern Russia that remembrance even unites people of different political persuasions. A presentist approach also emphasises the traditional behavioural values promoted by the myth of an heroic people. This is evident in the Soviet and post-Soviet stress on *vospitanie*, the moral education that inculcates in the younger generation a belief system propagated by the state as both patriotic and traditional, while ensuring the continuation of such widely desirable national characteristics. This conservative attitude to moral values tends to produce an ideological status quo, which could eventually lead to the stagnation of memory and commemorative practices.

Ernst Renan appreciated that a nation's shared past could also include shared suffering: 'Where national memories are concerned, griefs are of more value than triumphs, for they impose duties, and require a common effort.'[16] As in the case of Masada, a strong nation is often confirmed through martyrdom, as a sacrifice made in the common interest underlines the value of the nation today as something (still) worth fighting for, while also legitimising the continuation of ceremonies of remembrance sponsored by the state, notably Victory Day, the popular Russian equivalent of VE Day, which falls annually on 9 May. This argument justifies collateral damage in the war for the sake of a positive outcome. The overpowering commemorative narrative constructed by the Soviet state nipped in the bud any potential questioning surrounding the huge losses incurred in the war by presenting the dead as heroes and martyrs, who sacrificed their lives for their country and its communist ideology. Frequent reference is still made in Russia to the nation's gratitude to the millions who gave their lives in the war for the sake of their descendants and the country's future. In this way a cult of ancestors has been built up, linking the past with a shared vision of a brighter future, where a blurring of time lines promotes historical continuity over the decades.

National identity is never more important than in wartime, but is also evident in any period when a society needs cohesion and a common goal. It is often in peacetime that a war myth is invoked in countries experiencing internal or external challenges. The use of the national war myth as a metaphor for nationhood by the ruling elite in order to promote social and political cohesion may be expected particularly in an authoritarian society such as the Soviet Union. Created during the Cold War in a period of perceived external threat and re-created in twenty-first century Russia to rally a nation facing possible disintegration from within, the national war myth fills the state's need for a simple and positive message of a victorious nation. Within the national meta-narrative cultivated by the two war cults of the Brezhnev and Putin eras, the local war myth of Malaia zemlia has flourished.

The myth of Malaia zemlia offered an ideal political tool to the Soviet elite of the Brezhnev era thanks to its simple ingredients of a town occupied by the enemy, the daring night-time landings by a handful of men and the defence of the beach-head against all odds until the positive climax of the liberation. Added to this was the presence of the charismatic future general secretary. With details of thousands of Soviet deaths, alleged collaboration and betrayal strategically omitted, here was a narrative ripe for exploitation by the state. Like the overriding national war myth, it focused on the simple facts of the invasion by the deceitful enemy and the struggle of the people against all odds under the guidance of the communist leadership, until victory was finally won.

A myth can help a nation or community to make sense of the past, and leaders to justify present actions, by deploying a simple code which taps into the patriotic pride of the population. A modern war myth is therefore much richer than just an agreed narrative due to the inclusion of its own special tropes, rituals and symbols. The coded language in which it is often expressed, full of emotional imagery and local significance, is commonly appropriated by individuals. Where those more familiar with the war in northern France may still speak of the 'Dunkirk spirit' in reference to the solidarity of troops in mortal danger and those who went to save them, the people of Novorossiisk have their own set phrases that continue today, for example 'the sacred land soaked in blood'. Rather like Dunkirk, the very name of Malaia zemlia can convey the motivating emotional message of small numbers stranded on the beach in the face of a strong enemy holding the upper ground. The word *zemlia* (land) has connotations of homeland, of dry land as seen from the sea, a land inhabited by compatriots, *zemliaki*, rather than the foreign invader. The expression *Malaia zemlia* hence gives the impression of an island, a small homeland, while the rest of Soviet territory was referred to as *Bol'shaia zemlia* (the 'Large Land'). The implication was that ordinary people lived on the mainland, while Malaia zemlia was set apart for occupation by an heroic species, the *Malozemel'tsy*, the troops fighting on Malaia zemlia. The heroic troops and the ground on and for which they fought are clearly more important features of the myth than the finer points of the battle itself.

It also helps a myth to have one specific and common enemy, in this case the 'fascist occupiers', who may be targeted by leaders past and present to deflect criticism from themselves in a process of unification of the people. In fact the derogatory label 'fascist' is still commonly employed by Russians in relation to any perceived enemy, in an evident continuity of vocabulary from the Soviet Union to modern Russia. A distinct binary attitude to others is employed by those in authority even today, with people or other countries often classified as either enemies or friends of the state. Once cleansed of the enemy, the new town of Novorossiisk rose from the ashes of the old and the war narrative of Malaia zemlia took on the properties of a foundation myth.

Although nobody would expect a modern war myth to refer to fictitious gods or a snake-haired gorgon, myths may be confused with legends and deemed by some to be false representations of the past. Just like the detractors of Brezhnev's memoirs, others may point out the inconsistencies in the myth of 1940 in Britain, the year that saw the evacuation of the Allies from the beaches of northern France at Dunkirk, the Battle of Britain and the London Blitz. When the historical facts are examined minutely, it is easy to claim that this is a deceptive myth, the product of a deliberately misleading top-down propaganda campaign.[17] Any meticulous comparison may conclude that a myth is a false representation, thus privileging 'real' history as an objective discipline over the perceived fabrications existing as 'mere' myth. War myths may appeal to the heart rather than the head, invoking emotion rather than inviting analysis, but they are largely based on historical facts, however embellished or streamlined after the event. A modern war myth is not a made-up legend: sufficient factual evidence exists, chronicled in the archives, to prove that the main narrative of the myth of Malaia zemlia or of 1940 in Britain is actually just a different representation of history, if sometimes from the perspective of the 'little' man or woman whom history has until recently tended to forget. In this light, recent approaches have been more sympathetic to the war myth which built up around 1940. Seeing little value in a debunking exercise, scholars are now tending to examine rather the subsequent appropriation and ownership of the myth by the people, studying it as a social construction in its own right rather than a web of deceit, and trying to understand its effect on the present.[18]

A myth has the ability to select and emphasise the highlights, spurning the minutiae so valuable to Western historians tunnelling through the archives. In view of this mythical tradition, some versions of Soviet history may seem to Western eyes to be hugely distorted, sometimes allotting more space to smaller events – often those deemed to have more ideological significance – than events that may be key in the longer term, as time expands and contracts flexibly with little regard to linear chronology. Many Soviet and even more modern Russian history books have been deployed with propaganda purposes in mind, as the state has selected the official canon of war history and encouraged interpretations of the past to serve its own ideological ends.

By virtue of their collective compilation, war myths may inevitably lose some of the historical detail in the simplification process; moreover, myths compiled gradually will contain only those elements deemed to have current or future utility. Any small historical inaccuracy is not too important for the self-perception of a community, as long as the overall narrative is unambiguous and broadly based on fact.[19] However, urban legends, the contemporary version of their classical counterparts which have a more tenuous connection to reality, are also present in today's Novorossiisk, if not part of the main war myth.

I perceive a war myth as a corpus of tradition, a community's cultural heritage, rather than historical fact or fiction. If we are truly to get under the skin of a nation or community, it is essential to recognise the importance of the evolution of a war myth. Understanding this publicly shared remembrance linked to communal identity reveals how people relate to the past as it is incorporated into everyday life. I do not wish to undermine or expose the falsity of the myth of Malaia zemlia, but rather seek to understand and explain the myth as the contemporary heritage of cultural politics from the Brezhnev to the Putin era. Although my evidence suggests that the events relating to the myth of Malaia zemlia are based largely on what I deem to be historical fact, it does not really matter if all aspects of the myth are entirely true. The important thing is that the people of Novorossiisk widely accept this myth as part of their social and cultural background; it helps them to make sense of their local history with an emotional and moral appeal lacking in the dry detail of the history text-books.

The local war myth of Malaia zemlia has developed both in Novorossiisk and countrywide against a complex historical and ideological backdrop in which distinct shifts in the state attitude to war memory are evident. State-sponsored remembrance of the war in the Soviet Union was scant and strictly managed in the immediate postwar years. The authoritarian Stalin regime disapproved of public remembrance, fearing criticism of the Nazi-Soviet non-aggression pact of 1939, the Soviet Union's poor preparation for invasion and its weak handling of the early months of the war. The state did, however, confer the title of Hero City of the Soviet Union on Leningrad, Stalingrad, Sevastopol' and Odessa on 1 May 1945, in much the same way as the island of Malta and its citizens were collectively recognised by the award of the George Cross for withstanding a prolonged siege. Soviet hero cities were not, however, as common as the hundreds of smaller towns in France awarded the communal Croix de Guerre for their role in World War II.

At the end of the war, victory was celebrated nationally on 9 May 1945, but the anniversary of Victory Day became a normal working day from 1947.[20] After Stalin's death in 1953 the relative thaw of the Khrushchev period saw some easing of the restrictions on remembrance and Kiev became the fifth hero city in 1961. However, it was not until the twentieth anniversary of the end of the war in 1965 that the official attitude to memory started to undergo more substantial change following the accession of Brezhnev. During the Brezhnev era the regime created a countrywide war cult – a memorial environment through which remembrance of the war was encouraged – with substantial media coverage of war memory, the prolific building of monuments, the increased scale of memorial rituals, the publication of war memoirs and the military-patriotic education of children and students. Victory Day became a public holiday again in a political climate which actively promoted commemoration of the past. Under Brezhnev Moscow (1965), Brest Fortress (1965), Novorossiisk (1973), Kerch' (1973), Minsk (1974) and Tula (1976) were added to the ranks of hero cities.

Although a further two hero cities (Murmansk and Smolensk) were named in 1985 to mark the fortieth anniversary of the end of the war, the state deployment of war memory as a political tool changed markedly after Brezhnev's death in an apparent backlash against an overemphasis on the state-sponsored war myth, which had obscured what some saw as factual history and verged on the absurd in his final years. With Gorbachev's policy of *glasnost'* (openness) in the late 1980s came a period of increasing official transparency and questioning about the past, leading to some painful revelations about the war. The aftermath of the collapse of the Soviet Union in 1991 saw a debate about the importance attached to war memory: the military parade on Moscow's Red Square was ended under El'tsin in 1992, but reinstated in 1995, if on a lesser scale than previously.[21] The collapse of the Russian economy in the 1990s meant also that there was little money or indeed appetite for memory matters, which seemed to lose their political priority, leading to some lean years of casual public forgetting as the country battled to forge a new ideological future. However, a new century and a new president brought in another change of policy. Declaring on Victory Day, 2000, that memory of Soviet victory in the war would 'help our generation to build a strong and prosperous country',[22] Vladimir Putin once again brought state-led collective remembrance to the fore. Since then, Russia has experienced a second war cult which has returned remembrance of the war to the heart of domestic politics just as living witnesses are disappearing. In the twenty-first century memory politics has emerged as a potent unifying tool for the country with its slogans and symbolism, not least in relation to recent military action in Ukraine.

Strong leadership and war cults leave little scope for independence and it is tempting to assume with regard to an authoritarian nation that the state is responsible for the construction and dissemination of a war myth. Even under these prevailing conditions, however, this book reveals opportunities for individual proactivity and spontaneity in remembrance. After all, it is the individual who does the actual remembering within the context of the local community of remembrance; it is individuals who shaped the myth in the first place, and who, in turn, are now shaped by it. The situation with regard to the war myth in Novorossiisk therefore calls for the adoption of a more integrated and nuanced approach to the memorial processes that recognises the role of different sectors of society at all hierarchical levels, linking state, civic society and the individual. Although these different stake-holders often reinforce the memory message, conflicting narratives are sometimes heard, giving rise to a more three-dimensional, multivocal memorial environment. In view of the various political, sociological and cultural influences at play, it is necessary to examine throughout who exactly is involved in the processes of construction and propagation of the myth of Malaia zemlia.

Novorossiisk lies within the Krasnodar Region, around 1,500 kilometres south of Moscow – only two hours away from the influence of the capital by plane, but far enough away to have developed its own identity and unique modes of commemoration. A state-centric approach focusing on the memory message from Moscow does not always concur with the position in provincial Novorossiisk, where traditional Russian burial and mourning ceremonies, and customs dating back centuries rather than mere decades live on in churches and cemeteries alongside the triumphalist façade of Victory Day. In this book I reveal the most personal and private aspects at the heart of remembrance in my exploration of the complex and ongoing relationship between commemoration of the war at the local and the national level.

PART I

WAR CORRESPONDENCE AND MEMOIRS

THE CONSTRUCTION OF THE WAR MYTH THROUGH LITERATURE

J'ai plus de souvenirs que si j'avais mille ans.
Un gros meuble à tiroirs encombré de bilans,
De vers, de billets doux, de procès, de romances,
Avec de lourds cheveux roulés dans des quittances,
Cache moins de secrets que mon triste cerveau.
C'est une pyramide, un immense caveau,
Qui contient plus de morts que la fosse commune.
Je suis un cimetière abhorré de la lune.[1]

Librarians in Novorossiisk have sometimes surprised me by giving me copies of old war memoirs to help with this book. Why would they part with them so readily? Because these – to me – valuable gifts are simply redundant to them. It seems that they have rather too many for their readers' needs these days: over the last ten years only elderly men, they say, would very occasionally take them down from the shelves, blow away the dust and take them home for a few days, like old friends. They used them as a portal to a past time, out of nostalgia, perhaps, for their long deceased comrades-in-arms who had written or featured in these slim volumes – the *Malozemel'tsy* themselves: those who had served on Malaia zemlia. Those local memoirs that I have seen are certainly well-thumbed, though, a testament to the important role they once played in the community. And so we, in turn, must wind the clock back to 1943 and start at the very beginning, when the myth of Malaia zemlia was in its gestation period.

In the construction of a modern war myth all actors in and observers of the event in question have a potential role to play and hence a possible claim to ownership of public memory. In the case of Malaia zemlia, written personal accounts of war correspondents during the campaign and memoirs of veterans after the event were central to the evolution of the war myth. Undoubtedly the most influential of these narratives was the book *Malaia zemlia* by the general secretary of the Communist Party of the Soviet Union, Leonid Brezhnev, published in 1978. Although this work won Brezhnev the Lenin Prize for literature, recent evidence reveals that the work was ghost-authored, the subject of political machinations by Brezhnev's inner circle. However, Brezhnev's slim volume was only one of a series of written accounts which together were instrumental in the formation of the textually mediated myth of Malaia zemlia.

In the process of construction of a war myth, the gradual homogenisation of different individual accounts over time can produce an unambiguous narrative from a single perspective and with a consistent message of unquestionable heroism. Samuel Hynes' study of European memoirs of World War I, for example, demonstrates that individual memories undergo a process of selection, gradually converging to determine an agreed version that informs social remembrance, such that, over time, 'a complete, coherent story emerges'.[2] This may be regarded as a process of natural selection, whereby dominant narratives with a strong common element and persuasive rhetorical style prevail. The process of myth making also depends on the weighting and trust attached to different accounts, with eventual common agreement on what material is selected and what is omitted from the myth. This mechanism for the construction of a war myth provides a plausible framework for the development of the myth of Malaia zemlia, albeit largely dependent on forces from below in the form of the individual narratives that are aggregated and homogenised.

However, this war myth was constructed in the Soviet Union, an authoritarian state with a restricted and inward-looking culture. Like all literature, war memoirs were subject to the scrutiny of the official censor charged with the protection of state secrets, Glavlit, and the interest of the KGB (the state security service).[3] Furthermore, writers had to be authorised members of the national Writers' Union,[4] while the Communist Party of the Soviet Union kept a watchful eye on the political content of publications. Any deviation from the party line in the strict environment of a one-party state resulted in penalties ranging from the 'arrest' of manuscripts or their author, to expulsion from the Writers' Union or even the country.

Writers were expected to work within the parameters of the prevalent literary system of socialist realism, employed as a tool to educate the masses in communist ideology. The relationship between literature and official 'truth' as demanded by the Communist Party was at the crux of this formulaic literary system imposed by stringent state censorship on writers, if sometimes with their own pre-emptive collaboration. Following a meeting with writers in 1932, Stalin dictated that: 'The artist ought to show life truthfully. And if he shows our life truthfully, he cannot fail to show it moving to socialism.'[5] After the First Congress of Soviet Writers in 1934, Andrei Zhdanov, the chief Communist Party spokesman on cultural affairs, further stated:

> Truthfulness and historical concreteness of artistic representation must be combined with the task of ideological renewal and education of the workers in the spirit of socialism.[6]

Using this cultural tool to educate the masses in communist ideology, the writer's duty was to signpost with optimism the bright ideological future, 'portraying Soviet life, not as it was in reality, but as it should become'.[7]

Life was therefore seen as a constant fight, moving towards victory of the workers both politically and in the war, in order to guarantee socialism in the utopian postwar future just beyond the horizon. An integral part of this process was the moral and political education of the younger generation in communist ideology, where literature would provide role models of young people coming to full political consciousness under the guidance of older mentors. The 'master plot' of socialist realist works, as analysed by Katerina Clark, emphasises the heroic actions and self-sacrifice of communists, often young men or women, whose death renders them both timeless and immortal. Furthermore, any female companion included in a socialist realist narrative was usually an assistant in furthering the ideological cause, rather than a mere love interest.[8]

The problem to be overcome in the practical deployment of the theory of socialist realism was that present endeavours did not adequately represent the glorious future to come: the Soviet Union struggled with its economy, industry and collectivised agricultural system and the standard of living of most citizens left much to be desired. It was therefore necessary to indicate the implied reality of the future in the present, based on exploits in the past, leading to a blurring of the time-line in the service of the promised land.[9] As the protagonist develops into an ideal communist, 'past, present and future are crammed together in the process of a person becoming someone better'.[10] A canonised literary 'Great Time' was invoked, which conferred an exalted status on people who had played a major role in selected past exploits, including the October Revolution, the Civil War and Napoleon's defeat in 1812.[11] To these examples may be added the thirteenth-century character of Aleksandr Nevskii, mythologised in Eizenshtein's film and Prokof'ev's music of 1938, which effected an implied comparison between the courageous forces of mediaeval Rus' and its Soviet counterpart. In a recycling of historical precedents, an heroic age from the past was repeated in the present as a foretaste of the messianic age to come. For war correspondents, as the passage of time was virtually irrelevant, victory became totally predictable as just a staging post in the building of socialism.

The state's demand to place a positive spin on wartime and postwar literature is at complete odds with the cynical, less censored products of other wars. Many World War I poets in the West were able to comment on the chaos of war and the futility of mass death, which would not have been permitted in the Soviet sphere. Notably, Siegfried Sassoon invoked the bewildering experience of modern, total warfare, which could never be forgotten, while employing his own concept of time in a very different way from that demanded by socialist realism. Time, it seems, flows differently during a war. To Sassoon, Time (often capitalised in his works) is both personified and polarised, taking part in the battle and capable of acting on the side of either God or the enemy. As with socialist realism, Sassoon's military time is distorted, seeming to expand or contract as in a war myth. However, although Sassoon sometimes merges past, present and future into one, as with socialist realism, he also describes a distinct temporal separation between 'now' and 'tomorrow' in a distinctly binary approach. Time, it appears, is devious, capable of acting as either friend or foe. It steals chunks of lives by stopping the clock entirely during a war, then, once in the battlefield, it hastens the start of the actual engagement, only to slow down again during peacetime.[12]

Socialist realism may not have been as subtle as Sassoon's poetry, but it was almost universally applied. Re-invoking in the present epic moments in the past, it was ideally suited to the creation of war myths for use in both the present and the future. In this way, the old Russian tradition of myth making and repetitive story-telling merged with the new Soviet requirement for conformity. With its mythological treatment of time, its adulation of (politically conscious) heroes and the formulaic process of its production, socialist realism was a perfect framework for enforcing the uniformity of narration and interpretation demanded by myth.[13] As historical time was compressed, myth became fiction and fiction fact, such that there were no barriers to performing mythical feats in the present to be celebrated in the future. The optimistic slant placed on wartime feats would often render them unrecognisable to those who were portrayed in the resulting narrative. Emphasis was also placed on the location of an event,[14] so that not only the Motherland (*Rodina*) became sacred, but also the individual battlefields soaked in the blood of heroes.

Western readers might therefore assume that under the didactic guidelines of socialist realism there would be a monolithic attitude to the process of memory production, even if some Western material permeated the borders of the Soviet Union. In fact, there was some variation within this top-down environment, as the official attitude to war memory oscillated over the years depending on the internal and external political climate. Approval from above for individual and group forays into memory was therefore affected by periods of frost and thaw, often negotiated thanks to some degree of compromise between the state and its would-be memoirists. In a country grappling with Stalin's wartime legacy, enduring a hot-and-cold attitude to the process of de-Stalinisation under Khrushchev and Brezhnev, there was no guarantee that the war myth would remain constant or coherent indefinitely, or that its tone would remain static.

In democratic societies the agreed form and content of a myth usually provide reinforcement and confirmation to all agents involved, namely the individual, state and society in general. However, such mutual ownership of the war myth by multiple actors in the Soviet

Union was compromised within a dynamic memorial environment. Thus the war myth as propagated by the dominating agency of the state sometimes differed from the memory of the individuals formulating the bottom-up accounts, who were often discouraged from publishing their already heavily censored war memoirs. Moreover, once Brezhnev's connection with Malaia zemlia had become an integral part of the war cult, it was so dominant that it even influenced the official interpretation of history, while dictating the content of other published memoirs. Shaped by the myth according to Brezhnev, individual veterans and the groups to which they belonged lost ownership of their own memories in the culmination of a complex process that is not adequately described within the normative Western model of memory formation.

Distortion of memory was caused not only by the overwhelming influence of the state, particularly with respect to the role of Stalin's leadership during the war, but also by the natural process of forgetting common to all retrospective demands on memory. Furthermore, whether for ideological or social reasons, the character of memoirs may change depending upon how long after the event they were written; the individual memoirist may find it easier to remember specific events shortly after the war, but, for the statesman, more historical perspective is available at a greater distance from the actual event. Similarly, later memoirs tend to be more reflective, as the benefit of hindsight better enables the location of an individual's story within the collective as one person's life intersects with history.[15]

This part of the book concentrates on war correspondence from the front and memoirs by veterans, all culturally specific literary devices to be interpreted as products of their era within the Soviet literature of the period. The myth was born early in the actual campaign of 1943 and the first tranche of individual memories was then collected together prior to the emergence of a cohesive war myth with the publication of Brezhnev's memoirs. Later memoirs were more uniform, modelled on the dominant state template, thereby locating individual accounts within the overarching myth by then owned by the state.

If a distinction is made between 'collected' and 'collective' memory, it is possible to propose a considerably more sophisticated mechanism for the construction of the war myth in Novorossiisk than that proposed by Hynes. The simple collation and aggregation of individual memories to produce collected memory was followed by a state-sponsored collective representation still residing today in the national consciousness. Rather than just a vague homogenisation of accounts, there were four discrete stages in the construction of the myth of Malaia zemlia, based on the interacting influences of bottom-up popular memory and top-down state ideology:

(1) the birth of the myth through the attribution of a name and its dissemination by war correspondents;
(2) the collection of individual memories into one coherent form by memoirist Georgii Sokolov;
(3) the construction of the official state-owned war myth by Brezhnev; and
(4) the complete convergence and homogenisation of the myth according to Brezhnev.

As mentioned previously, the myth of Malaia zemlia represents just one specific example of a local Soviet war myth, and yet this myth came to be known nationwide above all others during the years of the Brezhnev war cult. Although in many ways typical of myths constructed rapidly during the war, the myth of Malaia zemlia already showed some exaggerated claims to longlasting fame lacking in other cases. A comparison with the development of the myth of the siege of Leningrad, one of the first hero cities of the Soviet Union, shows some considerable variation in tone of the two local war myths. If there is substantial disillusionment in the face of war in literature describing the Western Front in World War I, and a wish by Leningraders to reveal fully the stories of heroism and human weakness in their war myth,[16] what, then, is the tone of the incipient myth of Malaia zemlia and the motives of the memoirists recalling the campaign?

It is this type of evidence which demonstrates the massaging and manipulation of war memory that served the presentist political aims of the Soviet state. Furthermore, I show that the original bottom-up mechanism for the construction of the myth was overtaken by the overarching dominance of the state war cult of the Brezhnev era, within which memories were mutated and relocated. The influence of the state on war memory was eventually more powerful in the construction of the war myth than that of groups of veterans, even locally in Novorossiisk with its own unique claim to the myth. Finally, I show that the production of memory is not necessarily the same as its reception, proving that the myth of Malaia zemlia disseminated nationwide was dominated so much by the persona of the general secretary himself, that, with Brezhnev's death in 1982, the memorial climate changed entirely.

CHAPTER 2

A MYTH IS BORN: WAR CORRESPONDENCE FROM MALAIA ZEMLIA

Море всегда неспокойно,
И берег тревожен крутой,
Сверкает во мгле освещенный
Кусочек земли дорогой,
Волна набегает и брызжет,
Ночной караван – под огнем.
Но берег к нам ближе и ближе,
К нему мы упорно плывем.

Плывем мы, – хоть падает в море
Близ нас не последний снаряд, –
Туда, где на склонах предгорья
Товарищи наши не спят.
Вот берег причальный и тропка,
Родные деревья в пыли,
Высокие гордые сопки –
Хранители 'Малой земли'.[1]

Paul Carell, the German historian of World War II on the Eastern Front, claims that it was Leonid Brezhnev who gave the beach-head of Malaia zemlia its popular name.[2] Although this may be understandable in view of Brezhnev's strong link with the campaign, there is no other evidence to confirm Carell's statement, nor does Brezhnev's name feature in contemporaneous communiqués from war correspondents. In contrast, N.V. Kolesov contends that the name of Malaia zemlia became widely known only after the liberation of Novorossiisk in September 1943, implying that it was familiar to a smaller circle of people even before then.

> At that time, in the war years, the names of 'Myskhako' and 'Malaia zemlia' were known only to those who fought in the Caucasus. The first reports about the landings at Myskhako were published only after the liberation of Novorossiisk in September 1943.[3]

So who named this small area of recaptured Soviet territory and when did the name 'Malaia zemlia' first appear in popular Soviet consciousness?

With the notable exceptions of Vietnam and Iraq, war myths are rarely negative in the consciousness of those constructing or propagating them.[4] A myth is more likely to be built in the aftermath of victory, with the benefit of hindsight and reflection enabling its positive positioning within the agreed national narrative of the war. Even the Allied retreat from Dunkirk in 1940 is mythologised as a positive event thanks to the patriotic fleet of small ships rushing to the rescue of the troops stranded on the beaches of northern France. A myth started during the actual event may help the participants make sense of a difficult situation. As in the case of the London Blitz, troops and civilians encouraged by a myth are motivated to fight on, when the only alternative would be to admit defeat.[5] Similarly, evidence indicates that the myth of Malaia zemlia was articulated by the armed forces and formulated, if only locally, by journalists present on the beach-head even as the campaign was unfolding, only to be reinforced and relocated decades later within the national master-narrative of the war.

According to Jeffrey Brooks, the role of the war correspondent as part of the state propaganda machine was to promulgate the sole objective of 'victory over the invaders' by means of a holy, patriotic war.[6] Widely considered to be a branch of politics, journalism was intended both to inspire the troops and to maintain discipline.[7] However, all information disseminated by the media was controlled by the Soviet Information Bureau, Sovinformbiuro, which disseminated reports through TASS, the official state news agency.[8] In the interests of public motivation and cohesion, reports were often far from truthful and barely credible in the case of Soviet losses, especially in the difficult early days of the war, when bad news was rarely reported in the press or on the radio.[9] Only good news was encouraged, sometimes supported by photographs, helping to form positive memories for after the war. Konstantin Simonov describes the work in his memoirs:

> Our job as war correspondents, as patriots and as writers was to find, in the mass of wartime actions, not that which spoke about the difficulties of today, but that which spoke about the promises of a better future, about the triumphant end.[10]

In this vein, war correspondents and the Soviet propaganda machine harvested examples of the self-sacrifice of heroes (such as the young 'martyr' Zoia Kosmodem'ianskaia), who were immediately mythologised in order to boost the morale of the people.[11] The Red Army may have been losing the larger campaigns, but successful small-scale exploits and occasional triumphs rendered the gloomy overall story more palatable.

Little journalistic licence was allowed under this climate of stringent censorship: indeed, a war correspondent had to be skilled in navigating 'the treacherous waters of communication between the state and a largely mistrustful readership'.[12] The public was probably aware of some official deception, if not of the details of any omissions, while the journalists themselves were at risk of losing more than their jobs if they deviated from the official line. Out of public sight, however, negotiations often took place between correspondents anxious to publish the truth about Soviet losses and warn the public about the advancing enemy, and editors wishing to avoid too much criticism from the censor. In some rare cases the editors, as middlemen, sided with the journalists, publishing very occasionally without the censor's approval.[13] Although the regulation of writers was slightly relaxed during the war years, offering more independence for journalists than previously,[14] socialist realism continued to influence war correspondents, dictating the overall tone of newspaper articles.[15]

At the onset of war, civilian writers and poets were drafted in to work on military newspapers, with most holding army ranks, while others were enlisted from the armed forces.[16] The most enduringly famous of the war correspondents on Malaia zemlia was Major (later Colonel) Sergei Borzenko, whose dispatches regularly appeared in the pages of the 18th Army's weekly newspaper, *Znamia Rodiny*. Although not of the same national stature as Il'ia Erenburg, Vasilii Grossman or Konstantin Simonov, well-known war correspondents for the national military paper *Krasnaia zvezda*, Borzenko took part in military action and was later named a Hero of the Soviet Union, going on to work for the national newspaper *Pravda* and to write his memoirs in the postwar period.[17] When Novorossiisk was finally liberated in September 1943, an influx of reporters sent telegraphic dispatches back to *Pravda* and *Izvestiia* in Moscow, including Anatolii Sofronov, who would later write a fictional play about the Malaia zemlia campaign.[18] Other correspondence from the front includes articles by army officers, notably *Izvestiia's* Captain N. Petrov and *Znamia Rodiny* 'special correspondents', usually Captain A. Svetov and Senior Lieutenant (later Captain) Boris Miliavskii.

Memoirists Georgii Sokolov and Grigorii Bondar' claim that the name 'Malaia zemlia' was used from the earliest days of the campaign.[19] Similarly, A.F. Galatenko, the captain of a motor launch taking marine infantry from Gelendzhik across the bay to Myskhako during the earliest days of the landings, refers to 'the battle for the small strip of shoreline reclaimed from the enemy, which [...] was still simply called the beach-head, but which a few days later came to be known as Malaia zemlia'.[20] Retrospective claims on memory are hard to evaluate, but it is possible that the name may have been used amongst the troops within the first few weeks of the February landings. However, wartime communiqués still referred only to the 'Novorossiisk front'. Even when the area of Malaia zemlia was under discussion, it was not named. This is the case in an article about enemy action, which appeared in *The Times* of London, filed by a special correspondent in Stockholm during the fierce fighting of April 1943:

> Most of the aggressive air activity by the Axis is being directed at present against the Russian positions south of Novorossiisk and the adjacent bases on the Black Sea shore, so as to ease the strain on the garrison at Novorossiisk. This garrison has been fighting since March to prevent being hemmed in between the mountains and the Black Sea.[21]

In contrast, a letter written home from the front by a certain E.D. Goncharov in the weeks before his death on 4 May 1943 refers specifically to Malaia zemlia.[22] Contemporaneous songs and poetry use the name,[23] while the first press report from the front mentioning Malaia zemlia appeared in newsprint, as Kolesov suggests, in the local pages of *Znamia Rodiny* in June 1943,[24] well into the seven-month campaign which had started with the tentative February landings. The name of 'Malaia zemlia' only became public thanks to the military press once there was good news to tell and victory was in sight, at least for the Soviet North Caucasian 18th Army, after the favourable conclusion of the critical April battles around Novorossiisk. The name 'Malaia zemlia' was not in general use, however, until after the liberation of the town in September 1943, when it appeared in only one article in *Pravda* concentrating on the specific location of the troops in and around the village of Myskhako just outside Novorossiisk.[25] Thus the myth of Malaia zemlia appears to have been born amongst the armed forces serving on the beach-head months before full knowledge of the nature of the campaign and its popular name had become widespread.

Such rapid myth creation was not exceptional during World War II. Winston Churchill's famous lines, 'Never in the field of human conflict was so much owed by so many to so few', epitomised the myth of the Battle of Britain at its height in the summer of 1940. Similarly, the London Blitz was so named almost before it began and, once started in earnest, was immediately mythologised.[26] Like the Blitz, the war myth around the siege of Leningrad (1941–44) concentrated on the community spirit of ordinary citizens and the continuation of family life in a key city under bombardment. Any similarities between London and Leningrad were superficial, however, as were the circumstances of the besieged Soviet city and the small Black Sea coastal strip outside Novorossiisk. Although both were surrounded by German forces and with escape possible only across the water, the differences were more significant. The siege of Leningrad, the important second city of the Soviet Union, lasted four times longer than the 225-day campaign on the provincial beach-head of Malaia zemlia. During that time, Leningrad was still occupied by a large number of its prewar population of civilians, whereas Malaia zemlia involved only troops, mainly soldiers from the 18th Army and the marine infantry,[27] as most of the citizens in and around Novorossiisk had been evacuated, interned or executed in 1942 as the enemy advanced on and then captured the town.[28]

The myth of besieged Leningrad developed through local media during the actual event.[29] Radio played a large role in the dissemination of information and in boosting morale in addition to the newspapers,[30] whereas its use on Malaia zemlia was largely restricted to military purposes. Troops on Malaia zemlia had not only the army newspaper to hand, but also *Polundra*, a morale-boosting sheet of articles, cartoons and sketches. Produced by the Communist Party propaganda team in the caves and bunkers housing the military headquarters and field hospital, *Polundra* was credited as the brainchild of librarian Mariia Pedenko.[31] A modest propaganda news-sheet, *Novorossiiskii partizan*, also appeared in print runs of up to 1,000. Published by the state's Sovinformbiuro over 43 editions from November 1942 to September 1943, it was dropped from planes to resistance fighters on the ground, being passed from hand to hand by the partisans roaming the hills around the town.[32]

The myth of the siege of Leningrad became widespread nationally even in its early days. By July 1943, around the time the name 'Malaia zemlia' was appearing regularly in the local military press, the city newspaper *Leningradskaia pravda* spoke about the *'boevaia sem'ia'* (military family), indicative of the community spirit of Leningraders, all in it together, rather like Londoners in the Blitz.[33] The same article also makes it clear that the whole nation was aware of the struggle: 'The whole Soviet people are carefully following our fight and work.' It seems that the siege of Leningrad, started in September 1941, had already become a national myth well before Malaia zemlia was present in the popular consciousness. However, evidence suggests that Malaia zemlia was even further along the road to epic mythical status than Leningrad, as, even while the campaign was still being waged, future memory of it was being invoked. In an article of June 1943 referring already to *'pamiat' o Maloi zemle'* (memory of Malaia zemlia), the war correspondents Svetov and Miliavskii claim that the fruits of Malaia zemlia would inspire the memory of both civilians and veterans:

> There will come the day when once again people here will drink wonderful juice from the fruit of the vineyards. And from the 'Malaia zemlia' glass people will become as drunk as former soldiers on their memories. This is not just a lovely dream. [...] Flowers will bloom in the gardens here. [...] That is for tomorrow. But today war is being waged on 'Malaia zemlia'.[34]

A myth normally involves memory of the past in the present. Here, in contrast, future memory of the present was invoked not merely as a hopeful dream, but as a quite detailed prediction along the socialist realist lines outlined by Clark, where there is 'no collision [. . .] between "is" (or "present") and "ought to be" (or "epic past" – or future)'.[35] As an example of the blurring of time boundaries, and in an extreme statement unusual even for the Soviet Union, war dispatches firmly place Malaia zemlia within an historical continuum linking the difficult wartime present with a bright future in the aftermath of predicted victory. Looking ahead to the future, while looking back to the war itself, Svetov and Miliavskii's article smoothly spans the years, already nominating Malaia zemlia as the subject of a future war myth and analysing the process of potential myth making. In a similar, if even more exaggerated way, Winston Churchill skipped forward across the centuries just before the start of the Battle of Britain in 1940 to lay claim to the future myth, while continuing to motivate the country at a dark time in the war:

> If the British Empire and its Commonwealth last for a thousand years, men will still say, 'This was their finest hour'.

Unlike the normal situation in wartime papers, this Soviet article aligns itself with Churchill in stressing by implication the hardship of the battle at the time of writing, in contrast to the promised victory ahead.

However, at virtually the same time, the focus of Leningraders after two years of siege was fixed on the present and the more immediate future. Articles on the awarding to civilians of medals for the defence of Leningrad, which could easily have been written in a similarly epic vein, made no mention of future memory or an historical continuum.[36] Indeed, in June and July 1943, *Leningradskaia pravda* took a different, less triumphant tone, pointing to struggles still to come and the serious lessons to be learned in the future from history:

> It is not in the character of the defenders of Leningrad to give in to self-deception, reassure themselves about the achievement, to boast about their services in the past. No! We analyse the past seriously, absorb its experience and at the same time look ahead vigilantly. But ahead of us lie new trials, new difficulties, decisive battles with the enemy.[37]

Both Soviet articles reveal the immediate problems of conflict rather more truthfully than would have been expected at the beginning of the war. Furthermore, in an article about children finishing the academic year in June 1943, the same Leningrad paper gives only pragmatic details of everyday life, rather than taking the opportunity to elaborate on the memories of these children as adults in a utopian socialist future.[38] This omission reflects the overwhelming emphasis on survival in the present to the detriment of enforced ideology embracing the future.

The only 1943 article in *Leningradskaia pravda* to mention memory of the heroic past in the future attributes any success to Stalin's 'titanic will' rather than to military prowess:

> When future historians come to study this time, they will above all be amazed at the unity, the strength, the endurance of the citizens of Leningrad, whose thoughts and actions are permanently directed by the titanic will of that great genius – Stalin.[39]

In contrast, one of the more popular songs about Malaia zemlia cited in *Znamia Rodiny* compared the troops to the giants more often found in classical legends:

> Споем же о тех великанах,
> Что ходят по 'Малой земле',
> О людях, в борьбе неустанных,
> По крепости равных скале.[40]

> Let us sing of those giants
> Who walk on 'Malaia zemlia',
> Of people, not exhausted by battle,
> As strong as a rock.

There is a marked difference between these verses in the attribution of success: to Stalin in the case of Leningrad, and to the military heroes on Malaia zemlia. Malaia zemlia, then, benefited more than Leningrad from its physical distance and political independence from Moscow as this poem fails to toe the party line. Mentions of Stalin in the press had decreased significantly during the months of defeat and retreat from November 1941 to the end of 1942. While Soviet forces were being pushed back, Stalin waited in the wings. At this stage in the war, more press columns were devoted to the generals, especially Georgii Zhukov, the troops and even the correspondents themselves, in an overlapping of interests of the military and the journalists.[41] Although censorship had increased with the onset of war, literary critics became gradually less demanding, such that there was more freedom and authority for journalists from the end of 1941 to 1943, as reflected in the song about Malaia zemlia, where the 'giants' of Malaia zemlia boast an exaggerated stature similar to that of Stalin himself. However, once the tide of the war had changed after the victory at Stalingrad, previous conditions were re-asserted as mentions and photographs of Stalin reappeared in the press with the re-establishment of his cult of personality towards the end of the war.[42] This is reflected in the *Leningradskaia pravda* article of July 1943,[43] demonstrating the closeness of the second capital to the political influence of the centre, in comparison with the relative freedom of expression in the same month of *Znamia Rodiny* on the periphery, still to be reined back into the Stalin-centric fold.[44]

Journalists were also able to privilege the role of the individual over the state in the development of morale-boosting mythology in the first two years of the war. While not mentioning Stalin by name, *Znamia Rodiny* refers rather to the many individual communist heroes on Malaia zemlia, with the dedicated troops dubbed *'dvazhdy kommunisty'* ('doubly communists') and *'trizhdy partiinye'* ('thrice party-minded'), linking their heroism with their political ideals as in socialist realism, though without reference to their political leader.[45] All the same, *Znamia Rodiny* correspondents Svetov and Miliavskii make use of Soviet clichés in describing Malaia zemlia as 'one of the most unforgettable pages in the history of the war'.[46] Articles and photographs of individual Malaia zemlia heroes in July and August 1943 appear to confirm the statement that 'stories of its heroic defenders will pass down from generation to generation'.[47] The oath taken by the troops before departure for Malaia zemlia was similarly invoked to place the heroes of the campaign in a genealogical continuum of strong Soviet men.[48]

According to the military press, the great desire of the troops was to reunite their small beach-head with the rest of the country.[49] The trope of liberation and reunification was also incorporated into predictions for the not too distant future:

> There will come the day when 'the Small' will merge with the large Soviet land. But it will always remain Small in the memory of the men who recaptured it from the Hun. Nor will it die in the memory of those who will benefit from its fruits, breathe its air, live freely and happily beneath its sky.[50]

Therefore, when Novorossiisk was finally liberated on 16 September 1943, Borzenko was able to write about the accomplishment of what had already been predicted by the embryonic myth, while diplomatically uniting Stalin's image with that of communism by affirming that the victory had been achieved thanks to Stalin's leadership and Lenin's communist ideology:

> The epic Malaia zemlia campaign is over. Everyone who stepped onto its shores was a hero. [. . .] The burning Small Land was thirsting for reunion with the Large Soviet land, and this time has come to pass. [. . .] Malaia zemlia has been united with the mainland. Soldiers and sailors took off their caps and marched victoriously past the monument to V.I. Lenin, the name of Stalin on their lips.[51]

Furthermore, in the same article, Borzenko lauded the decisive role of the landing troops: 'The Malaia zemlia landing troops played a large role.' Although this judgment cannot be doubted, Borzenko was one of the commentators who, in the Brezhnev era, helped to build up the myth of Malaia zemlia by exaggerating this role and thereby the strategic significance of the military campaign in Novorossiisk.

A folkloric mechanism for the future construction of collective memory of the past was identified in romantic vein by Svetov and Miliavskii as early as July 1943 in the culmination of an article about a concert of poetry and songs on Malaia zemlia. These home-grown concerts were mainly staged outdoors on quieter evenings,[52] unlike their more famous counterparts in Leningrad, which occasionally boasted the music of Shostakovich in its concert halls. Concluding the article, Svetov and Miliavskii employ socialist realist theory to extrapolate from the present situation to the future, drawing a parallel between the construction of the war myth and that of a memorial to the recent, but already – according to them – legendary events on Malaia zemlia:

> 'Malaia zemlia' is one of the most glorious pages of the Great Patriotic War. Generations will remain grateful for the stories of steadfastness and selfless courage of its heroic defenders for the sake of the motherland. That is why the folk-tale, song and proverb transmitted from mouth to mouth are already carving a monument not made by hands to those unparalleled events taking place in our own age.[53]

Recalling the troops' songs and poems about Malaia zemlia, this memorial is not a monument physically created by human hands, but constructed by the more traditional, oral means of evolution of classical myths. In using the phrase *'nerukotvornyi pamiat''* ('a memorial not built by hands'), Svetov and Miliavskii invoke the classical literary source of Aleksandr Pushkin's famous poem 'Ia pamiatnik sebe vozdvig nerukotvornyi' ('I created a monument to myself not built by hands'), 1836, in which Pushkin predicts his own immortality thanks to the enduring legacy of his poetry. Pushkin's poem recalls Gavriil Derzhavin's 'Pamiatnik' ('The monument'), 1796, while Derzhavin in turn refers back to Horace's 'Exegi monumentum' ('I have made a monument'), 23 BC.[54] Thus allusions to enduring remembrance of Malaia zemlia were made two months before the liberation of Novorossiisk in the context of the canon of traditional Russian poetry and the classical legends of ancient Rome, in a fashion typical of socialist realism both with its reference to 'Great Time' and the compression of time.

All three poems claim that the poet's oeuvre builds an everlasting monument to himself, a creation that will outlast any physically constructed monument.[55] In using the expression 'nerukotvornyi pamiat'' during the Malaia zemlia campaign, the war correspondents are already looking ahead to the future, according to the norms of Soviet culture, when its memory will have attained mythical status on a par with the classical legends, while postulating a traditional mechanism rather than textual mediation. Just as an historical continuum is an integral part of socialist realism, so a continuum of literary excellence connects Pushkin to Derzhavin and to Horace before them, effecting an implicit comparison between the mythical greatness of the exploits on Malaia zemlia with the feats of the classical heroes. It is also possible to read into the allusion a bold claim by the authors that their work is of a similarly high literary standard. In an interesting juxtaposition of folkloric and high culture and, despite its appearance in the printed press, the article concludes that the oral tradition of propagation, by 'folk-tale, song and proverb', is more enduring than any physical monument that may be erected in the future in memory of the dead. This claim can only be supported by a detailed study of the relative efficacy of the main methods for the propagation of memory considered in later chapters.

War correspondence from Malaia zemlia broadly followed the national guidelines on socialist realism, if marginally behind the trend with respect to the lauding of Stalin. By Victory Day the local Communist Party newspaper, *Novorossiiskii rabochii* (*The Novorossiisk Worker*), reflected the re-integration of Malaia zemlia with the Bol'shaia zemlia: it was completely at one with the national press with its large photograph of Stalin on the front page and full of official national and international news courtesy of the Soviet Information Bureau.[56] However, this was at the expense of the new-born mythical identity of Malaia zemlia, which was mentioned only briefly on an inside page two days later. It would have to wait until Brezhnev came to power to become a fully-fledged war myth.

CHAPTER 3

EARLY MEMOIR LITERATURE

Да, были люди в наше время,
Могучее, лихое племя.[1]

Many of the North Caucasian 18th Army were either born locally or chose to remain in the Krasnodar region after the war, with some veterans even choosing to settle in Novorossiisk.[2] For this reason, the incipient myth of Malaia zemlia remained for several years far more localised than the myth of the siege of Leningrad or the London Blitz. Despite the far-reaching claims of war correspondents Svetov and Miliavskii, it is difficult to gauge the effectiveness of the oral propagation of memory in the aftermath of war. Although Elena Zubkova notes considerable nostalgia for the front and its camaraderie elsewhere in the Soviet Union, observing that veterans remained in touch through informal meetings in cafés, snack bars, and beer halls, it is questionable whether this so-called 'Blue Danube' network was operational in Novorossiisk in the three postwar years before it was closed down by the state.[3] All but annihilated by German and Soviet artillery during the military action of 1942 to 1943, the town had to be both rebuilt and repopulated after the war, doubtless exacerbating any postwar fatigue and compromising physical and emotional recovery such that it is unlikely that veterans in Novorossiisk managed to see much of each other in the difficult postwar period.[4] As in Leningrad, the trials of everyday life in the postwar Soviet Union were pressing to the exclusion of virtually every other activity. Oral memory was relatively slow to develop, as veterans to a great extent survived their recent wartime experiences by not speaking widely about them, even within the family.[5]

Jay Winter proposes a valid mechanism in the West for the expansion of memory over time from the individual to the wider social circle, as groups of the bereaved create memorial ceremonies to express and assuage their joint loss.[6] This type of process, whereby 'individuals can express and compare their memories with the experience of contemporaries, can begin to formulate a shared language and identify common themes', was even slower in the Soviet Union, thanks to restrictive state dominance. The recounting of war stories was discouraged by Stalin and it is probable that discussions about the war were confined to the immediate social circle, although bonds were doubtless forged through mourning.[7] Catherine Merridale finds that, even though private conversations could not be controlled, any attempt by the individual to spread memory was hampered, sometimes by self-censorship, under such oppressive political conditions. The bereaved often accommodated their own memories within Soviet ideology, although individual memories may not always have coincided with the politically correct version, especially in the case of minorities, leading to a complex process of myth building between sometimes competing images.[8] It was not until years after the war that formal reunions of former comrades-in-arms were able to create a shared identity and play a key role in promoting remembrance activities. Only at this late stage could individual loss finally evolve into public remembering, which was eventually assimilated into the national narrative as patriotism.

Nor did the official postwar climate welcome war memoirs, only a few of which were published by veterans during Stalin's rule.[9] Observing that Stalin did not want to risk personal humiliation by criticism of his wartime leadership or the questioning of officially established war myths, Lazar Lazarev quotes the official line that 'it was too early to be writing memoirs so soon after these great events, at a time when passions were still too much aroused, and thus the memoirs would not have the required objectivity'.[10]

After the death of Stalin in 1953 and following Khrushchev's attack on Stalin's war record in 1956, a temporary thaw permitting some degree of remembrance led to the publication in 1959 of Konstantin Simonov's popular war novel, *Zhivye i mertvye* (*The Living and the Dead*). This was made into a film in 1964, an addition to the many iconic war films which saw huge box-office success, notably Mikhail Kalatozov's *Letiat zhuravli* (*The Cranes are Flying*), 1957, and Grigorii Chukhrai's *Ballada o soldate* (*The Ballad of a Soldier*), 1959.[11] The 1956 radio programme in search of the heroes of Brest Fortress mutated into the successful Saturday evening television series *Rasskazy o geroizme* (*Tales of Heroism*), which started in 1962 and ran for a decade.[12] Its war veteran host, Sergei Smirnov, also published books based on the series, with a mention of 'the famous Malaia zemlia' in the context of the war's greatest battles. Claiming to be exposing the truth about the war, this programme broke through previous barriers to public discussion by opening up debate on hitherto closed subjects. In this way ordinary Soviet citizens learned, for example, of the harsh treatment by Stalin of Soviet soldiers taken as prisoners of war in 1941 through no fault of their own. At times, though, it was deemed to be rather too open in its discussions, falling foul of both the KGB and the Communist Party in the mid-1960s.[13]

Taking advantage of the thaw, some war memoirs by high-ranking military commanders started to appear towards the end of the 1950s, for example General Chuikov's 1959 memoir, which in a politically correct manner highlighted Khrushchev's role in the Battle of Stalingrad.[14] In Leningrad, too, memoirs of individual citizens were published from 1957, serving to increase local identity.[15] Very few memoirs specifically about Malaia zemlia were published in this period, however, although the more general war in the Black Sea and the Caucasus was more widely covered.[16] With continuing swings in the party's attitude to memoirs, the national memory climate again became more welcoming from the early 1960s, although the prevalent communist ideology dictated a highly standardised approach, with some distortion in the rendering of the historical past. Memoirs were also reliant on a good memory, as most military personnel had not been allowed to keep a diary or notes about their war service, in contrast with civilians, journalists and writers who later benefited from their wartime documents.[17] Most memoirs were produced by officers, as in the West, rather than by other ranks, whose command of literary language was usually more tenuous.

While in Leningrad in the 1960s most of the memoirs were published by civilians, only military personnel had been present during the Malaia zemlia campaign. Georgii Sokolov, a twice-wounded captain commanding the 165th Marine Infantry Reconnaissance Brigade, had spent virtually the whole 225 days of the campaign on Malaia zemlia, latterly working as editor of a front-line newspaper.[18] Although Sokolov, as a privileged military veteran, had written his first short books of war memoirs in 1949 and 1954,[19] it is his later, longer works that remain on the library shelves in Novorossiisk. The first of these was produced only after Sokolov had collected together the addresses of many of his former comrades-in-arms such that he was able to organise the first reunion of just over 60 *Malozemel'tsy* in September 1963, on the twentieth anniversary of the liberation of Novorossiisk.[20] Like the television programme *Tales of Heroism*, this first reunion provided a valuable forum for the assembly and exchange of war memories, enabling Sokolov to expand his personal perspective. After a period of enforced latency, this meeting proved to be the catalyst for other *Malozemel'tsy* to contribute their own stories, while correcting inaccuracies and expanding on Sokolov's original to enable him to publish a work of collected short stories in 1967.[21]

Eighteen years after his first publication, the time was indeed ripe for a completely new version of Sokolov's memoirs. As soon as Brezhnev came to power at the end of 1964, following his ousting of Khrushchev, the flourishing of the memory climate was apparent. A book of Brezhnev's first important speech about the war was published for export and Victory Day was reinstated in 1965, with its new *minuta molchaniia* (minute's silence) ritual introduced to all Soviet radio and television channels, which would later include a specific tribute to the heroes of the Malaia zemlia campaign.[22] Television increasingly brought war memory to the masses, with the series *Vyzyvaem ogon' na sebia* (*We Draw Fire on Ourselves*) and Smirnov's *Podvig* (*The Exploit*) both starting in 1965. The latter, in particular, focused on the stories of individuals and their regiments.[23]

Although under Khrushchev's leadership the publication of memoirs had coincided with periods of thaw with respect to de-Stalinisation, Brezhnev introduced a degree of re-Stalinisation with increased censorship and repression of writers.[24] Paradoxically, at the same time the publication of memoirs by top military commanders was encouraged after 1965. During this period the local newspaper in Novorossiisk often published articles submitted by high-ranking veterans of the Malaia zemlia campaign, notably Vice Admiral Kholostiakov. However, approval by a special commission was necessary.[25] All memoirs were referred to Voenizdat (the military publishing house), having to conform strictly with the official master narrative attributing victory to a united people that saved not only eastern Europe, but the whole of Europe, from the fascist enemy.[26]

In the context of a growing war cult, Sokolov's work, *Malaia zemlia: Rasskazy i ocherki* (*Malaia zemlia: Stories and Essays*) of 1967 was one of many memoirs to appear across the country. Published in the regional capital of Krasnodar, the book measures 21 by 13 centimetres, comprising 408 pages. While the red and cream hard-backed cover proclaims its Soviet provenance, the frontispiece reflects the military theme through the black and white image of a sailor in the act of throwing a grenade, machine-gun in hand and dagger in belt. The publishers obviously envisaged substantial local interest, in view of the relatively high quality and price of the book (85 kopecks), with an initial print run of 50,000. Their confidence was rewarded: Sokolov was made a member of the Writers' Union as a result of the first full edition of his memoirs, and the book ran to a further nine editions, with key updates in 1971, 1979 and 1985, some of the subsequent editions being published centrally in Moscow and with print runs as large as 200,000.[27]

The book's 31 chapters include an introduction by the author and a supportive, validating epilogue, 'Pamiat' serdtsa' ('Remembrance from the Heart'), by Colonel A. Ryzhov, Hero of the Soviet Union and former commandant of the political section on Malaia zemlia. Ryzhov praises Sokolov for his wartime service, while also mentioning the author's efforts over several years to trace the veterans of Malaia zemlia.[28] The bulk of the book, 23 chapters in all, is devoted to a series of broadly chronological discrete stories about individual people and events. It is noteworthy that, in line with national trends, Stalin appears rarely in the work, with merit being given rather to individuals even over military units. Collating the memories of his former comrades, Sokolov's work narrates in the third person the exploits of both officers and other ranks, living and dead, many of whom had been made Heroes of the Soviet Union. Not only decorated heroes, but also heroes conforming to socialist realism, they are often writers and sometimes musicians. Although serious in tone, the work is lightened by conversations, some of them reminiscences of the home life left behind and many of them between the protagonist of the particular episode and his senior officer, a mentor in the socialist realist mould.

Women also feature in the work, often medical orderlies, although one chapter is devoted to Klavochka, the morale-boosting 'postman' who risks her life carrying the mail in her leather bag to and from Malaia zemlia in the nightly boat convoy over the bay from Gelendzhik, the nearby port remaining in unoccupied Soviet territory.[29] In the story of Klavochka, Sokolov narrates how the boat she was in one night was sunk by enemy fire and everybody thought that she had drowned. Their relief was immense when she appeared the next day, having survived being thrown into the water. Another boat had apparently picked her up shortly afterwards and delivered her to Malaia zemlia, where she was welcomed, although the mail had suffered badly from the incident. Sokolov admits in a later edition that he had invented the ending to this chapter, being convinced that Klavochka had indeed drowned that night. His editors, however, preferred a happier ending and persuaded Sokolov to keep her alive as an example of female heroism. According to the author, it was only much later that he learned that Klavochka had indeed survived and married a local headmaster after the war.[30] Presumably it was only in 1979 that he felt able to admit this historical duplicity. Here is an example of the delicate equilibrium maintained during the Brezhnev era, when authors and editors charted unknown waters and where historical accuracy was compromised in the interests of presentist politics, leading to a dynamic outcome as writers tacked to port or starboard according to the prevailing political wind.

Sokolov describes the exploits of one unusually young hero in the chapter 'U iungi tozhe serdtse moriaka' ('A Sea-cadet also had the Heart of a Sailor'), about 15-year-old Viktor Chalenko.[31] Young 'Vitia' was already part of the national mythology of Malaia zemlia, as his story had appeared in the official state history of the war in 1961.[32] Son of a fisherman and a natural seaman, Vitia joined the navy straight from school in 1942, following the marine infantry to Malaia zemlia in February 1943. One week into the campaign, during the battle for the village of Myskhako, the agile Vitia managed to approach and destroy an enemy machine-gun nest by hand-grenade attack, losing his life in the consequent explosions. This spontaneous heroic action is an example of the reality of the times, when the rigid Soviet prewar rules ceased to apply and 'both troops and officers learned the necessity of making independent decisions and acting on them without specific, detailed orders from above'.[33]

Vitia was not forgotten amidst the chaos of war, as he left behind in his notebook a letter to his mother, written in pencil:

> If I should die on active service, I ask the leader of the political section, Vershinin, and Senior Lt. Kunytsin to go to my home in Eisk and tell my mother that her son died fighting for the liberation of the Motherland. Please give her my Komsomol card, my medal, this notebook and my sailor's cap, that she may keep them in memory of her son, the sailor.
>
> 15-year-old sailor, Viktor Chalenko[34]

Although Vitia's two mentors, Vershinin and Kunitsyn, both died in the fierce April engagements on Malaia zemlia, his request was eventually fulfilled and a school named after him in his home town. The following year, a street in Novorossiisk was also named in honour of this young Hero of the Soviet Union.[35]

With death an inevitable part of war and self-sacrifice an integral aspect of the prevalent socialist realism, Sokolov does not flinch from examining the tragedy of the fall of young combatants. Despite the realism of the narration, he avoids, however, any consequent ethical or moral dilemmas such as those that arose in similar circumstances in the trenches of World War I and gave rise to a degree of cynicism in subsequent Western memoir literature about the waste of young lives, often attributed to poor military leadership.[36] This type of critical examination of a dystopian war would not have been allowed in the Soviet Union, where censors demanded rather instances of the triumphant success associated with heroic self-sacrifice.

While the main body of Sokolov's work is narrated in the third person, the final six chapters of the book cover his postwar encounters with former comrades, which are narrated in the first person by the author. Written during the Cold War, the chapter 'Tsvetok Korei' ('The Flower of Korea') is both unusual in providing some retrospective analysis and revealing as a political statement in comparing the troops of Malaia zemlia fighting the 'fascist occupiers' with the North Koreans waging their own war of independence against the 'American imperialist' invaders.[37] This chapter is the only one in the book in which Sokolov considers the Malaia zemlia campaign from a presentist political perspective, emphasising the ravages of capitalism in what appears to be a concocted tale. Furthermore, in a convoluted comparison of capitalism and communism, the still devastated Chemin des Dames, a World War I battlefield in France, is contrasted with the green and regenerated area of Malaia zemlia during the period of the Korean War (1950–3). This comparison renews the socialist realist symbolism found in the wartime articles of Svetov and Miliavskii of the perfect future built as a result of the Malaia zemlia campaign.[38] The latter thereby takes its place in an historical continuum of wars against the invader over the previous half-century, in a specific instance of a national pattern of artificial associations between the present and great moments in Soviet history.[39]

Sokolov's democratic bottom-up venture both determines the form of the memoirs and their content, while ignoring the weighting attached to any one individual's memory by virtue of their social position or military rank. Sokolov, with the official censor, had the opportunity to remove any stories not conforming to his own and the state's ideal of the heroic myth they wished to construct on behalf of others. Through his unifying pen, these collected memoirs offer a varied yet coherent account of the Malaia zemlia campaign, conveying the single ideological message necessary for a myth. With one dominant voice pervading a work written from several different perspectives, Sokolov's memoirs may be considered 'collected' rather than 'collective' memory. In fact, later editions of Sokolov's memoirs contain the names of well over 200 individuals.[40] Just as the former comrades-in-arms reinforced their group identity at the first official reunion in 1963, so that identity was maintained through Sokolov's work, with his epilogue 'Twenty Years Later' describing their interaction on the twentieth anniversary of the liberation of Novorossiisk as a synthesis of the preceding individual stories.[41]

While Sokolov's book of collected memories of Malaia zemlia was not published until 1967, in Leningrad a similar book of stories written during the siege, *900 Days*, had been published ten years previously. This was the first major volume about the city, as works about the siege of Leningrad had been actively discouraged by Stalin, who had only permitted histories which portrayed the siege in the context of the war as a whole, thus denying any possibility of heroism not directly linked to his own command.[42] However, *900 Days* was not a work under a single authorship, rather a multi-voiced anthology of civilians' experiences of the blockade. This anthology was not to be followed until the thaw and the war cult permitted a wider collection, *Blokadnaia kniga* (*Book of the Siege*), published in 1979. Although the latter was under the sole authorship of Ales Adamovich and Daniil Granin, it differs from Sokolov's book in that it represents the authors' hundreds of (heavily censored) interviews with citizens of Leningrad, including some diary extracts in its substantial 44 chapters (496 pages).[43] Thus the work simply records a collection of sometimes brief interviews, using the words of those interviewed, unlike Sokolov's memoirs, which relate episodes from the war in the words of the author, including the literary device of conversations which render the work more immediate and personal.

Furthermore, these two Leningrad works were devoted entirely to civilians during the siege, whereas Sokolov's work was exclusively based on the memories of military personnel, albeit occasionally mentioning civilians. Treading a fine balance between the party and the individual, Sokolov recognises the initiative and heroism of individuals, in common with the earlier works on Leningrad which, from the civilian perspective, focus on family life in the city.[44] With the family one of the key tropes of Soviet wartime propaganda, Sokolov's more intimate conversations between the troops often relate to those left behind, or plans for a happy family future together, sometimes, however, thwarted by events. Moreover, in common with *Blokadnaia kniga*, it is to the family that Sokolov attributes his motivation for writing his work, stating that his book is intended for the young reader.[45] This was in line with the tenets of socialist realism, re-iterated by Zhdanov in 1946, shortly after the relative liberalism of the war years, whereby its didactic function was to offer communist role-models of physical and moral heroism to the younger generation.[46] This concept of social moral education (*vospitanie*), particularly applied to young people by means of the war narrative, exists to this day, if latterly without its overt ideological connotations.

At the end of the book, Ryzhov applauds Sokolov for fulfilling his military and literary duty in writing up these memoirs of comrades. Dedicating his work as a '*pamiatnik*' ('monument') to those who gave their lives, Sokolov appears to have considered his work to be a creative tribute, a monument in the Pushkinian literary tradition. In this case, however, it was not intended as a monument to himself as its creator, but rather as a memorial to his fallen comrades.[47]

However well Sokolov crafted a coherent narrative from collected personal memories, the position of the individual within the construction of the war myth remains complex. Surely individual memories must remain personal, as people are not able to share others' discrete memories, despite their potentially collective experience of past events. However, in the case of veterans of the same campaign, it is possible that individuals may retain similar, if not perfectly uniform, memories of a past event, which, however subjectively they may affect the individual, can nevertheless result in a collective representation of individual memories. All shared a similar type of experience, such that their individual memories offer the complementary perspectives collected by Sokolov, reinforced by their mutual interaction over reunions, where any differences could be discussed and mutual agreement reached. It seems that groups develop shared stories to define their identity and in order that members may find a common significance in their own memorial narratives.[48] It is probable, therefore, that contestation by any individual of the final version would be limited by the overriding strength of group identity.

Sokolov's first published collected version of the myth achieved a convergence of story and tone, by bringing the private memories of witnesses into the public domain as socially constructed memory with a consistent and self-confirming heroic tone and no element of defeatism or disillusionment present.[49] Concentrating on the human side of history in the shape of the nationally recognised Heroes of the Soviet Union emerging from the campaign, and some, but by no means all those characters singled out by the original war correspondents, the collaborative work speaks more authoritatively than the voice of any one individual. These discrete memories, freely given to Sokolov and formulated collectively, became subsumed into the overall myth under construction, as ownership of war memory passed into the public domain in the Krasnodar region.

CHAPTER 4

BREZHNEV'S WAR MEMOIRS

Old men forget; yet all shall be forgot,
But he'll remember, with advantages,
What feats he did that day.[1]

Individual memories continued to become collective property during the 1970s, when popular memory of the war was very much influenced by the television programme *Ot vsei dushi* (*From the Bottom of my Heart*). Travelling around the country to highlight previously unknown ordinary heroes of the recent past, the programme emotionally evoked memory of the war and immediate postwar years, serving to reunite veterans separated for decades. This family show was presented from 1972 to 1978 by the well-known actress Valentina Leont'eva, a survivor of the siege of Leningrad, reaching not only individual families in their homes, but also provincial audiences assembled in local palaces of culture.[2]

Denis Kozlov has suggested that the nationwide manifestation of an interest in history was due to the fact that it was a more 'culturally acceptable' subject of discussion in Soviet society than internal or external politics, which invariably strayed into the realm of uncertainty.[3] This may have been true for the politically conscious intelligentsia, but *From the Bottom of my Heart* was riveting viewing for the masses, as everybody in the country could identify with the courage and death toll of the war. The preoccupation with history did not only concern the recent war, however, but still encompassed a general concentration on and even idealisation of the past.[4] Although socialist realism was by then less stringently applied, the identification of historical continuities remained a developed literary form, recalling both the wartime article by Svetov and Miliavskii and Sokolov's convoluted comparison of the Korean War and both world wars of the twentieth century.[5]

The propagation of war memory through a burgeoning war cult during the late 1960s and early 1970s reinforced Brezhnev's own political position as a high-ranking veteran. By the end of the 1970s, according to Hedrick Smith, a Western journalist based in Moscow, Soviet cultural life had become 'saturated with the war theme'.[6] While Catherine Merridale condemns the whole Brezhnev era as 'a golden age of concrete and hot air, an era of state-sponsored multivolume histories of the war, of solemn speeches of commemoration, handouts, new medals, and the mass design and construction of memorials', there was substantial popular support in the early years for a policy which aimed to unify the country. Merridale refers to the gratitude of successive generations for a 'hero-myth' giving them a sense of purpose in the face of foreign antagonism, whilst at home Lisa Kirschenbaum has argued that the cult may have diverted the intelligentsia's attention from state clamp-downs on freedom of speech following the arrest and trial of dissident writers Iulii Daniel' and Andrei Siniavskii in 1965–66 and the persecution of Aleksandr Solzhenitsyn from 1969 to 1974. Nina Tumarkin similarly attributes the growing war cult to the state's wish to 'mobilize loyalty [and] maintain order', in what could have become an explosive situation amongst people questioning the whole ideology of communism. The cult helped also in the identification of an unambiguous Western enemy. In view of Brezhnev's appropriation of the 'great victory' for the Soviet people alone, with the denigration of the other wartime allies, it is probable that any conscious political target of the cult was the capitalist West as a whole, particularly at the height of the Cold War, with distraction from internal politics a useful by-product.[7]

It is difficult to establish the main instigating agent for the growth of the war cult: Brezhnev himself, the ruling elite or the ordinary people. If the cult had been established, as suggested by Tumarkin, early in the Brezhnev regime, many aspects of it resonated with the average citizen in the late 1960s.[8] Indeed, we shall see in Chapter 10 that the year 1968 was pivotal in the development of remembrance in Novorossiisk. The war cult was widely disseminated not only through literature, but also via the Communist Party's Komsomol organisation for young people and the programme of monumental commemoration which expanded during the 1970s. Certainly the overall dogmatic environment regulated the production of culture, encouraging on the one hand while restricting content on the other. Television programmes about the war were genuinely popular in the country, although it is indisputable that the general secretary took advantage of the memory environment to establish further his own military and leadership credentials, evidence for which is examined in Part II. It may be deduced that Brezhnev encouraged the originally largely popular development of the war cult for his own personal ends, while also aiming to unify the country politically through the intergenerational propagation of war memory. With Brezhnev's physical and mental decline towards the end of the 1970s, however, it seems that the cult was employed as a tool for self-protection amongst the ruling elite. Playing to Brezhnev's vanity and cult of personality within the war cult, his political comrades awarded him a series of medals in what appears to have been a concerted campaign to keep him in power whilst protecting the governmental status quo. Thus Brezhnev was awarded a Hero of the Soviet Union star on his birthday on four different occasions: in December 1966, 1976, 1978 and 1981.[9] However, for our purposes, it is the recently uncovered plotting around the production and dissemination of Brezhnev's war memoirs which sheds light on the most relevant machinations of Brezhnev's inner-circle in the late 1970s.

With memory of an heroic victory cementing the population and the leadership together, more and more veterans were encouraged to produce their war memoirs in the 1970s, in marked contrast to the general restrictive literary environment. Memoirists' freedom to publish in principle did not, however, imply a total freedom of content. Authors were supposed to support the party line on the war, adhering to the material in the official history books and situating their works within the state's master-narrative, which by then attributed victory to the party and the people working together against fascism, rather than to Stalin or even the military commanders.[10] However, official history was, in turn, mutually reliant on memoir literature, such that a dubious edifice of incontestable mythology of the war was generated, with a vicious circle linking history and political ideology.

The postwar memoirs of Sergei Borzenko provide a useful example in the case of Malaia zemlia; they also emphasise the growing position of Brezhnev within the myth, whilst serving to promote Borzenko's own reputation through his (indirect) association with Brezhnev thanks to his work on Malaia zemlia as a war correspondent. As early as 1958, Borzenko lionised Brezhnev as colonel in charge of the political section of the 18th Army, a senior representative of the party, in a chapter dated 1943:

> Brezhnev was the soldiers' favourite. He knew their moods and thoughts, knew how to make a joke at the right time and inflamed their thirst for heroic deeds. The landing troops knew him by sight, and in the noise and din of battle they were able to distinguish his authoritative, calm voice.[11]

Borzenko also reveals that Brezhnev had his own validating encounter with danger at the front when knocked unconscious as the boat he was taking from Gelendzhik to Malaia zemlia hit a mine, the tone of the section suggesting that Brezhnev was never far from the sound of battle.[12] The same information is recycled word for word in later works by Borzenko, although local newspaper articles before 1966 make no mention at all of Brezhnev's role on Malaia zemlia.

In a case of what Roger Markwick terms 'institutionalized mendacity', Borzenko's at best exaggerated and at worst inaccurate 'memory' is cited as historical fact in the official history of the war, published in 1961, even before Brezhnev had ousted Khrushchev and started the war cult.[13] This is perhaps an indication of Brezhnev's growing influence or simply the desire of an ambitious writer to flatter the chairman of the Presidium of the Supreme Soviet. Nonetheless, Malaia zemlia and Novorossiisk featured only briefly in Soviet histories of the war: the official six-volume publication (1960–5) contained only four pages about Malaia zemlia, a mere 0.1 per cent of the whole. Reading in places more like a myth than an historical record in the fact-dominated Western sense, more space is allocated to the young hero Viktor Chalenko than to Brezhnev. Whether benign mythology or indeed institutionalised mendacity, Soviet historiography since the October Revolution certainly played a political function that must be acknowledged when situating Soviet-era works on Malaia zemlia in their historical context. This degree of mythology in the official history paved the way for further aggrandisement, as a vicious circle developed whereby only 'facts' already in print were allowed to be deployed or cited in future history texts.[14]

With memoirs officially sanctioned, the censor remained busy, 'neutralising', for example, any potentially embarrassing comments on the defeats of the early weeks of the war.[15] Authors, forewarned, therefore avoided sensitive topics, producing sometimes less than honest, formulaic works, full of sentimental clichés about the 'sacred' battle with no comments of an anti-war nature. Few, if any, of these memoirs went as far as Sokolov in synthesis, being content with description rather than analysis.[16] In contrast, the anti-war character of literature in the West was prevalent towards the end of the Vietnam War. Commenting on the noticeable difference, Hedrick Smith observed:

> Official propaganda treatment of war [. . .] is vastly greater than in the West. Because of Vietnam, war is an extremely divisive issue in America, but in the Soviet Union, it is an unchallenged unifying element that serves to justify many of today's policies.[17]

During the decade from 1967 to 1977 Voenizdat published memoirs by the nationally famous Marshals Rokossovskii, Konev and Zhukov, although Khrushchev had to step in to overrule a KGB move to prevent publication of Zhukov's memoirs.[18] Zhukov, highly respected during the war and the veritable symbol of military victory, paid tribute to Brezhnev by inserting a few lines in his memoirs about seeking Brezhnev's military advice in April 1943:

> We wanted to ask the advice of the head of the political section of the 18th Army, L.I. Brezhnev [. . .]; Brezhnev had been here numerous times and was familiar with the situation, but at that moment he was on the Little Land where extremely fierce fighting was going on.[19]

An historical debate has ensued about this paragraph. According to Zhukov's daughter, Mariia, her father had never heard of Brezhnev during the war, a claim supported by Roi Medvedev, an unflinching Brezhnev critic, who held this passage to have been fabricated when Zhukov's editor was 'advised from above' ('*po sovetu svyshe*') to insert a paragraph about seeking Brezhnev's advice.[20] In contrast, however,

Aleksandr Khinshtein unconvincingly pushes all possibilities to their limits in order to give Brezhnev the benefit of the doubt, whilst accepting that Brezhnev probably asked Zhukov not to forget his role in his memoirs.[21] This is the likely scenario, as, in a similar vein, Orlando Figes cites the case of the documentary war film *A Soldier Went* (*Shel soldat*), 1975, based on Konstantin Simonov's interviews with veterans, which was not passed by the censors until a sequence paying homage to Brezhnev as a war leader had been inserted.[22]

It seems probable that Brezhnev facilitated the publication of memoirs by those who had fought in his sphere of the war in the Krasnodar and eastern Black Sea region, particularly A.A. Grechko, the commander of the North Caucasian 18th Army and Vice Admiral Kholostiakov.[23] The main memoirs of Malaia zemlia in this period were by Lt Gen I.S. Shiian, who wrote in detail about the partisans. Following the national trend and in contrast to Sokolov's work, Shiian's works were published centrally by Voenizdat and were introduced by the now famous Sergei Borzenko.[24]

Brezhnev's own war service on Malaia zemlia became increasingly highlighted and exaggerated in representations of the war. Borzenko had written in *Pravda* as early as 1968 that Brezhnev was on a par with the main hero of the Malaia zemlia landings, Major Tsezar' Kunikov. It is probable that Borzenko, always closely linked with reporting and commentary about Malaia zemlia, was able to promote his own career by his association with and flattery of Brezhnev.[25] Further excessive claims at this time about Brezhnev's military prowess are found in two documentary films crediting Brezhnev as 'one of the people who planned and executed the landings in Novorossiisk' prior to its liberation.[26] By 1976, Brezhnev's volume of speeches and articles was being referred to in a history book as 'an item of documentary material'.[27]

Anatolii Sofronov, another former war correspondent familiar with the Novorossiisk front, also promulgated Brezhnev's role fictionally.[28] While his play, *Deviatyi val* (*Storm Force 9*), 1968–73, includes some real historical characters, the chief protagonist is not a military leader, but a certain Colonel Berezhnov, a party official on Malaia zemlia clearly intended as a fictional representation of Brezhnev, whose main function is to check that all the troops carry their party cards, at the same time boosting their morale. Reminding his audience of the importance of the transmission of war memory, Berezhnov concludes the play with the words: 'Memory [...] is propagated from generation to generation. We shall never forget the heroes. Eternal glory to them.' Reinforcing the by then mythical qualities of Brezhnev as a wartime political leader, the name 'Berezhnov', barely changed from that of Brezhnev, signifies by implication the attributes expected of a great statesman: caring and solicitous of others, careful and thrifty economically. A photograph in a review of the play's premiere in Uzbekistan in 1975, on the thirtieth anniversary of the end of the war, further underlines the identification of Berezhnov with Brezhnev, as the actor playing Berezhnov looks remarkably similar to Brezhnev himself. Emphasising not only the importance attached to the brotherhood of different nationalities in the war, particularly relevant outside Russia, the review also reiterates the nationally required theme of the importance of the party during the campaign through the role of the political commissar. Once again the historical importance of Malaia zemlia is inflated, with Novorossiisk dubbed 'the Stalingrad of the Caucasus' by virtue of its deemed strategic significance for the outcome of the war.[29]

Brezhnev's connection with Malaia zemlia was disseminated even further than Uzbekistan: Brezhnev gave a gift to Fidel Castro on his visit to Cuba in January 1974 of a book of pictures of Malaia zemlia produced by former 18th Army war artist, P.Ia. Kirpichev.[30] Thus, during the 1970s, the status and significance of Malaia zemlia in the national and even international consciousness increased considerably, thanks to Brezhnev's association with the campaign. Whereas Stalin had opposed any propagation of the myth of the siege of Leningrad in order to retain his own reputation, Brezhnev actively promoted his connection with Novorossiisk and Malaia zemlia, finally resulting in the publication of his own war memoirs.

By 1977, with his physical and mental health deteriorating, Brezhnev's growing cult of personality depended increasingly upon his popularity with veterans and his reputation as a modest, wise and organised wartime leader, the desirable qualities typical of a mature mentor in the socialist realist mould. Although some consider that Brezhnev's dominant cult of personality was reminiscent of Stalin's, in that he gave the impression that he was controlling every aspect of government,[31] Brezhnev's leadership style was in fact much more democratic. Collective decision making allowed for a substantial delegation of responsibility, which won him more supporters than enemies amongst the ruling elite, the Politbiuro. Brezhnev had, however, been astute enough early in his leadership to defuse any potential threats to his leadership. Iurii Andropov (who would eventually succeed him), for example, was demoted early in Brezhnev's leadership from the secretariat of the Central Committee of the Communist Party to become chairman of the KGB. Known increasingly for his legendary vanity and love of military awards, Brezhnev was honoured on his seventieth birthday in December 1976 with yet another war medal and more flattering films.[32] It was the following month, January 1977, on the journey to Tula, the latest in the growing list of hero cities of the Soviet Union, that the plot to write Brezhnev's war memoirs was hatched by his closest allies.

Popular debate about the authorship of Brezhnev's memoirs has flourished over the last few years, with Russians anxious to elucidate the 'truth' about their provenance.[33] The man apparently behind their inception was Konstantin Chernenko,[34] leader of the Soviet Union after Andropov, then a member of the inner-circle of the Politbiuro and Brezhnev's 'political shadow'.[35] Anxious to please the general secretary, who, it seems, had the habit of boring colleagues with his wartime stories while freely admitting that he had no writing skills, Chernenko enlisted the support of Leonid Zamiatin, head of the state news agency, TASS. A team of ghost-writers was signed up, notably Anatolii Agranovskii of *Izvestiia*, Arkadii Sakhnin of *Novyi mir*, Aleksandr Murzin of *Pravda* and Vladimir Gubarev, science correspondent for *Pravda*. Each had responsibility for a part of the memoirs; for example, Gubarev wrote about Brezhnev and Soviet space developments in *Kosmicheskii oktiabr'* (*Cosmic October*). Russian scholars now agree that Sakhnin started and Agranovskii completed *Malaia zemlia*.[36]

With Brezhnev refusing to take part in the project, according to Brezhnev detractor Leonid Mlechin, the writers had to use archival material and trace his former comrades-in-arms, such as Sergei Pakhomov, Brezhnev's wartime deputy. Once the text was approved by Zamiatin and Chernenko, only four or five copies were typed up in what amounted to a top-secret military strategy, being kept deliberately from Andropov at the KGB. No explanation for this is given, but no doubt the commissioners of the work remembered the relatively recent controversy leading up to the publication in the West of Khrushchev's war memoirs in 1970, in which Andropov was also implicated.[37]

As soon as the work was finished, Brezhnev asked for it to be published immediately in the literary journal *Novyi mir*, entailing a last-minute cut-and-paste exercise in 500,000 copies to replace the intended middle section of the next edition with *Malaia zemlia*.[38] Brezhnev's work finally appeared in February 1978, on the thirty-fifth anniversary of the Malaia zemlia landings. It was reproduced in *Literaturnaia gazeta* and locally in *Novorossiiskii rabochii* a week later.[39] *Malaia zemlia* was followed later the same year by the two other sections of the original trilogy, *Vozrozhdenie* (*Regeneration*) and *Tselina* (*The Virgin Lands*). After the appearance of Brezhnev's *Malaia zemlia* in the press, several books followed.[40] The main publication of two sections of Brezhnev's memoirs, *Malaia zemlia. Vozrozhdenie*, was a paperback clearly produced for mass consumption, priced cheaply at 24 kopecks and measuring 22 by 14 centimetres.[41] With a wartime picture of the troops on the cover and a current image of Brezhnev as the frontispiece, the scene was set by a photograph of Brezhnev in uniform with the troops during the war. Just less than half of the book's 94 pages (39 in all) relate to Malaia zemlia, with the second half, *Vozrozhdenie*, covering immediate postwar events.

The popularity of Brezhnev's work was guaranteed, extending to several editions. With an overall print run of 15 million over 20 editions, it appeared in over 100 countries in 65 languages.[42] An article about it even appeared in *The Times* of London a couple of weeks after its publication, recording the fact that Brezhnev had received the Order of Victory for his 'great contribution' to the Soviet victory in World War II. This was apparently presented by Mikhail Suslov of the Politbiuro, citing Brezhnev's participation in the 'bloody battles of the legendary Malaya Zemlya'.[43]

In contrast to Sokolov's substantial memoirs published 11 years previously, Brezhnev's work was concise – short enough to fill only four pages of the broadsheet *Novorossiiskii rabochii*. The print run for the first book published locally was similarly modest, at 3,000 rather than the 50,000 copies of Sokolov's 1967 edition. This edition of *Malaia zemlia* was a correspondingly small hard-back volume measuring only 15 by 10 centimetres, with 136 pages, produced in time for the thirty-fifth anniversary of the liberation of Novorossiisk in September 1978.[44] Its quality was proclaimed by the glossy, maroon cover, boasting a photograph of landing troops, with a picture of Brezhnev opposite his signature in maroon as the frontispiece, and further photographs of the campaign inside the front and back covers. At 35 kopecks, it was cheaper than Sokolov's 85-kopeck edition.

Despite the indirect source of much of the information they contain, Brezhnev's work agrees with Sokolov's to reinforce the myth of Malaia zemlia through several key tropes. Brezhnev emphasises the name of the beach-head, quoting from a letter claimed to have been written by himself to the troops and copied to Stalin: 'The small piece of land outside Novorossiisk retaken by us from the enemy [...] we named "Malaia zemlia"'.[45] The small area of the re-conquered territory is stressed by both authors. Sokolov writes without elaboration of the troops 'on a small area of land'.[46] Brezhnev, in contrast, highlights the significance of the name in an elevated literary style indicative of the authorship of his memoirs:

> It is certainly small – less than 30 square kilometres. And it is great, as only a scrap of land can become great when it is soaked with the blood of selfless heroes.[47]

Continuing to evoke the empathy of his readers, he explains the meaning of defending this small piece of Soviet land, portrayed as a small section of the Motherland and thus a smaller representation of the Soviet Union:

> It may be small, but it is ours, Soviet land, soaked with our sweat and our blood, and we shall never under any circumstances return it to the enemy.[48]

Sokolov goes even further, stressing the troops' positive wish to rejoin Malaia zemlia with the mainland: 'The *Malozemel'tsy* cherished a dream to unite the Small with the Large.'[49]

While both authors agree on the significance of the coastal strip, there is a distinct difference in the tone of two respective memoirs. Sokolov remains optimistic throughout, while Brezhnev emphasises negatively the sense of isolation and separation from the mainland, writing rather of the constant hardship and mortal danger. As his memoirs are written in the first person, in contrast to Sokolov's third-person account, this may be interpreted as a testament to Brezhnev's own implied courage. Indeed, the whole tone of the work is set in the introductory passage, when, promoting his own bravery, Brezhnev repeats the story published by Borzenko of the mine explosion which left him unconscious on the night of his arrival by boat on the beach-head.[50] Sokolov's more positive approach is demonstrated by the inclusion in his memoirs of several songs sung by the troops, some of which look forward to victory.[51] Brezhnev, however, despite the literary provenance of his memoirs, only resorts to verse when speaking of the death of a comrade in the political section, when the man standing next to him in a dug-out was blown up, again serving to promote Brezhnev's reputation as a brave soldier.[52] Where Sokolov concentrates on several individual acts of heroism, Brezhnev focuses largely on his own interaction with the troops and his role in boosting their morale, which largely took place in relatively safe bunkers.

Although Brezhnev's memoirs were produced by committee, they do not demonstrate the variety of perspectives inherent in a collaborative venture such as Sokolov's. Both memoirs have a performative style, with substantial amounts of fictionalised dialogue between characters. However, with only one main protagonist in Brezhnev's work, it has even more cohesion than Sokolov's collected work.

With Brezhnev's influential position as leader of the Soviet Union, his memoirs were far more significant than Sokolov's collected work in shaping the national myth of Malaia zemlia, which thus attained a higher status than its brief mention in the history books warranted. Reactions to Brezhnev's memoirs were mixed. Andropov's response to a political *fait accompli* was to telephone the 'author' in hospital to express his rapture.[53] The national press immediately provided extensive coverage, praising Brezhnev as a military and literary hero,[54] and commenting on the high level of interest within the Soviet Union.[55] As early as 29 March 1978 a conference with over a thousand delegates, mainly party officials, was held in Rostov-on-Don in order to scrutinise and approve Brezhnev's conclusions.[56] In the introduction to the published proceedings, the work's political importance is highlighted:

> Workers of the Don region rate highly the memoirs of Comrade L.I. Brezhnev, 'Malaia zemlia'. [. . .] They agreed unanimously and wholeheartedly that the publication of the book 'Malaia zemlia'

> was the most important socio-political event in the life of our country.[57]

The work was not only acclaimed for its political content, however. Subsequent conferences held across the Soviet Union from Tashkent to Tbilisi proclaimed its literary merit. Praise was also attributed to Brezhnev by Ukrainian scholars for both the literary style and historical veracity of his memoirs, despite the fact that he had used the services of a team of ghost-writers for the project. Furthermore, scholars at a conference held at the Institute for World Literature in the Moscow Academy of Sciences favourably compared Brezhnev's work with the oeuvre of Aleksandr Pushkin.[58] Brezhnev's memoirs were also awarded the Lenin Prize for Literature in 1979, for 'their popularity and their educative influence on the mass of readers'.[59] The myth of Malaia zemlia once again caught the attention of *The Times*:

> The engagement received little mention in Soviet war histories until the late 1960s, when President Brezhnev's image began to predominate. Now it is treated as a major turning point in the war, alongside the battle of Stalingrad and the siege of Leningrad, with Mr Brezhnev's role receiving special attention in official accounts and memoirs.
>
> Mr Brezhnev's own description of the battle, in which he is officially said to have come close to death, was given the country's top literary prize. A song about it is now frequently played on Moscow radio.[60]

Some subdued criticism was also evident at home. Brezhnev's wife, Viktoriia Petrovna, is alleged by Zamiatin to have said that he should not have accepted the prize.[61] More generally, following the controversy over Khrushchev's memoirs and the fact that Stalin, the leader of the country during the war, had not published memoirs himself, it may have been viewed an extreme move for Brezhnev, albeit already leader of the country for over 13 years, to promote himself so boldly in what was clearly a bid for political one-upmanship. Moreover, although ghost-writing and group-authorship was widely practised amongst the country's highest-ranking politicians, in this case newspaper editors disapproved of the rumoured non-payment of the anonymous writers who had earned him 'hundreds of thousands of roubles', while allegedly embellishing Brezhnev's military career.[62] Popular opinion judged the issue with yet another Brezhnev *anekdot*, one of a wealth of relatively good-natured popular jokes told at the expense of the general secretary and his war cult:

> Brezhnev found an extremely positive review of his *Malaia zemlia* in the national press. He hurriedly summoned an aide and asked if he had read the book. 'Yes', replied the aide. 'And what did you think about it?', asked Brezhnev. 'Amazing!' replied the aide. Seeking confirmation, Brezhnev went through the same daunting interrogation with two further, increasingly frightened officials. In the face of unanimous positive response, Brezhnev declared: 'Well, in that case, I really must read it myself!'[63]

As Brezhnev's personal memoirs depended on a team of ghost-writers, their credibility as an historical document or even a witness account may rightly be questioned. It is likely that Sokolov's memoirs are more accurate than Brezhnev's, as a first edition was recorded in 1949, relatively soon after the war, although Sokolov admits that he lost his notes during the liberation of Novorossiisk.[64] Although arguably historically more useful,[65] Sokolov does make occasional mistakes, notably the exact date of the February landings, whilst claiming that *Malozemel'tsy* never forget.[66] If Brezhnev's work was inaccurate, it may possibly be attributed to the fact that it, like Sokolov's, was a collaborative venture, although not in the same sense. Brezhnev had already suffered a stroke by the time it was written, so that the drafts were read to him while he was ill and probably not mentally alert in hospital.[67] Being written by a third party, it was reliant on other memoirs and contemporaneous news reports, which were often themselves inaccurate. The frequency of his visits has also been questioned: Roi Medvedev claims that Brezhnev only crossed twice to Malaia zemlia, while Novorossiisk historian Tamara Iurina cites records showing up to 11 visits.[68] Other sections of the memoirs were obviously politically motivated, for example the continued propagation of the myth that Brezhnev's military advice was sought by Marshal Zhukov.[69]

However, despite criticism of factual errors and claims of exaggeration of the role of Brezhnev, his memoirs went on to influence the nation as a whole. By 1978, the story of Malaia zemlia was firmly established in the national consciousness, showing more characteristics of a drama than of an historical account. Under the domination of Brezhnev's memoirs, one authoritative voice prevailed, rather than the coherent collection authored by Sokolov or the multiplicity of perspectives normally encountered in historical publications in the West. Encouraged by the pervading war cult, one ideological meaning was attached by Brezhnev to the campaign, with motivation for its success attributed solely and subjectively to the heroism of communist troops. No doubt, disillusionment or cynicism features, and there is no objectivity or room for differences in its interpretation.

Malaia zemlia is remembered nationally mainly thanks to Brezhnev's overpowering top-down intervention, rather than Sokolov's bottom-up project, which remained largely local. Especially in the Krasnodar region around Novorossiisk, Brezhnev's memoirs were praised as a literary monument not only to the defenders of Malaia zemlia, but to the whole Soviet people:

> a monument, created by a man who has lived through all that the heroes of his work lived through, comprehending entirely the greatness of the feat not only of his comrades-in-arms, but of the whole Soviet people.[70]

However, if Brezhnev's volume is considered to be a monument, it is, like Pushkin's poem, a literary monument to himself, the central character in the work created in his dotage, rather than to his fallen comrades, as in the case of Sokolov. If Brezhnev propagated the myth of Malaia zemlia through his memoirs, he also used them to construct a mythological version of himself for posterity. Just before his death, quotations from Brezhnev's work were engraved on the giant Malaia zemlia memorial erected in Novorossiisk by the state in 1982, guaranteeing Brezhnev and his memoirs a certain degree of physical, if geographically limited, immortality.

CHAPTER 5

BEYOND BREZHNEV AND BREZHNEVISM

> Memory is never shaped in a vacuum; the motives of memory are never pure.[1]

After its publication, Brezhnev's volume of memoirs, *Malaia zemlia*, went on to dominate remembrance of the war in Novorossiisk, canonising the war myth according to Brezhnev. Its dissemination increased in momentum across the country, affecting individual Soviet citizens of all ages, particularly those exposed to political lessons in schools and universities, and veterans wishing to contribute their own memoirs to the war myth. As a consequence of the domination of Brezhnev's memoirs came a period of homogenisation of memory of Malaia zemlia through further memoirs, from 1978 until shortly after Brezhnev's death in November 1982.

Despite the minor nature of the Malaia zemlia campaign, its significance and Brezhnev's role were systematically exaggerated, becoming a major part of the official story of the war. Brezhnev's master-narrative became the authoritative work on the Malaia zemlia campaign, studied by academics and the subject of numerous scholarly works. Roi Medvedev recalls:

> It was necessary to consider him an intellectual, a talented man able to write books, interesting books. These books had to be studied in school. This was a characteristic of the regime.[2]

Immediately after its publication, school teachers were involved in the propagation of Brezhnev's *Malaia zemlia*, being encouraged by the Ministry of Education to include mandatory courses on its content for children in Young Pioneer and Komsomol summer camps. In the light of the work's 'most important significance for the communist education of the Soviet people', the young generation was targeted for the 'moral' and 'spiritual' education it offered. Furthermore, following a series of training conferences for teachers over the summer period, the memoirs featured prominently in the academic curriculum from September 1978. The exact nature of the approach to Brezhnev's work was detailed for every school year, being included in the schemes of work from even the youngest classes. This was an eminently attractive myth, used by the elite to rewrite the past, thanks to its so-called 'importance as an historical document'. With 'examples of mass heroism', 'analysis of historical facts' and the demonstration of the 'leading role of the Communist Party' in the war, its 'truthful, factual' account provided exemplar material for history and politics lessons for younger pupils, while its artistic merit guaranteed it a place in the study of twentieth-century literature for older students alongside such luminaries as Fadeev, Sholokhov, Tvardovskii and Simonov. In the case of university students, *Malaia zemlia* appeared in the ubiquitous courses on the history of the Communist Party in the Soviet Union.[3] Teachers' lesson plans and students' work were inspected by the Komsomol, guaranteeing compliance by lecturers and students alike. Even outside school, children were taken on educational tours of Malaia zemlia and its memorials,[4] while the recommendation of the book for reading at home with subsequent homework ensured the engagement of parents.[5] This relatively minor military campaign, virtually overlooked in earlier official history books of the war, had become by 1978 an integral part of the school and university curriculum, leading to sales of Brezhnev's memoirs of about one million copies annually.[6]

Michael Shudson observes from a Western perspective that, once canonised in the curriculum, a 'work accumulates a self-perpetuating rhetorical power', gathering an expanding circle of validating proponents and followers: 'It gathers partisans, partisans beget schools, schools beget cultural authority, cultural authority begets an established tradition.'[7] In the case of Brezhnev's memoirs, however, although the outcome was the same, it was achieved through a different mechanism from that observed in the dissemination of Western literature.

In Brezhnev's case, the cultural authority and canonisation were established from above *before* the work became widely known to the masses. Once actively promoted in schools and universities, the authority of Brezhnev's *Malaia zemlia* was set in the concrete of socialist realist iconography.

The film appeared, a play followed and *Malaia zemlia* was produced as a record version, read by well-known actors.[8] Popular songs about the heroic campaign sprang up,[9] some included in a musical produced in 1979,[10] while Sofronov had his play set to music in an oratorio by K. Akimov, *V serdtse i v pamiati* (*In Heart and Memory*), based on Brezhnev's memoirs.[11] In a probable attempt to align himself with the correspondent's flattering comments, Brezhnev 'recalls' in his memoirs the contribution of Sergei Borzenko, working alongside political worker Mariia Pedenko and the poet Pavel Kogan. This 'memory' is flawed, however, as Kogan was killed in the fighting immediately following the German occupation of Novorossiisk in September 1942, well before the Malaia zemlia campaign started, and Brezhnev did not arrive on Malaia zemlia until April 1943.[12] Despite this, the invented incident features in the musical adaptation of Brezhnev's memoirs, which further propagates Brezhnev's version of events. Although this musical was in the same sentimental vein as Sofronov's play, composer Iurii Levitin and lyricists E. Dolmatovskii and Iu. Miliutin did not attempt to fictionalise the protagonist. Rather, the narrator, book of memoirs in hand which he quotes extensively throughout the musical, represents the author Brezhnev himself. While the start of the musical is relatively faithful to the book, commencing with Brezhnev's arrival on Malaia zemlia after his boat struck a mine, the campaign is further embellished by the introduction of sentimental and patriotic songs. The musical starts with Shostakovich's *Novorossiisk Chimes*, the 18th Army gathers in Gelendzhik to a stirring military march, while later more solemn music proclaims a funereal tribute to Major Kunikov.

The most nationalistic sentiment is reserved for political worker Mariia Pedenko's song about the birch tree, a symbol of the Soviet Union. A woman also featured in the dramatised version of *Malaia zemlia*. Sofronov's play included the female spiritual companion demanded by socialist realism, a certain Masha Kuzina, a kind-hearted character who tended the sick, like Mariia.[13] In Levitin's musical, Mariia dies during the fighting, only to re-appear at the end as a representative of the three million party members who fell during the war. The cult of Mariia Pedenko gained ground in the 1970s, spawned by the cult of Brezhnev, an example of an individual whose identity was re-shaped in line with the war myth according to Brezhnev. Far from dying on Malaia zemlia, though, Pedenko was wounded during the liberation of Novorossiisk, only to settle in Kiev after the war until her actual death in 1957.[14]

In his memoirs, Brezhnev recognises Pedenko's morale-boosting contribution to the Malaia zemlia campaign, where she not only undertook clerical and librarian duties, but also worked as an 'agitator', a member of the political section, in the production and dissemination of the locally produced news-sheet, *Polundra*. The name for this publication derived from the battle-cry shouted by sailors and marine infantry. Previously interpreted as a warning – Watch out! Get down! –, on Malaia zemlia it was intended as the more positive encouragement – 'Let's go!' –, often followed by the word *'Vpered!'* (onwards), the Russian equivalent of the French *'en avant'*.

Pedenko had already published her memoirs in the form of her wartime diary shortly after the war, but it was not until her contribution was publicly recognised by Brezhnev that she was included in the official war cult.[15] Georgii Sokolov notes that Brezhnev had recalled Mariia during the reunion of 18th Army veterans in Moscow in May 1970, saying:

> Do you remember Mariia Pedenko? A girl in the political section of the 255th Marine Infantry Brigade? For me, her face was the personification of many women who fought shoulder to shoulder with the men.[16]

Following Brezhnev's lead, Sokolov went on to include her story, 'Ryzhaia Polundra' ('Redheaded Polundra'), in his later memoirs,[17] with further comments about her belatedly recognised role in the introduction and epilogue.[18] An academic article published in Ukraine the following year confirmed her new status as Brezhnev's protégée, quoting extensively from his memoirs.[19] Pedenko's own novel, drafted in 1952, was published posthumously in 1980. *"Polundra, Krasnoflotsy!"* (*"Polundra, Red Navy Sailors!"*) was based on Pedenko's time on Malaia zemlia, and included Brezhnev's words about her in the introduction.[20] It has been found that memory of women participants in the war relied mainly on private, oral accounts.[21] This may well have been the case for many women in the Soviet Red Army, whose public voices were silenced due to the perceived stigma of alleged sexual promiscuity during the war. Thanks to Brezhnev, however, Mariia Pedenko was singled out from several women on Malaia zemlia, with her place in the myth further propagated by Sofronov, Levitin and Sokolov.

Pedenko's is not the only story to have been revived by Brezhnev. Due to the overriding influence of Brezhnev's memoirs, many responses were spawned and individuals re-defined within Brezhnev's master-narrative, leading to a second stage of homogenisation of memory according to the myth propagated by Brezhnev. Many publishers jumped on the memorial band-wagon, recycling and re-working material from Brezhnev's *Malaia zemlia*. For example, a new guide-book to Novorossiisk with substantial extracts from Brezhnev's memoirs was published in 1978.[22] A further book wrapped the text of Brezhnev's memoirs around glossy photographs of Brezhnev's visit to Novorossiisk in 1974, with one whole page dedicated to Mariia Pedenko's place in Brezhnev's memoirs.[23]

Following the appearance of Brezhnev's memoirs, several veterans of Malaia zemlia suddenly published their own memoirs, once the door had been opened to them. The snowball effect launched by the publication of Brezhnev's authoritative text is a factor in the construction and propagation of a war myth unique to Malaia zemlia in the Soviet Union of the period, serving to validate Brezhnev's story and exaggerate its importance. This continuing myth-building process, where the existing myth influences the individual, is diametrically opposed to the initial mechanism, whereby several individuals contributed to the construction of the original myth. A whole series of such memoirs was published in the Krasnodar region between 1978 and 1985 in the series *Ratnyi podvig Novorossiiska* (*Novorossiisk's Military Feat*), with the stated aim of setting the war events in Novorossiisk alongside those of other better-known hero cities.[24] The series continued well after Brezhnev's death in 1982, probably due to the local interest generated by the regionally published works. Identical in size, format and style,[25] the covers of the books embrace a small variety of different colours to distinguish them from each other. The series was branded by the motif across the top of each edition of the Defence Line monument erected in September 1978 in the north-east of Novorossiisk, months after the publication of Brezhnev's memoirs.

This concrete arch across the main road to Gelendzhik depicts a series of socialist realist fists, each clenching a stick grenade.

Uniformity of the individual books was further guaranteed by a distinguished editorial team including the memoirist Georgii Sokolov and other senior *Ratnyi podvig* authors: A.P. Marfin, V.T. Protsenko and G.A. Pshenianik. This elite group managed to navigate the increased censorship of the time, ensuring that the content of each work conformed to the growing myth.[26] With a modest print-run of 25,000 per book and priced between 15 and 30 kopecks, memoirs in the series were written mainly by officers, with the notable exception of Viktor Kaida, a marine infantry rating who settled in Novorossiisk after the war. Other authors were former and existing marine infantry officers, Black Sea Fleet officers or pilots. All were men, although Mariia Pedenko's wartime diary, originally published in Kiev, was re-published in the *Ratnyi podvig* series as *Frontovoi dnevnik* (*Frontline Diary*).

Most of the works contain substantial passages of conversation with comrades, ostensibly recalled almost 40 years after the event. These render the books more accessible, while also padding out the meagre content in the case of Viktor Kaida. In contrast, Grigorii Bondar', who had become a rear admiral by the time he wrote his memoirs, has a more thoughtful, literary style, filling three times as many pages as Kaida. Overall there is much material in common. Several books mention Tsezar' Kunikov in Gelendzhik before the landings and his untimely death, although his name was only a legend to most.[27] The self-sacrifice of young Viktor Chalenko appears in Bondar''s memoirs,[28] while other episodes also bear the hallmark of Sokolov's earlier accounts.

It is no surprise that the enemy occurs in every work. Referred to as Fritzes, Hitlerites or simply fascists, they are depicted as weak and drunk, uncommitted to their cause. On the other hand, the Soviet troops hold the moral high ground throughout, winning through thanks to their 'iron courage' as they fought 'for the honour, freedom and independence of their dear Motherland'.[29] Bondar' selects several close encounters with Germans to make his point. He was involved in the capture of a weak German prisoner, who became an informant for the Soviets without much persuasion. A Romanian defector is also mentioned, admired for his 'peasant practicality' by Bondar' in his persistent attempts to desert in search of better treatment from the Soviets.[30] Sympathy is also shown for a German pilot shot down in flames, who was unwilling to face capture, having apparently been told that the Soviets would cut out his heart and liver and eat them.[31] The propaganda war was fought by both sides, it appears. The enemy dropped leaflets onto Soviet troops with 'forged' photos of Soviet officers who wrote in favour of the Germans. In return, Bondar' and a political officer hid a radio on the slopes of Mount Koldun close to enemy lines, through which they broadcast propaganda messages. These included letters written allegedly by German prisoners of war about the stupidity of conflict and the great political unity of the Soviet people defending their Motherland.[32]

All authors describe dangerous situations where they came close to death. Galatenko reinforces the nightly threat of torpedo and shell fire when crossing the bay from Gelendzhik.[33] On land, Kaida was surprised by two Germans when entering an apparently empty shack, only escaping death by the timely intervention of his comrades.[34] In his own drama, Bondar' describes the struggle to access water from the sole well in Myskhako (the so-called Well of Life), which was under constant fire from enemy troops holding the higher ground.[35] Bombing and strafing by German aircraft was a constant danger to everyone based on Malaia zemlia.

Once the fiercest battles of April were over, there was time for some relaxation. Formal concerts and poetry reading were organised by the political department. Bondar' recalls singing and dancing to a record player in the cellar under the wine factory in Myskhako, while Galatenko includes a photograph of a concert in the open air, with guitar, accordion and saxophone.[36] It was during their free time that the troops missed their homes most. Bondar' describes conversations about their families, noting that it was the women that the men discussed most. However, it seems that there were actually several women on Malaia zemlia, not only Mariia Pedenko. Most were volunteers, including radio operators, telephonists, nurses and field medical orderlies, mechanics, meteorologists, librarians and interpreters, with many in the political section. There were even two female officers on the beach-head – one medical sub-lieutenant and one lieutenant in a marine infantry rifle platoon. In a chapter entitled 'Nashi frontovye podrugi' ('Our Female Friends at the Front'), Bondar' includes an extended analysis of women's roles, giving several examples by name, and noting his admiration for their courageous behaviour in the cold and wet trenches, carrying rations and communications equipment into action and wounded men off the battlefield.[37] Grigor'ev refers to Mariia Pedenko's production of the May Day issue of *Polundra*, with the help of artists contributing humorous cartoons and sketches, including Vladimir Tsigal', who was later responsible for the design of the Malaia zemlia memorial complex.[38]

One significant feature of the *Ratnyi podvig Novorossiiska* books is several pages of black and white photographs, which usually include a picture of Brezhnev among the troops as well as the standard photograph of Major Kunikov before the landings. As a series of memoirs influenced by the myth according to Brezhnev, wherein each individual author relocates his own story, Brezhnev's appearance in these works is virtually mandatory, with some apt quotations from his memoirs. Even Savitskii, a former pilot, who would not have met Brezhnev during the war, speaks of his memoirs with authority.[39] Most memoirists include a tribute to Brezhnev, who was apparently recalled by them all, thereby reinforcing and further endorsing Brezhnev's memoirs in a spiral of myth making. Indeed, it has been alleged that the mature myth according to Brezhnev generated many more 'witnesses' who actually believed the fabrications that they wrote.[40] For example, Galatenko boosts Brezhnev's reputation as a wise commander, recalling him making a useful suggestion on the training of troops:

> Colonel Brezhnev requested the sailors to help the landing troops with respect to the crossing and landings. He says that you already have previous experience in landing operations, which should be shared with our troops and commanders.[41]

Reinforcing the argument for homogeneity of content as well as form, Kaida relates in his book published a few months later how Brezhnev recommended the passing on of experience from sailors to soldiers:

> Leonid Il'ich suggested directing experienced *Malozemel'tsy* sailors to instruct the soldiers who were taking part for the first time in such a difficult military operation as landings from the sea.[42]

In a more personal passage, Grigor'ev recalls giving Brezhnev a guided tour of the trench network. Apparently, having congratulated the troops on their defensive preparations, the colonel went on to request a steam bath, which, it seems, was made available.[43] Widening the scope, Bondar' not only recalls Brezhnev on Malaia zemlia, but also met him as leader of the Soviet Union. Other memoirists similarly recall meetings with Brezhnev in 1974 and on key anniversaries.[44]

In the *Ratnyi podvig Novorossiiska* series individuals clearly demonstrate a tendency to smooth out differences for the sake of simplification and coherence of the war myth. Lisa Kirschenbaum similarly finds the increasing appropriation of the war myth by survivors in their own accounts towards the end of the Brezhnev era, although none of them would have claimed to meet Brezhnev during their military service.[45] This phenomenon was not unique to the Soviet Union, however, as a similar merging of individual experience with the myth has been found in the case of Britain during World War II.[46]

While earlier memoirs were produced by veterans with a genuine gift and motivation for writing, most of these later authors were not talented writers. As little more than political pawns, they do not stand out amongst the memoirists of Malaia zemlia, their identity being subsumed by the overarching state ownership of the war narrative, and their own real stories transformed into myth. Thus, by the time of Brezhnev's death, there was a state of total visible convergence of published war memoirs in Novorossiisk, due largely to state coercion and under the complete ownership of the state. In view of the state's didactic attitude to the production of culture, it is not surprising that the myth of Malaia zemlia developed in this way. The formulaic nature of socialist realism which led to the uniformity of literary form observed in many memoirs facilitated myth creation by their very homogeneity.

The overt inflation of Brezhnev's role in his memoirs and the self-aggrandising monumentalisation of war memory drew criticism from both dissident and Western scholars immediately after Brezhnev's death.[47] Michael Ignatieff, for example, is scathing of the war cult of the Brezhnev era:

> Compared to the other great battles, the fight for Novorossisk would have been a minor skirmish had it not been for the fact that a young party propaganda officer named Leonid Brezhnev played a minor and inglorious role in the rear. [. . .] When masters invent tradition, they have the past re-written as the history of their own glorious beginnings.[48]

From a more personal point of view, Zhores Medvedev recalls both the campaign and Brezhnev's memoirs:

> Brezhnev's attempts to rewrite the history of the war were a source of derision amongst the military. As his 'personality cult' became more insistent, so he was more and more often described as an outstanding military leader who had played an active part in the most important battles of the war. This was simply not true. The battle which took place near Novorossiisk in 1943, where he was the deputy of the commander for political work [. . .] was part of a not very successful military operation and not one of the crucial battles of the war as it is depicted in works written to elevate Brezhnev's role. I am in a position to form an independent opinion about this isolated section of the Southern front [. . .] for as a seventeen-year-old private in the infantry I was in the same army at the same place.[49]

This comment demonstrates the superficial validity of the memories of two different people of the same event. In the face of Brezhnev's dominant narrative, though, Medvedev's opinion from the point of view of a hospitalised junior soldier would count for little. However, his opinion four decades after the events carried more scholarly authority in the West. Roi Medvedev is similarly scathing of the 'forged' memoirs, while Lazar Lazarev condemns Brezhnev's memoirs as a 'ghost-written biography, which included a glowing, fictionalised account of his own modest wartime service as a military commissar'.[50]

The literary response within the Soviet Union after Brezhnev's death was more muted but equally pervasive. If Brezhnev had defined other memoirists involved with the Malaia zemlia campaign for his own purposes, it was Brezhnev who was later re-defined by the memoirists. On the national level, the section relating to Brezhnev in Borzenko's original article on Malaia zemlia written in 1943 no longer appears in a collection of wartime dispatches published in 1982, while a later version of Zhukov's memoirs has the questionable paragraph about seeking Brezhnev's opinion removed.[51]

Locally, however, the response was less severe. Sokolov retains in all later editions of his memoirs the same brief passage about the kind and modest Colonel Brezhnev, narrated by the young Vasilii Zelentsov, to whom Brezhnev issues his party card:

> A colonel is sitting at the table. Thinnish, but with bushy, black eyebrows. He's wearing a simple soldier's uniform and greatcoat. He turns to me, smiling. His eyebrows lift a little, and I can see his bright, jolly eyes. [. . .] And do you know who that colonel was? [. . .] Brezhnev, the head of our landing army's political section.[52]

Similarly, the passage describes Brezhnev's rallying speeches on the beach-head and retains the part about Brezhnev having been blown out of his boat by a mine.

It is the epilogues of Sokolov's memoirs, however, which clearly demonstrate the rise and fall of Brezhnev's cult of personality. In his final chapter of the 1967 edition, 'Dvadtsat' let spustia' ('Twenty Years Later'), four lines are devoted to Brezhnev, by then general secretary of the Communist Party of the Soviet Union, who joined the veterans for the first major reunion on Malaia zemlia in 1963.[53] This section was repeated verbatim in the 1971 edition of the book.[54] By 1979, Brezhnev's memoirs were cited in the prologue by Admiral Kholostiakov, who 'recalled' that Brezhnev took part in the actual planning of the landings, aligning both himself and Sokolov with Brezhnev's version of events.[55] By then, the Malaia zemlia campaign was so famous that Kholostiakov compares it favourably with the Battle of Stalingrad. In Sokolov's epilogue, 'Tridtsat' let spustia' ('Thirty Years Later'), Brezhnev makes an early appearance in the second paragraph, by virtue of his attendance at reunions and his visit to Novorossiisk in 1974, which permeates the rest of the epilogue and will be considered in detail in Part II. Exaggerating the number of times Brezhnev crossed to Malaia zemlia and emphasising the danger involved, Sokolov repeats the story of Brezhnev's boat hitting a mine. Details of his party work on the beach-head follow, with the information that Brezhnev never forgot a name or a face. Furthermore, Sokolov attributes to Brezhnev in this edition the suggestion that he supplement his original book of memoirs with the input of his comrades-in-arms. Brezhnev is given credit for supplying Sokolov with a list of addresses for this reason and also with helping in the organisation of the first reunion in 1963. Thus Brezhnev is characterised alongside other leading military officers as a brave soldier, a trusty comrade and an organised leader.[56]

Memory of the past has an important function in the building of an identity in the present. James Wertsch observes that, for an individual's identity, memory is more likely to privilege accuracy, while for a country it is based rather on the need for a politically usable past.[57] In Sokolov's case, however, as in the *Ratnyi podvig Novorossiiska* memoirs, accuracy seems to have been discarded by the individual memoirist for the sake of toeing the party line in the context of group and national identity. There may be two possible reasons for the homogeneity of memoirs after the appearance of Brezhnev's works, especially in relation to Brezhnev himself. This may simply be caused by unconscious reactions to an almost subliminal influence on memory caused by pervasive propaganda and its formulaic language – the defining framework for the war cult of the Brezhnev era. Wertsch demonstrates how, in some cases, 'a text can structure meaning, communication and even thought', while 'another author's words may be appropriated by the recipient who then passes them on as his own words'.[58] This type of unconscious organic influence may be recognised in media content, with television and press coverage in the Soviet Union probably subjecting the malleable memory of an individual citizen (who may not even have read Brezhnev's memoirs) to the dominance of the collective. A more likely mechanism in the case of memoirists, though, is that they employed a proactive response indicative of a degree of self-serving political awareness. In this way, the pragmatic memoirist probably effected a deliberate reconstruction of personal memory, encouraged or coerced by the censor, to accommodate the unwritten literary guidelines of the era.

It is noticeable that Sokolov carefully crafted different editions of his memoirs to situate them within the memorial climate of the Soviet Union over nearly two decades, changing them proactively to suit the presentist attitude of the state. By Sokolov's final edition, published in 1985, most of the material is similar to previous versions, except the epilogue, 'Sorok let spustia' ('Forty Years Later'). Here, in complete contrast, Sokolov removes every reference to Brezhnev, although he retains most other sections from both 'Twenty Years Later' and 'Thirty Years Later'.[59] In a similar way, two of the later memoirs in the series *Ratnyi podvig Novorossiiska*, published after Brezhnev's death, contain no references to him, in contrast to earlier works in the series. These reactions to the death of the agent of the centralised myth suggests that the predominant influence on memoir literature relating to

Brezhnev from 1978 to 1982 was the proactive type, residing mainly in the hands of the author, rather than an unconscious reaction to an overwhelming influence from above. Having largely removed Brezhnev from his memoirs by 1985, Sokolov finally left a probably more truthful version than Brezhnev's own memoirs for posterity, demonstrating greater integrity as a memorial to his fallen comrades.[60]

The influence of Brezhnev's memoirs was so overwhelming during his leadership that they permitted no contestation, clouding and distorting history for the sake of political utility. In the end though, Brezhnev's exaggerated claims probably served to sound the death-knell for the war cult. After his death, the public attitude to Brezhnev in the capital hardened, following disclosures in 1987 by Soviet historians that his wartime exploits had been greatly exaggerated in *Malaia zemlia*, causing one letter-writer to state: 'The work is not worth keeping in public libraries and the war museum since, as everyone knows, Brezhnev never wrote it.' With Brezhnev written out of his own myth, copies of his memoirs were in fact removed from school libraries and destroyed, while references to Malaia zemlia in the introduction to television's minute's silence were cut.[61] Thanks to Brezhnev, Malaia zemlia had become a national and international subject of derision and a sad symbol of the stagnation of the Brezhnev era.

The myth that during the war years had promised so much in comparison with the myth of the siege of Leningrad had, it seemed, died an early literary death. As a victim of its own hyped-up success, it had exaggerated the past to such an extent that its rapid construction was followed by an even swifter deconstruction. The carpet was pulled out from under the lesser authors of the *Ratnyi podvig Novorossiiska* series and only Sokolov managed to regain his once-compromised integrity. In complete contrast, the myth of the siege of Leningrad, built upon more solid historical foundations, continued to attract growing public credibility once the stranglehold of the Soviet elite had been released. For Malaia zemlia, though, the remembrance process would have to rely on a different, non-literary mechanism if it was to survive at all.

PART II

LEONID BREZHNEV

LOCAL LEGEND OR NATIONAL STATESMAN?

> People, their deeds and works, are remembered by history only if they succeed as story. Their lives may be told and retold as legend, altered to fit the needs of succeeding generations.[1]

A bronze statue of Leonid Brezhnev appeared in the centre of Novorossiisk in 2004, decades after other statues to the general secretary had been removed from public spaces across the country. The new statue was erected for the thirtieth anniversary of Brezhnev's visit to Novorossiisk in 1974, when he presented the Gold Star to the new Hero City of the Soviet Union. This statue reveals the human characteristics of the general secretary in an artistic representation of a local legend which has developed around the event. It encapsulates the personal rather than the political side of this historic relationship, serving to define the current identity of Novorossiisk with respect to Brezhnev. The Brezhnev statue is grounded in local society and is thus more specific than national memory, which barely recognises the event to which it refers. National and local views of Brezhnev's place in history are not necessarily in opposition however, but offer complementary perspectives of the general secretary, seen from a distance or in close detail as if through opposite ends of a telescope.

This type of relationship has been explored with regard to Germany by Alon Confino, in search of common ground between local and national myths. Through the idealistic concept of *Heimat* (home) in

German society, he successfully links the local with the national, demonstrating an overlapping of symbolism such that local memory may sometimes appropriate the national, while the national may acquire and revive different local meanings. In this way, Confino inverts traditional, presentist scholarship which sees national interests always moulding local ones, to examine how local issues may shape nationhood in a convergence of interests.[2]

The *Heimat* approach in Germany embraces both local and national connotations. Although it is particularly useful in the case of Germany, to date scholarship has barely addressed this degree of complexity in the construction of local identity within the often overpowering Soviet myth of the Great Patriotic War.[3] On the local level the concept of *Heimat* is similar to that of *Malaia zemlia*: a small place that one can call home. However, the troops on Malaia zemlia saw the rest of the country as different, *Bol'shaia zemlia*, accepting that their beach-head was only one small part of a larger whole and hoping for a reunification of the two as the enemy was expelled.[4] There is no opposition between these two concepts, though, which dovetail together perfectly. The early myth of Malaia zemlia was simply an expression of a strong local identity which would later be subsumed within the national war myth, as we have seen earlier with memoir literature.

In this part we return to Novorossiisk to examine growing scrutiny of the local war myth and Brezhnev's role within it in the town where he saw war service. Brezhnev's visit in 1974 so affected the hero city's perception of its own status within history that an eventual divergence in interpretation of Brezhnev's association with Malaia zemlia arose between national and local audiences. The visit shows characteristics of what Aleksandr Etkind terms a 'memory event'.[5] This type of secondary phenomenon occurs some time after the original, historic event, but is dependent upon memory of the original for its impact and (re-)interpretation. A more familiar example of a memory event is the fall of the Berlin Wall, which invites comparison with the original event of its construction and also led to its own sequence of anniversaries. Brezhnev's visit to Novorossiisk in 1974 was both secondary to and a product of his presence in the original Malaia zemlia campaign, in turn giving rise to its own memorial consequences in a series of reverberations through time. Chapters in this part examine the Brezhnev visit, the agency and mechanism of subsequent reverberations and the extent of any consequent re-interpretation and divergence from national collective memory.

The public persona of Brezhnev, which had been carefully constructed during the war cult only to be deconstructed nationally shortly after Brezhnev's death, was re-constructed in Novorossiisk alone after the fall of communism, overriding the connection still ingrained in national collective memory between Brezhnev and his state-sponsored myth of Malaia zemlia. With a national re-assessment of Brezhnev around his centenary in 2006, however, a more empathetic and nostalgic sentiment has arisen nationally, which is closer in some aspects to the view consistently held in Novorossiisk.

Recent publications reveal a certain nostalgia for the Brezhnev era of stability and international power amongst some commentators, with criticism of a period of political and economic stagnation by others.[6] It is not only some members of the older generation who would welcome a return to the conditions of 'developed socialism' under Brezhnev, but also President Putin, who has publicly lamented the collapse of the Soviet Union and reintroduced the Soviet national anthem with new words. War memory in contemporary Russia is also an integral part of the wave of nostalgia for the past that is gripping the country. Indeed, Putin's policy of expansionism in Ukraine may be interpreted as a neo-imperialistic attempt to turn back the clock. It appears that the war cult is not merely used to validate the present, but also marks a campaign to return to some of the social and political values of the past by the promotion of collective remembrance.

The onset of a new war cult in the twenty-first century has led to a rapprochement of perceptions of Malaia zemlia nationally and locally, albeit allowing for a revised role for the general secretary in the public consciousness. The protracted debate around the adoption of the Brezhnev statue suggests that this artistic representation of Brezhnev's place in the war myth is one significant indicator of the current mnemonic identity of Novorossiisk with respect to its relationship with Leonid Brezhnev.

CHAPTER 6

BREZHNEV COMES TO TOWN

Figure 6.1 Heroes' Square, Novorossiisk (photograph by the author)

Twenty-eight years after the naming of the first Hero Cities of the Soviet Union, Novorossiisk eventually joined their ranks on 14 September 1973. On Heroes' Square a wall was erected overnight to mark the award so that, by the next day, the words 'Hero City' were evident, made of cement at first, with a later inscription carved in granite. The national press reported a celebratory rally of thousands of workers in the town, with a special sitting of the town's Communist Party Committee, the Gorkom. The country was reminded of the reason for the honour, while in the local newspaper, *Novorossiiskii rabochii*, a brief history of the campaign was provided by Georgii Sokolov, the authoritative memoirist of Malaia zemlia.[1]

The scholarly verdict in the West was less laudatory. Observing the noticeable escalation of the war cult at the beginning of the 1970s, Nina Tumarkin finds that 'there is no question that Novorossiisk was given the honored title of hero city exclusively because of the Brezhnev connection'.[2] It is indeed indisputable that Brezhnev was closely involved with the award at this specific time, in view of his letter of congratulations written on 15 September 1973, which was reported nationwide in *Pravda* the following day, the thirtieth anniversary of the liberation of Novorossiisk:

> Dear Comrades!
> Today is one of the most significant days in the history of the glorious town of Novorossiisk! Together with you, I feel sincere joy and pride in my links with the awarding to Novorossiisk of the supreme and honourable title of Hero City.
>
> L.I. Brezhnev[3]

However, when interviewed, a former head of culture in Novorossiisk claimed that Brezhnev had needed some prompting from the town, which had sent delegations to Moscow over a period of five years prior to 1973 to lobby his aide, Viktor Golikov. They backed up the town's claim to fame with a portfolio of historical evidence supplied by the Novorossiisk museum director, Evgeniia Makarovna. Personal contacts were apparently deemed crucial to manoeuvring through the minefield of Soviet politics, and Golikov would no doubt have felt sympathetic to the cause, being a native of Novorossiisk and former headmaster of School Number Seven, who in his political career worked alongside Brezhnev for nearly 30 years. In a newspaper interview shortly before his death, Golikov recalled: 'I did everything for Novorossiisk that I considered useful and necessary.'[4] It is likely that Brezhnev was not too hard to persuade of the utility of war memory in view of his close connection with the two towns made hero cities on the same day: both Novorossiisk and then Kerch' had been liberated by the 18th Army in 1943. In his newspaper article,

Sokolov stressed the pride of Novorossiisk in its connections with Brezhnev. The evidence therefore points to Novorossiisk's having been honoured as a hero city mainly due to the Brezhnev connection, albeit in a slightly more complex way than has previously been assumed.[5]

Brezhnev had written his letter of congratulations from the Crimea and did not capitalise politically on his links with Novorossiisk by visiting the town that month. Neither had Brezhnev visited Novorossiisk when the town was awarded the Order of the Great Patriotic War (first class) in May 1966, less than two years after he had become leader of the Soviet Union. As the momentum of the war cult built up in the late 1960s, however, Brezhnev started to attend 18th Army veterans' reunions in Moscow, notably on the twenty-fifth anniversary of Victory Day in 1970.[6] However, although Brezhnev's name had been associated with Novorossiisk in the national press from 1966, the town had to wait until September 1974 for Brezhnev to return to Novorossiisk and present personally the hero city's gold star.

The official marking of the award of hero city status in both 1973 and 1974 enabled the town to celebrate the occasions in two different ways. While the festivities of September 1973 were devoted solely to the award, the events of 1974 focused on the person of Brezhnev himself, consolidating his position with regard to Novorossiisk both in the past and in the present, with more significant consequences for the future than simply the gold star he brought with him.

Brezhnev, accompanied by Golikov and two other aides, left for Novorossiisk on 6 September 1974 from Moscow's Vnukovo Airport,[7] with the tone of his visit to Malaia zemlia having been set in the national press. Articles in *Izvestiia* reminded readers of the significance of the campaign and the constant danger to those on the ground:

> So what was Malaia zemlia, then? It was the landings; then standing in trenches nearly up to your knees in hot, spent cartridges, with the cold water of the Tsemes Bay behind you; it was when you could never retreat by even one step.[8]

The final line refers to Stalin's infamous 'Not one step back' Order Number 227 of July 1942, intended to ensure that soldiers in the Red Army did not have the option to retreat. Those that did were often placed in penal battalions or even executed for cowardice. Establishing Brezhnev's credentials under these testing conditions, the correspondent writes:

> In the hottest days on Malaia zemlia, Colonel L.I. Brezhnev, Head of the Political Section of the 18th Army, was often to be seen. In the hardest days he was alongside the troops.[9]

According to TASS, Brezhnev flew from Moscow to Anapa, where he changed from an aeroplane to a helicopter for the final leg of his journey to Novorossiisk. His welcome committee at the aerodrome on the site of Malaia zemlia consisted of several veterans and the head of the neighbouring Stavropol' Region, a certain Mikhail Gorbachev. The official reception over, the delegation proceeded straight to the stele of remembrance on the sea shore at Stanichka, where photographs show them walking to the shore where the landings had taken place.[10]

Photographs of Brezhnev, the monuments and crowds testify to the atmosphere of the occasion, where veterans wearing medals reportedly joined 'tens of thousands' of citizens on the newly cleaned streets to greet the general secretary. Brezhnev then visited significant monuments and sites in the Malaia zemlia hinterland near the village of Myskahko outside Novorossiisk, including the wine cellar in the main building of the communal vineyard, which had acted as the headquarters of the 83rd Marine Infantry Brigade and where Brezhnev had 'once talked with the heroes of Malaia zemlia'.[11]

Figure 6.2 Brezhnev's Wine Cellar Bunker in Myskhako (photographs by the author)

Figure 6.3 The Spot in Myskhako Where Brezhnev Planted a Tree in 1974: 'This Tree was Planted on 6 September 1974 by L.I. Brezhnev' (photograph by the author)

After planting a memorial tree in the so-called Dolina smerti (The Valley of Death) in Myskahko, Brezhnev's historical tour ended back in the town centre with a visit to the monument to the Unknown Sailor and the laying of flowers at the eternal flame on Heroes' Square.[12]

The following day, the official correspondent described further 'tens of thousands' of citizens carrying red flags and banners, all heading for the 'Trud' Stadium:

> We are walking in a dense flood of people to the stadium on this notable day, 7 September 1974. [. . .] Workers from the cement factories and the port, sailors, builders and teachers [. . .] are carrying bouquets of bright flowers, grown on the rocky slopes of Tsemes Bay. The dress uniforms of officers and generals are sparkling with awards and medals.[13]

As Brezhnev mounted the podium in the stadium, he was apparently greeted with a standing ovation, captured by press photographers, before speaking at length to the assembled crowd and finally presenting the gold star to the town.[14]

In his speech, which was recorded for posterity,[15] Brezhnev outlined – in the literary tradition of socialist realism – Novorossiisk's military and political past, emphasising the continuity of the devotion of its citizens to communism and the building of socialism. He praised the town's role in 1905 in setting up the first Council of Deputies in the country; its loyalty during the 1917 revolution; the deliberate scuttling in 1918 of a squadron of ships rather than allowing them to fall into the hands of 'Imperial Germany'; and the rout of the White Guards in 1920 which precipitated their flight from the country at the end of the civil war. Reminding the audience of the lasting impression made by the 1943 episode on all participants, Brezhnev noted the durability of memory, again invoking prime examples of Soviet history to enhance the status of the Malaia zemlia campaign:

> If a man has been a direct participant in some important event or other of his times, an event which comes to be the most important turning point in world history, this remains in his consciousness for all his life. It is comparable with the October socialist revolution and the civil war for our party's older generation.[16]

Further inflating local events, Brezhnev set them in the context of the strategic battle for the northern Caucasus with its rich supplies of oil. He also referred to the overall campaign in the Don region, thus expanding the significance of the 'bastion' of Novorossiisk and enabling a realistic comparison with Stalingrad, an uncontroversial example of a hero city.

Acknowledging creative artists in general, Brezhnev singled out the war correspondent Sergei Borzenko with poet Pavel Kogan for 'their fighting, passionate words'; sculptors of monuments; and Dmitrii Shostakovich, composer of the *Novorossiisk Chimes*. Creative work was also evident throughout the visit. Local and national interests combined in the showing of the film *Pamiat' navsegda* (*Memory is Forever*) in Novorossiisk's 'Moscow' cinema, showing Brezhnev meeting 18th Army veterans. Furthermore, on the day of Brezhnev's arrival, a group of workers was called to the cinema studios to film another documentary, *Bitva za Novorossiisk* (*The Battle for Novorossiisk*), presumably to add retrospective credence alongside other shots of Brezhnev's visit. This artistic response to Brezhnev's visit ensured its national coverage, incorporated two years later into documentaries marking the general secretary's seventieth birthday.[17] It is worth noting that, while photographs and sound recordings of Brezhnev's visit provide a valuable record, they could have been staged or edited to a certain extent. The sheer number of similar images, however, indicates that press reports are widely accurate, if referring sometimes to obviously staged meetings with workers and veterans to guide the interpretation of readers.

The tone of Brezhnev's speech and further meetings was not only military and retrospective, however. It was evident throughout the visit that not only war memory was at play, as Brezhnev also praised the role of local industry in the country's economy: Novorossiisk apparently produced 'one quarter of the national tonnage of cement', while the port was 'well-known internationally'. Visits were made to the growing port and the 'Proletariat' cement works, where Brezhnev was reportedly 'welcomed everywhere by thousands of residents'. National and local journalists highlighted the postwar regeneration that had brought new life to the ruined town, with the vision of a prosperous future implied by the building of a new school and a maternity hospital with 200 beds.[18]

This new emphasis on the future appears to have left the townspeople with no little responsibility. According to the press, the response from Novorossiisk was to express a wish to work even harder to fulfil the tasks of the five-year plan,[19] with a certain P. Belen'kin of the 'October' cement works promising 'shock work' tactics: 'To the supreme award from the Motherland, the cement workers of our factory will respond with supreme productivity.'[20] Belen'kin reminded readers of progress since the war: 'Our factory lay in ruins. In 1948 the citizens of Novorossiisk decided to build a new cement factory on the site of the former one.' By the following year, the new factory produced its first cement, in the context of a countrywide determination to rebuild factories and increase productivity: 'We worked as excellently as we fought in the war.' In this way the fight against the invader during the Great Patriotic War was likened in 1974 to the fight for socialism and the inherent economic productivity attributed to communist ideology. However, in a tacit acknowledgement of the benefits of capitalism and Western investment, Brezhnev also visited the new Pepsi-Cola factory built with American finance.[21] While the national media covered mainly the history behind the award of hero city status, the local emphasis was firmly on the present and even the future.

In the case of events of national interest taking place in Novorossiisk, such as Brezhnev's visit, the official communiqués were written in Moscow, then telegraphed to Novorossiisk for minor 'correction' by local journalists.[22] With TASS firmly in control, in what was standard practice at the time, no local interpretation or deviation from the official line was possible. Although the Novorossiisk press reproduced the TASS reports from Moscow during Brezhnev's stay in Novorossiisk, local reporting after the visitors had left was in a different vein. In Novorossiisk it was possible to see the monuments on Malaia zemlia on a daily basis, which may have caused them to have less impact than when their photographs were seen in Moscow in *Pravda* or *Izvestiia*. In contrast, Brezhnev's interest in the town's postwar regeneration, housing and employment was of more interest locally than in the distant capital. However, official memory of the war and of Brezhnev's role on Malaia zemlia remained identical. Brezhnev's visit endorsed the new hero city, while the town professed particular thanks to the general secretary for its new status, thus promoting Brezhnev's own growing cult of personality through his historical connection with the Malaia zemlia campaign.

For a few years after Brezhnev's visit its memory lived on in Novorossiisk. A full account of the event was published the following year,[23] while nationally the war cult increased to a climax with the publication of Brezhnev's memoirs in 1978. The 1979 edition of Sokolov's memoirs covered Brezhnev's visit in depth in the final chapter, 'Thirty Years Later'.[24] Similarly, memoirists Grigor'ev, Savitskii and Grezin recalled 7 September 1974 in the *Ratnyi podvig Novorossiiska* series of memoirs.[25] Grigor'ev described the mood in the stadium as Brezhnev appeared on the podium:

> There we were in the stadium. Everyone was rooted to the spot in expectation. Suddenly a wave of animation swept through the stadium. Thousands of people stood up, as enthusiastic applause broke out.[26]

According to Sergei Kudryashov, there is always the danger that the experiences of memoirists become 'fixed', being 'committed to memory, at later points in time', so leading to biased recollections.[27] Although this is noticeable when witnesses repeat the assertions of previous memoirists, in this case it is less likely, as these recollections are supported by photographs, newspaper reports and the testimony of others present at the time. However, these memoirs represent the final phase of adulation of Brezhnev both nationally and locally, as the war cult was dismantled centrally on Brezhnev's death in 1982. By 1985, Sokolov had removed all references to Brezhnev's visit, 'forgetting' this event, while expanding instead on the mood in the town when it was named a hero city in 1973.[28] Although the visit of Brezhnev to Novorossiisk had caused the press and other media to reflect on the Malaia zemlia campaign for a time, its lasting repercussions did not become apparent until 25 years later, by which time many aspects of the visit had developed into local legend.

CHAPTER 7

THE GODFATHER

Figure 7.1 *Malaia zemlia* by Aleksandr Kamper (picture copyright of Aleksandr Kamper; photographed by the author and published with the permission of the artist)

Artist Aleksandr Kamper works near the Valley of Death in the village of Myskhako. On his studio wall hangs a collage entitled *Malaia zemlia*, composed from an old, torn canvas depicting a beach, which could well be the beach-head at Malaia zemlia. The frontispiece of Brezhnev's volume of memoirs is mounted on a hill overlooking the shore, rather as Mount Koldun overlooks the battlefield outside Novorossiisk. According to the artist, this work represents state-sponsored memory of Malaia zemlia, with Brezhnev's book depicted as a monument overlooking an act of remembrance in which the viewer is taking part. Kamper interprets the holes in the picture as gaps in official memory of the Malaia zemlia campaign, which have inhibited informed remembrance, thanks to Brezhnev's overpowering intervention of the 1970s. According to Kamper's explanation, Malaia zemlia is remembered almost exclusively thanks to Brezhnev, but because of Brezhnev's domination that memory has remained incomplete, overpowered by his memoirs to the extent that the full, factual picture has been prevented from emerging.

My research shows that this may well be true on the national, mythical level, despite the emergence of more recent historical perspectives on the war which have influenced the picture since Brezhnev's death. On the local level, however, the gaps have been filled in two different ways: by hard historical facts derived from material and documentary evidence; and by local legend. Recently unearthed artefacts shed considerable light on the engagement, while schools' local history courses and an authoritative recent history of the campaign by local academic Tamara Iurina serve to propagate a more detailed narrative.[1] Education of the young is covered in Part IV; the rest of this part, in contrast, will examine how a local legend sprang up around Brezhnev's visit, such that local memory of this event as an addendum in its own right to the wartime campaign has reverberated through the town since 1999.

Brezhnev's visit to Novorossiisk marked a notable bifurcation of attitude both to Malaia zemlia and to Brezhnev himself on the national and local levels. For the country as a whole, the visit had a single significance: the bestowing of the gold star of the hero city on the town, thereby ratifying the award of 1973. This event was connected to the war alone, such that Brezhnev's name is integrally linked to that of Malaia zemlia and the war myth he constructed around it. Despite the subsequent deconstruction of both the Brezhnev-era war cult and Brezhnev's cult of personality, this is the perception of Brezhnev and Malaia zemlia that has remained ingrained in the older generation, with the publication of Brezhnev's over-inflated memoirs providing evidence for this public interpretation. Gorbachev's period of *perestroika* (restructuring and reform) in the late 1980s, the fall of the Soviet

Union in 1991 and the difficult decade thereafter saw the national demise of the official war myth. Only *Izvestiia* marked the significant fiftieth anniversary of the end of the war with a sarcastic article about Malaia zemlia, indicative of the scornful attitude to Brezhnev's memoirs still extant in society years after his death, a view that continues to this day, dormant in the minds of those old enough to remember the Brezhnev era.[2]

In Novorossiisk, however, the Brezhnev connection was evolving along a different path, as Brezhnev's visit of 1974 largely superseded the formal award of hero city status the previous year. Brezhnev's visit was a personal triumph for himself and the town, with the general secretary's charisma in the present more than eclipsing distant memories of his wartime service on Malaia zemlia. Winning over officials, veterans and the public alike, Brezhnev's character and overt identification with Novorossiisk endeared him to the population, who claimed him as their own. Here was the real Leonid Il'ich, acting and speaking spontaneously and at close quarters, rather than the official statesman observed from afar on the television. If Brezhnev's wartime function on Malaia zemlia had played a minor role in shaping the postwar town, this visit of the general secretary would influence the development of the newly nominated hero city for a further 30 years, whilst marking a reconstruction of the persona of Brezhnev with the establishment of a burgeoning local legend in the process.

In 1999, towards the culmination of an era of instability, Novorossiisk looked back to a heyday in the town's history as the twenty-fifth anniversary of Brezhnev's visit approached. A key investigative newspaper article in *Novorossiiskii rabochii* exposed new evidence from witnesses that had been suppressed in 1974 in favour of the TASS reports which had dominated the press.[3] It is this first public examination of the significant event which both expressed and continued to formulate local opinion on Brezhnev in the town, as the press still delves into 'hidden' aspects of Brezhnev's now legendary visit.

It is not always possible to believe everything that was recorded in the Soviet press at the time of the actual event. On this occasion, though, many citizens were present at official events, and others actually met the general secretary and heard his speeches. News did – and still does – travel fast in this provincial town: it is important not to underestimate the strong network of interconnections among residents in this relatively parochial place Several of my interviewees had either witnessed Brezhnev's visit or had heard about it from other family members. Eleven respondents aged from around 50 to well over 80 expressed pride and pleasure that they had seen Brezhnev, and a further five had heard about the occasion at second hand. Memories reinforce one another, tending in this case to support Kudryashov's view that they had been committed to memory at the time and then permanently fixed and laid down in the mind.[4] It is probable that they are genuine, as these accounts confirm the main story while differing in points of detail, as would be expected from a variety of respondents spanning a broad age spectrum who had met Brezhnev under slightly different circumstances. Klavdiya, for example, was in the first class at school, while Stepan was already an elderly veteran at the time. Alena recalls how Brezhnev 'gave her his hand' from his car, while he was on foot when Mariya saw him. Lev saw Brezhnev on the road in his open car and then in the stadium, where he waved his flag along with the crowd. Vasilisa met Brezhnev at her workplace, the *sovkhoz* (communal vineyard) in Myskhako, where 'he came to our corpus and talked to us'. Her colleague Darya, now in her nineties, was one of the workers lucky enough to meet Brezhnev at the aerodrome, standing alongside two women with babies:

> He came up to us with open arms and greeted us [...] He gave presents to the children, writing on them 'a present from Grandfather Brezhnev'. [...] The next day we [...] gathered in the vineyard where we worked and we were all really happy. He got out of the car and said 'thank you'.

This story has been passed down through Darya's family with photographic clarity, mediated by a contemporaneous photograph depicting a bent old woman giving flowers to the general secretary, taken when Brezhnev visited Mar'ina roshcha, another outlying village across the bay from Myskhako. This iconic photograph was widely disseminated in Novorossiisk and included in a book of photographs of Brezhnev's visit edited by his aide Viktor Golikov and published four years later.[5] According to Darya's granddaughter, she likes to imagine that this woman is indeed her own elderly grandmother, hardly conscious of the fact that the original woman was much older than her grandmother at the time, if nonetheless resembling her now, decades later. This example of what Marianne Hirsch terms 'post-memory' demonstrates the appropriation of a real memory by a younger generation who did not experience the event, with the projection of a later image onto an earlier one in a 'merging of people and times'.[6] In this case, the woman in the photograph that has passed into local history has been claimed by another, younger individual in her attempt to reconstruct her own picture of that event.[7] This small-scale social construct has produced a sense of familial ownership of public memory, which here is on a purely emotional level and without any rational basis, a product of the cultural environment surrounding Brezhnev's visit.

Brezhnev was not only the subject of photographs in 1974, but also used the occasion to gift some of his own wartime photographs to the Novorossiisk museum. Evdokiia Prialkina, then director of the museum, remembers Brezhnev's arrival in September, 'immediately surrounded by women', in what was apparently the norm. It seems that Brezhnev was a great hit with the opposite sex, embracing them on his departure: 'a real man', as recalled by Larisa Kolbasina, the current director. Both women were struck by Brezhnev's insistence on simplicity: 'No need for fine-sounding words, such as "Dear Leonid Il'ich, we are very pleased ..."'.[8]

It is noteworthy that considerably more female than male respondents in my survey spontaneously contributed their memories of Brezhnev's visit. This may demonstrate a reflection of the demographics of the ordinary citizens who encountered the general secretary, combined with the greater proportion of women in my interview sample. This phenomenon should, however, be compared with published local memoirs of the war, which were largely written and consumed by men who had played an active part. Memory of Brezhnev's visit in 1974 was claimed by the population as a whole, with the women more vocally endorsing Brezhnev's masculinity.

The outcome of the visit was that the museum was given a new building with extra exhibition space in the town centre – some of which is still used to recall Brezhnev's visit to Novorossiisk. It is this type of aid which remains firmly in the minds of witnesses and has informed the opinion of many of the residents of Novorossiisk today, including newcomers to the town. Brezhnev's interest in the town's industry was emphasised in the local press shortly after his visit, with substantially more coverage of his meetings in the port, the cement factories and the new Pepsi-Cola factory than evident in the national press.

When I first spoke to people in Novorossiisk about the town's attitude to Brezhnev I was told by the archivist of the Maritime Academy that I would not find anyone in Novorossiisk with a bad word to say about Brezhnev. And this, incredibly, seems to be largely true: Brezhnev certainly seems to enjoy more popularity in Novorossiisk than elsewhere in Russia. Forty per cent of my interviewees, aged from 18 to their late eighties, volunteered this opinion without prompting, including Tamara Iurina, Professor of History at the Novorossiisk branch of the Moscow Institute for Economics and the Humanities. Interestingly, of these 49 subjects, at least seven were relative newcomers to the town, who had assimilated this attitude to Brezhnev since their arrival, providing evidence for the efficiency of propagation of the postwar aspect of the Brezhnev myth. Furthermore, the majority of my subjects who volunteered this information reminded me not of Brezhnev's role on Malaia zemlia or his communist ideology, but of the postwar support afforded to the almost annihilated town thanks to Brezhnev's intervention. Although younger respondents voiced more general approval of Brezhnev's help to Novorossiisk, more mature interviewees specifically credited Brezhnev with improving infrastructure (particularly the new trolley-bus lines), supporting the cement factories, expanding the port and building better accommodation for the townspeople. Three respondents cited this aid as an excuse for Brezhnev's not having visited the town in 1973 as soon as it was made a hero city, 'recalling' that Brezhnev had stated that he would only return to the town once Novorossiisk looked worthy of its new status. Although this is reinforced by Brezhnev's favourable comments on the excellent appearance of the town in his speech of 7 September 1974, a recent publication refers to Brezhnev's more disparaging remarks about the town on a visit to the 'Proletariat' cement works later the same day, when the 'head of state observed that the appearance of the town was not commensurate with its status as a hero city and that it would be necessary to solve the overall problems of Novorossiisk (with the building of housing, schools, hospitals and roads) at the national level'.[9]

Evidence suggests that state aid to Novorossiisk was supplied in one way or another from the late 1960s onwards throughout the first decade of the Brezhnev regime – assistance seen by many in Novorossiisk as proof of Brezhnev's special relationship with the town. However, it is possible to postulate a rationale and mechanism for preferential development without Brezhnev's intentional intervention. As early as 1945, Novorossiisk was identified as one of 15 major towns that had suffered most severely from enemy action and were therefore in need of substantial state support for their regeneration.[10] Like most hero cities, Novorossiisk was a key industrial centre with its cement works; its strategic position on the Black Sea also made Novorossiisk an ideal location for the export of wood from the interior of the region and oil from the Caucasus or Caspian regions, rendering development of the port and its infrastructure an economic priority for the Soviet Union. This led to a marked increase in population in the postwar years, requiring in turn the construction of new living accommodation and concomitant social amenities, until the town's appearance was indeed considered to be commensurate with its status as a hero city.[11] It is probable that more aid was forthcoming after Novorossiisk became a hero city, due to its significance as a tourist destination for Soviets and its transient population of many visitors to the port from overseas.

The fact that Viktor Golikov had the ear of the general secretary and was himself regularly lobbied by Iurii Semenov, the chair of the town's strategic developmental committee, the Gorispolkom, resulted in the approval by the state of 35 million roubles for Novorossiisk from 1968 to 1975.[12] It seems likely that Novorossiisk would not have received this amount of aid had it not been a hero city of the Soviet Union, which itself was dependent upon the Brezhnev connection. Ivo Mijnssen goes even further in concluding that the link with Brezhnev was 'absolutely decisive' for the town's economic development in the late 1960s and 1970s.[13] Other factors were also involved, but the evidence certainly points to an exercise in mutual promotion between Brezhnev and Novorossiisk.

This perceived favouritism by Brezhnev in the first half of the 1970s served to increase the status of the town with respect to other cities in the region, promoting some jealousy on the part of the leaders of Krasnodar, the regional capital.[14] However, Novorossiisk continued to receive state aid, despite the fact that its own leadership had been denigrated for economic incompetence by the regional authorities in Krasnodar in the late 1960s.[15] Furthermore, it must be concluded that the illogical decision to build the first Soviet Pepsi-Cola factory in Novorossiisk was indeed a sign of Brezhnev's favouritism, as asserted by three middle-aged male interviewees.[16] The town has never been able to rely on a stable source of drinking water, a problem which is not totally resolved to this day,[17] rendering it a dubious contender for American investment, despite its strategic position on the Black Sea. Although kilometres of extra piping and a reservoir were constructed in the 1950s and 1960s, many in the town were still relying on water from wells and springs, despite a surge in population in the decades after the war. By 1968 a crisis situation had developed following a drought during the spring months such that two tankers were commissioned to work round the clock to bring fresh water by sea from Tuapse and Sochi along the coast. Construction of more wide-calibre pipes and underground reservoirs started later that year, using the 'voluntary' unpaid labour of thirsty residents to help dig the new trenches in their days off work, an example of the *subbotnik* (Saturday) system, whereby workers gave up one Saturday a month for the common good.[18] Eight of my respondents credited Brezhnev himself with sending the tankers and providing the financial support necessary for this enormous project.

Once the water was flowing, and despite ongoing supply problems, the Pepsi-Cola factory was constructed in Novorossiisk when trade links with the United States were initiated during a period of détente in Cold War relationships. The contract between Pepsico and the Soviet Union was signed when American representatives of the company met Alexei Kosygin in 1968. Kosygin was premier of the Soviet Union as chair of the Council of Ministers who worked alongside Brezhnev, the chair of the Central Committee of the Communist Party. It was largely Kosygin who was responsible for the introduction of reforms in an effort to modernise the economy and expand industry. This contract was a coup both in economic terms and in the field of foreign relations. Both sides benefited: the Soviet Union was allowed to produce an increasingly popular Western product, while the United States gained the right to import one litre of Stolichnaya vodka in return for every litre of Pepsi concentrate exported. It was probably no coincidence that the factory was completed in 1974, a few months before Brezhnev's visit, nor surprising that he was given credit locally for the the new plant in Novorossiisk, although it seems that he was probably not the main instigator of the project.[19]

Figure 7.2 The Well of Life Monument (photograph by the author)

However, Brezhnev's connection with drinks and drinking water operates also at the more subtle level of local legend. It is documented that, when he was taken to the Valley of Death outside Myskhako, he was shown the Well of Life, where the defenders of Malaia zemlia had gone at night to fetch precious drinking water in the face of fire from Germans holding the upper ground.[20] In an incident reminiscent of Jesus' encounter with the Samaritan woman at the well, television cameras following Brezhnev showed how he was re-introduced to a grey-haired woman, who as a young girl during the war had given him water from a bucket at the height of the battle.[21] This unexpected meeting apparently reduced Brezhnev to tears, supporting the claim of elderly Lyudmila that Brezhnev had uncharacteristically declined the wine or vodka he was offered on that occasion, preferring to walk off, alone with his memories, to drink water from the well.

Figure 7.3 The Water-Giver (photograph by Sergei Krasnolobov and used with his permission)

The links between Brezhnev and drinking water as a symbol of life and renewal are potent. The arrival of mains water, claimed to be thanks to Brezhnev's intervention, was celebrated in 1973 by the erection of a statue on the promenade, *Dariashchaia vodu* (the Water-Giver), the only statue to mains water in Russia.[22] The original sculpture was replaced in 2006, on the reconstruction of the promenade, by a more elegant version by sculptor Aleksandr Suvorov, under the direction of the mayor of Novorossiisk and with money donated by businesses, reinforcing the town's continued gratitude for a stable supply of drinking water.

A female with softly sculpted features, the statue kneels in thanks and supplication with cupped hands holding water outstretched towards the sea, whence the water originally came. Offering the water to the people, she allows it to sprinkle into the pool at her feet, the source of a fountain, the first in Novorossiisk, which would not have been possible before the advent of the mains supply.[23] Galina Krympokha, former archivist at the Maritime Academy, attributed the original statue to funds from Brezhnev himself, while Petr, a senior architect, connects the statue with Brezhnev's instructions to send water to the town by tankers and its ongoing importance as a result of the fragility of the supply even today. Reflecting the primitive emphasis on the gift of life through water, the statue continues to be linked with Brezhnev by some residents in his symbolic role of a beneficent water god, complementing that of benefactor and patron to the town.

Evidence for changes in the attitude of the hero city to its patron may be found in promotional photograph albums of Novorossiisk published over the last three decades. 1978s edition was edited by Viktor Golikov, who seems to have been responsible both for Brezhnev's visit and the promotion of Novorossiisk in the 1970s. It is therefore not surprising that it contains several pages dedicated both to Brezhnev's wartime role and his 1974 visit. By 1998, however, there was little interest in the general secretary, such that the equivalent publication had only one wartime photograph including Brezhnev in a total of 14, with no indication of his visit or his connection with the conferment of hero city status, in line with the more derogatory national understanding of Brezhnev's role. Following renewed interest in his visit, however, the latest luxury edition, published in 2012, indicates a reversal of attitude, with just one small photograph of Brezhnev on Malaia zemlia in 1943 amongst a total of 46, while his visit in 1974 is given much greater coverage alongside images indicating the increased status of the town as an industrial centre.[24]

In contrast to the national attitude to Novorossiisk, it is clear that not only war memory is at work locally today. Brezhnev's postwar role in Novorossiisk linked to his visit is indeed considered now to be more meaningful than his time on Malaia zemlia or his once-famous war memoirs. Brezhnev put this provincial town on the map of the Soviet Union to the extent that interviewee Vyacheslav likened him to Lenin; he was deemed a 'godsend' by a priest; and described as the town's 'godfather' by the regional manager in charge of maintenance and planning of monuments in Novorossiisk. Over the years, personal and public memories have been incorporated into the larger cultural narrative so that even newcomers are inculcated with a duty of thanks to Brezhnev, who, according to all my respondents, did more than any other statesman for Novorossiisk. The town's popular sentiment is summed up by former Museum Director Prialkina:

If you ask anyone about Brezhnev today, they will talk about 'the era of stagnation', linking it with Brezhnev. This may be the political verdict of his rule. But in Novorossiisk we acknowledge the truth that, for us, we want to remember with sincerity Leonid Il'ich, the man who did more than anybody else for the development of our town.[25]

CHAPTER 8

THE MAKING OF A MODERN LEGEND

> Надоело говорить и спорить,
> И любить усталые глаза …
> В флибустьерском дальнем море
> Бригантина подымает паруса …[1]

Exactly a decade after the publication of Brezhnev's memoirs the state, under the leadership of the same Mikhail Gorbachev who had met Brezhnev in Novorossiisk in 1974, decided to tear down the statue in Moscow erected on his death:

> Where a monument to Leonid I. Brezhnev once stood, there is now an uneven sidewalk, covered with a dusting of snow and frozen dirt. The large black Cyrillic letters that spelled out his name on a nearby metal and concrete billboard have been erased.[2]

With Brezhnev consigned to national political oblivion and Moscow's Brezhnev Square renamed,[3] the war cult of the Brezhnev era was formally dismantled. Indeed, following his discredited predecessors, two marble statues of Brezhnev are now to be found off the beaten track in Moscow's Muzeon sculpture park, adjacent to Gorkii Park, where they are relegated to the periphery next to the portable toilets in a corner full of superfluous Lenins and Stalins. These busts depict a statesman fallen from his pedestal, both literally and metaphorically, reinforcing the inflexibility in interpretation of monuments, which are rarely able to accommodate changes in the political scenery around them.[4]

In the light of Brezhnev's national fall from grace as a victim of Gorbachev's revised official narrative of the Brezhnev era, it is all the more remarkable that public opinion in Novorossiisk would be so out of tune with the capital as to consider a new monument to Brezhnev in the twenty-first century. The political debate and a decision-making process revealing flexibility in interpretation of a superficially static monument shed light on the attitude to Brezhnev and the local interpretation of his role in the history of the hero city he created and patronised.

So interlinked are the reputations of Novorossiisk and Brezhnev that in 2004, exactly 30 years after his famous visit of 1974, the town decided to erect the only public monument to Brezhnev in the whole of Russia. Brezhnev was already integrally linked with the large Malaia zemlia memorial complex, completed at his instigation in 1982 and studded with quotations from his memoirs. Since 1974 he had also been linked with the cluster of monuments in the Valley of Death, but more recent proposals to name a street after Brezhnev had come to nothing.[5] This new statue would mark a further reverberation of the 1974 event, catapulting memory of Brezhnev's connection with Novorossiisk and Malaia zemlia well into the twenty-first century. The process of decision making around the commissioning and erection of the statue acted as a catalyst for renewed discussion of both Brezhnev's role in the war and the visit itself, setting off an after-shock of further reverberations and some revision of memory during the heated debate involving local and regional officials and the public. The conclusion of what may be viewed in retrospect as a protracted seven-year heritage controversy would eventually fix the collective image of Brezhnev within the identity of Novorossiisk, thereby formalising the rift between the national and the local view of Brezhnev's links with the hero city.

New monuments in Novorossiisk are normally subject to planning permission granted by the Krasnodar Region. Smaller planning applications may be decided locally by the regional manager in charge of maintenance and planning of monuments in Novorossiisk, while larger projects such as the Brezhnev statue need to be accepted by the regional council as a whole. The decision-making situation is complicated by the multi-layered structure of local government in Russia. Within the town itself, the local *duma*, or town council, makes policy decisions, which are then implemented by the municipality's head of administration, the town's chief executive officer, popularly known as the mayor, who heads the local authorities. The most influential mayor of Novorossiisk in recent times has been Vladimir Siniagovskii, who served from 2003 to 2016 and was named an 'honoured citizen' of the town in 2009. Siniagovskii, a member of President Putin's United Russia political party, was elected to the national parliament in 2016 to represent Novorossiisk. His successor, and the majority of town councillors in the *duma*, are also members of the same party.[6] The other relatively large party in local and national politics are the old-style communists, still retaining some popularity since the collapse of the Soviet Union. The mayor of Novorossiisk has six deputies responsible for different areas of administration.

The first proposal for a statue to Brezhnev by a Novorossiisk member of the regional council in Krasnodar was rejected following one of several disagreements between the region and the town, but a second proposal was accepted in 2004.[7] The successful project was sponsored by Dmitrii Shishov, a communist member of the regional council in Krasnodar, who not only had a vested ideological interest in reviving the connection of Novorossiisk with the longstanding general secretary of the Communist Party of the Soviet Union, but also the financial funds to back it. However, despite the support of the mayor of Novorossiisk and another member of the Communist Party on the Novorossiisk town council, the vote to erect the statue was by no means unanimous.

The leader of the minority Democratic Union voted against the statue, referring to the perceived lack of democracy in the country and suggesting that the decision to erect it was only to be expected 'in a country of slaves', made by 'people who have no need of freedom'.[8] This minority opinion reinforced a controversial letter from a certain Mikhail Prorok published by newspaper *Novorossiiskii rabochii* when the statue was first mooted early in 2004. Citing the oppression of dissidents and ethnic minorities during the Brezhnev era as a reason not to erect the statue, he claimed that Novorossiisk would have developed naturally in the past without the alleged support from the general secretary.[9] The newspaper was deluged with responses, the majority of those published arguing robustly for the erection of the statue on the grounds of the postwar aid given by Brezhnev to Novorossiisk, with only one (published) letter reminding readers of the waste of lives in unpopular wars in Czechoslovakia and Afghanistan under Brezhnev. Furthermore, one writer, Vladimir Aleksandrovich, was particularly indignant about the number of undeserved awards worn by Brezhnev in his latter years: 'He had more decorations than a New Year tree.'[10]

The statue was first proposed about a year before it was actually erected, but the arts committee charged with its implementation was still making the most important decisions on its form and site three weeks before the envisaged dedication date.[11] On 23 August 2004 the sculptor, Nikolai Bugaev from Krasnodar, presented a scale model which won the support of committee members, sponsor Shishov and other local businessmen funding the project, pending final approval from the mayor.[12] However, a prolonged debate failed to reach a conclusion about the best site for Brezhnev. It was decided not to stand him on a main road near the sea, as this would entail cutting down too many trees. More importantly, a site on Malaia zemlia itself was also excluded, not only because the relatively small statue would fade into insignificance beside the huge Brezhnev-era Malaia zemlia memorial on the shore, but also because of fears that this would reinforce 'past mistakes', when Brezhnev's role in the campaign had been inflated, which would reflect badly on both Brezhnev's memory and the identity of Novorossiisk itself.[13] This strategic political decision no longer overtly to associate Brezhnev with Malaia zemlia marked the formalisation of the rift between opinion in Novorossiisk and the national attitude to Brezhnev.

Local opinion was voiced by Tigran Martirosian, former chief executive of the commercial port and honoured citizen of Novorossiisk since 1997, who felt that Brezhnev's role after the war was far more important in the town's socio-economic development than his war service, an argument that was incomprehensible to the national press, who could only see Brezhnev's infamous connection with Malaia zemlia as the impetus for the monument. Following due consideration of political, historical and green issues, it was therefore decided to site the statue somewhere in the centre, in a place to be determined by the mayor, possibly on a crossroads with connections to Lenin.[14] Two days later, the mayor agreed that the postwar argument prevailed, stating: 'The people of Novorossiisk remember, know and value Leonid Il'ich's contribution to the development of Novorossiisk.'[15] With this in mind and possibly to put the communists in their place, he overruled links with Lenin and decided on a spot even closer to the centre, on the avenue Ulitsa Novorossiiskoi respubliki.

The final stages in the sculpture of the statue were hurried – it was reported that the sculptor hardly slept for the final two weeks of the project – but Brezhnev was finally lowered into position just in time for the official dedication of the statue on the anniversary of the liberation of Novorossiisk in 1943, 16 September. It may be questioned why this date was chosen, in view of the desire to avoid links with the war, but it also represented the culmination of Novorossiisk's 'town days', lasting from about 11 to 16 September annually. Although 7 September, the date of Brezhnev's famous speech, or 12 September, the date of the town's foundation, may have been more suitable, it is unlikely that the statue would have been ready, in view of its hasty completion at the end of the decision-making process. Brezhnev's grandson, Andrei, was invited to the ceremony. Fighting off autograph hunters from Brezhnev admirers, he declared himself 'shocked' to receive the invitation: 'I never would have thought that, with our current leaders, anyone would have the idea of erecting a monument to my grandfather.'[16]

The national press expressed equal surprise to be faced with a bronze statue depicting not the decrepit general secretary remembered by the joke-tellers, well into his dotage with a chest covered in medals, but a much younger Brezhnev in civilian clothes, stepping out in fluid motion on his pedestal with knee bent, casually loosened tie, jacket slung over his shoulder. Shishov declared that he and the sculptor 'wanted to depict Brezhnev not as a leader, but as a person [...] much loved in Novorossiisk'.[17] This is not a statesman or a war hero, but a normal human being, shown strolling through the town. Furthermore, in contrast to the huge Malaia zemlia war memorial, or even the statue of Lenin in the town centre, this bronze monument is on a more realistic human scale, being just over two metres tall and standing on a red granite pedestal 1.8 metres high. This statue represents the simple, very human Brezhnev who public opinion perceives came to award the gold star as an old friend of the town,[18] albeit, as pointed out by the chair of the Novorossiisk Historical Association, rather younger than the statesman who had visited in 1974, and substantially older than the wartime colonel.[19]

Brezhnev's character as recognised in Novorossiisk is implied by the working title of the statue: 'A man walking through the town'.

Figure 8.1 The Brezhnev Statue, Novorossiisk (photograph by the author)

Outsiders, however, had to pose the question 'through which town?', as they linked Brezhnev solely with his army uniform and military service on Malaia zemlia.[20] The statue portrays Brezhnev's mythical modesty, simplicity and his respect for the town and its citizens, referred to by four older respondants, just as several war memoirs refer formulaically to Brezhnev's love for the troops and their love and respect for him in return.[21] Elderly interviewees Anna, Mariya and Vasilisa even giggled as they recalled how handsome Brezhnev looked in his younger days, remembering his common, populist touch, while Raisa Sokolova, the museum's chief archivist, has a portrait of the younger Brezhnev hanging on her office wall – a place where the current leader of the country would normally hang. Perhaps people are actively looking for examples of Brezhnev's more positive characteristics as if in denial of any weakness of character evident in Brezhnev's later years. If Brezhnev propagated the myth of Malaia zemlia through his memoirs, so Novorossiisk is now propagating through this statue the image of the charismatic man still loved by local collective memory – the mythical Brezhnev in his prime, before his physical and mental decline.

William Tompson, Edwin Bacon and Mark Sandle have posited a plausible periodisation of the Brezhnev era which may serve to explain the apparent difference in recollection of Brezhnev between Novorossiisk and the rest of the country.[22] The citizens of Novorossiisk saw Brezhnev at his peak, a memory of the 1974 visit fixed in the new statue, which took place months before his first stroke led to a steady deterioration in his physical and mental stamina. In contrast, it appears that the older generation of the rest of the country recalls the later, ailing Brezhnev – confused, highly dependent and open to flattery. This apparent change in character is discussed by Sergei Semanov in a nuanced defence of the general secretary, contrasting the old man of the caricatures, with slurred speech, thick eyebrows and weighed down with medals, with the genuine patriot who remained 'less hysterical' than Khrushchev, less cruel than Stalin and less corrupt than present-day politicians, if lacking in decisiveness and somewhat weak-willed.[23]

The centenary of Brezhnev's birth in 2006 provided an opportunity for a national reappraisal of the legacy of his lengthy term in office, with a protracted debate in *Literaturnaia gazeta*, the appearance of new biographies and the publication of a plethora of survey data. In an attempt to get to grips with the apparent paradoxes of the era, the national press contrasted the stern realities of Soviet tanks entering Czechoslovakia, the war in Afghanistan, domestic censorship, the repression of dissidents and the non-availability of beer, with leadership in space exploration and, on the ground, the germination of a middle class, free and improving education and health services, high levels of employment and personal security, the building of new housing stock, development of industry and steady economic development.[24] Some recent Russian works remain as critical of Brezhnev today as Gorbachev and historians Roi and Zhores Medvedev in the past; Leonid Mlechin, for example, highlights the stagnation of the Brezhnev era and mocks Brezhnev's wartime role.[25] Despite this, a more nuanced and empathetic view is coming into fashion, with the benefit of greater historical perspective and a political climate that is searching for positive aspects of the Soviet past.[26] Most recently, Aleksandr Khinshtein's biography of Brezhnev defends an era of stability, while others argue that twenty-first century wars, widespread corruption, the removal of free state benefits, high levels of unemployment and homelessness make the Brezhnev era seem like a golden age of the past. As Khinshtein points out, there is a dichotomy between the current mood of nostalgia for the Brezhnev era and continuing criticism of its economic, political and social stagnation.[27] Some nostalgia for the time when the Soviet Union was regarded as a significant world power is certainly evident in recent official surveys and is probably indicative of the political conservatism of the Putin regime. There have even been re-interpretations of the 'stagnation' label aimed at Brezhnev, emphasising rather the stability, peace and calm enjoyed in the country for the first time in the twentieth century.[28]

One possible answer to this apparent paradox lies in the periodisation of the era that is the subject of increasing nostalgia amongst the older generation, for whom it represented their youth. While it is tempting to suggest that the nostalgia may be predominantly reserved for the early part of the era, with the criticism aimed largely at the latter years, the official survey data is not so discriminating.[29] In the specific case of Novorossiisk, however, many residents maintain that Brezhnev's personal patronage led to a change in gear in the developmental progress of this town in the early 1970s.[30] In contrast, the later era of national stagnation was overseen by the older Brezhnev who instigated the construction of a spate of what some scholars deem to be unnecessarily large war memorials, including those at Stalingrad and Malaia zemlia, and 'wrote' his memoirs, which still link Novorossiisk and Brezhnev in the mind of a generation.

Otto Boele has claimed that the erection of the Brezhnev statue in Novorossiisk developed from of a sense of nostalgia for the Brezhnev era amongst people of a certain age.[31] However, my research indicates that much more than nostalgia for an era was behind its erection. The protracted town council and media debate indicates that the majority of those involved, both elected councillors and the public across a wide age-range, speak of their affection for and gratitude to Brezhnev himself, rather than the Soviet regime he represented. This reveals a further dichotomy, whereby the people of Novorossiisk are now apparently sufficiently at ease with the Brezhnev connection to separate the politics of the era from the character of its leader, applauding his good traits while not seeming totally blind to his faults, and still telling the same Brezhnev jokes as elsewhere. Remembered no longer for the memoirs that put Novorossiisk on the map, but rather for his postwar contribution to the town, Brezhnev is now regarded in Novorossiisk if not with absolutely uncritical worship, certainly with empathy on a human scale, like his statue. In agreement with local historian Tamara Iurina, several more informed respondents offered a relatively balanced retrospective view of Brezhnev as a man who had definitely been on Malaia zemlia, simply doing his duty courageously in the war, while probably not deserving four Hero of the Soviet Union medals. Furthermore, ten interviewees across the age spectrum agreed with Iurina that Brezhnev was so busy leading the country in the 1970s that he had to have professional help with his memoirs, just like many other leading statesmen of the era.[32]

Re-location of the Brezhnev Statue

With memory of Brezhnev formalised and stable in Novorossiisk, if different from that in the rest of the country, the news that it had been decided to move the statue less than six years after its installation on Ulitsa Novorossiiskoi respubliki marked the start of a public debate to determine the new site and, with it, a battle for the ownership of the similarly re-positioned memory of Brezhnev's connection with Novorossiisk. Even if the issues remained local with an agreed positioning of memory, the significance of the statue and its location were still hotly debated in a decision-making process that provides a fascinating case-study in local politics of remembrance.

Monuments are usually expected to stay in one place for well over a human lifetime, despite any potential need for re-interpretation as the political climate changes. Their very longevity has led Jan Assmann to see 'objectivised culture' as being even more permanent in society and better at reinforcing social identity than orally transmitted memory, a view endorsed by Mikhail Yampolsky.[33] On the other hand, Paul Connerton, arguing from a postmodern temporal perspective, points to increasing human longevity, which renders the lifespan of objects such as monuments increasingly insignificant with respect to their human counterparts.[34] In any case, six years cannot be regarded as a long time from the point of view of a statue or the community in which it stands. Furthermore, Connerton has argued that, once monumentalised, the subject of a memorial may safely be forgotten, partly because the scale and relative instability of modern city space undermine it as a focal point.[35] The latter may be true in the case of the modest Brezhnev monument although perhaps Connerton, with modern American cities rather than provincial Russia in mind, is not familiar with the enormous scale of many Soviet edifices. Certainly, the gigantic Malaia zemlia war memorial at Stanichka stands immovable and unconquerable in the face of changes to the promenade nearby, a testament to the stability in both space and time of many Soviet monuments and confirming Yampolsky's position.

The small Brezhnev statue was definitely not forgotten for long, with the 2004 debate on its siting clearly unfinished business, thereby defying Connerton's assertion that monuments quickly fade into the background. When it had been originally positioned no-one had counted on the rapidity of the mayor's extensive urban renewal programme along the promenade and Ulitsa Novorossiiskoi respubliki, bulldozing everything in its path; nor of the subsequent erection in December 2008 just metres from the Brezhnev statue of an enormous column commemorating the short-lived independent revolutionary Novorossiisk Republic of 1905 after which the avenue was named.[36] Bearing in mind the monument to the town's founder nearer the sea at the bottom of the avenue, the road was becoming increasingly crowded with memorial statues with arguably conflicting symbolism, such that the small 'alien' Brezhnev statue was at risk of being 'swallowed' in the shadow of the double-headed eagle on the new column.[37]

Katharine Hodgkin and Susannah Radstone properly question who has the right to decide where a memorial should be sited possibly years after the event it commemorates, in view of potentially conflicting political, economic and emotional interests.[38] In this case, with different vested interests of various groups of citizens, it was decided to reassure the public by the convening of a committee of experts to advise on the best site for the monument's re-location. To allay potential public concern, an open consultation for citizens was announced, with a full-scale media debate launched on local television and in the press.[39] Although the monument was built with private money, the original sponsors do not seem to have been consulted, although, towards the end of the discussions, the issue was also debated in the local *duma*.

It was necessary firstly to establish if the statue should be moved at all and, if so, then to where. There was some initial conflict between the committee of experts on the one hand and ordinary citizens on the other: the former was under the mayor's remit to find a suitable alternative location, while the latter, mainly the elderly and financially-conscious largely anti-communist younger residents, vociferously questioned the sense of the move at all, citing in letters to *Novorossiiskii rabochii* the projected financial burden on the town of 500,000 roubles for the exercise, while warning of the worst excesses of communism.[40] Despite their differences, however, most parties were united in wishing to retain the statue in Novorossiisk due to Brezhnev's strong connection with the hero city, at the same time rejecting calls to place him on Malaia zemlia for the very reasons discussed in 2004.

It became obvious through local television coverage in February 2009 that the committee of experts was seriously advocating a move from the centre of the town to the periphery, namely to a small square in front of the Hotel Brigantina on Anapa Shosse, the main road entering Novorossiisk from the north-west.[41] The justification for this proposed move stemmed paradoxically from the informal character of the statue itself. Whereas on its erection the statue was described as depicting Brezhnev's beloved simplicity and modesty, it was conveniently recalled in 2009 that it could also convey something more temporally and locationally specific to the town, based bizarrely on the hotel in which Brezhnev stayed on his 1974 visit, the Hotel Brigantina.

Back in 1974 the national press had made no mention of where Brezhnev stayed, but since 1999 attention has been firmly focused on this aspect of his visit, which has become almost as important as his official schedule. According to journalist Tat'iana Besedina, the proposed hotel among the vineyards of Abrau-Diurso, the champagne-producing region of the Black Sea coast, at that time offered insufficient suites of a suitably high standard. Furthermore, the long, winding road from the hotel to Novorossiisk was deemed by his staff to be uncomfortable for the general secretary. For these reasons, on the day before Brezhnev's arrival, they suddenly started to assess other options in Novorossiisk itself, finally deciding on the Hotel Brigantina, which offered luxury suites, if not luxury furniture within them. In a last-minute compromise, the better quality furniture from the rejected hotel in Abrau-Diurso was rapidly transferred to suite 309 of the Hotel Brigantina, displacing existing guests.[42]

According to the local press, the statue commemorates the evening of 6 September 1974, when local social memory holds that Brezhnev gave his bodyguards the slip to stroll down the road from the hotel towards the town centre. He apparently popped into a shop, 'striking the assistants dumb with surprise', and then 'bumped into someone or other in the street' where he exchanged a few words incognito. It is this simple rumour, unmentioned in the official TASS reports of Brezhnev's visit, which has become a living legend in Novorossiisk since it appeared in the public domain in 1999, a generation after an alleged evening stroll whose actual occurrence seems highly improbable, in view of the tight security arrangements around the general secretary's visit.[43]

A wealth of alleged details has been built up around the walk, with some sources claiming that an old woman engaged Brezhnev in conversation; although she did not recognise the general secretary, she spoke well of him, saying that she had known him during the war, thereby moving Brezhnev to tears.[44] In view of its similarity with Brezhnev's documented meeting with old women in Myskhako and at Mar'ina roshcha, it is probable that this detail is in fact an incorrect compilation of circumstances. Eyewitnesses to Brezhnev's alleged walk are hard to find, just as very few ordinary soldiers or marines seem to have met Brezhnev on Malaia zemlia during the war.[45] This is an example of a narrative trope whereby an important personage dons common dress to mingle with the people. It indicates the people's wish to believe the best of their often distant rulers and in England may be traced back to Richard the Lionheart.[46] Here is a potent example of the robustness of a legend, even when faced with virtually no evidence of individual corroborative memory, perhaps just a wish that has developed into collective consciousness and so-called historical fact. What matters is the social memory that has developed, a perception of the past expressed by some in the town as a coherent narrative. Jeffrey Olick points out that public memory is not necessarily located in the mind of any one person, such that, in this case, the legend is based on a collective representation of Brezhnev's positive qualities which underline his love for the town and its citizens.[47] Gillian Bennett and Paul Smith argue plausibly that such 'contemporary legends', while untrue by definition, are 'generally believed by gullible people', indicating the reinforcing nature of rumour on a large scale whose original source cannot be identified and which can therefore be neither confirmed nor disproved. According to Bennett and Smith, such legends 'appear to be substantiated, though they are ultimately unsubstantiated (and probably unsubstantiatable)'.[48] It seems that this urban legend which did not arise until 1999 informed the representation of Brezhnev in the statue erected in 2004, thereby taking on a long-lasting life of its own which has fixed it in official memory. Thus the interpretation of the statue reinforces the local perception of Brezhnev as a man of the people, an indication of the power of memory as a social construction.

It does not necessarily matter to the residents of Novorossiisk whether the story is true or not: in either case the legend depicts the Brezhnev they own, whose characteristic traits are transmitted both by the media and the statue itself, helping to fix the role of Brezhnev in local remembrance in an agreed episode within the town's past. In this respect the legend of Brezhnev's evening stroll differs from the war myth projected in his memoirs of Malaia zemlia, whose veracity was subject to substantial doubt.

With this legend in mind, the re-location committee remained adamant that the Brigantina location was more historically justified than anywhere else in Novorossiisk for the statue. However, many residents of Novorossiisk, especially the older generation, preferred Brezhnev's presence in the centre, where it was convenient to pop by, lay flowers and pay their respects. After all, they argued, Brezhnev did not only walk in the vicinity of his hotel, but brought the gold star to Heroes' Square in the centre of the town. The committee stuck to its guns, however, strengthening its argument with the fact that, unlike the town centre or the promenade, there are no significant monuments in the area where Novorossiisk is entered from the north-west, deeming the Brezhnev statue to be a prime attraction for incoming tourists.[49]

The role of the press in the protracted debate was key in offering an opportunity to ordinary citizens to have their say through letters and online comments. When interviewed, the editor of *Novorossiiskii rabochii* saw the role of Novorossiisk's most popular daily newspaper as a platform for public debate. Indeed, emotive letters and articles on both sides of the argument were published in the paper in the spring of 2009.[50] On the other hand, the mayor's official publication, *Novorossiiskie vesti*, targeting the educated middle class, acted as a mouth-piece for the opinions of its editor, Sergei Novikov, key proponent of the move to the Brigantina.[51] The town that was always united in its love of Brezhnev was thus divided over where to put him, in an open battle over the ownership of public memory. In the end, the argument favoured by the committee of experts won the day, aesthetically linking the Soviet statesman with the concrete Soviet-era hotel. In October 2009 a *postanovlenie* (notice of intent) appeared in *Novorossiiskie vesti* signalling the decision to relocate the statue to the square in front of the Brigantina.[52]

However, a further notice reversing this decision appeared four weeks later, apparently following a deluge of adverse comments from citizens. It was therefore assumed that the statue would, after all, remain in its original position, with the solitary response on the official town website exclaiming 'Thank God!'.[53] This was still not the final word on the affair, however. Seven months later it became apparent that the statue would, after all, be moved, but not very far, staying on the same avenue where the majority of citizens had demanded he remain. Moreover, in a further about-turn, Brezhnev would be rotated through 180° to face the sea, appeasing those who still preferred to connect him with his role on Malaia zemlia, while officially billed as for architectural reasons.[54] Following the 18-month decision-making process, Brezhnev was finally moved to his new location 200 metres from the original site in July 2010.

If the committee thought that it should have been the main decision-making body in the process, it was wrong, having been over-ruled by the mayor, with backing from the town council. My interviews with two key committee members eight months later demonstrated that the decision remained controversial, with one claiming that the mayor had succumbed to political pressure from several older citizens who had lobbied him directly by telephone. Ten of my interviewees with no connection to

Figure 8.2 The Relocated Brezhnev Statue (photograph by the author)

politics indeed perceived the decision to have been made by the mayor, while nine others saw the discussions as reflecting communal will, perhaps facilitated by the public debate in *Novorossiiskii rabochii*, whose editor felt that his paper had played the key role as 'the defender of truth' in the town. The very fact that such a prolonged and complex debate took place underlines the fact that social myth and memory may be collective, but that their significance remains personal and debatable. This analysis of the issues of agency in memory construction does not indicate a clear-cut case of top-down or bottom-up decision making, but demonstrates the important role of the mayor, who, according to the local press, did occasionally over-rule previous decisions.[55] In the case of the statue, it appears that the mayor apparently rejected the officially appointed committee and acted according to the wishes of those people who had lobbied him directly in the old Soviet way, in an act of political self-defence. It seems that the case was swung by older citizens, more emotionally connected with the Brezhnev image, and more used to the old-fashioned, direct approach which had occasionally succeeded in the past with petitions to the tsar or even Stalin. Their last-minute intervention prevailed over the much-vaunted democratic discussions in the media or the planned, more academic debate of the committee of experts.

The paradox of the twists and turns of the debate with its many last-minute decisions represents the success of informality over the more formal approach and a victory of political utility over historical accuracy, following a decision-making process that seems to have moved one step forwards towards democracy and two steps back to the old Soviet ways. The statue's location was influenced not by the appointed 'trustees of memory',[56] but by the generation that remembered Brezhnev's visit, who selected their own image of Brezhnev's link with Novorossiisk to be projected to their successors. It seems that the mayor's political power for the present and the foreseeable future is built on the past, employing a more traditional, patriarchal type of authority and manipulating social remembrance for his own political utility, much as Brezhnev did himself.

Most of my respondents were not too concerned with the re-location and remained philosophical or even pleased about the outcome, although their positive verdict had much to do with the general refurbishment of the area and the installation of new gardens and a fountain. Young Elvira and Viktor, in his late sixties, thought the affair to have been unnecessarily protracted, while Boris, a veteran of the war in

Afghanistan, considered the whole debate to have been a *'potoploka'* (a quagmire), blaming the *duma* for the outcome rather than the local authorities. Other citizens expressed sentiments that would seem totally out of place in the capital: one contributor to a newspaper accorded Brezhnev god-like status by referring to the 'blasphemy' of moving his statue, while 'Anya' saw the re-location as traumatic as the exhumation and re-interment of a close friend: 'Poor Brezhnev – he should be left in peace after his death.'[57]

For the moment, Brezhnev has settled into his current position. Despite the fact that several trees have been cut down to improve the line of sight from the sea – trees that have suddenly been judged 'unstable', but which in 2004 were hotly defended – the whole avenue, with its new fountain on the original spot of the monument, looks pleasingly open and symmetrical. The tall Novorossiisk Republic column in the centre is flanked by the smaller monuments to the founding father and to Brezhnev, effecting an implicit comparison between Nikolai Raevskii, the town's nineteenth-century founder, and Brezhnev, its twentieth-century patron. Similarly, the symbol of the state in the form of the double-headed eagle atop the new monument complements the smaller statesman, linking the first bright days of communist ideology with the later days of stagnating socialism. In a re-signifying of space in the town centre there is now an historical continuum along the central reservation of the avenue, with an arrow of time running from the town's foundation in 1838, via the 1905 republic to the Brezhnev era, such that the street may be read as a spatial memorial device within the topography of the modern town, where the image of Brezhnev on a human scale and with a human lifespan seems totally in proportion.

Now that the memory controversy is over and interest in it gradually wanes with the death of the older generation who fought with and for Brezhnev, it is possible that he may rest in rather too much peace as the statue fades comfortably into the memorial background of the town, as Connerton would suggest.[58] Although popular as a background for wedding photographs,[59] it is notable that the statue is not to be found on the tourist trail catering for the few cruise ship passengers from England and the United States occasionally visiting the town.[60] The role of the tour leader is crucial in setting the mood and selecting the itinerary for tourists. According to guide Kseniya, she does not want to mention the statue to tourists, as she connects Brezhnev with his memoirs which she believes are false. Visitors are therefore shown the impressive Malaia zemlia memorial complex, which still evokes emotion, although its inscriptions are often no longer recalled to be quotations from Brezhnev's memoirs. The Brezhnev connection apparently remains Novorossiisk's private secret as far as foreigners are concerned, despite the fact that many of them would have heard of the former leader of the Soviet Union, demonstrating some continuing embarrassment on the part of some, at least, in Novorossiisk about the notorious *Malaia zemlia* memoirs.

If 2004 led to a debate about Brezhnev's character and 2006 to a re-appraisal of his political legacy, the 2009 discussion focused on whether Brezhnev should remain in the centre of town or on the periphery, while confirming the re-positioning of memory to privilege the 1974 visit over Brezhnev's wartime role in 1943. Thanks to the continuing impact of the visit and its perceived economic consequences on the local consciousness, a decade of reverberations took place from 1999 to 2009, long after the 1974 visit, itself three decades after the Malaia zemlia campaign which originally saw Brezhnev's involvement and led to the conferment of hero city status on the town. With this background still dominating public opinion, particularly amongst the older generation, Brezhnev was eventually deemed too important to be relegated to the outskirts of the town, which gave rise to a new commemorative discourse of the legendary walk in a revision of social remembrance, such that Novorossiisk now officially commemorates the charismatic private man rather than the statesman or soldier. This is in contrast to, but complements, memory of the general secretary elsewhere in the country which has remained caricaturised and largely static since his death, if with some softening evident around the time of his centenary. In Novorossiisk, it is Brezhnev's perceived largesse and his more intimate side which are recalled: personal conversations and informal repartee. In line with the rest of the country, however, the Brezhnev era is loved or hated in equal measure by those who remember it, another facet of the town's paradoxical identification with the man, if not always with the state he represented.

Brezhnev's once-dominant wartime role may be on the wane in the local narrative, but it is still subject to political exploitation on a modest scale. Most notably, the mayor of Novorossiisk distributed specially reprinted copies of Brezhnev's *Malaia zemlia* to veterans during the 2002 local election campaign.[61] Two middle-aged women gave me bags of metal badges issued by the mayor since 2010 as rewards to children accompanying parents and grandparents to political meetings. In 2010 the young Colonel Brezhnev was one of a series of local Heroes of the Soviet Union on the badges, linking the forthcoming sixty-fifth anniversary of Victory Day with local elections in Novorossiisk. In a further series issued before the parliamentary elections, Brezhnev was depicted as the older statesman in a series of Soviet and Russian leaders from Tsar Aleksandr to Prime Minister Putin who had visited Novorossiisk. Whereas in the first series, the image of the genuine hero Tsezar' Kunikov is juxtaposed against the giant Malaia zemlia memorial, in the later series, it is the Soviet leader who is clearly linked with the monument erected at his instigation. These badges use Brezhnev as a political tool to attract both the young and the elderly, just as Brezhnev himself employed his connection with Malaia zemlia for his own political ends.

In contrast, the main political driver for the re-location of the Brezhnev statue was simply the mayor's rather sudden plans for urban regeneration, which altered the physical and political landscape around the statue to the extent that its very meaning was subject to a process of re-examination. The debate over the positioning of the new statue in Novorossiisk indicates that there is room for some individuality and personalisation within a local myth. Following a heritage controversy that exposed differences of opinion towards memory of Brezhnev and his role with respect to Novorossiisk, Brezhnev's position nonetheless remains central both physically and metaphorically to the town's identity today. The statue has enabled differences between memory of the elderly statesman and the younger private person to be publicly resolved in Novorossiisk. Largely thanks to memories of 1974 fixed in the minds of older citizens and now crystallised in the statue, the town has collectively selected the image of Brezhnev to be propagated to future generations: that of an energetic man in the prime of life rather than the caricature of the overseer of a period of stagnation, embraced by much of the rest of Russia. This significant difference between the local and the national verdict of history underlines the importance of personal contact and direct communication with the general secretary in an era when attitudes were generally formed and dictated by the more remote official mass media, which were instrumental in building up the war cult and disseminating Brezhnev's memoirs nationwide. In contrast, Brezhnev's 1974 visit to Novorossiisk was key in determining the town's current interpretation of their own Leonid Il'ich, largely by means of the legends which have grown up around this charismatic and very human being.

CHAPTER 9

THE STATE COMES TO TOWN AGAIN

Figure 9.1 *Land for Sale: Malaia zemlia* by Aleksandr Kamper (picture reproduced with the artist's permission)

Aleksandr Kamper's latest creative comment on Malaia zemlia is a photograph of an area near the site of the landings, allegedly being sold as building plots for more holiday homes for wealthy Muscovites who may never even have heard of the campaign. In a statement about the abuse of the integrity of the war myth, Kamper has placed this photograph over the red letters of the title page of a book of what seems to be Brezhnev's memoirs, appearing to be part of what is regarded by many as the 'sacred' earth beneath. By this artistic device, the collage condemns the sale of this piece of local memory: 'Land for sale: Malaia zemlia'. There is no doubt that the pace of recent development has caused some controversy in Novorossiisk.[1] Interviewee Alisa was horrified at what she saw as the desecration of sacred land, although Artem, a professional who works in Myskhako, perceived only the economic benefits to the area.

While the physical land of Malaia zemlia is for sale to the highest bidder, memory of both Brezhnev and the campaign itself remains useful, more often than not for reasons of political expediency. Under President Vladimir Putin the commemorative politics of the state are subject to renewed intensification, which, far from conflicting with local memorial interests, actively promotes them in Novorossiisk, resulting in a basic harmony of approach which fosters the local war myth as in the Brezhnev era. While this may not be true in other towns or regions of the former Soviet Union,[2] the war myth in Novorossiisk is evolving as a consensus of local and national political interests, with some notable differences from the case at the height of the Brezhnev-era war cult.

The increasing use of war symbolism as in the mayor's badges is one indication of the nationwide impact of a second war cult under Putin.[3] Scholars argue that the narrative of war victory is possibly the only theme, historical or otherwise, that can unite Russians today: the inherent social control and consequent solidarity are arguably even more necessary to the political elite in Russia in the early twenty-first century than in the Brezhnev era, when one official ideology united the Soviet Union.[4] It has been suggested that top-down nationalism is often a reaction to a period of social transition.[5] This may have been one reason for the start of the war cult in Russia following the years of economic and political uncertainty of *perestroika* and the 1990s. More recently, however, the image of a strong and united nation is politically useful in the face of increasing criticism from abroad over Russian intervention in Ukraine and Syria.

If Putin's war cult may be deemed a top-down response to the uncertainty of the Gorbachev and El'tsin leaderships or a challenging foreign policy, the cult of the more politically stable Brezhnev era may be attributed rather to the character of the general secretary himself and the desire of his political colleagues to retain their places in government. However ridiculed the figure of the elderly statesman, the monuments erected nationwide and his re-introduction of Victory Day celebrations were popular, while the re-intensification of the latter under Putin probably contributes to some extent to the conservative wave of nostalgia for the Brezhnev era. It is notable that Putin himself also admits to 'a clear respect, even nostalgia' for the past,[6] stating that the fall of the Soviet Union was the 'greatest geopolitical catastrophe' of the twentieth century.[7] Scholars have documented general and specific similarities between the policies of Putin and Brezhnev: Bacon and Sandle see a number of parallels under Putin with the Brezhnev years,[8] while Khinshtein regards Putin as Brezhnev's natural and even more successful successor.[9]

On 29 August 2011 *Novorossiiskii rabochii* reported that crowds thronged around the Brezhnev statue in Novorossiisk to watch the arrival of Prime Minister Putin astride a Harley-Davidson motorbike, a mode of transport that defines his leadership character as more macho and youth-oriented by far than Brezhnev's sedate procession through the streets by open-topped car in 1974. Hand firmly on the throttle rather than waving to the crowds, the black leather-clad Putin led a cavalcade of a thousand rock bikers, in contrast to Brezhnev's retinue of elderly Soviet dignitaries. Putin's companions on this occasion were members of the Night Wolves bikers' club, whose leader was given the Order of Honour by Putin for his 'active work in patriotic upbringing of the young', while being sanctioned by the USA in December 2014 for the club's overtly nationalistic role in the Ukraine crisis.[10]

Putin's visit coincided with a rock concert, not a military occasion nor for a commemorative event; he nonetheless used it to deploy war rhetoric in the interests of nationalistic politics. From the museum ship 'Mikhail Kutuzov', once one of the most powerful cruisers of the Soviet navy, the prime minister reminded the audience of the military campaign to liberate occupied Novorossiisk, urging them to remember 'the heroes who fought to regain the town at enormous cost'. Putin recalled that the heroic landing troops who freed Novorossiisk had for their motto *'dvizhenie tol'ko vpered!'* ('moving only forwards!'). His words were seized upon as a political slogan by local and national media in the light of the forthcoming general election of December 2011.[11] Referring probably to Stalin's notorious 'Not one step back' Order Number 227, its use indirectly confirms accusations by some scholars of a return to a degree of Stalinism under Putin. Spectators at the rock concert were treated to an extravagant pyrotechnic display illuminating a reconstruction of the liberation of Novorossiisk, including the fiery death of many of the enemy. 'Pervyi kanal', the official state television channel, confirmed the spurious connection of the concert with the war, recalling that the anniversary of the liberation of Novorossiisk was less than three weeks away.[12]

President Putin did not visit Novorossiisk on the seventieth anniversary of the landings in February 2013, although he had been in Stalingrad the previous day, a definite indication that one hero city is more important than another. However, Putin did visit Novorossiisk in 2010, when he arrived just before Victory Day to give a television interview and an impromptu walkabout which I witnessed.[13] In contrast with Brezhnev's solo evening stroll from the Hotel Brigantina, Putin's 200-metre walk was in the presence of regional governor Aleksandr Tkachev and a strong security guard. Although apparently spontaneous, the walkabout was both well-managed and consummately professional, responding to demands from the crowd for Putin's personal appearance. The prime minister was clearly idolised by the waiting women in much the same way that a younger Brezhnev had appealed to the female workers of Novorossiisk in 1974, although Putin betrayed no trace of Brezhnev's mythical modesty.

It is notable, however, that Putin made no mention of either the general secretary or Malaia zemlia on his visits to Novorossiisk, preferring instead to speak about victory and heroism in general rather than in specific terms, thus giving the impression that Brezhnev has been written out of the official state narrative. In contrast, in an apparently concerted campaign of re-recognition of the political utility of the war myth in Novorossiisk on the national level, President Dmitrii Medvedev noted in his blog-post the day after Putin's walkabout that his own grandfather had fought on Malaia zemlia.

> My grandfather, Afanasii Fedorovich Medvedev, volunteered for front-line service in 1941, and fought on Malaia zemlia, just outside Novorossiisk. Whenever he spoke about this, there were always tears in his eyes, and he seemed to re-live the whole experience on each occasion.[14]

Furthermore, in his online biography, Medvedev records, with a trace of humour, that his grandfather had, however, never met Brezhnev during his time on Malaia zemlia, reinforcing common scepticism about Brezhnev's inflated wartime role.

> Actually, he never met Brezhnev, but he was really there. According to his memories, it was a real inferno.[15]

Thus Malaia zemlia was again on the official agenda as part of the increasing momentum of the new national war cult, providing wartime credentials for the president's family. However, President Medvedev made no reported comments on the war when visiting Novorossiisk during a tour of military bases in the south of Russia in 2009, suggesting that the war cult is driven largely by Putin's impetus.[16]

While investigating opinion about Brezhnev's *Malaia zemlia* memoirs today, more than 30 years after Brezhnev's death, I interviewed 35 subjects in other parts of Russia, with no connection to Novorossiisk. Of these, nobody under the age of 40 had heard of Malaia zemlia at all, showing that it is not part of the war myth for the younger generations. The cut-off date of birth after which subjects had no knowledge of Malaia zemliia appears to be around 1967. Although three subjects in their late forties had not heard of Malaia zemlia either, a convincing majority, 86 per cent of those over 40, who would all have been over the age of 15 and in full-time education or employment before Brezhnev's death, still connected the name of Malaia zemlia irreverently with boring lessons of Soviet political ideology and a wealth of Brezhnev jokes, the popular antidote to repetitive ideological pronouncements on the part of the elite, in much the same way as illustrated by Medvedev's comments. It is apparent that, for them, Novorossiisk's gold star is considered to be as phoney as the awards hanging on Brezhnev's chest when he visited Novorossiisk in 1974.

President Putin may have avoided mentioning the Brezhnev connection, perhaps wishing to avoid adverse comparison between the two statesmen. However, his own family's challenging wartime experience in Leningrad, where his father was wounded by shrapnel and his mother narrowly escaped starvation, adds strength to Putin's image of dutiful son and father within the war cult. Thanks to his own personal connection with the war and his promotion of the war myth, the president could almost be deemed a hero in both past and modern terms.[17]

If Putin is regarded as a masculine leader, it is in a different mould from the popular perception of Brezhnev in Novorossiisk, which was based on his actual wartime service as well as his alleged promotion of the town economically. Brezhnev possessed a modest, common touch which resonated with the people then, deploying his war medals where motorcycle imagery is more likely to appeal to younger Russians today. However, Brezhnev had genuine links with Novorossiisk, rather than merely visiting the town for overtly political reasons. Similarly, popular scepticism about Brezhnev's war memoirs and Putin's KGB past detract from their cults of personality vis-à-vis the war myth. Although with vastly different leadership styles, both men enjoyed in their prime a wide following and a lengthy term of office in which to establish a strategic political use of remembrance of the war.

During the Malaia zemlia campaign, one concern voiced by the troops was the isolation of the beach-head from the rest of the country (*Bol'shaia zemlia*), and the wish to re-join the two to form a complete whole. Despite the geographical reunion in 1943, the national and local attitudes to the campaign were not always aligned over the next 70 years. Whereas state and town were united in the significance of Malaia zemlia during the war cult of the Brezhnev era, a gulf in interpretation arose after Brezhnev's death, only for them to become largely reconciled with the re-appropriation of the local war myth by the state under Putin.

Despite the continuing overwhelming influence of the state on the interpretation of the past, there is growing demand for the revision of history in twenty-first century Russia with scope for local detail which may not totally match the national narrative. Underneath the simplified headlines there exists a deeper, more complex interaction of national and local understanding with respect to Brezhnev and Malaia zemlia. While Putin's interpretation of the war myth retains only the single unmired fact of the liberation of Novorossiisk from German occupation, locally it has developed further nuance and legend over the years thanks to the recent re-examination of popular memory of Brezhnev's significant visit to Novorossiisk in 1974 upon the erection of the new statue. The result of the re-location of public memory is that the nation and the town now own two complementary myths regarding Brezhnev's link to Novorossiisk.

PART III

RESPECT FOR THE DEAD

RITUAL AND MONUMENTAL REMEMBRANCE

В молчании застыли все вокруг:
Куранты бьют мерно в тиши,
И гордо рвется к небу Вечный огонь.

Его зажгли мы в память всех людей,
Отдавших за Родину жизнь.
Этот великий подвиг
В наших живет сердцах.[1]

Every hour on the hour since 1960, from the first hesitant notes on the celeste to the final triumphant orchestral crescendo, the strains of Dmitrii Shostakovich's *Novorossiisk Chimes* have rung out across Heroes' Square, where the tomb of the Heroes of the Soviet Union killed during the Malaia zemlia campaign has stood since 1946.[2] Commissioned in the name of the citizens of Novorossiisk by the secretary of the town's Communist Party, Shostakovich's requiem for the fallen heroes indicates not only the inevitable passing of time, but also links past and present in its regular remembrance of those who fell on Malaia zemlia.[3] Heroes' Square is widely considered to be the most sacred area of Novorossiisk with regard to the war myth. Groups of schoolchildren and students are often to be found at the memorials, while local dignitaries and important visitors gather there for formal ceremonies and rituals of remembrance.

We have seen in Part I that, despite the accounts of personal heroism in Sokolov's memoirs and the *Ratnyi podvig Novorossiiska* series, propagation of the local war myth through literature was highly influenced by the state in the form of Brezhnev's authoritative *Malaia zemlia* memoirs. A greater local perspective was added to the myth with the erection of the Brezhnev statue. However, remembrance in Novorossiisk is not simply a case of lionising Brezhnev's role in the myth or of top-down ideology in action at a local level. Even within the constraints of the Soviet Union, there was much more scope for the proactive agency of the individual and the local dimension of commemoration in the case of rituals of remembrance and the design of monuments. And, surprisingly, individualism in these areas still exists in Novorossiisk – an attribute apparently highly valued in a hero city where respect for the dead of Malaia zemlia is almost as much a part of daily life as the monuments lining its streets.

The maintenance of these monuments and the continuation of the annual ritualistic ceremonies of remembrance taking place around them are evidence of what society deems its duty to remember the past. This continued commitment to honour the war dead is not unique to Novorossiisk or even to Russia. Many aspects of remembrance are universal, as communities still pay homage to those who gave their lives for what is held to be a worthy cause, and to pass on this respect to future generations. In my analysis of the dynamics and mechanism of this strong social reaction in Novorossiisk, I demonstrate that, even in the Soviet Union, the politics of remembrance were not entirely centralised, with some scope for different towns to develop and customise their own memorial practices and sculptures. In contrast to the largely uniform pan-Soviet Victory Day celebrations, the ritual of Beskozyrka, started locally in 1968, serves to emphasise the unique memorial identity of Novorossiisk. Quite surprisingly, this longstanding tradition, now fully incorporated into the myth of Malaia zemlia, was developed not by town authorities, but at the instigation of the inventive members of a small youth club at the height of the Brezhnev-era war cult. An examination of the development of Beskozyrka in Chapter 10 highlights the key role played by the younger generation in the propagation of the local war myth.

A regular repetition of memorial practice may comfort those who grieve, confirm a love of nation and town in many, if also tending to alienate members of the younger generation. Furthermore, any inertia associated with a tradition, even one strongly linked with local identity, risks leading to stagnation, as evidenced by the decline in attendance at ceremonies of remembrance in some countries. This is largely due to the death of veterans and their families, added to the disinterest of the younger generation. In the case of Novorossiisk, however, I show that the population in general displays an increasing empathy with and respect for the courage of the troops. This phenomenon is thanks to national and local conditions under which the war myth is thriving, such that this continuing legacy of the youth of 1968, far from being discarded after Brezhnev's death like many other aspects of the Soviet war cult, is increasingly relevant to the identity of the contemporary hero city of Novorossiisk.

Monumental commemoration of the dead is central to remembrance across the globe, but the states of the former Soviet Union as a whole have rather more than their fair share of World War II memorials to their war dead. At the end of the Soviet era, deaths of armed forces personnel and civilians were estimated to be around 20 million. And that estimate has risen considerably ever since until it is now closer to 30 million, representing at least 20 per cent of the population as a whole – a figure indicative of the huge scale of casualties inflicted on this occupied country.[4]

In Chapter 11 I explore through the framework of societal entropy the role of physical space and symbolic spatiality in creating and sustaining memory of the fallen. Modern Novorossiisk represents a mnemonic social construct, with over 200 monuments commemorating those who fell on Malaia zemlia arranged across the town and in surrounding areas to define this special site of memory. Monumental remembrance in Novorossiisk is largely identified by its topography, as Malaia zemlia is a geographically discrete area, where the former battle zone is cradled within the contours of the Caucasian foothills. As in some of the battlefields of Western Europe, significant decisions have been made either to develop or to retain the ravaged landscape. The topography of the hero city not only dictated some of the military action, but also planning decisions about the erection of monuments. My analysis of the decision-making processes follows on from the examination in Part II of the debate around the Brezhnev statue. In the case of war monuments, the state has played a major role in some instances, whereas in others responsibility is delegated to the Krasnodar Region or even the mayor of

Novorossiisk. My research into the urban cultural history of the hero city sheds light on the changing priorities of both state and town over the years since the war, as monuments from different eras make their imprint on the landscape, leaving a visual reminder of the battle lines in the context of the history of Novorossiisk since its foundation in the nineteenth century.

There is a tension between today's official memory and some degree of forgetting, either unintentional or selective. Monuments seen on a regular basis may fade into the habitual landscape, while there is also evidence of some official and unofficial embarrassment at other aspects of the war which may have been conveniently omitted from the popularly accepted myth of Malaia zemlia. This collective narrative is not able to accommodate every single sub-group in a potentially polyphonic memorial situation. In Chapter 12 I analyse the opposition between mainstream memory, which dictates the official mnemonic identity of Novorossiisk and is located visibly in and around the town centre, and some aspects of popular remembrance on the fringes of organised society, often situated on the geographical periphery. In particular, opinion and practice in the modern centre of Novorossiisk is compared with that in the *sel'skii okrug* (rural outlying district) of Myskhako, standing on the site of the worst of the Malaia zemlia battle.

Today's renewed emphasis in President Putin's Russia on ritual and monumental remembrance implies societal agreement on the interpretation of memory. However, the dead who are remembered remain individuals within the agreed collective narrative, whose personal remembrance is also important to their familial descendants. This dichotomy raises the question of how to locate the individual within a war myth – both individual victims of war and the individuals remembering them today, for whom collective remembrance may not be an adequate or accurate representation of their feelings or attitude to events of the past. I demonstrate that not all the fallen can be accommodated or respected within the simple war myth, revealing different categories of war dead. The town's relationship with the fallen troops may seem straightforward, but deeper searching exposes the ongoing challenges to respect afforded to innocent civilians and the enemy. Cases on the periphery of the town and of active memory are examined, including a disputed Holocaust event in Novorossiisk, an example of the sensitive issues with which citizens of former occupied Soviet states are grappling today.

The interaction of mythical and historical time is a key aspect of the dynamics of any myth-making process. We have seen in Part I the machinations of the Soviet cultural authorities to establish control over the abstract concept of time in the production of literary memoirs according to the guidelines of socialist realism. Although the intricacies of the psychology and the neuroscience of memory are beyond the scope of this book, it is important to recognise that memory remains a temporal concept, dependent on time in three ways. Firstly, as demonstrated in Part I, the substance and detail of memory is time dependent, changing with the political tide which may potentially imbue the war myth with different meanings; secondly, it is able to recall the past in the present, almost unconsciously relating the former to the latter, with time itself able to expand or contract flexibly on the part of both society and the individual remembering the past; and, thirdly, the passage of time can wipe away traces of the past, scattering personal memories and eroding memorials with a corresponding increase in entropy as time marches inexorably onwards. In establishing the dynamics of the transmission of the war myth, I show that the rich culture of memorial traditions in Novorossiisk merges to produce a unique perception of mythical time, which interacts with and occasionally dominates historical time, thus exposing the true complexity of the process of myth making in the Soviet Union and modern Russia.

CHAPTER 10

HATS OFF TO HEROES: THE BESKOZYRKA RITUAL

> So many fearless young sailors in pea-jackets and caps perished in the deep. So many times we saw dead sailors' caps floating on the sea.[1]

Conventional wisdom – sometimes erroneously – holds that, under the circumstances of a war cult, the state controls remembrance centrally. This is definitely the case with Victory Day celebrations on 9 May, which remain popular across post-Soviet Russia today since their reincarnation under Brezhnev in 1965.[2] From a presentist point of view, Eric Hobsbawm proposes a hegemonic mechanism for commemorative tradition, which provides little scope for public debate or individual input. According to this politics of memory approach, the state alone is responsible for inventing traditions. Hobsbawm sees the ruling elite introducing rituals and symbols 'which seek to inculcate certain values and norms of behaviour by repetition, which automatically implies continuity with the past'.[3] This theory correctly describes the situation regarding Victory Day and its relatively new attendant invented tradition of the St George ribbon, a symbol of war memory that has proved particularly successful since its introduction by the state in 2005 in capturing and moulding the national mood. Today there remains a general lack of dissent surrounding war memory by the public, who would probably mount a public outcry if this traditional holiday were ended. The high degree of popular support for Victory Day signifies the substantial convergence under President Putin of a manipulative state and a society relatively happy to be manipulated.

However, despite the outward impression of a state juggernaut pushing through its own agenda with respect to commemoration of the war, I contend that the position is far from straightforward. Catherine Merridale finds that, in the Soviet Union, state repression of potential alternative, personal remembrance was particularly noticeable during the grand military parades, which 'were designed to overwhelm, to drown individual memory in the clamour of patriotic ceremonial'.[4] And yet an alternative mode of commemoration with its own symbol unique to maritime Novorossiisk was indeed invented in Brezhnev's Soviet Union, its origins rooted in a provincial bottom-up memory movement. The ceremonies and practices around Victory Day in modern Russia will be examined in more detail in Part IV. In contrast, this chapter concentrates on the local Beskozyrka tradition, named after a simple sailor's cap.

In this ceremony, it is the *beskozyrka* which acts as the focal point of respect for the individual within the collective in an annual ritual of remembrance of the dead which is altogether more sober than Victory Day. The Beskozyrka ritual was invented in 1968 not by the national elite responsible for Victory Day celebrations, but by a small group of young Novorossiisk residents. However, this Soviet youth group was also no doubt under the influence of the state's burgeoning war cult shortly after Brezhnev's appointment as the country's leader in 1964.

The change in state policy to promote the war myth and associated remembrance was anticipated in Novorossiisk in 1963, when the local Communist Party newspaper, *Novorossiiskii rabochii*, filled a whole page with war memories. Two years later the same paper was exceptionally published on a Sunday, devoting its whole four-page edition to the revived Victory Day celebrations.[5] With a build-up of the memorial climate nationally and locally during the mid-1960s, the time was ripe for a new form of commemoration in Novorossiisk. In January 1968 a ten-line paragraph appeared in the youth section of *Novorossiiskii rabochii*, advertising *Operatsiia 'Beskozyrka'* (Operation 'Beskozyrka'), a procession taking the 'torch of glory', lit from the eternal flame on Heroes' Square, to the site of the Malaia zemlia landings in the small hours of 4 February, in commemoration of the twenty-fifth anniversary of the start of the battle.[6]

The youth group promoted by *Novorossiiskii rabochii* was inspired by the creation in 1962 of a literary club for young readers, *Klub iunykh kommunarov* (the Young Commune Members' Club) by *Komsomol'skaia Pravda*, the official mouthpiece of the Communist Party's youth movement, the Komsomol.[7] The Novorossiisk off-shoot of the readers' club was named 'Shkhuna rovesnikov' (the Schooner 'Young Contemporaries'), possibly after *Rovesnik*, the Komsomol magazine for teenagers which was popular in the 1960s.[8] The 'Shkhuna rovesnikov' may well have been modelled on the crew of a real ship on the Bering Sea, the *Seskor*, who had started a literary journal from their cabin.[9] The Novorossiisk club encouraged its teenage members (so-called *Shkhunatiki*) to form the land-based crew of an imaginary schooner, incorporating a system of ranks, an oath of adherence and passwords for meetings. The founding captain and self-proclaimed helmsman of the 'Shkhuna rovesnikov' was the novice *Novorossiiskii rabochii* journalist, Konstantin Podyma. Gathering his crew in November 1965 through a new youth page in *Novorossiiskii rabochii*, the 19-year-old invited all 'romantics' and 'fantasists' to set sail with him on a journey of dreams, discussion and self-discovery.[10] Thus started the weekly meetings in their 'cabin' in the *Novorossiiskii rabochii* offices,[11] leading to a series of romantic exploits deemed by a former *Shkhunatik* to be typical of the eccentricity of the club members.

Although the *Shkhunatiki* may in retrospect consider themselves to have been atypical of their generation, they were probably rather the product of their times and cultural environment, with relatively normal family backgrounds including peasants, accountants, workers in the port, doctors and managers in industry. Some of the young people's parents also worked for the Communist Party. Indeed, according to Gleb Tsipursky's analysis, most of the readers of *Komsomol'skaia Pravda* in the early 1960s represented 'conformist youth', who identified with the values propagated by the newspaper, including the strong sense of patriotism disseminated from above, a view extrapolated by Jeffrey Brooks to the relationship between the press and the Soviet population in general in the early Brezhnev years.[12] However, it is evident that this local club brought its own creative interpretation to the pervading examples in national youth publications.

Members of the 'Shkhuna rovesnikov' revelled in an atmosphere of literary romanticism, adopting as their hero the poet Pavel Kogan, who met his death outside Novorossiisk in September 1942. The young people regularly spent the night changing a red flag on the summit of Sakharnaia golova, the hill where he was killed in battle.[13] This interest in Kogan is a local reflection of the influence of the romantic poetry and song which became fashionable with young people in the post-Stalin era of the 1950s and 1960s, when student anthems included Kogan's 'Brigantina' (1937), typical of the 'bardic song' of the thaw years. Exotic heroes including the sea captains featured in Kogan's work and the romantic pirates of the open seas were popular heroes in this new genre.[14] It has even been suggested that 'Brigantina' is Kogan's tribute to Nikolai Gumilev, the poet well known for his Wanderlust.[15] No doubt the escapism inherent in Kogan's poetry and the perceived freedom of a sea captain were attractive to shore-bound teenagers with little chance of significant travel. It therefore comes as no surprise that, with their combination of idealistic romanticism and respect for the war dead, the group decided to mark the anniversary of the landings in 1968 in a special way, framing themselves within the pervading memorial context. Their idea was to commemorate unburied troops who had died at sea by carrying a sailor's peakless uniform cap (the eponymous *beskozyrka*) four kilometres through the streets of the town just after midnight. The hat would then be ceremonially lowered into the sea at Stanichka, surrounded by wreaths of flowers.

This ceremony is also a reflection of the increasing focus on military-patriotic youth training in the Brezhnev era, strongly endorsed by the Komsomol organisation. Membership of the Komsomol was expected for schoolchildren and students aged from 14 to 28 who became members of a primary cell, the bottom layer of a complex hierarchy of management mirroring the Communist Party organisation. Komsomol activities centred on the war cult were highly controlled by nationalist sympathisers and encouraged by novels and memoirs about the war. Furthermore, young people were taken to visit war sites and monuments as part of their moral upbringing (*vospitanie*).[16]

Novorossiisk teenagers were possibly even more exposed to memory of the war than many of their peers. According to Klara, a former member of the 'Shkhuna rovesnikov', the young postwar generation of Novorossiisk in the late 1960s were exposed to stories of wartime exploits in books, the press and the family. Moreover, when I was fortunate enough to interview him, Podyma claimed that the *Shkhunatiki* would routinely find grenades, shell cases and human remains, breeding a feeling of involvement in the war myth from childhood and a sense of identification with the young partisans who had fought outside Novorossiisk during the war.

However, Podyma and two female *Shkhunatiki* categorically dismiss suggestions of direct Komsomol influence on the original Beskozyrka ceremony, although it is probable that the overwhelming state propaganda machine of their youth went largely unnoticed due to its ubiquitous nature. They do, however, acknowledge Communist Party support from the editor of *Novorossiiskii rabochii*, Grigorii Pogibel', a member of the Gorkom, the town committee of the Communist Party, who provided premises for their meetings. He also encouraged the already independent youngsters to plan the ceremony themselves, while nonetheless checking on the organisational details.[17] Rather more direct input into the meetings is recalled, however, by Viktor Saloshenko, second secretary of the Novorossiisk Komsomol Committee at the time, who claims to have implemented all the organisation of which he deemed the young people incapable. He also suggests that, without his official Komsomol presence at all meetings of the 'Shkhuna rovesnikov', its members risked being taken for dissidents by the KGB.[18]

Klara admits that it took time for the authorities to come to terms with the group's sometimes unusual projects, although Podyma believes that the Komsomol was unwilling to help in the early days because of the absence of prestigious veterans from the first ceremony. This difficulty may reflect not only the status that the veterans would bring to the event, but possibly points to a problem with permission for a group procession. Veterans were among the few categories of citizens allowed to gather together in public at the time – an important privilege granted to those from whom the state needed absolute loyalty for the credibility of the war cult.[19] Podyma alleges that there was some peripheral involvement from the KGB, whose border guards set up searchlights along the shore to light up their proceedings,[20] a claim disputed by Klara. In the light of competing memories and the lack of decisive evidence from Komsomol records, it is difficult to gauge with certainty the degree of influence from above. The Beskozyrka movement may possibly have been the product of an organised campaign by the Komsomol leadership, which, under the influence of the national memorial climate, tapped into the enthusiasm and inventiveness of the younger generation. In today's Novorossiisk, however, the credit for its inception is placed squarely with the inventive young people themselves.

The first Beskozyrka ceremony was a modest affair, involving only 22 young people and six adults; the cap was carried by Elena Ostapenko, a former nurse on Malaia zemlia.[21] The newly invented ritual then faltered for a time, being banned by a Communist Party bureaucrat the following year, despite its patriotic intent and the countrywide encouragement of youth initiatives.[22] Party concern may have been due to a degree of nervousness about crowds of young people gathering together following the protest events in Moscow against the invasion of Czechoslovakia in 1968, as, although the ceremony was permitted officially in 1970, it was restricted to a much smaller area.[23] Thanks to the intervention of influential veterans and the Gorkom, local Komsomol officials were apparently finally convinced of the value of the ceremony and gave it their approval in 1971.[24] By the outing of the third Beskozyrka the number of participants had increased dramatically to a critical mass of 5,000, such that by 1973 the press was already referring to it as an established tradition.[25]

The rise in popularity of the Beskozyrka ritual during the 1970s mirrored the development of the war cult nationwide. The early Beskozyrka tradition was apparently welcomed by both young and old, fusing the patriotic commemoration desired by the older generation with the romance of a secret society attractive to its young inventors. Sokolov recalls the emotion evoked by the ceremony as veterans silently remembered their fallen comrades, linked with their gratitude for the opportunity to pass on this memory to the younger generation.[26] In contrast, the main aspect of Beskozyrka apparently enjoyed by the younger generation was the night-time torchlit procession and the secrecy of a complex system of passwords.[27] Here was an adventure in keeping with the romantic leanings of the *Shkhunatiki*, nurtured by the state emphasis on 'romantic militarism', exemplified by the publication from 1964 to 1990 of a series of biographies of romantic figures in history, *Plamennye revoliutsionery* (*Fiery Revolutionaries*).[28] Furthermore, the system of ranks and the military parade of Beskozyrka reflected official war cult values, which promoted a convergence of generations that would ensure the ceremony's success.

A Changing Tradition or a Tradition of Change?

The juxtaposition of the concept of longstanding tradition with a relatively young state such as post-Soviet Russia may seem paradoxical, particularly bearing in mind the unsettled years of *perestroika* and the 1990s, when Beskozyrka struggled to survive. Eric Hobsbawm suggests that newly invented traditions may be more widespread during periods of rapid social change and modernisation to which older established traditions may succumb.[29] In contrast, I contend that the comfort of any tradition, whether old or young, is particularly welcome within an environment rendered unstable by war, political or financial crisis. According to Edward Shils, it is the very normativeness of tradition that acts as 'the inertial force which holds society in a given form over time'.[30] Similarly, Paul Connerton sees the importance of ritual mainly in its invariance over time.[31] Maurice Halbwachs confirms that rituals tend to remain constant over time, even when society as a whole is in the process of change, as, especially in these circumstances, people tend to cling to tradition for the perceived security it offers.[32]

On the other hand, any inertia associated with a tradition, even one strongly linked with local identity, risks leading to stagnation. There is the related risk that the ritual may become static and boring, with over-reliance on what Paul Connerton calls 'habit-memory', leading to popular apathy rather than a proactive commitment to remember.[33] This is certainly not the case in Novorossiisk, though, where I have found that a society *can* successfully adapt an old tradition for new conditions by grafting new rituals or language onto the original ceremony of commemoration. In fact, it is perhaps not surprising that an analysis of the development of the Beskozyrka tradition over nearly five decades reveals gradual changes in the ritual. The organisers of Beskozyrka have adopted a process of re-invention and rejuvenation, enabling each generation to place its own stamp on the ritual, while serving to prevent stagnation and promote local identity. The series of changes in Beskozyrka has been established not merely as the passive response typical of a comfortably apathetic society, but in a proactive attempt to attract young people and propagate war memory across the generations. Furthermore, in view of the scale and frequency of these innovations, it seems that the concept of change in the Beskozyrka ritual has become an invented tradition in its own right.

With even younger children and their parents in mind, the time was brought forward firstly to the afternoon and then the evening of 3 February, better facilitating cross-generational transmission. Raisa Sokolova describes the addition of a solemn oath to the proceedings in 1978, the tenth anniversary of the tradition and the week during which Brezhnev's memoirs were published.[34] Repeating the oath made by Major Kunikov's troops prior to battle, the young people swore to become a living memorial to those who had given their lives. The original marine infantry had sworn to die for their country:

> We will give up our own will, strength and blood, drop by drop, for the life and happiness of the people, for you, our beloved Motherland![35]

After the event, their historic success was reinforced in a dispatch from the War Council:

> Your fathers, mothers, wives and children will be proud of your defence, courage and heroism. We know that this small area of land will become great and will bring about the liberation of our fathers, mothers, wives and children groaning under the fascist yoke.[36]

The heroes of Malaia zemlia were thus situated in a mythical historical continuum, charged with ensuring the freedom of their children, the generation responsible for the invention of the Beskozrka ceremony. In contrast, the oath made by the Beskozyrka carriers in 1980 principally reflected the prevailing ideology of the Brezhnev era, as participants vowed to strive to work hard to fulfil communist ideals, including the stringent economic demands of the tenth five-year plan.[37] It is perhaps not surprising that, in a ceremony with links to the general secretary's wartime service, political ideology further complicated the simple war myth. Despite an ostensible wish to commemorate the past, this pragmatic consideration of the political environment confirms that, towards the end of the Brezhnev era, national political concerns barely connected with war memory had taken over the local myth of Malaia zemlia.

In the early years after the fall of the Soviet Union interest in Beskozyrka waned in line with national trends after Gorbachev had dismantled the Brezhnev-era war cult.[38] Newspaper reports of the ritual are scarce, with nothing about Beskozyrka in the local press in 1993, the fiftieth anniversary of the landings. Several of my respondents mentioned that Beskozyrka in its original form barely survived during this period. Marta, a former member of the 'Shkhuna rovesnikov', blamed this decline on the end of the Komsomol organisation, which had apparently continued to endorse the ceremony since 1971. However, a retired headmistress recalls that 100 children from each of the local schools were invited during the 1990s to the town's theatre for a different type of commemoration involving about 5,000 annually, reinforcing Marta's claim that the town's head of culture and other founding members of the ceremony kept the ritual alive. This is plausible, since, following the town council's decision to take over responsibility for the ritual, it was back to full strength in 1998 for its thirtieth anniversary.[39]

For over 50 years the fact that *two* landings had actually taken place in 1943 was rarely recalled, as the war myth privileged the successful Malaia zemlia campaign over the failed landings at Iuzhnaia Ozereika. Since 1996 *two* torches have been lit and *two* hats carried to the beaches: the first to Malaia zemlia in the usual fashion, and the second transported by tank to the more distant Iuzhnaia Ozereika, where the ritual has evolved slightly differently, with its own committed following.

The twenty-first century has seen a partial return under President Putin to more conservative Soviet values, a renewed emphasis on *vospitanie* and the development of a new war cult. Once again, politicians promote a common interest in social coherence and continuity with the Soviet past, presenting the people with an image of a strong and united nation. As will be shown in Part IV, the involvement of the younger generation is central to current policy for the propagation of the war myth, utilising many of the strategies of the Brezhnev era.

My observations indicate that the majority of Russians of all ages welcome the associated ceremonies and ritual reminiscent of the Brezhnev era, particularly Victory Day in May.[40] However the notoriously cold weather in February provides a ready-made excuse for inhabitants of Novorossiisk to stay indoors and not attend Beskozyrka. Some respondents in their thirties and early forties search for further reasons for non-attendance, explaining how they would like to join in the procession, but would find it difficult to get there in the rush-hour traffic; moreover, they claim that their children are tired after school. Possibly with this in mind, the organisers introduced in 2010 a newly invented

Figure 10.1 'Beskozyrka' at the Eternal Flame on Heroes' Square (photograph by the author)

off-shoot of Beskozyrka, *Svecha v okne*, the 'Candle in the Window' movement, whereby those staying at home are encouraged to show their solidarity with the marchers outside. Those in the actual procession carry red glass lanterns containing a small candle. This is replicated in the homes of those not able or willing to join in the ceremony by placing a lit candle in the window as the procession passes by. Heavily promoted by the town council on posters and in newspaper advertisements, this modern idea is reminiscent of other ceremonies of remembrance worldwide. In Britain, for example, crowds holding candles gathered around local war memorials while lights were dimmed indoors on the centenary of the start of World War I. According to female respondents of all ages, this new supplementary invented tradition is particularly popular amongst women not wishing to venture outdoors, and involves far more people than ever before, even if they do not demonstrate the commitment of those taking part in the cold. Like the addendum of the St George ribbon to Victory Day, this is an innovation grafted onto an older, established tradition, having the effect of enriching, rejuvenating and refreshing the ritual, rendering it more attractive to the younger generation and their parents.

A new daytime Beskozyrka especially for children has been introduced, attracting a further audience of 4,700 young people,[41] a cohort of citizens not able to deploy excuses when taken to the ceremony by their teachers, as their families respond to a complex mixture of social expectation and freedom to attend. Continuing the tradition of innovation ingrained in the Beskozyrka ritual, a further ceremony started in 2016, whereby schoolchildren launch white ballons containing small paper seagulls at the Malaia zemlia memorial. This 'White Seagulls' movement once again encourages the active participation of the youngest generation during this special day.[42]

With their memorial duty dispatched, the children then watch a reconstruction of the landings at Malaia zemlia, repeated annually since 2011. Such historical events have also become very popular globally, ranging from the Battle of Hastings to civil war events in Britain and the United States. Napoleon's defeat at the Battle of Waterloo is reconstructed annually in Belgium, just as, in Russia, the re-enactment of the turning point in the Napoleonic war at the Battle of Borodino attracts large crowds. War memory in twenty-first century Russia increasingly refers to less controversial ubiquitous heroism rather than to the more specific examples still being cited in the 1990s. Any potentially problematic issues, such as continuing this tradition from the Soviet Union to modern Russia, are overcome by an increasing simplification of the memory message to one of popular patriotism and the dismissal of side-issues that may threaten to disrupt its coherence. In contrast, there is considerable local geographical detail in the reconstructions of the 1943 landings, which bring to life the generalisms of the national war myth with some local historical accuracy.[43]

A re-enactment on the actual battle site can be a very powerful means of propagating a war myth, while still representing a relatively passive experience for the large audience. In contrast, the more intimate group in Iuzhnaia Ozereika witnessed a different spectacle in 2011. In a seemingly spontaneous gesture, the *beskozyrka* bearer, young marine Ivan Ognev, attracted gasps of admiration from spectators as he strode into the sea up to his shoulders to deposit the hat on the waves. An exchange of messages in an online forum established that he had gone into the water of his own accord, in a surge of empathy with the original landing troops, and with no orders from above, effectively bringing the myth to life.[44] In the light of this personal tribute in braving the winter waves, it

Figure 10.2 Re-enactment of the Landings (1) (photograph by Anatolii Pozdniakov and published with his permission)

Figure 10.3 The *Beskozyrka* Bearer Lays the Hat and Wreath in the Sea (photograph by Anatolii Pozdniakov and published with his permission)

appears that the romanticism of the young founders of Beskozyrka lives on, at least in Iuzhnaia Ozereika, where there remains some scope on the fringe for the individual in organised remembrance today.

However, this originally spontaneous part of the ceremony has now been incorporated into the main ritual at Malaia zemlia, an indication perhaps of the increasingly centralised control of Beskozyrka, both administratively in the organisation by the town council, and physically in the ranks of Cossacks holding the spectators at bay. Such top-down intervention has prompted some negative comments in online discussions about over-organisation and the desecration of genuine memory for the sake of political utility.[45]

What started out as a series of sometimes minor innovations and refinements to the invented tradition of Beskozyrka has become a tradition of invented change in its own right. Even in 2012, more changes were still being promised by the press:

> From year to year the movement [. . .] does not change, but on each occasion the programme acquires new memorial components. This year will be no exception.[46]

Despite the innovations, there is comfort in the continuity of symbolism in the Beskozyrka tradition. With candles, caps and ribbons, its interpretation and essence remain constant, although the consistency of symbolism permits only one interpretation of the past, in accord with the conventions of the war myth, albeit widely endorsed by the local population. My observations and interviews indicate that Beskozyrka still appeals to the same members of society: teachers, cadets and veterans, although the first actors would hardly recognise the scale of today's operation and the veterans are becoming fewer. With the participation of schools, the interest of parents is guaranteed, with some young families new to Novorossiisk learning about Beskozyrka and coming to appreciate local history thanks to their children, as in the case of the original inventors.

In contrast, responsibility for the Beskozyrka ritual, founded by and traditionally associated with the young people of Novorossiisk, was taken over in 1999 by the regional youth committee in Krasnodar, this time involving a committee *for* youth rather than the younger generation themselves, who thereby appear to have lost their ownership of the ceremony. The following year, Beskozyrka became known as a pan-Russian operation, its name today emphasising its roots: The Pan-Russian Patriotic Youth Movement 'Beskozyrka'.[47] Despite the implicit geographical expansion, attendees are largely local, with the financial burden of the ceremony falling on the town of Novorossiisk, whose mayor now takes responsibility for its implementation, possibly reflecting some local rivalry over the ownership of memory between the hero city of Novorossiisk and the regional centre of Krasnodar. The 2011 advertising pamphlet, published by the region, confirms the continued emphasis on youth participation, although there is no mention of its young founders and their vision, indicating perhaps that the authorities are anxious to take all the credit.

Despite this omission, Podyma, a prolific inventor of tradition both in Novorossiisk and Moscow, has numerous publications on Beskozyrka and other less well-known memorial rituals to his credit, including one to commemorate those who died on the first night of the war in June 1941.[48] For over 40 years he consistently propagated the myth of Malaia zemlia, building up a legend around the 'Shkhuna rovesnikov', which, he claims, spread from Novorossiisk to other 'outposts' around the Soviet Union.[49] At the same time he nurtured his own personality cult as its 'romantic' founder and only true guardian of memory.[50] In Novorossiisk Podyma's name has become just as recognised as those of the real heroes of Malaia zemlia. While children learn about the history of Kunikov and his landing troops, older interviewees are equally likely to speak about the propagation of memory through Podyma's Beskozyrka ritual, which has also been assimilated into the local history of the town, albeit a generation younger than the war itself.

In the Russian Orthodox tradition, the exact site of burial is a vital focus for socially prescribed mourning.[51] In the case of soldiers lost at sea, with no obvious monument or grave for the individual bereaved family to visit, the simple sailor's cap floating on the waves provides the only focal point for tributes of flowers and the expression of emotion, much as the eternal flame for the Unknown Soldier provides a focus for memorial tribute in Moscow.

The original Beskozyrka ceremony also served to fill a ceremonial vacuum in the Soviet Union. Celebrations in February are not uncommon in other societies to alleviate the tedium and hardship of the long winter before the days lengthen and the signs of spring appear. In a

Figure 10.4 Konstantin Podyma (photograph by Irina Nikitina and published with her permission)

blend of Christian and pagan tradition, many countries hold a carnival week in February before the onset of the rigours of Lent, although the traditional Russian carnival *Maslenitsa* was banned in Soviet times. Beskozyrka is neither joyous nor food-orientated, but does involve those elements of flame and liturgy more often associated with church ritual. Similarly, the sailor's hat is borne in procession and laid on the waves in an act resembling an offering to the memory of the landing troops.

Reinforcing this interpretation, elderly Sonia throws sweets and biscuits into the sea behind the hat and the wreaths, as her own small sacrifice to the dead.

Secular commemoration and organised religion have much in common, with the sacralised war myth becoming almost a surrogate religion or faith system in Novorossiisk. Candles are very often lit in a Russian Orthodox church in an act of memory and are carried by President Putin in official services of remembrance. The quasi-religious symbolism of the liturgy and ritual of Beskozyrka is evident in the symbols of light and fire, the imagery of sacrifice and martyrdom. According to journalist Evgenii Rozhanskii, each small flame in the 'living sea' of candles in the Beskozyrka procession represents 'the soul of a dead soldier'. With implicit religious symbolism, the new Candle in the Window movement now effectively brings the sacred memorial ritual into the secular home, using the symbolism of the candle to shed light on memory. Russian families have traditionally placed a candle in the corner of a room to illuminate a holy icon, creating their own spiritual space for private worship. The placing of the candle on a windowsill, visible from the outside, breaches any remaining barriers between the collective and the private with respect to memory.[52]

Although few Soviet soldiers in the war were overt Christians, the Orthodox Church today is very close to the state, a situation accepted by veterans and encouraged by Putin, who ensures that priests pray for the war dead.[53] The joint influence of State and Church should aid in principle both the maintenance of the war myth and the inculcation of conservative moral values. However, some of my male respondents did not feel the necessity for the presence of a priest at Beskozyrka, stressing the mixture of faiths and ethnicities of the original troops and viewing it as a purely secular occasion. Local priest Father Georgii Fedorenko considers his presence at Beskozyrka to be vital, though, claiming that 95 per cent of the population of Novorossiisk are Orthodox believers. He has been invited by the mayor to attend in an official capacity for several years, demonstrating the increasing importance of the Church in Russia both socially and politically. While wearing his own military medals, Father Georgii's role remains largely symbolic, as he is not usually invited to speak, in contrast to his input on other memorial occasions, such as re-interments.[54]

There is no doubt that religion does play a part in remembrance today, but, according to my evidence, that part is largely in the personal sphere, for example when individuals pay their respects to the fallen by their gravesides on *Den' pamiati i skorby* (the Day of Remembrance and Sorrow) on 22 June, the more solemn anniversary of the start of the war in the Soviet Union in 1941, when a priest is usually present. As John Bodnar found with remembrance of the Vietnam War, there is a marked difference in tone between private commemoration concentrating on the pain of loss, and the larger, official ceremonies which employ generalised expressions of martyrdom, sacred duty and patriotism.[55]

Issues of personal mourning may no longer be applicable so long after the war, but individuals must still make a choice whether or not to attend a traditional ritual, even if subject to group pressure. The evidence in Novorossiisk demonstrates a strong commitment by attendees to the Beskozyrka ceremony in the face of often daunting weather conditions which serve only to strengthen the bond between those remembering and those remembered. Most participants in the Beskozyrka tradition are not simply passive spectators, but are able to justify their presence, usually accepting some physical discomfort as an aid to their interpretation of the ritual. This may not always be true for those simply watching a reconstruction, but it remains the case for those making the longer journey to the beach at Iuzhnaia Ozereika outside Novorossiisk. Here, the genuinely involved younger participants are compared favourably with the original *Shkhunatiki* by Galina Krympokha, who is credited with keeping the 'Shkhuna rovesnikov' and its crew afloat over the long years since its inception: 'There are no indifferent eyes there.'[56]

It is possible that the current wave of nostalgia for the Soviet Union plays a role in the popularity amongst older people of rituals of remembrance dating back to the Brezhnev era. In contrast, there is evidence that some young adults may have experienced enough of the Beskozyrka tradition following years of enforced participation as schoolchildren. However, the tradition is re-fuelled with fresh blood as eight newcomers to the area I interviewed seemed keen to attend the ceremony, while locals bring friends from further afield to experience it at first hand, attracted by the unique maritime connotations of the ritual.

It is clear that there remains a place today for traditional ritualistic ceremony in this modern, youth-oriented society, despite the fact that an established tradition may be regarded as a sign of conservatism in a society, as it simply maintains the status quo. In Novorossiisk the combination of the new state-sponsored war cult of the Putin era, with the influence of the more reactionary, provincial older generations, is sufficient to counteract the sometimes anti-traditional attitude of young people.

Although currently larger than ever, the numbers attending Beskozyrka remain substantially smaller than those celebrating Victory Day in Novorossiisk, mainly due to the different nature of the remembrance involved. As a celebration of national victory in 1945, Victory Day is less solemn than Beskozyrka, although a requiem for the dead is held early on Victory Day, before the start of the main celebrations. Citizens feel that Victory Day is a different type of event: national, happier and more celebratory, while Beskozyrka demands a more thoughtful approach to memory, which, according to some respondents, comes directly from the romantic soul of the young people of Novorossiisk.

The continuing sense of identification with Beskozyrka of the younger generation, with the gratitude and participation of many of their elders, maintains a sense of social cohesion that may easily have died out with other traditions during the 1990s. Furthermore, its original, specifically local, interpretation endures, despite and also thanks to a series of changes; these are usually regarded as elements of creative enrichment of the ceremony and more recently take their inspiration from commemorative norms worldwide rather than a small local youth club. Shils may regard originality as the enemy of tradition,[57] but in Novorossiisk it has helped to avoid any dilution of meaning and has guaranteed the longstanding popularity of Beskozyrka, which is now at an all-time high, with no sign of ritual fatigue. Official council figures state that between 15,000 and 20,000 participants in 2011 remembered the heroes of 1943,[58] while Deputy Mayor Maiorova suggested that a record 23,500 attended the ceremony in 2013. According to the official town website, a staggering 44,000 took part in 2017.[59] The fact that nearly 20 per cent of the total population of the town is involved in some way is an indication of the growing popularity of the tradition. Although Beskozyrka remains a ceremony reinforcing local identity, Podyma claimed a decade ago that over 350,000 people had taken part in the ceremony since its inception and visitors from 270 other towns have taken part over the years.[60] In 2011, for example, delegates were invited from other hero cities to take part in a series of events and a ritual on a much larger scale, while coverage on the national television news confirmed the status and identity of Novorossiisk nationwide.[61] In recent years, however, the only visiting delegations to Novorossiisk have been from the regional capital, Krasnodar. The considerable local and national media hype serves to convince many younger respondents that Beskozyrka is famous worldwide, such that they express naive surprise that it remains unknown in Western Europe.

For today's ritual, it is the town council which bears the brunt of, and takes the credit for, the organisation of Beskozyrka. This indicates a new uncompromising recognition of the significance of the ceremony on the part of the town. It is in this respect that responsibility for the propagation of memory has changed most significantly, with the original transmission of Beskozyrka by the younger generation now centralised and controlled by the local authorities, and the only remaining spark of individuality and spontaneity on the periphery now formally incorporated into the official mainstream narrative at Malaia zemlia. The mnemonic vicious circle may have been broken through the tradition of change, but Soviet society's traditional values are increasingly being projected through ritual onto the younger Russian generation, subject today to domination and determination by the elite who now organise Beskozyrka, rather than the romantic young idealists of 1968.

Young people in Novorossiisk appear today to be less able or willing to use their own initiative about remembrance practices than in the Brezhnev era. What started as a rare example of a bottom-up ritual in the Soviet Union, albeit under the not insignificant influence of the Brezhnev-era war cult and probably the Komsomol leadership, has become more like the top-down type of invented tradition described by Hobsbawm, with its stress on the propagation of social values through the war myth. As Russia experiences a second war cult under Putin, the Soviet emphasis on patriotism and moral education of the young are once again in evidence, affording national and local conditions under which this unique remembrance ritual is thriving and where increasing empathy with the landing troops is demonstrated. It is notable also that, although started under Brezhnev, this ceremony has no connection with the former general secretary, focusing instead on the individuals who died, and thus serves to deflect attention from his memoirs. There may be a growing audience of schoolchildren to ensure its future propagation, but, nonetheless, the tradition would not last unless enjoying popular approval from the public as a whole. The proactive maintenance of this tradition with its regular re-invention helps to define the mnemonic identity of the hero city of Novorossiisk and ensures that the myth of Malaia zemlia remains at the heart of the local community.

This case shows that it is not sufficient to accept state domination without consideration of the local 'community of memory', which is perhaps more conscious of its own past than of national history.[62] This type of social remembrance is potentially more meaningful to groups and individuals as it is designed and customised by the local community and implemented through ritual close to home. The Beskozyrka tradition does not seek to contest the national narrative, but represents a special subset of memorial behaviour which commemorates the myth of Malaia zemlia within the national war myth. It is evident that there does not have to be a binary opposition or power struggle between state and popular expressions of collective memory, as in the case of memory of the war in Vietnam.[63] The Beskozyrka tradition is not at all conflictual, being accepted throughout the country as specific to Novorossiisk.

From the point of view of nationwide commemorative events, Novorossiisk is typical of contemporary Russian society. However, the ceremony here shows several idiosyncratic features, proving that remembrance was capable of taking on a distinctly local form, even under the centralised and authoritarian conditions prevalent in the Soviet Union. It is largely the unique Beskozyrka ceremony which distinguishes Novorossiisk from other hero cities of the former Soviet Union. Unlike the infamous Brezhnev connection, this special distinction is welcomed by the people of Novorossiisk, who still profess an admiration for the tradition of romanticism and spontaneity associated with war memory from below.

The Time and Tide of Memory

Confiding her personal thoughts during the remembrance ceremony of Beskozyrka, middle-aged Klavdiya remarks: 'I think behind my eyes: I try to imagine it, from films and books, how awful it was: explosions, how they lived. It must have been very hard.' This statement demonstrates that, even though today's rituals of remembrance represent a highly organised communal experience, they nonetheless offer the opportunity for an individual, if silent, response. This is a good example of trans-temporal empathy promoted by a successful memorial ritual, whereby each person's imagination may be converted into a time machine capable of linking two distant moments in time by the act of memory.

The return to the past through anamnestic recall raises the question of the complex temporality of memory with respect to historical time – time which is often perceived as linear and unidirectional, but, where the annual rhythm of memorial anniversaries is concerned, may also be perceived as cyclical, leading the participant's memory back to the original event on a regular basis. During the Beskoyrka reconstructions a reversal of time is apparent on the very same space where the landings took place, reducing the perceived relative time gap between past and present with a resultant increase in identification between present-day participants and the original troops. In this respect, Klavdiya's testimony shows that 'the past becomes something experienced, rather than understood or examined'.[64]

Monuments tend to preserve the past in the present in much the same way as ritualistic tradition, where cyclical temporal movement gives the impression of static time around the monumental focus of rituals. However, instead of time merely standing still, Mikhail Yampolsky argues persuasively for a special flow of time around a monument:

> A monument creates around itself a kind of special temporal expanse in which time moves differently than in other places, a sort of mystical protective zone that surrounds the monument and is apparently connected with the experience of temporal metamorphosis.[65]

In the case of Novorossiisk, those taking part in the Beskozyrka ritual act as time-travellers, approaching the Malaia zemlia monument from the present, crossing the timeless space around it, to arrive in the past via the Brezhnev era as they reach the monument itself. In this way the monument in the shape of the prow of a motor launch, erected in 1982, seems transformed back into the original craft it represents, while the sculpted depictions of the original 1943 landing troops on its sides are transformed into the ranks of the modern soldiers reconstructing the landings. This blurring of time zones evident even today is reminiscent of the deployment of socialist realism in Soviet literature, which recycled

Figure 10.5 Re-enactment of the Landings (2) (photograph by Anatolii Pozdniakov and published with his permission)

heroic historical precedents as a fore-taste of the implied reality to come, thus merging present time with past and promised future.[66] The static monument and the memory it channels may have outlived the heroes, but still transmit the timeless testimony of non-contestable patriotic heroism to be valued in the present and future and appreciated by all stake-holders in the Beskozyrka ritual.

According to memoirist Georgii Sokolov, the *beskozyrka* floating on the water is carried by the same waves as in 1943, themselves depicted as insensitive carriers of memory of those who lost their lives: 'They will never return, no, these lads will never return to shore. Only the senseless waves beat on the shore, remembering the past . . . .'[67] Thus the sea itself is deemed to be an agent in the apparent closing of the temporal gap between 1943 and today. Not only the waves recall the night, apparently. Mariya, a classmate of Konstantin Podyma, feels that nature as a whole sees the need to reproduce the conditions of 1943 in tribute to the troops. An aspect of the war myth expressed by respondents of all ages includes the legendary icy wind and stormy weather every year on the night of 3–4 February.[68] Podyma himself stated on one of his last visits to Novorossiisk: 'It is appointed by nature that it is always foul weather on 3 February in Novorossiisk, with wind, rain, and bitter cold which penetrates to the bones.'[69] In a masterpiece of understatement, *Novorossiiskii rabochii* proclaims: 'On this day, tradition is religiously observed not only by citizens, but also by the weather. A warm wind never blows on 3 February.'[70] Women, particularly, refer to wearing layers of clothes for the ceremony, while some men endorse the sentiment expressed by a *Novorossiiskii rabochii* journalist: 'The harsh weather reminded descendants of the conditions experienced by Kunikov's troops landing in the icy waves of the Black Sea.'[71] Podyma, describing in 1975 the first Beskozyrka seven years previously, emphasised the similarities: 'The February night was freezing and windy. Exactly the same as many years ago . . . .' Even the password on that night reflected the prevalent winter wind in Novorossiisk – *Nord ost* (north-easterly).[72] In 2012, myth became reality, as hardy citizens turned out in unprecedented temperatures:

> There is never good weather on 3 February. Never! But this year the temperature plunged even below yesterday's −15°C, with wind too, a change from the usual more tolerable −3°C.[73]

An annual, cyclical and quasi-biological ritualistic chronology promotes an illusion of timelessness and permanence, linking past and present time while offering both continuity and stability.[74] It is as if traditional time stands still, while historical time marches on regardless. However, thanks to the continuing tradition of innovations associated with the Beskozyrka ritual, serving to give the impression of a renewed ceremony every year, the danger of stagnation associated with circular ritualistic time is not so marked in Novorossiisk.

Over the years since the war, the addenda to the myth of Malaia zemlia, with their own ritualistic chronology, have been incorporated in tandem with the original, producing a uniquely complex local memorial time running alongside the national. The annual cycle of anniversaries is quite demanding: the town library and museum keep a special calendar so that nobody and nothing is forgotten.[75] Not only specifically war-related anniversaries have an impact on people's consciousness – respondents also mention other significant maritime dates, including *Morskoi uzel* (the Sailor's Knot) and *Den' Flota* (Navy Day).

The inauguration of wartime monuments hinged on the most well-known anniversaries, many of them having been completed in a significant year after the war. Similarly, books dealing with local history or traditions tend to be published in key years. The Beskozyrka tradition, which was started on the twenty-fifth anniversary of the landings, has its own anniversary, too. One recent book, for instance, links the thirty-fifth anniversary of the landings with the tenth anniversary of Beskozyrka itself, giving almost equal importance to both, so indicating that the mythical time of ritualistic tradition has virtually converged with linear historical time.[76] A newspaper article in 2007 completely misunderstands the dates, though, confusing the commemoration with the actual historical event, and stating that 2007 would see the thirty-ninth anniversary of the landings, rather than the thirty-ninth anniversary of Beskozyrka.[77] It is tempting to infer that the journalist was a relatively young person, for whom the fixed temporal horizon of 1968 seemed just as far away as 1943, such that real time and mythical time have actually converged. Certainly, it provides further evidence that, for some at least, the act of commemoration has become more significant than the distant event it commemorates, while also suggesting that memory of the Malaia zemlia campaign in Novorossiisk is indeed incomplete without the Beskozyrka tradition.

Jan Assmann considers memorial rituals themselves to be suspended from the onward movement of linear time, forming 'islands of time', or 'memorial spaces', rather like the Malaia zemlia monument standing in its own protective space and time. Assmann's reading is supported by Eviatar Zerubavel's observation that what is historically worthy of remembrance appears amplified in time with respect to the mundane, suggesting that time appears to slow down at key points in the calendar. From a similar perspective, Christine Boyer visualises days of remembrance as 'blank' spaces in the calendar.[78] My research indicates that time is experienced differently by locals at Beskozyrka and on Victory Day. The latter is always a holiday from work, loved by all and celebrated by families together, both a 'blank' and a red-letter day. On the other hand, Beskozyrka breaks the established socio-temporal order, eating into free time on a long February evening, when many families would prefer to be at home. They would much rather be strolling the streets on 9 May than 3 February, suggesting that Beskozyrka does not have the same impact as an 'island' on the memorial calendar as Victory Day. Young Maksim even admitted that he had to be reminded at the last minute that Beskozyrka was happening, which would never be the case with Victory Day. Since 2010, even the private time of those not taking part in the procession outside has been invaded by ritualistic time thanks to the Candle in the Window movement, which also demands extra memorial space as the Beskozyrka ritual expands into people's homes.

There is no doubting the spatial and temporal expansion of Beskozyrka. What started out as a small-scale evening event now takes up the whole of the day and evening on 3 February, and most of the previous day too, as increasing numbers of delegates from other towns are invited to take part in an ever-longer programme of events in a growing statement of local identity. Furthermore, schools devote the whole month of February to patriotism, the new top topic of the Russian curriculum, almost seamlessly linking history of the landings on 3 February with Defender of the Fatherland Day (*Den' zashchitnika Otechestva*) on 23 February. Similarly, the colonisation of time by wartime memorial dates impinges on other existing anniversaries in Novorossiisk. The anniversary of the 1943 liberation falls on 16 September, just days later than the anniversary of the town's foundation on 12 September (1838). A joint poster advertises a full week of celebrations and processions, merging the original foundation of the town with its postwar re-foundation thanks to the liberation. Here, the more recent memory predominates, with the St George ribbon and other military symbolism covering all advertising material for both anniversaries.

It is clear that mythical time seems to be measured and perceived differently from historical time. But I have shown that commemorative time, reinforced by political will, seems to have the power to expand flexibly, to colonise adjacent days and even weeks, while occasionally dominating historical time. This is a key factor in the establishment of cross-generational empathy and identity so evident at the Beskozyrka ceremony. It is probable that, with the death of the last veterans, time may eventually run in a more linear fashion, when historical rather than mythical time rules memory of the Great Patriotic War and Malaia zemlia finally becomes distant local history in Novorossiisk.

CHAPTER 11

MYTH AND MONUMENTS: THE PLACE OF THE DEAD

Мы были большими, как время.
Мы были живыми, как время.
Теперь —
мы в легендах прославленных дней.
Теперь —
мы в поэмах и прозе.
Теперь —
мы в граните и бронзе
Теперь —
мы в безмолвье могильных камней.[1]

On my very first day as a visitor to Novorossiisk in 1999 I was taken to view the most iconic and powerful of monuments – the Malaia zemlia memorial complex at Stanichka. Here, at the site where thousands of Soviet, Russian and foreign tourists have been introduced to the war myth over the years, I listened to the simplified story of the seven-month campaign and first became aware of the war in Novorossiisk.

As I stood in the shadow of the gigantic monument, my feet were on Malaia zemlia, and yet Malaia zemlia itself, the site of the protracted battle, does not appear on any maps. In his memoirs Brezhnev famously defined this small area as an abstract concept rather than a geographical entity:

Figure 11.1 The Malaia zemlia Memorial at Stanichka (1982) (photograph by the author)

> In a geographical sense, Malaia zemlia does not exist. If you want to understand it further, you should clearly imagine this rocky area of dry land right up against the water. It measured six kilometres along the front line with a depth of four and a half kilometres in all.[2]

The mythical identity of Novorossiisk is linked to a specific space around the area of Stanichka to the south of the town centre, where the Malaia zemlia memorial complex now stands. But Brezhnev's Malaia zemlia also extended further south and west to Myskhako, a village just outside the town, and even further inland to the forested slopes of Mount Koldun. The modern town of Novorossiisk has developed around this geographically limited memorial site, its public space a dynamic testament to the priorities of the community and a reflection of the collective will to promote and maintain respect for the dead.

This chapter examines the role of monuments in and around Novorossiisk in creating and sustaining the war myth, while honouring the dead both individually and collectively. In it I analyse dense layers of accumulated memories through their spatial inter-relationships to shed light on the changing priorities of both state and town over the years since the war, as successive generations have projected their own vision of the memorial role of urban space. In the twenty-first century this strong geographical identity is easier to preserve than living memory. With natural lapses of memory and the death of war veterans, each successive generation becomes further removed temporally, if not spatially, from the events of 1943. As personal memory gives way to social commemoration around the main war memorials, monumental remembrance has become more important to the town than oral testimony or memoirs.

The dissipation of direct memory with the passage of time indeed presents a challenge to remembrance. In this respect, memory behaves in a similar fashion to the thermodynamic concept of entropy. Entropy may be described as the probability of a closed system of existing in a particular state, or simply its degree of disorder.[3] Highly organised solids possess a low entropy, while more randomly organised fluids are higher in entropy. Entropy increases naturally with time, as organisation of a system inevitably decreases, unless energy is expended in counteracting the resultant disorder.[4] I shall invoke the concept of 'societal entropy' as a useful tool for analysing the effects of the relentless flow of physical time since the war in Novorossiisk. Without man-made intervention, the passage of time and natural increase in entropy would lead eventually to the complete atomisation of memory, resulting in collective forgetting. When external agencies intervene in the natural process, however, time can appear to stand still, and even go into reverse, as order is re-imposed on the natural process of decay. This process of reorganisation and entropy decrease demands the input of considerable social energy: from the state in the form of a dominant war cult; from a community with the collective will to retain memory of the past through ritualistic and monumental remembrance; and even from exceptionally motivated individuals. I shall show that considerable energy in the form of finance and planning is expended by the local community in maintaining and even enriching its ritualistic and monumental tradition. Most local war memorials are maintained rather than being allowed to fall into disrepair, demonstrating that war memory in Novorossiisk exhibits an unnaturally low entropy status, a reflection of the strong social desire to combat the effects of naturally increasing entropy in a concerted undertaking not to forget the war dead.

In the first months after the end of the war, Novorossiisk was named by the Council of Ministers as one of the 15 Russian cities structurally most badly affected by the conflict and therefore given priority for rebuilding.[5] During the invasion in 1942 and the liberation of the port in September 1943, 96.5 per cent of its buildings had been flattened and its infrastructure totally destroyed by both German and Soviet bombardment.[6] As was the case with many key towns in northern France and Germany, complete reconstruction was necessary. The postwar visionaries established a creative committee to come up with a regeneration plan: architect Boris Iofan, well respected for his work in Moscow in the 1930s, was appointed to lead this proposed drive to resurrect the town from the rubble. This was the first step in the construction of order out of the high-entropy chaos of war, as Iofan took advantage of the total destruction to design a new town along Haussmannian lines. Concentrating on the living rather than the dead, he drew up plans for new single-storeyed houses linked by a system of roads 100 metres wide radiating out from what remained of Ulitsa Sovetov, the town's main street before the occupation. Iofan proposed a new central square close to the shore in the southern part of the town, where the local council, port authorities, central post office, museum and library would be sited, alongside a theatre for 1,000 people. This new, functional centre would be complemented by another open space even closer to the sea, which would be semicircular in shape in order to house a huge commemorative panorama depicting the liberation of the town.[7]

This postwar vision included gardens, parks and sports centres. Iofan also considered commercial transport, linking the train and sea stations. Everything was carefully planned to take into consideration the topography of the town: details were incorporated such as the judicious planting of trees to protect the centre from the vicious north-easterly winds from the mountains. However, with some tension between the abstract plan and postwar reality, this grand design never came to fruition – there was simply not enough money in the state budget to support such an ambitious project, with the demands for regeneration across the country and the push to establish control over eastern Europe. In the end, all that could be afforded was a central avenue around what is now known as Pushkin Square, where citizens could stroll on high days and holidays. Large-scale housing developments, hospitals, parks and roads for these citizens had to wait for a few years, but nonetheless most of the major work had been completed by 1960. By then 300,000 trees and bushes had been planted around the new avenues and parks, where the growing population went to relax as the pressures of postwar life decreased.[8]

However, residents who had gradually returned to what was left of their town, supplemented by those veterans of the 18th Army who wished to remain in the area, were adamant that at least one central space was too sacred to delay even for one year: a proper tomb for the heroes of the Malaia zemlia campaign was deemed a priority.[9] The remains of Major Kunikov and the others who had earned the title 'Hero of the Soviet Union' were re-interred in 1946 close to the shore near what had been the town centre, on what would become known as Ploshchad' Geroev (Heroes' Square).[10] Over the years Heroes' Square has been gradually developed to become the centre of remembrance in Novorossiisk. In 1958 the town became only the third in the Soviet Union to have an eternal flame, following Leningrad and Sevastopol', with the latter acting as the source of the flame lit next to the heroes' grave in Novorossiisk, thereby linking the two

Figure 11.2 The Eternal Flame on Heroes' Square (1958) (photograph by Sergei Krasnolobov and reproduced with his permission)

maritime towns. The eternal flames in Moscow and Stalingrad were not introduced until 1967, considerably later than in Novorossiisk.

During the Khrushchev years, a few more monuments started to appear on the urban landscape. Testifying to the maritime nature of the battle, a striking memorial to the Unknown Sailor was erected on the promenade in 1961, the ribbons of his *beskozyrka* flowing

Figure 11.3 Monument to the Unknown Sailor (1961) (photograph by the author)

prominently behind his head. A further monument to all the troops who fell during the seven-month campaign appeared in Myskhako in 1962.

However, to local outrage, the Krasnodar regional authorities refused a request from the people of Novorossiisk for a more substantial monument on the actual site of the landings.[11] A further demand from key veterans of

Figure 11.4 Memorial Stele at Stanichka (1963) (photograph by the author)

Novorossiisk was sent directly to Brezhnev himself, as a veteran of the action on Malaia zemlia, leading to the erection in 1963 of a commemorative concrete stele at Stanichka, on the twentieth anniversary of the landings. Etched on its sides was a brief history of the campaign with the names of all those troops involved in the battle who were made Heroes of the Soviet Union. For years, this stele stood alone on the shore, standing guard over what had become the sacred site of the landings. The beach and the ground behind it were left untouched, with the softened contours of the trenches and dugouts a moving testament to the battle.

The mythical identity of the hero city of Novorossiisk was largely established during the Brezhnev-era war cult, when many more monuments were erected and new streets named. As a sign of this state influence, a concrete motor torpedo boat appeared in 1968 on the shoreline for the twenty-fifth anniversary of the landings, representing the fleet of small craft that had transported the marine infantry troops to the shore in the wintry early hours of 4 February 1943.

Figure 11.5 The Motor Torpedo Boat Monument (1968) (photograph by the author)

A further cluster of monuments was erected in Myskhako when Brezhnev visited Novorossiisk in 1974. The Explosion sculpture represents the mythical 1.2 tonnes of enemy metal that rained down on each of the Soviet troops on Malaia zemlia. This sculpture vividly depicts the high-entropy chaos of battle, its shards of metal fused together randomly in a static representation of a dangerously turbulent situation, where death is just around the corner. In contrast to the Explosion monument, most of the main memorials are sculpted from concrete in the style favoured by the state, socialist realism, where the subjects are usually young, muscular, square-jawed ethnic Russians. This unusual sculpture stands next to a map of the battle lines and the Calendar monument, where large steles represent the consecutive days of the fiercest fighting in April 1943.

Figure 11.6 The Explosion Monument in Myskhako (1974) (photograph by the author)

Figure 11.7 The Calendar Monument in Myskhako (1974) (photograph by the author)

The accumulation of mnemonic symbolism in the urban space during the Brezhnev era facilitated the transmission of the agreed narrative of Malaia zemlia to the younger generation, especially as the uniquely local significance of the visual narrative was evident. As the population of Novorossiisk grew in the 1960s and 1970s, many new streets were named in memory of the fallen. New blocks of flats were built in the area of Stanichka, re-named after Major Kunikov, the leader of the landing troops. Similarly, the long Ulitsa Geroev desantnikov (Landing Troop Heroes Street) is a constant reminder of all the heroes, while other streets are named after Sniper Rubakho, Viktor Chalenko, Lieutenant Schmidt and Admiral Sipiagin. One construction, the Sailor with the Grenade monument, depicts the *Malozemelets* Viktor Kaida, the memoirist, immediately recognisable to many in Novorossiisk as he settled here after the war.

Erected in 1972, the Sailor with the Grenade monument marks the wartime boundary of Malaia zemlia and occupied Novorossiisk. Inscribed on the side of this monument is an outline map showing the front lines on either side of the occupied town. It is complemented by a second, larger monument on the other side of the bay, representing the front line to the east of Novorossiisk. The latter is one of another specially designed group of monuments erected as a result of the state's growing recognition of the political utility of war memorials. Large monuments formed a significant aspect of state ideology during the war cult of the Brezhnev era. Along with an avalanche of war memoirs and an escalation of the scale of annual Victory Day celebrations, state-sponsored remembrance of the war became a politically unifying feature of late socialism. The erection of monuments was incorporated into the state 'Plan for the Construction of Monuments with Federal Significance between 1967 and 1970'.[12] In response to this countrywide initiative, the Novorossiisk local authorities recommended a project which would finally lead to the construction of a proper memorial complex at Stanichka.

Not content with just one monument, they requested three, to be arranged in an equilateral triangle around the Tsemes Bay. This project was both ideologically and financially extravagant, linking the maritime history of the town from World War I to World War II. When eventually completed, this state-funded initiative resulted in an harmonious composition set around the bay, with each monument situated five kilometres from the others. The first component of the trilogy was planned to stand outside the town to the east, on a cliff high over the bay. This monument commemorates the deliberate scuttling of the Black Sea Fleet in 1918 on the orders of Lenin, to prevent the ships falling into German hands following the Treaty of Brest-Litovsk. Moving in an anti-clockwise direction, the second monument was the Defence Line arch, which was completed in 1978 to complement the Sailor with the Grenade across the bay, marking the opposite front lines. The third and largest monument would be the long-anticipated gigantic Malaia zemlia monument on the beach at Stanichka.

Figure 11.8 Sailor with the Grenade Monument (1972) (photograph by the author)

Architect Vladimir Tsigal' worked on this monument for years. News of the grandiose project even reached London via the Moscow correspondent of *The Times*.

> The Soviet authorities have ordered the construction of a massive monument at the site of a once little-known Second World War battle in which President Brezhnev took part.
>
> The monument will be a vast panoramic depiction of the engagement at Malaya Zemlya, near Novorossiysk on the north-east coast of the Black Sea, where Soviet forces prevented German landings in 1943, an official bulletin said. The decree did not mention Mr Brezhnev, then a political commissar with the rank of colonel, but it is thought almost certain that he will get a prominent place in the panorama.[13]

The Times was correct. During the years between the planning and fulfilment of the project, Brezhnev's memoirs had been published, and the decision was taken to incorporate some of his quotations on the side of the new monument. The wait was embarrassing for both the government and the town, but finally the monument was officially inaugurated in September 1982, on the 39th anniversary of the liberation of Novorossiisk in 1943. The delays were critical: by then Brezhnev was not able to attend due to ill health, and he died two months later, never having seen this final testament to his wartime service and indeed his entire cult of personality.

The Brezhnev-era war cult had, in its twilight years, seen a spate of what some scholars deem to be unnecessarily large war memorials across the Soviet Union, visible symbols of the power of the state. Nina Tumarkin criticises the 'vulgarity and gigantism' of memorial complexes, while Scott Palmer refers to their 'pharaonic excess'. Even Soviet citizens themselves dared to criticise these edifices. Former war correspondent and famous author Konstantin Simonov saw the huge monument at Stalingrad as tasteless: 'An authentic heroic monument should always be as modest as the heroes themselves.'[14]

However, the reception in Novorossiisk was more favourable, as the new memorial complex rapidly became a potent symbol of the hero city. The Malaia zemlia monument, towering over the shore-line at 22 metres high, cements the sense of place. It represents a stylistic motor launch, which replicates in concrete the abstract triangular shape across the bay: in fact, this monument is affectionately known in Novorossiisk as the *nos korablia* (ship's prow). On the external walls, groups of sculpted figures depict the landing troops storming the beach from their craft. Inside the monument visitors mount a steep staircase towards the pinnacle. Here, a memory capsule containing the names of all the dead Soviet troops of Malaia zemlia is located inside an artificial red 'beating' heart, the apex of the remembrance process in Novorossiisk. Along the sides of the ascending and descending staircases are bas-reliefs of the heroes of the Soviet Union involved in the battle, including both Major Kunikov and Colonel Brezhnev. Both internal and external walls of the monument are studded with quotations from Brezhnev's memoirs, sealing in concrete his links with the town of Novorossiisk.

The state is responsible for the monument's upkeep, while local authority architects are responsible for the area around it. In order to preserve the Malalia zemlia memorial in its own space-time zone, the conservation area around it has been left totally uncultivated, the ground

Figure 11.9 The Malaia zemlia Memorial (1982) (photograph by the author)

still retaining the lines of the trenches and dugouts established by the landing troops in the first days of the campaign.[15] The whole area was curtained off from nearby buildings by a line of 225 poplars, representing the number of days the land was defended. Time may have stood still in the protected area, but it moved rather too quickly on the perimeter. The expected lifespan of the trees was curtailed by the adverse climate in a triumph of entropic decay over man-made order. Likened by *Novorossiiskii rabochii* to the fallen landing troops, the dead trees were replaced by young ash trees in 2010, prized for their robustness in extremes of weather, and sourced, ironically, from Berlin.[16] Continuing the simile, the head of the council's environmental department observed that the landing troops also wore green, and that the red autumnal leaves of the ashes recall the spilled blood of the brave troops. Today, the thin ranks of young trees stand guard over the sacred site of Malaia zemlia, screening it from the quotidian, thanks to the new generation of local councillors who are actively endorsing the renewed national cult of war memory under President Putin.

Figure 11.10 The Malaia zemlia Memorial and its Immediate Environment (photograph by the author)

The spilled blood of the landing troops is a popular ingredient of the war myth. I have also observed the widespread assertion that the poppies flourishing on the rough ground of the Malaia zemlia memorial complex are symbolic of this blood. This may be compared with the symbolism attached to red poppies as vehicles of memory in Great Britain. Ten respondents confirmed that Malaia zemlia is regarded as sacred ground precisely because the land is soaked with blood: anointed through the spilling of heroes' blood, Malaia zemlia has thus acquired the status of holy land. Religious superstition is also evident in flowers placed on one large stone near the monument. Reminiscent of a shrine, this stone is deemed by young manager Anton to be the site of the miraculous oozing of the blood of heroes from the earth on which they fell, as if in recognition of their martyrdom.

Russian tradition holds the earth of graves as sacred, with implications for the sanctity of war memory in Novorossiisk through the soil.[17] This is not unique to Russia, though: tourists on D-Day battlefield tours around the Normandy beaches or on the World War I trail from Ypres to the Somme also refer to 'sacred ground' when encountering war memorials and cemeteries testifying compellingly to mass sacrifice.[18] In the opinion of Caroline Winter, 'the Western Front has become a sacred landscape of remembrance, and its battlefields and memorials are now regarded as the equivalent of shrines and holy sites'.[19] A geographically specific sanctity was also recognised by Georgii Sokolov: 'Malaia zemlia [. . .] is a sacred place for Black Sea troops', with even a sniper's rifle acquiring religious significance for a new generation of soldiers.[20] This sentiment was embedded in the war myth upon the award of hero city status to the town in 1973: 'You live on sacred earth, where the blood of defenders of the Fatherland has poured onto every stone', which was captured in the popular song 'Malaia zemlia, sviashchennaia zemlia' ('Malaia zemlia, sacred land') of the same year.[21] Even now, many citizens of Novorossiisk avoid swimming in the sea near the Malaia zemlia monument, as even the sea bed is deemed by some to be sacred ground.[22]

Remembrance of the war in Novorossiisk is guaranteed across the former Soviet Union not only by Brezhnev's memoirs, but also through its 'sacred' earth. Soil from all the hero cities is found at key war memorials in major cities, spreading the concept of sacrificial glory to places far beyond their own immediate region. Soil from Novorossiisk was geographically dispersed to be honoured and respected across

Figure 11.11 Earth from Novorossiisk in Irkutsk (Siberia) (photograph by the author)

the country, and can be found today around monuments in city centres ranging from Moscow's Aleksandrovskii Garden to Irkutsk in Siberia.

However, this perceived sacred ground is under the bizarre threat of development in the form of a cathedral complex to be built on Malaia zemlia. Grandiose plans for the project indicate a tall main church with further smaller buildings around it. The concept of a sacred site apparently varies from person to person, as objections to the construction around the memorial complex abound. Some residents are concerned about the destruction of the land for ecological reasons; others do not wish to see the Malaia zemlia monument diminished by this planned intrusion into its sacred space.[23]

However sacred it may remain to some residents, the functional urban landscape must tread a fine balance between the need to remember and the need to forget.[24] Paul Connerton identifies an inherent failure of war memorials, contending that, once erected, their presence assists communities to discontinue their duty of remembrance. In Novorossiisk, the 200 war monuments and 42 streets named after war heroes present a real risk to memory inflation and consequent devaluation, with the possibility that they may gradually fade into the expanding townscape and be taken for granted.[25] Although the powerful Malaia zemlia complex is deliberately kept apart from the encroachment of new buildings, the spatial impact of the Valley of Death complex in Myskhako has been diminished by the intrusive presence of an avenue of large, dark trees and a development of new houses. The Calendar monument still dominates the small area, however, to the detriment of the Explosion monument, which appears much diminished due to the urbanisation of the once-rural area.

With the Brezhnev memorial statue a notable exception, monuments, once placed in their permanent position, normally remain there as a testament to the war myth, even if human memory starts to fail. However, the natural increase in entropy with time also predicts the gradual decay of stone and concrete. Shelley's poem 'Ozymandias' (1817) expresses this inexorable process, depicting a monument subsumed by entropy, whose decaying remains serve only to emphasise the dominance of time over the memory of a once-powerful ruler.[26] In contrast, monuments that are well maintained can demonstrate both the desire of a community to retain memory and, transcending time, the importance to the community of the event or people commemorated.

Novorossiisk is growing around its Soviet-era monuments and the town council has had to make key decisions about their role in the modern landscape. Towns often rely on old buildings as an everyday reminder of their history. This is not the case in Novorossiisk, however, where most prewar buildings were completely destroyed during the war. In the period of postwar reconstruction it was decided by the state to retain unaltered the shelled former palace of culture as a monument to the damage inflicted on the town rather like Dom Pavlova in Stalingrad or the old Coventry Cathedral in England.[27] Also under the protection of the Ministry of Culture, on the other side of the main road stands the rusty skeleton of a railway coach bearing the marks of hundreds of bullets. These two monuments have been left deliberately unreconstructed, powerful symbols of the destructive chaos of war.

There was a danger in the lean decade of the 1990s of many other monuments falling into permanent disrepair, but this is certainly not the case in today's Novorossiisk, where most show signs not of decay, but rather of well-planned restoration. Although the state controls the maintenance of some major Brezhnev-era memorials, the upkeep of most is devolved to the regional department for the preservation of monuments, and thence to local agencies. Although the state's Ministry of Culture provided 1.4 million roubles in 2011 for the upkeep of monuments in Novorossiisk, this was insufficient. To plug the gap, the mayor holds public competitions to renovate monuments, while encouraging local firms and schools to sponsor the maintenance of their chosen memorial.[28] For example, although originally under state control, and then taken over by the region, the upkeep of the concrete motor torpedo boat erected in 1968 and standing astride the promenade is in the de facto hands of a well-known Novorossiisk company. More parochially, in Myskhako, the maintenance budget is stretched by the local authority's encouragement of volunteers to spend weekends in April sprucing up the monuments in this vestige of communism, the *subbotnik* day, dedicated to the refreshing of the war myth in time for the Victory Day celebrations in early May.

Thanks largely to former Mayor Siniagovskii, the memorial landscape of Novorossiisk is not entirely static, even 70 years after the war. A new generation of statues and memorials for the town centre is appearing and yet more are under public discussion, mainly due to the development of the new promenade, Siniagovskii's pet project. A new monument has recently been erected on the promenade to commemorate the exodus of the White Army from Novorossiisk towards the end of the civil war in 1920, while consultation is taking place about the popular demand from older residents for the erection of a monument to the *khamsa*, the small Black Sea fish, which, according to the local war myth, kept the partisan population from starvation during the World War II occupation.

Monuments demonstrate very low entropy both temporally and materially, while the present is fluid and ever-changing, always fading into the more entropic future. Unlike rituals, which may and do change, monuments and their associated space and time are generally more resistant to change. A monument's temporal stagnation neglects, however, the ravages that may be wrought by time itself, with its increase in entropy effecting a degradation as in the case of Ozymandias, which could well serve to diminish and alter its significance in the future. Moreover, a monument may reign in its own time-zone and space, but time moves on around it, during which its surroundings may change, potentially undermining the monument's meaning.

Like the new Brezhnev statue, most town-centre war memorials remain popular with residents. When one of the first simple memorials high on the slopes of Mount Koldun started to disintegrate, artist

Aleksandr Kamper designed a new monument, erected with his own resources in 2008. His successful attempt to take on the ravages of time and increasing entropy met with defeat, however, when the department for the preservation of monuments became involved and ordered him to remove the new monument on the grounds that it was not in keeping with the overall 'plan'. Kamper retaliated by accusing the local authorities of being guilty of 'designer' rather than 'genuine' memory, despite the fact that he had replaced the original modest obelisk with a large, red, Soviet-style metal star, possibly not to everyone's taste. After a second battle of Malaia zemlia, on this occasion a battle for the ownership of collective remembrance, during which Kamper won the support of the local press and its readers, his monument was eventually officially recognised in 2009.[29] Kamper's supporters believe that the officials should be grateful for his help, deeming them reluctant to spend limited resources on the proper maintenance of outlying memorials, while concentrating largely on the higher profile, central monuments. In this case, overwhelming popular support from below succeeded in overcoming the top-down organisation of monuments, which normally carries more weight than any bottom-up individualisation of memory.

These undercurrents on the periphery are not obvious to the relatively few Western tourists visiting Novorossiisk, who are introduced to a town that seems to some to be 'stuck in a Soviet time warp'.[30] Disembarking from their cruise ships for a few hours, visitors are whisked around the Valley of Death and the Malaia zemlia memorial complex.[31] Even ordinary Russians far from Novorossiisk see life in the hero city portrayed as revolving around the iconic Malaia zemlia monument in key scenes from the recent popular film *Marafon* (*The Marathon*),[32] while 80,000 tourists are estimated to visit the monument every summer.[33]

Over the years, the town of Novorossiisk has created its own monumental culture, which serves to define this unique urban site of memory, and has been partly responsible for creating the mythical identity of the town. It seems that the tradition of monumental memory in evidence in today's Novorossiisk has indeed overtaken the folkloric type of propagation of the war myth by 'folk-tale, song and proverb' claimed by war correspondents Svetov and Miliavskii to be more enduring than physical monuments.[34] Once carefully filtered, this is an eminently potent and marketable myth, both to outsiders and residents, with its unambiguous heroes and successful outcome. Thanks to the town's use of space and symbolic spatiality, the grand designs in the centre dominate Novorossiisk's mnemonic identity. It is fair to say that the town is doing (almost) everything in its power to maintain monumental memory of Malaia zemlia. Bottom-up individualisation exists on the periphery, but is discouraged by top-down bureaucracy. Veterans may be succumbing to the effects of ageing, but monuments, in this respect, are more permanent than living memory, thanks to careful preservation which reverses the natural increase of entropy with time. If this maintenance should be halted, when there are perhaps no longer the political will or financial resources available, then chaos would set in and monuments and memory gradually crumble.

CHAPTER 12

PEOPLE ON THE PERIPHERY

Над Бабьим Яром памятников нет.
Крутой обрыв, как грубое надгробье.
Мне страшно.[1]

Not only monuments but also dead bodies decay as they increase in entropy with time. This high-entropy state is also reflected in the wide distribution of the fallen on and around Malaia zemlia. The ongoing task of collecting together their scattered remains in order to pay due respect according to traditional values hence involves an organisational decrease in entropy. Although 37 communal graves have been established in Novorossiisk since 1943, the town still appears anxious to provide a fitting place of rest for all the fallen.[2] In 2010 all the war dead from the town cemetery on Myskhakskoe Shosse were transferred to a new burial place across the road with a view over Malaia zemlia.[3] New marble plaques list the names of over 2,500 war dead of several nationalities, including Armenians, Georgians, Ukrainians and the grandfather of the former president of Kabardino-Balkaria, Arsen Kanokov, gathered together in this probably now final resting place.

Not all lie in such salubrious circumstances, however. Sonia has spent her retirement years collecting money to ensure the decent burial of the fallen. This altruistic 'Mother Teresa' of Novorossiisk, according to her friends, raised the money for the construction of new crosses on the site of a dozen vandalised graves in Myskhako, testimony that not all show the same respect for memory of the dead. Following her intervention, cadets from the Maritime Academy in Novorossiisk have taken on responsibility for the upkeep of the graves. Similarly, Aleksandr Kamper discovered two metal plaques in a Myskhako school yard, discarded from a nearby monument. Having found temporary wooden boards in their place, with the names of the deceased written in marker pen, he successfully campaigned for the restoration of the original plaques.[4] The battle against entropy is apparently not yet over in the outlying areas.

Any high entropy, disorganised pattern of death is disturbing in the Russian tradition, where it is culturally important to bury a soldier near to home in order to complete the grieving process and enable remembrance to be conducted with both humanity and respect.[5] Relatives still come to Novorossiisk in search of information about their ancestors. I met Kirill, who had travelled to Myskhako from the Urals in 2010 in search of the final resting place of his father. The Ministry of Defence only started to set up a data-base of war graves after the fall of communism and there is no centralised agency in Russia to compare with the war graves commissions in other countries. However, thanks to the meticulous records of the Myskhako Veterans' Council, Kirill was shown the communal grave where his father lay and was able for the first time to mourn his death as a result of his pilgrimage. Five years later I encountered another tearful relative in search of a parent – this time an old Georgian woman, who had come to Myskhako with her daughter in search of her father's grave and who had found similar support from the Veterans' Council there.

According to local historian Tamara Iurina, it is impossible to quantify the number of dead in the campaign, with estimates ranging up to 30,000. What is undeniable, however, is that bodies continue to be exhumed, in a process lauded by the press, which sees the execution of search work a patriotic duty:[6]

> On the slopes of Mount Koldun and Sakharnaia golova outside Novorossiisk, and the Anonymous Heights around Iuzhnaia Ozereika, our soldiers' bones lie bleaching ... It is said that the war will not be considered finally over until the last fallen soldier is buried.[7]

Recently, over 40 bodies were found on the shore in a hitherto unknown communal grave dating from the first days of the Malaia zemlia campaign.[8] Sometimes bodies are found during excavations prior to building or reconstruction work; for example five skeletons were exhumed in 2009 under the auspices of the *Novorossiiskii tsentr poiskovykh rabot* (Novorossiisk Centre for Search Work) during the laying of foundations for a new school sports hall. Most exhumations, however, follow the location of bodies on Mount Koldun, which is constantly, if not entirely systematically, being searched by small groups of amateurs licensed by the Ministry of Defence. This type of activity has been taking place since the 1960s.[9] According to regional and state legislation, teams nowadays must be fully trained and accredited in the appropriate methodology;[10] they are financed jointly by the state, the region and the local authorities, with some voluntary contributions. In the wake of various terrorist attacks in Russia, President Putin wishes to introduce military supervision for search work, to ensure that no live ordnance falls into the wrong hands.[11] Official statistics show that 83 hand-grenades and 655 mortars were dug up in the area as recently as 2004.[12] The head of the Novorossiisk Historical Association confirmed the occasional discovery of 500kg unexploded bombs in outlying suburbs and both Alisa, an accountant, and Elena, a teacher, had heard of children losing limbs to unexploded devices.

Vladimir, an amateur archaeologist for over thirty years, was decorated in 2010 with the *Za razminirovanie* medal, awarded to those whose search work has led to the destruction of more than 3,000 explosive devices by experts called in when potentially dangerous finds are made. Vladimir is leader of the local branch of the regional search organisation *Nabat* (a funeral bell), which has several teenage members. He spends his weekends on Koldun searching with a metal detector for the bodies of dead soldiers in order to have them re-interred in a respectful and organised way. According to Vladimir, his sons often accompany him into the forests of Koldun, which he sees as an opportunity to pass on memory, expertise and a love of local history. He regards this activity not only as aiding the propagation and organisation of memory, however. In common with the inventors of Beskozyrka, Vladimir finds the whole adventure 'romantic', thanks to the combination of fresh air and nature during a night in the open 'by a campfire, under the starry sky'. It is this element of romanticism which has become synonymous with genuine and creative war memory from below in Novorossiisk, often to be found on the fringes of society and where young people are involved.

Recently exhumed Soviet bodies are re-interred every year in September, the anniversary of the liberation of Novorossiisk, in a tradition dating from 1998. Sixty-two were buried in the cemetery on Kabakhakha Hill overlooking Novorossiisk in 2012, with a further 25 in 2013, while 35 bodies discovered on Koldun were interred in 2010 in the communal grave in the centre of Myskhako.[13] This gradual but substantial decrease in entropy brings together the scattered remains of decaying bodies, so that they may finally be identified, if possible. The details and personal possessions of newly discovered soldiers are passed to the town museum's archivist, who works meticulously on the identification process, although by no means all are ever identified.[14] The names are then entered into a memory capsule inside the red heart which beats at the apex of the triangular Malaia zemlia monument, the pinnacle of centralised memory in Novorossiisk, both spatially and organisationally. In 1982, when the monument was originally dedicated, 5,000 names of the fallen were listed in the capsule. Every year, on 8 May, new names are added in what is called *Aktsiia pamiat'* (the Memory Movement). Reflecting the amount of search and identification work carried out recently on the site of Malaia zemlia and the slopes of Mount Koldun, a significant 991 new names were added in May 2012, with a further 23 on 16 September, the thirtieth anniversary of the erection of the monument, making a total of around 23,000 identified dead troops so far.[15] However, as it is estimated that up to 30,000 were killed on Malaia zemlia, there remains some way to go until all are found and afforded the official and central respect the town deems due to them.

Following lobbying by groups of amateur searchers, the state has recently committed to recognising the fact that thousands of bodies across Russia still remain where they fell in the war. The remains of the first 'unknown soldier' were laid in the Aleksandrovskii Garden alongside the Kremlin wall on 3 December 1966, at the start of the Brezhnev-era war cult. In 2014 the same day was officially named the Day of the Unknown Soldier, one further memorial date in the increasing calendar of special days of the Putin-era war cult.[16]

The complementary work of the official agencies (the regional planning department in charge of the maintenance of monuments, the town council and the museum) and enthusiastic amateur search workers should ensure, in theory, that each individual soldier may eventually be recognised and afforded due remembrance. However, some of the bodies discovered on Koldun are inevitably those of the enemy. Experienced searchers recognise that German soldiers were usually buried more carefully than the Soviets, and often wore crucifixes. Search organisations try to involve families in the repatriation and burial of their dead: a coachload of German relatives visited Novorossiisk in the 1990s, and a video documentary was made more recently by a further German family travelling to Myskhako to reclaim their ancestor.[17] If not repatriated, remains of Wehrmacht soldiers are passed on for re-interment to the Volksbund Deutsche Kriegsgräberfürsorge, the German war graves commission.[18] Since 2008, soldiers from the Kuban' front have been buried in a new German war cemetery outside Apsheronsk, the only one in the south of Russia,[19] as there is no German cemetery in Novorossiisk, due apparently to continuing prejudice against the occupiers. Although the searchers themselves claim to care equally for bodies from both sides, they accept that it would be hard for most locals to treat German soldiers with the empathy shown to the Soviets. It seems that the myth of Malaia zemlia is not yet ready to accommodate a German war cemetery in the town: German trees may be welcome in Novorossiisk, but German bodies offer only awkward and unwanted memories of the 'fascist occupiers' still popularly depicted with hatred.

One focus of revulsion for the enemy occupiers is a 20-metre obelisk at Volch'i Vorota, an isolated spot ten kilometres to the north-west of Novorossiisk, which commemorates the many nameless civilians who were taken there by the Gestapo and shot during the occupation of Novorossiisk in an action superficially similar to Holocaust events in Ukraine. Indeed, the very name of the monument, 'Nepokorennym' ('To The Unvanquished'), is reminiscent of the film *Nepokorennye* (*The Unvanquished*) about the execution of Kiev's Jews at Babii Iar in 1941.[20]

This monument was erected on the twentieth anniversary of the liberation of Novorossiisk in September 1963, one of the first to appear outside the town centre. It was one of two large monuments inaugurated in the same week, the other being the large stele at Stanichka. Both marked for the first time places where hundreds met their death. In contrast to the highly visible monument on the shore, however, it may be concluded that the outlying memorial obelisk did not attract much public attention, as it is not mentioned in the leading article of *Novorossiiskii rabochii's* anniversary edition, where other town-centre

Figure 12.1 Monument to The Unvanquished (1963) (photographs by the author)

monuments do feature.[21] The difference may be due purely to the location, but also possibly to the fact that the stele commemorates the deaths of service personnel, whereas the obelisk to The Unvanquished is a memorial to civilians. A short article a few days later refers to the thousand 'Soviet patriots' who were 'victims of a mass execution [by firing squad]'.[22] Similarly, the official entry in the Novorossiisk museum archives refers to a new monument 'erected on the place where the German fascist occupiers carried out a mass execution of residents of the town of Novorossiisk'. According to the plaque on the monument, it commemorates the 'residents of Novorossiisk and the landing troops of the Soviet Army who were tortured and shot on this spot in 1943 by the fascist occupiers', with no mention of the Jewish population of the town being specifically targeted by the enemy. In both cases the wording about the victims is as generalised as on the Holocaust memorial at Babii Iar, which refers only to the death of 'citizens of Kiev', a euphemism used to signify the town's Jewish population.[23]

I first heard of the monument's existence after 12 years of annual visits to Novorossiisk. This long-term silence may reflect its geographical position well outside the town, but also the fact that it is not commonly visited, situated also on the periphery of the war myth. A certain reticence about both the presence of the monument itself and the nature of the dead remains, evidence of some discomfort and possibly even of ongoing anti-Semitism in the town. Only four out of 124 respondents voluntarily mentioned the existence of this monument. The Jewish woman who first alerted me to its presence maintained that all those executed were Jews, while an historian was adamant that the victims were simply representative of all those civilians who stayed in the town during the German occupation: mainly ethnic minorities, including Jews, Greeks, Czechs and Tatars. Eremenko and Podyma claim that at least one member of the underground resistance was executed there, but another historian agreed that most were Jews, although usually given the blanket term of 'communists' in a half-hearted official denial of a Holocaust event in Novorossiisk.[24]

Scholars agree that memory of the war with respect to Jews in the Soviet Union is a troubled area. The lack of certainty about the monument to The Unvanquished is a reflection of widespread silence about the Holocaust and the experience of Jewish citizens in the country for decades after the war alongside a lack of monuments at the site of mass graves. Even during the Khrushchev and Brezhnev eras public debate about Jewish citizens was often couched in generalisms, with the use of euphemisms and 'coded' references. Substantial official anti-Semitism and suppression of information about the Holocaust led to the virtual elimination of specific reference to Jewishness, and many films, plays and poems about the fate of Jews in the war were banned or heavily censored.[25] Indeed, only two years after the erection of the Novorossiisk monument, Elie Wiesel observed amongst the Jewish community in the Soviet Union a constant fear of informers, finding Jewishness 'somewhere between a dirty word and a state secret'.[26] During the same period that saw the patriotic foundation of the Beskozyrka movement to commemorate the fallen landing troops of Malaia zemlia, a darker type of Russian nationalism was evident in the country,[27] probably partly responsible for the suppression of full details of a Holocaust event outside Novorossiisk. The continuing lack of explicit reference to Jews cannot be explained merely by the relatively small numbers of murdered Jews in comparison with overall Soviet deaths in the war. While it is possible that the Soviet population genuinely considered ethnicity to be irrelevant within an ideology that embraced internationalism, information about the fate of the Jews in the war was suppressed to the extent that it is only in the last two decades that knowledge of the Holocaust in the Soviet Union has become widely disseminated.[28] In Novorossiisk lessons on the mass execution of Soviet Jews are sometimes delivered in schools by the local Jewish community,[29] but do not feature specifically in the mainstream school curriculum.

It is quite plausible that the monument to The Unvanquished outside Novorossiisk does in fact recall a Holocaust event: in the light of an estimated total of 27,000 Jewish citizens exterminated by the Nazis in the Krasnodar Region, it is highly likely that such a massacre happened in Novorossiisk.[30] This particular event is not, however, included in *The Black Book* of mass executions of Jews in the Soviet Union, nor is there any reference to it in Soviet accounts, Iurina's recent history of the battle for Novorossiisk or the new historical guide to the town.[31] According to one informant, a war commission, reported in *Novorossiiskii rabochii* in January 1945, confirmed the deaths on this spot of 425 Red Army soldiers and some 60 civilian women and children in 1942 and 1943. However, the Novorossiisk library today refers to the deaths of 7,000 'peaceful citizens and prisoners of war', while the research website of the 'Babi Yars' organisation has claimed that 1,000 of the prewar population of 1,595 Jews in the town were shot here.[32] Although the latter two claims are not incompatible, the death of 1,000 Jews out of a total of 1,595 represents a substantial proportion (63 per cent) of the Jewish population of Novorossiisk, a statistically significant figure hidden in the library's overall number of 7,000 citizens out of an overall prewar population of over 109,000 (which represents only 6 per cent of the total number).[33]

If the background of the victims remains uncertain, so too does the date of the mass execution. The Babi Yars organisation has stated that the Jewish population in Novorossiisk was massacred on either 22 September or 16 October 1942,[34] shortly after the Germans took the town on 10 September 1942. Witness testimony, however, suggests that any remaining civilians in the town were either shot as partisans or fled the town during the period October 1942 to August 1943,[35] which would accord with the date (1943) on the monument's plaque. It is likely, therefore, that, although the monument is stated to commemorate the deaths of citizens plus some landing troops over a protracted period, it actually stands on the site of one mass execution of mainly Jewish civilians carried out in the early days of the occupation, while the mass grave was used for further non-Jewish victims during 1943.

According to one newspaper article, which as recently as 2005 makes no specific reference to Jews, the thousands who were summarily executed were mainly women and children, as most of the men had already left to join the army or had been dispatched to German forced labour camps.[36] In this respect, the monument to The Unvanquished belies the popular myth of Malaia zemlia, while the narrative of the events it recalls is similarly marginalised. Most monuments in Novorossiisk support the popular war myth, which extols individual and collective military heroism and martyrdom, rather than recalling the ignominious defeat and subsequent mass death of civilians. This indicates a myth composed of a comfortable, straightforward narrative around a usable past, from which any potentially embarrassing facts have been omitted, just as incidences of industrial unrest or corruption are often side-lined in Britain's war myth.[37] Indeed, two of the few interviewees who suggested that Novorossiisk did not really deserve its hero city status, young Anton and elderly Dmitrii, gave the reason that no civilians were present or suffered during the fighting, as opposed to the first tranches of 'genuine' hero cities.

The Jewish community is unable to commemorate its dead either individually or communally in the central and concrete fashion enjoyed by other ethnic minorities. In contrast, the ethnic Greek residents of Novorossiisk openly remember their own hero, the wartime pilot Vladimir Kokkinaki, whose bust stands in the middle of the town.

According to respondents of Greek ethnicity, on Victory Day they gather around the monument to lay tributes of remembrance, singing and dancing in the shade of the trees, while a plaque on the wall of the side-chapel of the Uspenskii sobor, the main Russian Orthodox church, lists 200 names of those of Greek ethnicity who died in the war.

Remembrance and respect for the dead of the Jewish community, however, exists on the periphery of official memory, evidence of prejudice and discomfort still to be found in certain hidden and sensitive areas of Novorossiisk's past, despite attempts by the Jewish community to incorporate itself into the mainstream war myth through an exhibition in the central Veterans' Council and to present itself as part of the town's rich ethnic heritage in the main children's library.[38] It is probable that the Jewish significance of the monument to The Unvanquished is implicitly acknowledged by many, including possible anti-Semites. It was desecrated in 2003, according to a Jewish information website, which openly accuses the town in general and *Novorossiiskii rabochii* in particular of racial intolerance, although other monuments with no minority ethnic connotations have been similarly vandalised.[39] Unlike

Figure 12.2 Monument to Vladimir Kokkinaki (1975) (photograph by the author)

the mainstream Soviet troops buried in Novorossiisk, the names of the civilian dead are not remembered. Some key characters in the myth of Malaia zemlia are Jewish, however: Tsezar' Kunikov, the commander of the landing troops, was of Jewish descent, while soldier and poet Pavel Kogan was certainly admired by the postwar younger generation, although his ethnicity was never overtly mentioned.

Whereas the press now reports some executions during the occupation,[40] evident embarrassment about the monument's significance was shown by the regional officer in charge of the planning and maintenance of monuments, who, when questioned, refused to discuss with me the event commemorated by the memorial. This type of reaction is confirmed by Stephen Lovell, who deems the topic of occupation awkward in view of 'current political concerns' which may imply allegations of collaboration with the enemy within occupied territory in the betrayal of Jewish civilians,[41] certainly not a part of the original war myth, but an area coming under increasing popular and academic scrutiny, particularly in western areas of the former Soviet Union, notably Ukraine and the Baltic states.[42]

During the war, the state placed its emphasis on military heroes rather than moral cowards. Little was said about collaboration in the early postwar years, with the notable exception of the first public war crimes trial, held in Krasnodar in 1943, which resulted in the executions of some Soviet citizens involved in the massacre of Jewish civilians in the town.[43] Collaboration during the occupation of Novorossiisk was acknowledged by local historian Anatolii, while young academic Sofiya confirmed that this is a research topic in local universities. My evidence suggests that collaboration with the enemy is suspected amongst some interviewees, if largely unspoken. Three respondents indicated that occupied cities in Ukraine became stigmatised due to an enemy presence which induced collaboration, while Novorossiisk was viewed as above 'contamination' thanks to the 'sacred' presence of the troops on Malaia zemlia, which placed the town above suspicion and on a par with Leningrad and Stalingrad. Only after several meetings did one female respondent trust me sufficiently to break an implicit taboo and voice the rumour that the Kuban' Cossacks had assisted enemy forces to enter and occupy Novorossiisk in 1942, in view of the fact that the town was defeated apparently without much opposition. This rumour was backed up by three futher informants, both male and female. It is alleged that the Soviet plans were betrayed to the German Abwehr, which led to the failure of the Iuzhnaia Ozereika landings.[44] The implication of Cossacks in the occupation is, however, at odds with the official current stance whereby Cossack forces are invited to take part in ceremonies of remembrance in an apparent political positioning of the identity of the town around its Cossack heritage as well as its maritime status, in what may represent a vying for position with Krasnodar, the regional capital and historically the base of the Kuban' Cossacks.[45] This conservative and potentially nationalistic re-alignment of the identity of the town has, however, provoked questions about the integrity of the inclusion of Cossacks in official ceremonies. Despite the strong development of the Cossack movement in southern Russia, they are not regarded as 'natives' of Novorossiisk, evidence of ongoing suspicion amongst some residents.[46] Furthermore, the issue of alleged Cossack collaboration has recently resulted in the re-naming of a street in the Cossack area of Borisovka named after General Shkuro, hanged as a war criminal in 1947 for his role alongside the Wehrmacht in Berlin.[47]

On the whole, however, the memory message in Novorossiisk demonstrates considerable consensus, with a common attitude to history underlined by a common geographical identity with respect to the war.[48] This remembrance exhibits the low societal entropy status typical of considerable organisation and centralisation, reflecting the energy expended to promote and maintain rituals and monuments by both state and society. Despite the overall control of the authorities, however, it is clear that there is still room on the fringe for the personalisation of memory, whether it concerns the family of a German soldier or the distant children of a Soviet battle victim. It is also the case that memory seems more personal in Myskhako, on the periphery of the control of the Novorossiisk authorities, but at the very centre of the worst of the battle. This close-knit community appears to care deeply and sincerely about the honour due to its war dead, seeing them as people rather than mere statistics. Away from the centre of Novorossiisk, the villagers retain a close connection with the earth, demonstrating a greater respect for old Russian burial traditions than huge Soviet monuments. Dissent, when it exists, serves only to promote the values of dignity and humanity in death and remembrance, which sometimes risk being forgotten in the official narrative. Official and unofficial interests often complement each other constructively, with a common mnemonic aim; on occasion, however, the tension between so-called 'designer' and 'genuine' memory is evident in the ongoing local debate over who is the true guardian of myth and memory.

PART IV

MEETINGS OF GENERATIONS

TEACHING THE YOUNG TO REMEMBER

Помните!
Через века,
через года, –
помните!
О тех,
кто уже не придет
никогда, –
помните![1]

A group of cynical young searchers for war artefacts outside modern St Petersburg is suddenly transported back through time to besieged wartime Leningrad. Their experience of the fear and hardship of soldiers in the trenches builds up cross-generational empathy and even love, which changes their moral perspective on the war. This is the fictional story-line of the film *My iz budushchego* (*We are from the Future*), 2008, drawn to my attention by eight younger interviewees, who claimed that it had influenced young people in Novorossiisk.[2] The film addresses the fact that some of the younger generation in Russia are becoming more diffident about the war with increasing temporal distance from historical events. At the same time the number of veterans and participants in the war is decreasing inexorably, rendering direct transmission of memory to the young less viable. Rather than letting the war myth fade into history, however, the town of Novorossiisk appears to be promoting social cohesion within the framework of a new state war cult through a series of educational measures designed to effect the successful transmission of the agreed local war myth from generation to generation.

Novorossiisk is typical of many towns across the country, where the effects of the Putin-era war cult are widely visible – indeed inescapable – in schools and on days of remembrance. This final part assesses the effectiveness of the intergenerational propagation of the war myth by an examination of the various mechanisms deployed by different social groups within the community of remembrance to educate the younger generation individually and collectively. This analysis of the relative influence of the various agencies promoting remembrance permits the construction of a hierarchical model of social interaction demonstrating the complexity of the memorial influences on society in general and young people in particular.

It is difficult to imagine the propagation of the war myth without interaction between members of the community. Different 'frames of remembrance' and 'spheres of influence' around a young citizen exist through agencies such as the state, the family and mainstream educational establishments.[3] Each individual is influenced by the various overlapping social circles of which they are a member, for example in the case of young people the school, youth club, local library or their own immediate and extended family, whilst they are also influenced more remotely by national and local mass media. A spectrum of different agencies of influence, from the individual to the state, may thus be invoked, incorporating a multitude of voices often reinforcing each other, but possibly varying in their attitude to memory. Each one of these agencies may offer a slightly different reading of the war myth, but, when put together, they establish a largely coherent overall narrative. However, it has long been recognised that the individual may not realise the full influence of these groups on the shaping of communal identity or even individual memory.[4]

The education of the young in the war myth takes place both formally and informally – in educational institutions, within the family and in the wider social circle. The aim of the final three chapters is to identify the most effective means of propagation to the younger generation, those who will in the future potentially bear responsibility for further transmission of the war myth. The formative influence of older generations on the young in the propagation of historical memory through conservative and conserving institutions, such as the family or museums, is well documented in scholarship, where the normative transmission of systems of beliefs and practices is recognised as the root of social cohesion.[5] I have observed that this is reinforced in Novorossiisk by a tendency for what I term 'reverse propagation', where the young transmit back the memory message to their elders, a spontaneous phenomenon which serves to consolidate and maintain the myth. In contrast, more modern influences such as the mass media and films may sometimes undermine the consistency of transmission, while a rejuvenation of the message has already been observed in ritualistic tradition.

Successful cross-generational transmission of memory depends on effective communication between generations, the opposite of any possible generation gap in society that may cause intergenerational tension and lack of understanding. In contrast to Western society, the postwar leaders of the Soviet Union vaunted the absence of a generation gap, actively encouraging 'meetings of generations' (*vstrechi pokolenii*) whereby the moral education (*vospitanie*) of young people was formally effected by their elders, often citing examples of wartime heroism and patriotism.[6]

Individual and collective remembrance of the war is propagated today at the confluence of generations, thanks to the renewed deployment of veterans in the *vospitanie* of the young alongside continuing moral and historical education by family members and teachers. The very act of transmission of the war myth serves to reinforce the identity of all citizens of Novorossiisk with respect to the Malaia zemlia campaign, linking them in a quasi-familial chain of memory to the landing troops.

CHAPTER 13

GENES AND GENERATIONS: INFORMAL TRANSMISSION OF MEMORY IN THE FAMILY

> Images and symbolic constructs of the past are imprinted, almost in the manner of genetic information, on our sensibility.[1]

In 2017, the hundredth anniversary of the October Revolution, a 200-tonne memory capsule was raised from the sea bed in Novorossiisk. Dreamt up and organised 50 years previously by the 'Shkhuna rovesnikov', it contained 'letters to the future' written by 118 adults and children to their descendants.[2] Among the memorial articles offered by the public and sealed in the capsule were several war medals, evidence that the propagation of war memory to future generations was deemed important by residents as early as 1967. The stainless steel capsule embedded in concrete also contained a recording made by Iurii Levitan, the famous Soviet newsreader associated with wartime broadcasts and the minute's silence introduced to radio in 1965, stating: 'Those who open it should be grateful to those who gave their lives so that you could live happily.'

It seems that these descendants concur: journalist Evgenii Lapin wrote in 2013 of the 'return to a duty of memory' as 'the most important task of patriotic education'.[3] And that widespread sense of responsibility for the transmission of memory to future generations has resulted in a second phase of this initiative. During the Beskozyrka ceremony in 2017, children from schools across the area deposited their own 'dispatches to descendants' into special boxes at the Malaia zemlia memorial, to be, once again, placed into a time capsule for a further 50 years. On this occasion, though, all mention of the 1917 revolution has been omitted from the attendant publicity, with World War II remaining the only historical connection.[4]

Through these time capsules, generations are mutually linked in two directions in the transmission of the war myth: looking backwards to their antecedents and forwards to their descendants in a chain of memory. Although the *Shkhunatiki* were only one generation removed from their parents who fought in the war, young people today are temporally more distant from the war experienced by their great-grandparents. With veterans becoming fewer, artefacts such as war medals, which bridge memorial distance, are increasingly significant in the propagation of the war myth if the past is to become closer in the imagination of the younger generation. While examining the mechanism and effectiveness of the familial transmission of the myth, this chapter analyses whether the family as an integral part of society, where physical proximity is often most marked, values and even needs its ancestors in order to retain its mnemonic identity. Information about the mechanism of familial propagation of the war myth was obtained from two perspectives: from discussions with younger respondents and with older generations. Some of these were war veterans, if with a variety of wartime experiences which together were far more complex than the simplified myth allows. They included military personnel, deportees and child internees. Personal interviews with 26 young adults aged 18 to 29 revealed that a substantial 58 per cent of subjects remembered having discussed the wartime role of their grandparents and great-grandparents with them, indicative of oral transmission of memory through meaningful conversations.

The close relationship of the present with the past is key to continued societal cohesion. The presentist position, whereby the present reshapes the past as governments and society's elite employ a preferred version of history for current utility, is the political side of the mnemonic coin. The opposite, anthropological side, sees rather the past forging present identity, whereby society interprets positive current social qualities as due to historical events, which so moulded the characteristics of their ancestors that they were then transmitted across the generations. This essentialist position is what I term the 'genetic' approach to desirable social attributes, founded on longstanding traditional familial values, which my research indicates is noticeable in Novorossiisk. There is an evident causal contradiction between the two positions, which are not, however, incompatible in this context, but indicative of the complexity of myth formation in the Soviet Union and modern Russia. This genetic position acknowledges forces already present for centuries within traditional Russian society, which act within the overpowering presentist environment of the state war cult to reinforce a potent local war myth.

Conversations within the family appear to be responsible for a 'genetic' construction of memory, a method of propagation typical of traditional pre-Soviet folkloric transmission, whereby older family members act as links in a memory chain which connects today's citizens genetically with the landing troops. Already in the nineteenth century the poet Mikhail Lermontov had referred to Russian soldiers at the Battle of Borodino as 'a mighty, spirited tribe',[5] underlining in the language of romanticism the positive military traits possessed by the soldiers which were passed down to their descendants. Two hundred years after Borodino and two days after his inauguration as president in May 2000, Valdimir Putin declared of the whole Russian people: 'We have become used to victory. This habit is in our blood.'[6] Putin held his 2012 election address, perhaps not by chance, on 23 February, Defender of the Fatherland Day, when Russian military courage is celebrated. Putin utilised this occasion to repeat his positive message:

> We are a victorious nation. This is in our genes, in our genetic code and it is transmitted from generation to generation.[7]

In contrast, Serguei Oushakine points to a link with the past through a more negative continuity, whereby generations are united in sadness through rituals of loss, symptomatic of a 'patriotism of despair'.[8] This claim refers largely to victims of more recent wars and is an aspect of genetic inheritance not observed now in the hero city of Novorossiisk, where Beskozyrka and commemorative requiems highlight gratitude today for victorious and justified death during the Great Patriotic War, rather than despair over the 'devalued military sacrifice' perceived in the wars in Afghanistan and Chechnia during the unstable final decades of the twentieth century.

In Novorossiisk the genetic belief system stresses continuity with the past – not with the Soviet Union in general, but rather through a local, familial connection which is also evident in the feeling of empathy with the landing troops demonstrated particularly at Beskozyrka.[9] Katharine Hodgkin and Susannah Radstone see decentred social memory as an inheritable property, transmitted by institutions rather than individuals, which then reinforce the relation between the individual and the social. This genetic mechanism attributes to society a will and a memory of its own which is independent of the individual within it.[10] However, my research indicates that the propagation of the war myth is linked to the transmission of a belief and behaviour system as if through cultural DNA, much as eye colour or blood group is transmitted from one generation to another. This is due partly to the strong sense of tradition in the town and partly to the educational memorial environment cultivated by the state, schools and the local authority as well as within the family unit. Many of my interviewees were able to point to their individual ancestors who had fought locally and subsequently settled in Novorossiisk, while respondents at both ends of the age spectrum claimed that they had inherited the hardy and heroic character of their forebears. Moreover, social memory in general is deemed by some to be transmissible through the blood-line in a similar fashion, with one town councillor regarding the war myth as 'our blood, our duty, future and past together'.

It is this perceived duty of memory which seems to motivate the older generations to educate younger family members in the tradition of commemorative practices, thereby nurturing a familial cultural heritage. Extrapolating from the individual to the community in general, the headmistress of School Number Six observed that the heroism typical of wartime is transmitted through ritual, as if 'caught' by the younger generation in the form of improved behaviour: *'geroicheskoe iavlenie diktuet povedenie'* ('an heroic event dictates behaviour'). Anatolii, a local historian, commented on this phenomenon, claiming that 'it is as if they drink it in their mothers' milk', while Boris, a former soldier in his forties, believes that the town's inhabitants 'were born' from Malaia zemlia, suggesting that the courageous qualities of the heroes are as desirable in a family as in a tribe or race. Indeed, Alina, a young teacher, sees the war myth as part of the town's 'living organism', whereby knowledge about Malaia zemlia is 'naturally' assimilated. Claims of a passive, informal assimilation of both heroic qualities and memory itself, much as first language acquisition, must, however, be questioned, due to the many more formal measures taken to ensure the socialisation of the young with respect to the myth of Malaia zemlia. Whatever the mechanism of transmission, the resulting sense of familial memory and cross-generational identification nurtured in the young is epitomised in the slogan ubiquitously displayed on school walls in Novorossiisk: '*Pobeda deda moia pobeda*' ('My grandfather's victory is my victory').

One manifestation of the intergenerational transmission of social values is the post-wedding ritual, where myth is effectively propagated as generations come together at local war memorials to lay flowers as a token of respect to the war dead.[11] Although in many cases the original meaning of this tradition has been lost, for the first postwar generation such visits in homage to the heroes were extremely important.[12] Most of those mainly female respondents who volunteered relevant information interpreted this pan-Russian tradition as a mark of gratitude and indebtedness to ancestors who had given their own lives so that their children and grandchildren would be able to live in freedom and happiness.[13] The sites most frequently visited are the main Malaia zemlia memorial complex and the smaller Valley of Death complex in Myskhako, where it is apparently usual for the bridegroom to pose at the base of a map of the Malaia zemlia campaign, while the bride climbs to the top for the photographs, in a pose suggesting the supremacy of the woman in the new family. Evdokiia Prialkina also refers to visits to the Well of Life monument in Myskhako, linking the only water source on Malaia zemlia with the successful future of young married couples. Justifying the local meaning behind the tradition using a further genetic trope, she claims that the characteristic of faithfulness is transmitted from the landing troops to the younger generation: 'It is as though the *Malozemel'tsy*, through their heroic lives, bequeath their faithfulness to young people in their life together.'[14] It is thus implied that the mutual loyalty of a married couple guarantees the continuity of life through their floral tributes to the war dead. Furthermore the Soviet postwar expression of lament at the death of millions of young soldiers, '*skol'ko ne rodilos' detei pogibshikh soldat*' ('How many soldiers' children were never born!'), quoted by Anna, a retired nurse, implicitly places a duty on the new family to replace both those who died and their unborn children. The war myth and the celebration of married life are thus linked with the necessity and ability, through water from the Well of Life, to procreate and propagate a new family.

Jay Winter views war memorials as sites of symbolic exchange, where the dead are figuratively brought home and where the living express a debt to the fallen.[15] In Russia, the flowers of the newly-weds are offered in thanks for the gift of life, both theirs and those of their yet unborn children, who may also inherit the heroic character of the war dead, in what seems to be almost a fertility ritual. From my discussions, however, the subtleness of interpretation of this tradition by the older generations is lost on the young, who seem to act out of custom alone, with no overt reference to the war except the use of monuments as a backdrop for wedding photographs, providing memory of a different kind for the new family unit.

In modern Novorossiisk there is evidence that the conservative values of the postwar years still exist, as many adults praise the return in the twenty-first century of aspects of *vospitanie* and patriotic education familiar from their own youth in the Komsomol or Young Pioneer organisations. Any potential generation gap is partly narrowed by this nostalgia for what parents and grandparents deem idealistic aspects of the Soviet past. However, despite the general strength of family bonds and the varied mechanisms by which the young are exposed to war memory in Novorossiisk, my research indicates that there are some families who do not pass on the memory tradition from one generation to another. One elderly man, a child during the war, blamed the family if a child is disaffected, seeing it as their clear duty to transmit memory, although teacher Nadezhda considered that young parents born at the time of change in the late eighties and early 1990s may have different values and little regard for remembrance. Furthermore, the headmaster of a secondary school observed that some children may live in small family units or atomised families who do not spend much time together, such that they are not exposed to an upbringing which includes discussions within the family about the war.

Those not observing memorial traditions were seen as abnormal by some of my respondents active in local affairs: families are accused of being 'illiterate' or 'bad parents', incapable of joining in the collective social movement for memory transfer, while others are considered '*nepravil'nye liudi*' ('not proper people'). This is an indication that an educated, well-brought-up young person is expected by society to think in a socially correct way about the war, due to the 'proper' promotion of socially accepted traditional values within the family. Any deviation that may threaten social cohesion invites condemnation.

A recent incident in which a group of six young dancers uploaded a video onto *YouTube* of themselves performing a twerk dance in front of the Malaia zemlia monument incurred the immediate wrath of the courts. It was not necessarily the suggestive dance that offended public decency, but the place in which such 'deviant' behaviour was displayed, which immediately called into question the moral upbringing of the perpetrators. Three of them were given light custodial sentences for 'mild hooliganism'. However, it was the parents of the youngest girl, still under the age of 18, who came in for most condemnation: they were accused of 'failing to perform parental duties for raising minors', and charged with 'failing to take measures to facilitate children's physical, intellectual, psychological, spiritual and moral growth'.[16]

Those parents wishing to imbue a sense of connection with the past in their children may employ family archives, letters, photographs and other artefacts, which render memory more vivid and tangible and engage younger generations more than a dry narration. Although some older respondents narrated their histories to me without any material props, others employed old photographs to mediate their account. In such instances, visual aids may act as aides-mémoire, partly dictating the rote repetition of narratives. I observed this with two older women, Sonia and Lyubov, who twice recounted their own memories of the war to me identically, on both occasions clutching photographs of themselves as young women.

The interaction of private memory with an official war myth is not straightforward. Harald Welzer's study of intergenerational family narrations finds that they can be gradually re-shaped over time due to re-evaluation and the need for a new meaning as changes in the political environment may affect the perceptions of both the narrator and the listening descendants.[17] Similarly, Raphael Samuel and Paul Thompson argue that mythical elements in both public and private memory form a continuing historical presence, being continually reshaped for the utility of an individual.[18] Retrospective re-positioning of one's own life story may enable the deployment of some historical perspective, as in the case of memoir literature. Kirschenbaum finds alongside this a common renegotiation of the narrator's identity in order to maintain the compatibility of individual and official memory.[19] Oral narratives become simpler over time, as any problems and ambiguity are removed and plots rearranged to form an idealised linear account, much as in the war myth in general and in local memoir literature.[20] Today's interviewer cannot wind back the clock to hear biographical tales told years ago. However, it is known that, whereas during the war soldiers would declare that they were fighting for Stalin, later memoirs declared that they were fighting for communism, while accounts today hold that the war was fought for the people (*narod*).

Consistency of narrative was demonstrated in one woman's account of her childhood in the war, related to me in identical terms on three different occasions, providing evidence of the rehearsed version of the past that she wished to propagate. There is no reason to doubt the general authenticity of Lyudmila's story, which was probably typical of many with such a powerful emotional investment in their personal history. Her father joined the army in the early days of the war, leaving his wife alone with two children. As the enemy advanced towards Novorossiisk, the family became separated; Lyudmila found herself in the care of her older brother living in a small cave in the hills outside the town, with, she chuckles, no proper toilet facilities. Her brother joined the partisans, while Lyudmila eventually went to Ukraine to try to find another member of the family; there, she was taken by the Germans and held in a camp for child internees until her liberation.

While there are clear parallels between accepted social memory and that of individuals, it is important to note the significance of the collective war myth for the individual within the dominant influence of the state war cult, despite the variety of wartime experiences of my interviewees. Groups often develop shared stories to define their identity and in order that members may find a common significance in their own memorial narratives which make use of a shared culture.[21] It has also been found that many individuals accommodated their own memories within Soviet ideology, although some managed to retain their individual histories despite an overriding state narrative,[22] leading to a difference between the memory of individuals and the state-propagated myth.[23]

This concurs with my findings of the subjective situation of some personal narratives within the collective myth, evidence of a complex interrelationship of private memory and public ideology, past and present. However, eight of my elderly interviewees' generally rather diffident and self-deprecating accounts of the war do not conform with Welzer's claim of a 'cumulative heroisation' of the protagonist over time, particularly those events related by two Crimean Tatars deported to Central Asia. Most of my older interviewees tended to place a positive spin on the end of their war stories, which always ended with the highlight of their career – that is where they were when the war ended on Victory Day 1945, or how they returned to Novorossiisk to build a new life after the war.

One respondent, an elderly retired teacher, spoke to me at length about her experience on Malaia zemlia as a worker in the political department alongside Mariia Pedenko, the memoirist. Vasilisa's detailed account included tales of singing and dancing on the streets after dark during the summer months of the campaign, when she longed once again for the forbidden freedom to wear a dress. More notable was Vasilisa's claim to have been present during an earlier incident when Soviet and enemy troops were dug in on opposite sides of a main road during the harsh April fighting. Apparently the Germans wanted to finish the engagement off quickly that week, driving the Soviets back into the sea, as a birthday present for Hitler. Some older interviewees mentioned that a Soviet artist left a different 'present' for Hitler on the enemy's side of the road during the night – a pencil sketch of the Führer characterised as a wild boar. There is no doubt that Vasilisa was indeed present on Malaia zemlia: this is confirmed in Sokolov's memoirs.[24] However, it is most improbable that she was involved in the birthday incident, if it indeed ever happened, when she was more likely to have been fully occupied in one of the makeshift first aid points further away from the front line. This reformulation of her own history is indicative of the influence of other accounts, which may have caused her gradually and probably unconsciously to alter her indirect memory over time and assimilate it into what she then transmitted as a direct memory.

This type of personal negotiation in order to make sense of the past is described in the case of Australian veterans by Alistair Thomson, who suggests that individuals strive to construct a personal back-story which helps to make them feel as comfortable as possible with their current identities. In order to do this, they must take into account the accepted cultural norms and language of the time, perhaps unconsciously repressing experiences which may be at odds with the expectations of modern society.[25] Individual memories narrated today may not always be totally reliable, but do represent a personal mnemonic construction within the official myth. It is impossible to measure in retrospect the accuracy of an individual's memory with regard to historical fact, but Michael Schudson, Paul Connerton and Daniel Schacter all emphasise the probability of increasing distortion and (sometimes selective) forgetting with the passing years. If detail is lost over time, it is also possible that the voiced memory of any pain or humiliation in the past is suppressed, whether consciously or unconsciously blocked by the narrator, giving rise to a more positive spin on the past than events actually merit.[26]

I found that those who took part in the war are largely happy to talk about their memories today, however stereotyped. In contrast, two elderly respondents stated that their parents had never mentioned the war to them. It is hard for children of parents who took part in the war to understand to what extent private family memory of the experience could endure under the oppressive political circumstances of the Soviet Union, when it was often impossible to reconcile public and private memory, especially but not exclusively where minorities were omitted from the official state narrative. Individual memories may not always have coincided with the politically correct state version, leading to a complex process of myth building between sometimes competing images.[27]

Silence on the part of older family members may also be indicative of the psychological scars that can understandably prevent discussion of some topics within the family.[28] It may be tempting to conclude that this silence is on the part of the older family members, but one teenager confided to me that she felt uncomfortable discussing her great-grandmother's wartime experiences with her, as she had been raped by occupying forces. The great-granddaughter's obvious discomfort was matched by that of a further student at the Moscow Institute for Economics and the Humanities in Novorossiisk, whose distress at her family's experiences during the war prompted her refusal to take part in a class on local history. Apart from these exceptional cases, no intergenerational tension or narratives counter to the accepted war myth were offered, such as found in Canada by Graham Carr.[29] My interviews with young and old alike pointed rather to cohesion, consensus and empathy across generations.

In a traditional society, memory often passes from grandparents to children, whose parents are usually busy working. The older generation takes responsibility for memorial practices and informal education, such that propagation of memory tends to skip the middle generation.[30] Correspondingly, a majority of 64 per cent of my younger interviewees mentioned the significant role of grandparents rather than parents in the transmission of memory, even if those grandparents were themselves too young to have been war veterans. This indicates that there is possibly more opportunity and desire for grandparents to discuss the war with children than for busy parents, especially in a more modern society with working mothers and sometimes a single parent. The ritual of oral narration may promote historical understanding and empathy in younger family members, binding generations together through memory. In contrast, younger generations may find the narratives of personal memories of the war by their grandparents and great-grandparents repetitive and performances rendered more irritating due to the natural forgetting of old people. However, with the mediation of mnemonic artefacts, family narratives remain subjective and personal, often possessing a sense of intimacy that cannot be reproduced in a more formal, collective environment. Strikingly, the headmistress of School Number Six claimed that some veterans find it more difficult to talk to their own family than to a class of schoolchildren. From the high percentage of veterans claiming to recount war memory to their grandchildren or others of a much younger generation, however, it appears that it may in fact prove easier to talk about the war to a young generation decades after the event than it was to talk to one's own children soon after the event.

Although they were not specifically asked, some middle-aged interviewees could also recall how they had heard from their own parents and grandparents about the war. Some recounted to me long and personal stories of their relations' wartime experiences in Novorossiisk gleaned from direct personal transmission and one woman recalled that her aunt had written her own memoirs of the war, which had been treasured in the family. Twenty per cent of subjects between the ages of 30 and 69 volunteered the fact that their father or grandfather had fought in the war, while 14 per cent offered the information that their parents or grandparents had talked to them about Malaia zemlia. In contrast, Zoya was sad that her parents had not talked openly about the war when she was young, and is now particularly eager to transmit family history to her own grandchildren. Thus the sense of a personal connection to the war remains strong for some families, thanks mainly to direct communication of memory transmitted by older generations.

As those with direct memory of the war die, current and future generations will be recipients only of indirect post-memory, when family influence may well diminish in favour of the official war myth. For the moment, though, several of my interviewees, both men and women, related how they personally propagate the story of Malaia zemlia to younger family members, often with their own subjective interpretation. Some parents and grandparents see it as natural to pass on memory about local history in the same way as their own parents. Mariya 'studies' the story of Malaia zemlia with her grandson using the same dated children's book that she used to read to her children.[31] Nikolai, like Klavdiya, takes advantage of the Beskozyrka ritual for conversations with his son about the war, while some employ Victory Day for this purpose. Vladimir uses the opportunity of weekends searching on Mount Koldun to discuss war memory with his teenage son. For younger parents, the monuments and street names in the town provide a vehicle for the transmission of memory. Nikolai and Varvara, for example, respond to their children's requests to read to them the information on monuments to heroes; for incomer Varvara, this activity teaches her about local history at the same time. Kristina is similarly prompted by questions about streets named after heroes, while others more proactively take their children to museums or for a tour of the historical sites. Many questions are prompted by school lessons, and provide the opportunity for family reinforcement. Families also contribute to school lessons by providing personal information for class discussion and websites. Many young parents claimed a sense of responsibility to pass on memory of Malaia zemlia to younger generations. For example Nina felt a duty to answer relevant questions: 'If the children say "let's remember", then parents must do so too.' However, not all have the time and Vyacheslav admitted that his children were simply not interested in family history.

James Fentress and Chris Wickham suggest that public memory is often in the control of men, with women taking a more private perspective. Most of the dead were male, as were the kinship groups formed after the war, while the mourners were typically female. They argue that older women may have less desire than men to remember the war publicly, as the war myth predominantly recalls male activities. Women are found to speak less about public space and more about domestic and family affairs, especially births, marriages and, most importantly in the context of war, deaths.[32] This generalisation may be questioned with respect to female memory of the Soviet Union at war by virtue of women's substantial participation in the conflict and their experience of life in an occupied country, as well as their wartime responsibility for industrial and agricultural production. However, it is notable that public expressions of female memory through memoir literature are rare in the Soviet Union and the position of potentially marginalised Soviet women in remembrance celebrations remains ambiguous.[33]

It is impossible to deduce from my interviews whether men or women are dominant in the intergenerational transmission of memory in the family, although women seem to be either more open about having had discussions at home and/or to have taken part in more discussions about the war. This concurs broadly with Artemi Romanov's findings about the perceived communication satisfaction gained by Russian grandparents in talking with their grandchildren: grandmothers tend to disclose more personal information, while grandfathers are more willing to talk about their opinion on historical events.[34] From my research it seems, however, that men may be more proactive in finding opportunities for discussion and interested in talking about the war in general, while women are more responsive to questioning and are more involved with school homework projects. Grandparents of both genders also play an important role.

'Reverse propagation', the more unusual but naturally-occurring means of intergenerational transmission of the war myth from younger to older family members, is opposite to the traditional mechanism of transmission from older to younger generations found in a society with little population mobility. This mechanism of intergenerational familial transmission is illustrated by a conversation documented by a journalist during the 2014 Beskozyrka ceremony, when an eight-year old boy was overheard telling his mother what he had been taught about the Malaia zemlia landings at school.[35] Six relative newcomers to Novorossiisk confirmed to me that they had learned about local war history from their children, who had in turn been taught about it at school. These examples also provide evidence that the history of Malaia zemlia is not widely known to people outside Novorossiisk, even though many older Russians recollect the name from Brezhnev's memoirs.

Conversations at home about the war may also be triggered by the amplification of military material in the mass media around Victory Day, reflected notably in the local press, which concentrates particularly on articles about individual veterans and their memories. According to Barbie Zelizer, the press is often an unrecognised agent of the propagation of memory, determining both the form and the content of its transmission.[36] In Novorossiisk, however, it is also a site of memory construction in its own right. The local press encourages investigative journalism in the 'exposure of truth' about the history of the war, while continuing to carry social interest stories about veterans and their past.[37]

War documentaries and fictional films old and modern invade the home in the Victory Day period, shown on both state and other television channels. Based on published television schedules, all such films shown in 2013 were of Russian or Soviet provenance.[38] This diet of war material is inescapable for three days, with the war classics probably welcomed by older citizens, if considered over-intrusive by Anton, a younger resident. Respondant Vera cited a television documentary about the fear in Russia that American war films such as *Saving Private Ryan* are too influential on young people who may fail to understand the role of the Soviet Union in the war.[39] Indeed, Stephen Norris points to the spate of new nationalistic and patriotic 'blockbusters' produced in Russia since the late 1990s, fuelling interest in tsarist Russia, World War II and some nostalgia for the Brezhnev era.[40] The film *We are from the Future* employs a version of socialist realism updated for modern Russia, mixing together past, present and future to re-frame the past in order to make it both relevant and educational for young people of the present. The audience experiences the same learning curve as the films' young protagonists, leaving all involved 'cleansed' by the narrative as they are subjected to the 'right', largely optimistic view of history deemed by director Andrei Maliukov to be politically useful.

Based on the resurgence of historical blockbusters in Russia and the West, Olga Kucherenko claims that most young people acquire their knowledge of history informally through films,[41] which probably serve to influence and even distort their understanding of the past. Furthermore, within the informal family circle, it is even possible that younger viewers may experience the 'prosthetic memory' described by Alison Landsberg, which offers a mechanism 'at the interface between a person and a historical narrative about the past' for the acquisition of powerful memories which were not actually experienced. According to Landsberg, films about history may evoke private feelings from a collective experience in the past such that the distinction between history and memory is blurred, whilst at the same time introducing an ethical dimension that may be absent from personal narrations or collective rituals of remembrance.[42] However, despite the huge popularity and accessibility of both home-produced and foreign films about World War II in general, my research in Novorossiisk demonstrates that the influence on young people of formal and informal education about specifically *local* history predominates.

Discussions about the war are not necessarily uniform across all families in Novorossiisk and children may have different degrees of exposure to direct narratives from an older generation. Furthermore, the family is not the only agent of propagation of the war myth, although two young parents pointed to the primacy of the family by virtue of direct and personal transmission, with emotional triggers guiding interpretation. The familial mechanism, where present, is always supplemented and complemented by experiences from other sources, including formal school lessons and extra-curricular activities. Indeed, many family conversations may not happen without some prompting from the mass media or other external agencies. Despite the pervading influence of the war cult, many interviewees, both men and women, contend that the family plays the largest role in the propagation of memory, arguing for a link between a child's upbringing and the transmission of the war myth, an indication of the importance of memory from below. Elizaveta, a young woman whose grandfather fought in the war, considered on the other hand that the family's role should be even more important than it is. In general, however, respondents apparently wish to uphold and transmit the memory and values of previous generations, viewing this as an indication of the patriotism of the family, which values its military ancestors and its own current mnemonic identity.

As direct memory of the war is fading, a family's own identity is cemented more by artefacts than by oral narration, but this still leaves room for an individuality of response to the state's war myth. Since 2013 young people of all ages have joined with adults on Victory Day in an overt demonstration of respect for their family 'heroes'. Following the popular military parade, this new procession unites generations, as marchers hold aloft sepia or black and white portraits of their ancestors who fought and often died in the war. This 'Immortal Regiment' (*'Bessmertnyi polk'*) movement was started in other regions of Russia in 2012, gradually spreading across the major cities of the country and being adopted in Novorossiisk the following year. Developing from an interactive online archive, its rapid evolution into a newly invented tradition marks an implicit recognition of the dwindling number of war veterans still able to participate in Victory Day.[43] Just as the Candle in the Window movement accompanying the Beskozyrka ritual has become an invented tradition in its own right, this addendum to the existing Victory Day tradition has served once again to rejuvenate the original ceremony, rendering it more relevant to children, while capturing the imagination of citizens of all ages through an explicit link to their own family history. The key role of the movement and the significance of the propagation of memory was recognised by the governor of the Krasnodar region on Victory Day 2016:

> Every family in the Kuban' has its own hero, its own member of the 'Immortal Regiment'. Summoned by their hearts, more and more people are joining the largest procession in the country, because it is a huge honour to march alongside the heroes of the Great Patriotic War. Their fearlessness and steadfastness, hardened in battle, saved the world from fascism. And it continues to save it from treacherous paths and false ideologies, from moral emptiness and self-betrayal. Today, our most important task is to transmit memory of the war to the next generations. This memory is our roots, our spiritual and moral support, which we should maintain for the sake of the future.[44]

This robust declaration aiming to drum up support for the new movement may not resonate with all citizens of Novorossiisk, however. Those with no interest in family history may ignore it, while those whose history has been lost thanks to the premature deaths of key members in or just after the war may feel excluded. From my observations, though, the Immortal Regiment is a popular and growing addition to Victory Day commemorations, validating once-private remembrance and bringing it out into the open to be merged successfully with public ceremonies of commemoration.

In the immediate postwar years, individuals sometimes found it hard to express their own experiences of the war to their children and to situate them within the overpowering influence of the state. Today the Russian state appears actively to encourage the private ownership of family history, which is publicly shared within the community of memory to reinforce the overarching war myth of a victorious nation. This overt convergence of memorial identity appears to be growing in popularity, courted and vaunted by a government seeking to unite the people. The risk of a dependence on a genetic identification with the past, however, is that it is more difficult to challenge in the future, being based on the mnemonic stasis typical of an identity built on past tribal exploits, a cult of ancestors and traditional moral characteristics.

CHAPTER 14

THE EDUCATIONAL ROLE OF VETERANS

To you from failing hands we throw
The torch; be yours to hold it high.[1]

A special guest at the central Veterans' Council in May 2010 was Prime Minister Putin, who took tea with a group of veterans on his visit to Novorossiisk,[2] just as Brezhnev had socialised with former 18th Army combatants during his visit in 1974.[3] Veterans of the Great Patriotic War are not only valued within the confines of the family circle, but have become increasingly esteemed within Russian society as a whole, which recognises the role they play in the propagation of the war myth to the young.

In the postwar years formal meetings of veterans were few, but, with a planned exhibition in the Novorossiisk museum on the fifteenth anniversary of the Malaia zemlia campaign in 1958, an official organisation for veterans of the Great Patriotic War was established to collect and organise exhibits. Crucially, at the time of the exhibition, veterans collectively and individually started publicly to recount their memories to young people under the auspices of the local Komsomol. Viktor Golikov, an historian by training, explained the reasoning behind this, stating that it was important for young people to learn about historical events from live witness testimony rather than from manuscripts or legends. The intention may have been laudable, but the reception by children of these often repetitive stories was not always positive.[4]

The duty of veterans as 'authorised witnesses' to educate the younger generation was also reflected in the stated motives for the publication of war memoirs during the war cult of the Brezhnev era. In exchange for their political loyalty the state implemented a new national policy for war veterans, such that, from 1965, veterans increasingly enjoyed privileged access to health services, housing, transport and sanatoria in line with the growing war cult in what Natalia Danilova terms a 'reciprocal contract'.[5]

Mark Edele suggests that clashes of veterans with Communist Party organisations often took place nationwide, thanks to the transfer of power from party organs to local veterans' clubs.[6] However, in Novorossiisk collaboration with the Komsomol developed, involving significant educational work by the Veterans' Council with young people in the Pioneers organisation.[7] Grassroots lobbying of Brezhnev by the public forced the government to acknowledge the preferred status of veterans by increasing their benefits, consolidating the mutually beneficial implicit social contract between the state and veterans of the Great Patriotic War. By 1978 they were entitled to interest-free loans for the construction of houses and an annual holiday, with a 50 per cent reduction on long-distance travel to state sanatoria, all supposedly in return for their public loyalty and educational role.

The status of veterans came under closer state scrutiny with the onset of the war in Afghanistan in 1979, resulting in veterans of the Great Patriotic War enjoying greater recognition and privileges than those of this later, less successful conflict.[8] The Novorossiisk Veterans' Council moved to new premises in 1981, where the central branch is still housed, and the first women joined the group in 1982, reflecting an increasing national recognition of the role of women in the war.[9] The preferred status of Great Patriotic War veterans was confirmed in the law 'On Veterans' in 1995, until the de facto failure of the reciprocal contract thanks to the economic crisis at the end of the 1990s, when many benefits were cancelled and the status of veterans devalued with the rouble.[10]

Today the reciprocity embedded in the implicit contract between veterans and the state is even more evident than in the Brezhnev era. The new war cult under Putin has led to a re-mobilisation of the few remaining veterans to appear in ceremonies of remembrance and to educate the young, such that it now appears that their public identity is linked predominantly with the war. Veterans are therefore in a position of key responsibility for the transmission of memory through the *vospitanie* of children, looking Janus-like in two directions: backwards to the past and forwards towards the younger generation. In a mutually beneficial role, they have become national treasures as probably the most important emotional ingredient of the war cult, to be wheeled out, bedecked with medals accrued over the years, by national and local politicians on every occasion connected with the Great Patriotic War, to the extent that I propose that there is now a veritable cult of veterans. In return, veterans have at last obtained the state and public acknowledgment they demanded during the final years of the twentieth century with a whole range of privileges amongst other less tangible marks of respect which provide evidence of their new, special position within society. However, it is their current status in comparison with the poorer treatment of veterans of more recent conflicts that reflects the importance attached to this particular group in their twilight years.

Victory Day celebrations are particularly significant, when every Great Patriotic War veteran receives an annual congratulatory letter from the president. Since 2013 younger citizens have been encouraged to pick up a postcard in a post office to send their thanks to a local veteran.[11] In Novorossiisk the mayor issues invitations to all local veterans to attend theatre performances and concerts, dinners and the main Victory Day procession, where they are placed in seats of honour. Gifts are showered on veterans at this time. To celebrate the sixty-fifth anniversary of Victory Day in 2010 the mayor of Novorossiisk gave every veteran in the town a collection of items full of symbolism to recall their war years, including a folded triangular 'letter from the front', writing paper and a pencil, a bar of soap, a pouch of rough tobacco with a box of matches, a canteen and a bottle of wine. This recent special treatment is evident in a campaign of banners and posters on buses, kiosks and walls put in place across the town by the local council: 'Dear veteran, your victory is eternal', 'Memory of your exploits will live forever' and 'Thank you for the victory, liberators of the town'. Improvements in their circumstances are also acknowledged by veterans themselves, and are linked by some younger interviewees to the fact that there are now very few remaining veterans and that the country is finally economically able to honour and care for them properly in their old age.

In 2010, for the sixty-fifth anniversary, the Novorossiisk town council supplemented golden signs marking the graves of veterans with new red plaques on the walls of the homes of living veterans. This gesture of respect was welcomed by three younger respondents, who for the first time were able to recognise and offer congratulations and help if necessary to their elderly neighbours, while those with cars were encouraged by posters throughout the town to 'pick up a veteran'. Sealing the social contract, most schools in Novorossiisk look after their sponsored veterans: teachers and children give support throughout the year by cleaning or shopping, and special gifts are offered on Victory Day, for example a new refrigerator full of food.

However the most important year-round work with veterans in the community is provided by the chain of Veterans' Councils in the region. According to a regional representative from Krasnodar, there were eight remaining Heroes of the Soviet Union living in the region in 2013, while the head of the town veterans' councils claimed that about 6,000 veterans of the Great Patriotic War still lived in Novorossiisk. In 2006 the responsibility for veterans' welfare was devolved to local authorities, although veterans of the Great Patriotic War still receive their pensions from the federal government.[12] Although many veterans still cling to the belief that the state has a 'moral duty' to compensate them for their valuable war service,[13] the ongoing social obligation to veterans in return for their role in the propagation of war memory is largely met by committed locals rather than any state mechanism. Funded partly by the region and partly by the town council,[14] the smaller area councils in and outside the town look after their local community veterans, who form what Jay Winter terms 'fictive kinship groups' or 'families of remembrance',[15] which promote common memorial interests whilst also comprising a mutually supportive social group.

In the outlying village of Myskhako, the head of the Veterans' Council has worked there on a part-time basis for 16 years for the tiny sum of 500 roubles per month. Her office is located in the main town council building, which also houses the post office, guaranteeing a stream of visitors who often stop by for a cup of tea and a chat. The central position of the office is convenient for collaborative work with staff responsible for youth affairs and the local mayor himself in adjacent offices. The veterans are all known personally to the officers of the Veterans' Council. Indeed, the organisation is so mutually supportive that it is difficult to distinguish between the veterans themselves and those slightly younger elderly people who help organise the series of activities throughout the year. Encouraged by the local mayor and councillor, the Veterans' Council contributes substantially to the morale of members through commemorative activities.

Over the period running up to Victory Day in early May vintage war films are shown in the palace of culture in Myskhako, to which veterans have free entry.[16] The library, also located in the palace of culture, similarly welcomes veterans, who not only still read the occasional book of war memoirs, but often attend anniversary parties organised by the Veterans' Council and librarians jointly. For example, children presented flowers to veteran Lyubov at a ceremony held in her honour, with a presentation showing images of her both today and as a young person in the war, stressing her current identity as that of a war veteran. Vasilisa, another Novorossiisk veteran, stated that she appreciates flowers given to her by children as an indication of their *vospitanie*. In return for this attention from the state, region and town, many veterans are conscious of their continuing implicit duty to educate (*vospityvat'*) children in a revived tradition harking back to the postwar Soviet Union.[17]

However, the most important sign of loyalty to the state in exchange for the receipt of benefits is the public appearance of veterans at ceremonies of remembrance, especially Victory Day, a cultural indicator of the influence of the current war cult. From my observations, most veterans appear to welcome the recent increase in pomp of the Victory Day celebrations, while some particularly appreciate the participation of young people, who, since 2005, have been encouraged by the state to distribute St George ribbons prior to and on Victory Day.[18] Flying from car bumpers, wing mirrors and aerials, these symbols of war memory are superficially reminiscent of British poppies or French *bleuets* (cornflowers), being offered in exchange for contributions to veterans' welfare charities.[19]

Like the poppy and the *bleuet*, the official St George ribbon website proclaims it as a symbol of remembrance, respect and thanks to veterans. However, the distribution of the Russian ribbons, through the support of the political youth organisation *Molodaia gvardiia* (The Young Guard) and the educational movement *Studencheskaia obshchina* (The Students' Society), is largely effected thanks to the involvement of young people. In this key respect, the distribution of the St George ribbon bears

Figure 14.1 Prime Minister Putin Wearing the St George Ribbon in Novorossiisk in May 2010 (photograph by Evgenii Nikitin, copyright of the author)

little resemblance to the work of often elderly members of the Royal British Legion.[20]

Wearing of the St George ribbon effects a sense of social unison on a national scale – what Benedict Anderson would term an 'imagined community' – emphasising a shared political, social and cultural background.[21] This recent addition to social remembrance increases the political utility of the celebrations through a public proclamation of social cohesion. The *lentochka* (ribbon) movement has been both praised and condemned as a top-down exercise in the intergenerational marketing of remembrance across the country and beyond, a potent symbol of the widespread propagation of the current war cult and its values.[22]

The *lentochka* movement has already gained the status of a tradition in Novorossiisk. Based upon the much older award made to military personnel in the reign of Catherine the Great and named after the patron saint of Russia, it is a further example of a newly invented tradition built on a past system that resonates particularly well in the current memory climate, as evidenced by its universal acceptance within a very short period of time. This national badge of membership is yet another invented tradition grafted onto an earlier, established ceremony. Like the Candle in the Window movement, it has the effect of enriching, rejuvenating and refreshing the Victory Day celebrations, thereby rendering them more attractive to a newly mobilised younger generation.

This symbol has been recycled for current mnemonic and political use, promoting shared ownership of memory and capable of stimulating a spectrum of nuances as each generation reads something slightly different into the ribbon. Vera, a headmistress, recognises it as a longstanding symbol that has recently been resurrected, supported by Sonia, who feels that it retains its association with the pre-revolutionary Cross of St George, with its implications of heroic exploits and love of the fatherland. The St George ribbon poster, distributed widely in the region in 2010, contains an overt reference to the great USSR at its centre, but the ribbon itself demonstrates military continuity from pre-revolutionary, through the Soviet period to the present.

Stephen Norris finds that the ribbon resonates well with veterans, who remember its use on Stalin's Order of Glory awarded to rank and file soldiers. Despite this, he argues persuasively that it successfully fills the national need for a symbol of war memory not tainted with Stalin.[23] The *lentochka* tradition appeared to be popular in Novorossiisk on my Victory Day visits in 2010 and 2015, when it was hard to see anybody without one. In addition to its fund-raising function, it is seen by many as an aid to memory in its own right. For example, veteran Vasilisa regards it as the declaration of a national wish to remember. A Novorossiisk newspaper journalist sees in the orange and black stripes a memory of the flame and smoke of war,[24] while Dmitrii recalls it as the ribbon worn on a Soviet sailor's cap, the legendary *beskozyrka*, whose symbolism needs no further explanation in this maritime town. It is not surprising that the ribbon that offers something for everyone should be so popular: indeed, Katherine Verdery argues that a political symbol is particularly potent 'not because everyone agrees on its meaning but because it compels interest despite divergent views of what it means'.[25] In an overt connection with the resistance to the occupation of the Soviet Union in 1941, it was even appropriated by pro-Russian fighters in Ukraine in 2014, not only as a symbol of memory and (Russian and Soviet) victory, but also of continued resistance to a government which some perceive to be illegitimate. In marked contrast, politically aware Elvira wishfully reads into the *lentochka* something particularly relevant to the domestic political climate: the gift of democracy from the Russian state to the people who crave it.

In the hands of energetic young people, the St George ribbon enables the propagation of memory from young people to the now passive oldest citizens, as the transmission of memory undergoes a process of reverse propagation. On Victory Day the memory message, with its new symbolism, defies the traditional propagation mechanism from older to younger generations, ensuring an evident solidarity between generations.

Through its attraction to young people, the *lentochka* movement introduces a new, youthful element into the already successful Victory Day celebrations. My observations indicate that young university students in bright red 'uniform' tee-shirts bearing the slogan *'Ia pomniu! Ia gorzhus'!'* ('I remember! I am proud!') seem to control the mayor's invited Victory Day audience, marshalling veterans as they hand to each a *lentochka* and an anniversary baseball cap. Victory Day, in this respect, has been appropriated by the new younger generation, not necessarily at their instigation, but apparently without coercion and with their tacit agreement, as evidenced by the enthusiasm with which they perform their duties. The Deputy Director of the Maritime Academy admitted that this may be exceptional behaviour, as his students do not always want to attend ceremonies of remembrance, deploying barely relevant excuses about lack of time. With their strong link to the military, however, students of the Maritime Academy seem bound by an inescapable social duty to be official representatives of their generation at Victory Day and other commemorative rituals.

If the official Victory Day ceremony in the centre of Novorossiisk is orchestrated by the local authority and largely in harmony with events on Red Square, less formality was observed on the town periphery in Myskhako in 2010. Veterans were gathered together in a brown military tent at a *soldatskii prival* (military field kitchen), feeding their nostalgia with wartime rations, mainly *kasha* (buckwheat porridge) washed down with quantities of vodka, all served by Cossacks. The old people gathered together in groups around the tables to sing war songs, pausing only at the interruptions of modern ring-tones as family members called to congratulate their own veteran. Such was the camaraderie among this community of remembrance that the pensioners seemed deaf to the official entertainment by children, local dancers and singers, in an example of overwhelming bottom-up ownership of a remembrance celebration by the oldest citizens. Eventually, the official speeches over, all participants came together on the same intergenerational wavelength as the vodka flowed, the officials retired and the unofficial dancing started. Apparently these veterans are not only enjoying their official role and recognition, but are happy to have taken full ownership of their new privileged social status in their twilight years.

CHAPTER 15

FORMAL EDUCATION OF THE YOUNGER GENERATION

> Детям своим
> расскажите о них,
> чтоб
> запомнили!
> Детям
> детей
> расскажите о них,
> чтобы тоже
> запомнили![1]

February 2013 marked the seventieth anniversary of the Malaia zemlia landings and the liberation of Stalingrad, currently known as Volgograd. To mark the occasion, Novorossiisk schoolchildren from five schools, university students and Cossack cadet soldiers took part in a Skype conference with counterparts in Volgograd. Organised and scripted in advance by the mayor's office, this 'tele-bridge' also linked Novorossiisk veterans with those of the Battle of Stalingrad in an explicit comparison of the two hero cities: 'Malaia zemlia – Mamaev kurgan'. With a spectrum of age ranges taking part, the event contrived to link themes appealing to the old using the modern technology attractive to the young, thereby effectively closing any virtual generation gap. The conference, 'The Patriotic Education of the Young on the Basis of an Heroic Past', claimed to instil patriotic values amongst young people, including a respect for the past and loyalty to their country, by its new approach to military-patriotic education and citizenship.

One of the ambiguities facing traditionalists wishing to propagate a war myth is the fact that history inevitably looks backwards to the past, whereas the tendency for the younger generation is to look forwards to the future. If not carefully nurtured in memorial tradition, the young may rebel against their elders, promoting a dismissal of the past with its inherent values. In contrast, successful propagation of a war myth may lead to a memorial vicious circle and consequent stagnation, leading eventually to unquestioning acceptance, which seems to be largely the case today in a younger generation inculcated with *vospitanie*. Older generations may tend to select the content, transmitting a simplified, positive message in order to promote cultural consensus and maintain the continuity of the war myth, although its interpretation may change slightly from generation to generation.

The renewed emphasis on moral education of the young has become almost synonymous to many respondents with the belief system of remembrance: in Novorossiisk well brought up young people are expected to pay respect to the dead in accordance with tradition. A *vospitannyi* young person today is deemed to be almost a clone of his or her Soviet counterpart, with the qualities of patriotism, respect, modesty and good moral behaviour both recalled and judged positively by older generations. According to Svetlana, an historian in her sixties, it is precisely these aspects of *vospitanie* that won the war, ideologically embedded through a unique type of patriotism expected of communists. There was a period during the 1990s when *vospitanie* and patriotism were not seen as so important, however, according to several respondents of all ages, who criticised the mass failure to maintain the war myth and remember the dead. Under the current war cult the state has driven a nationwide campaign to involve young people in patriotic activities, just as in the youth clubs, Young Pioneer and Komsomol organisations of the Soviet Union under Brezhnev.

The noticeable return to a more conservative style of education under Putin is exemplified by the re-introduction of school uniforms throughout Russia from September 2014. Today, once again, it is *vospitanie* that is viewed as both instilling patriotism and as a necessary foundation for the propagation of the war myth. *Vospitanie* is seen to be bred mainly by families and schools, while some recognise the role of social rituals and the local authorities. I have found that it is at the confluence of school and family that the war myth is most effectively transmitted.

Moral education of the young is effected in schools thanks to the new emphasis on patriotism, a topic now included in the school curriculum and dictated by the state, according to three head teachers, to the endorsement of many parents and grandparents.[2] A new syllabus for 'Patriotic Work' was introduced in Russian schools in 2010, following a state decision to prioritise citizenship in the school curriculum. This decision was endorsed by the regional authorities, such that each school is now responsible for designing and delivering its own courses. These include some material in common with other educational establishments across the country and some location-specific content. Furthermore, every school and the Maritime Academy have designated senior members of staff who are responsible for the design and implementation of the syllabus and for the *vospitanie* of the students.

A formal argument for the introduction of Patriotic Work into the curriculum forms the preface to the new syllabus for School Number Six and the Bekar School. It points to governmental concern at the loss of 'spiritual values' and growing 'social diffidence' during the period of economic and political changes in the 1990s. The document recognises that during this period the sense of patriotism and respect for Russian culture was much reduced, leading to a decrease in *vospitanie* of the younger generation.[3] Endorsing the government's educational findings, Catherine Merridale observes in the twenty-first century an increasing degree of collective amnesia in Russian society, where the young often lack any interest in the past, despite a stated desire to look back promoted by the new war cult.[4] There is also some reticence among the young about entering military service.[5] Moreover, there may be a potential conflict between the need to remember of survivors and their descendants, as the event remembered becomes increasingly alienated in time and space from those remembering.[6] Making no apologies for the ideological content of the new curriculum, the Bekar syllabus specifically bemoans the increase amongst young people of diffidence, self-centred individualism, cynicism, aggressiveness and lack of respect towards veterans, largely attributed to 'media propaganda [...] falsifying national history' and the propagation of non-Russian traditional values, with a commensurate decrease in the motivation of young people to join the armed services.

The aim of the new syllabus is to introduce 'a renewed emphasis on patriotic upbringing [*vospitanie*] as one of the most important educational tasks'. At the top of the list of themes is the 'desire to observe memory of dead troops', closely followed by the encouragement of 'respect for elderly people'; love for the town of Novorossiisk within the Russian Republic; 'pride in the Russian army' and its veterans, linked with a 'wish to serve one's Fatherland'; and the 'development of a sense of patriotism' based on 'the cultural and patriotic values of the glorious [. . .] military traditions of the Russian people', encouraging participation in regional and town commemorative events. The transfer of the war myth to the younger generation at school also takes place through a variety of other mechanisms: history lessons; a series of 'lessons in courage' ('*uroki muzhestva*'); dedicated class periods (*klassnye chasy*); local studies (*kraevedenie* or *Kubanovedenie*); and visits to libraries and museums, both in the school and the town.

History remains central to the school curriculum from an early age, often taught by specialists. The teaching of modern history in schools and universities has evolved over the decades since 1945, the subject of historical revisionism at the mercy of the political ideology of the state.[7] During Stalin's rule history lessons revolved around Leninist dogma and rote learning. Little was written about the war in the postwar years: archives were closed to researchers and questioning of the official version of the past was not encouraged. A subjective and dogmatic Stalinist version of the history of the war, full of distortions and omissions, finally appeared in 1963 with the publication of the multi-volume *The Great Patriotic War of the Soviet Union*. It depicted the devastating German invasion of the first few months of the war in 1941 in a less disastrous light, while also inflating the role of Stalin and the Communist Party at the expense of that of the military leaders and the Allies.[8] Party members became officially endorsed role models for young people in a string of selected exploits, reinforcing the impression of state-sponsored mythology rather than analytical history. For example, the work refers to a Komsomol member at Stalingrad who died whilst blowing up nine tanks,[9] an exploit similar to that of young Viktor Chalenko on Malaia zemlia. Some attempted revisionism and a cautious attempt at historical accuracy in Khrushchev's thaw of the early 1960s was followed by the intellectual conservatism and neo-Stalinism of the Brezhnev era. Aleksandr Nekrich's work of 1965, *1941, 22 iiunia* (*22 June 1941: Soviet Historians and the German Invasion*), was officially condemned and the author expelled from the Communist Party in 1967. An increase in censorship during the 1970s led to further clamp-downs on revisionist historians who had allegedly gone too far in the pursuit of historical accuracy.[10]

No wonder that oral memory was considered by some to be more accurate than that propagated by the state, a situation that is the opposite of that generally accepted in the West, but is still observed in Russia.[11] In general official memory had been so shaped by the narratives provided by their leaders that accounts of the war depended largely on mythology rather than accurate historical evidence until the Gorbachev years. An increase in interest in history in the mass media of the late 1980s, when previously taboo topics were gradually opened up to historical *glasnost'*, led to a plethora of revelations from 1988 to 1991.[12] Gorbachev himself appeared to encourage such openness about history:

> We have studied it, admitting miscalculations and mistakes, and learning lessons even from the difficult and tragic periods of our history. For us it is not acceptable to smooth out history. It already exists. And it is only a matter of showing it correctly. It is a matter of our honesty, responsibility and scientific approach.[13]

This new official attitude resulted in the evolution of a more questioning society after the fall of the Soviet Union in 1991. It remained short-lived, however. Igor Dolutskii's particularly influential anti-Stalinist, anti-communist school history textbook *Otechestvennaia istoriia XX vek* (*History of the Fatherland in the Twentieth Century*) was published in 1994, only to be removed from the Ministry of Education's list of approved books in 2003 following criticism of its less than positive treatment of the Great Patriotic War. Overseeing a return to state officialdom in history, Putin himself intervened in the discussions, demanding that school textbooks should help imbue patriotism amongst the young in the interests of social solidarity. After Dolutskii's extreme anti-Soviet work, more positive assessments were demanded in a textbook competition administered by the Ministry of Education, resulting in the publication of a new national favourite in 2007, Nikita Zagladin's *Istoriia Otechestva. XX vek* (*Twentieth Century History of the Fatherland*). Although Zagladin's previous work on global history, *Istoriia Rossi i mira v XX veke*, had continued the theme of the anti-Stalinism of the 1990s, his new prize-winning text failed to condemn the Soviet Union outright for its weaknesses during the war, choosing rather to recognise its successes in a more balanced and analytical style, more acceptable to a society looking for a sense of pride in their recent history.[14]

There is now one authorised history textbook used widely in Russia, including in senior classes in Novorossiisk schools. This book promotes an 'official' view of the past, nurturing a sense of national pride in Russian history. It seems to have a more balanced judgment on the strategic importance of Novorossiisk in the context of the whole war, by mentioning it briefly and only once, in a list of towns liberated in September 1943, as part of a chapter on the Great Patriotic War covering 43 pages.[15]

This uncontroversial textbook contrasts with another history book by A.V. Veka, which, according to one bookshop assistant, is popular in the town, if not used in schools.[16] This work, although making no mention at all of Novorossiisk, includes decidedly negative comments about Stalin, for example his absence from the centre of power in the first days of the war and his notorious 'Not one step back' order.[17] In complete contrast to the hype of Victory Day in Russia today, Veka attributes war victory to the Soviet people rather than to Stalin or his generals. Similarly treated are the controversial penal battalions (*shtrafnye batal'ony*) to which 'cowards and traitors' were dispatched, despite what the author deems the equally incompetent actions of their leaders.[18] This is an aspect of the war which some of my respondents wished to see fully exposed and dissected in the media, probably following a popular television series, *Shtrafbat*, aired in 2004, which prompted wide discussion and a wish to 'learn the truth' about the past.[19] The current vogue for national introspection appears to be in complete contrast to Stalin's fear of historical accuracy.

A whole spectrum of publications exists today, ranging from this example to the most conservative texts lauding the country's successes throughout and supporting the triumphal nationalism disseminated by Putin in his construction of a victorious continuity from the past through to the present. Exposés of the past may surface in some more liberal publications, but these are read largely by adults who grew up in the 1990s rather than by schoolchildren today. Historical revisionism during the Putin era has led to some overgeneralisation of events of the war in schools, such that children are socialised politically not to question in detail the accepted message of a victorious nation.

Works that counter the state-sponsored version have suffered since 2014, when a controversial law condemning the propagation of 'false' history came into force. As a result, books on World War II by military historian Antony Beevor have been removed from some regional libraries, accused of spreading a pro-Nazi message by his detailed examination of the role of Soviet troops.[20] It may be politically useful to disseminate a more generalised history when a detailed narrative risks detracting from the accepted war myth. *Novorossiiskii rabochii* actually bemoans the lack of specific information in modern school textbooks, appreciating that it is only because the town is a hero city that the myth is so strong and schools are able constructively to supplement the official books with solid local background.[21] Teacher Albina concurs that more concrete facts about the war are taught now than previously. Perhaps in Novorossiisk the myth of Malaia zemlia is so positive that it bears more detailed scrutiny in school lessons than many other local war myths. However, there is a potential danger of too close an examination of a myth that is so entwined with local identity. This myth is needed for a stable society and is increasingly likely to be defended robustly. Those questioning such widely accepted myths as the siege of Leningrad and even other blatantly propagandised Soviet war myths are simply not welcome in Novorossiisk: 'Don't mess with our history!', warns the local newspaper on the eve of Beskozyrka.[22] This recent vehement attack on revisionism gets to the core of the real issue: Don't mess with our identity!

Here there is little evidence of the degree of historical amnesia observed in the capital, where there is a distinct lack of engagement with the past on the part of the younger generation.[23] While my observations show evidence for the continuation of the local myth in provincial Novorossiisk, Catherine Merridale observes in the larger cities a clear generation gap, with older people recalling, albeit at some temporal distance, the 'dismal days of fake heroes and bogus achievements', while the younger generation demonstrates almost no understanding of the situation in which their parents were raised.[24] Merridale argues robustly that a lack of knowledge of the past breeds a failure to read any warning signs of a potential new dictatorship, a situation of collective amnesia which may in some ways suit the country's ruling elite. This insight suggests that a return to the domination of top-down manipulation of memory may flourish in the face of public apathy, linked to uncertainty about the constantly changing interpretations of the past.[25] From my findings in Novorossiisk, however, the state war cult is thriving not in the face of public apathy, but fuelled rather by a local self-interest in the promotion of the war myth, which boosts the status of the town regionally and nationally and inculcates a sense of pride which is passed on to the younger generation.

This pride is propagated also by school lessons in courage, which foster, by their very name, a positive genetic concept of military prowess. They concentrate on local patriotism in the war through films, seminars, essays and competitions. These lessons are mainly held during periods of the academic year when commemorative events take place locally, for example during January in the approach to Beskozyrka, leading up to Victory Day in May, and around the anniversary of the town's liberation in September. Starting in a narrow context, where the youngest pupils learn to 'love their small Motherland', the syllabus aims to develop military-patriotic consciousness through an appreciation of the local war myth. Children of all ages are taken on guided tours of the town's monuments; watch educational films on the history of Novorossiisk;[26] learn about the heroes of Malaia zemlia; read books about the war; build up exhibitions of memorabilia and literature, often collected from home; meet with former pupils now serving in the armed forces or as military cadets in the Maritime Academy and veterans of the war in Afghanistan; and take part in class competitions to produce creative work on the war theme.

There are no official textbooks in Novorossiisk for these lessons in courage, in contrast to the situation in the hero cities of Moscow and Volgograd. Although material suitable for the whole age spectrum is suggested in recommended lesson plans, the choice and delivery is largely left to the discretion of the individual class teacher. There is inevitably some repetition of material from year to year with the inherent risk of boredom amongst the older pupils, although one teacher at School Number 28 was praised by the town's official online news site for getting the pupils to use 'innovative technology' through the compilation of their own PowerPoint presentations.[27] This proactive approach appears, however, to be the exception rather than the rule in the face of the usual more didactic material.

A more personal approach is realised through the visit of local veterans to schools in a renewal of the Brezhnev-era system, when veterans would go into the classrooms on special commemorative occasions.[28] Only veterans of the Great Patriotic War are involved in such 'meetings of generations', which are often also held in local libraries, sometimes with specific aims formulated by the local authority's youth department as in the Skype conference with Volgograd. This practice allows a confluence of living generations that should, in theory, be more effective at propagating the war myth than films or books, although the age of the veterans today means that their presence is largely symbolic. There is evidence that veterans still welcome the experience of transmitting their memories to the younger generation; they may even find it easier to talk to unknown young people than to their own families. However, offering the same clichéd stories as in previous years, they may find it hard to make themselves heard or understood across what in reality is an almost insurmountable generation gap. While appreciating the importance of such meetings, teachers realise that veterans' narratives can fail to resonate with some pupils, particularly less than conscientious boys, who may be more attracted to war films depicting young men closer in age to themselves.

I have found that aspects of the patriotism syllabus that may be more effective include those where the young people have some control of the situation and are able to make their own choices. This applies across the age range; for example, one eight-year-old child became absorbed in a project on Malaia zemlia about which he had written three whole pages, while teenager Nikita had written a longer essay on his computer about Brezhnev's memoirs, demonstrating a notable exception to his peers in his interest.

Students at the Maritime Academy and the Moscow Institute for Economics and the Humanities also follow courses on local history, which remain largely popular, according to senior academics, such that some modules on Malaia zemlia are also broadcast on local television.[29] Unlike the school curriculum, local war history is set in the context of the whole of World War II in Maritime Academy courses on twentieth-century history. The head of the Faculty of History and Philosophy finds that about 50 per cent of student cadets choose to write essays or dissertations on Malaia zemlia, some of whom go on to write doctoral theses on related subjects. Not all students are equally motivated, however: apparently a minority demonstrates no real interest in local history, although Dr Denisov contends that it is the duty of the faculty to counteract any indifference. This is done partly by an emphasis on personal links, despite the fact that this area of history is becoming increasingly abstract, as family members who participated in the war have died and students are no longer able to discuss at first hand their roles in the war. The Maritime Academy has a policy of inviting cadets to do family research and to bring family photographs into the academy, where a substantial display of enlarged images was mounted in the entrance hall in 2010 to mark the sixty-fifth anniversary of Victory Day.

The linking of influences from both family and educational institutions is particularly effective in the transmission of memory. The onus is on the young people in both schools and the Maritime Academy to collect photographs, memoirs, letters and other artefacts, such that they have nominal responsibility for the propagation of the war myth, if actually required to do so by their teachers. The act of collection of such mnemonic material also prompts discussions in the home about the past, serving to revive family history at the instigation of the younger generation, another example of reverse propagation. The information collected by schoolchildren is either displayed for all to see, uploaded onto internet websites collating such data, or used as material for classroom presentation. By means of digital technology, old family photographs and other documents may be refreshed and brought to a wider audience, especially those parents of older classes invited into school to observe some lessons in courage.

In the past, a stark division between academic and popular history has been observed in Russia.[30] In today's schools and universities in Novorossiisk, however, there seems to be a greater merging of the two, as personal family stories are integrated into class history lessons. The aim of the syllabus 'to strengthen the role of the family in patriotic education' is apparently achieved through children taking home ideas from school and then returning with more information gathered from discussions within the family which may be shared with their peers to stimulate further collaborative study. This personal approach permits the incorporation of the individual family's history into the myth, enabling the construction of a unique bank of material in each school in the area. Information about family participants in the war may also be deposited in a growing number of nationally available online 'memory books', such as that linked to the Immortal Regiment movement, whose creation is probably prompted both by a fear of forgetting and the political environment of the war cult, while offering a site where more specific memory may be held in a largely uncensored environment.[31] Having captured huge numbers of testimonies, these memory banks, constructed from below and eminently accessible through the medium of modern technology attractive to the younger generation, may be seen by young people as more truthful, if more complex and multi-voiced, than the one-dimensional official war myth. Similarly, students often have internet access to information from other countries, leaving them with the difficult unfiltered decision of what information to trust.

Digital school archives complement the collections in school museums, which focus on specifically local material. Unlike English school archives, which often maintain a list of alumni who fell in the war, they largely contain artefacts collected in the immediate area. For example, the museum in School Number 27 in Myskhako was opened in 2007 thanks to the parent of a pupil who wished to have a space for his finds while conducting searches in the vicinity, whereas the museum in the Maritime Academy was created by *Shkhunatik* Galina Krympokha as a repository for records of the 'Shkhuna rovesnikov'.[32] Furthermore, the administrative head of Myskhako is planning a new museum there to cater for the increasing numbers of visitors to the village who are interested in its war history.

Schools also have their own small libraries, but the 19 public libraries in and around Novorossiisk work closely with teachers, especially with regard to the delivery of lessons in courage. Teachers sometimes walk their classes to the closest library for special occasions to make use of the better facilities and resources, and librarians sometimes go into schools to deliver lessons on the war. For example, a lesson in courage entitled 'Thanks to the heroes who died in battle' was delivered by librarians in School Number 11, while children in School Number 26 had a lesson in their local library called 'Let's meet by the Eternal Flame'.[33] Similarly, the patriotism syllabus for the Bekar School refers to library presentations such as 'The young heroes of Novorossiisk' and 'The streets of Novorossiisk are named after them'. The latter topic is seen as significant by librarians, as, through their children, it teaches newcomers to the town about the heroes of the past through the geography of the present in a further example of reverse propagation.

Schools similarly send children to the libraries to conduct independent research on local history, although one young respondent claimed never to have set foot inside a library during his school years. The role of libraries in the propagation of the war myth was welcomed by some parents: Klavdiya, for example, appreciated the gift by the children's library to seven-year-olds of different books on local war history that they could exchange with their class-mates. This type of education is important, according to librarians, because a survey conducted by the Novorossiisk Historical Association indicates that today's young people tend not to read many books, relying mainly on films, television and the internet for information. In response, the Novorossiisk central library has created a small cinema and a large audio-visual room, where I observed a group of Cossack cadets watching a film about Beskozyrka. On a smaller scale, the community library in Myskhako has a computer linked to a large screen, gifted by the councillor for Myskhako, which is suitable for group presentations on war history. A history club for young people also holds meetings in the central library and a catalogue of war-related works suitable for children has been posted on the central library's website in an attempt to attract younger readers to the library.[34]

Furthermore, one large room in the central library is devoted to *kraevedenie* (local area studies).[35] Rooted in the region, this subject has become increasingly important in the twenty-first century, probably viewed as a more humanistic antidote to the new post-Soviet history texts, which may have been deemed either too general or too negative in their revelations about the war. Librarians collate photograph albums and newspaper cuttings about the Novorossiisk area to cater for the research interests of students and the delivery of school lessons on the locality. Kraevedenie is also part of the school patriotism syllabus, if largely in a peaceful style. With its emphasis on cultural and environmental geography, it situates the Malaia zemlia campaign within the immediate area, reinforcing children's patriotic identification with this relatively small geographical area and highlighting the interconnectedness of a sense of place with the topography of Novorossiisk, its environment and the urban and political landscape.

There may be no alternative for young people *but* to remember, based on the substantial content of the patriotism syllabus in schools and the equivalent emphasis on local history in the institutions of higher education. However, the patriotic education of young people is not restricted to the classroom: perhaps the most noticeable role of schoolchildren and students in the town is their attendance at ceremonies of remembrance under the auspices of their educational establishments. It is expected by the local authorities that children from the Bekar School perform in a town concert for veterans just before the Beskozyrka ceremony, while most schools take members of older classes to the ritual itself. Schoolchildren are similarly expected by both the state and the local authorities to attend the traditional ritual at Heroes' Square early on 9 May. At the eternal flame the headmistress of School Number Six reads Robert Rozhdestvenskii's poem 'Requiem' before the playing of Shostakovich's *Novorossiisk Chimes* and the official minute's silence, after which the generations are united in their respect for the dead as children and veterans lay flowers together. Families also take children of all ages to the Victory Day commemorations, just as in the Brezhnev era, although Boris suggested that there is no longer a duty to attend. Aleksei recalled being dressed in a sailor suit on Victory Day in the 1960s. Nothing much seems to have changed in this respect: young boys and girls nowadays are sometimes dressed up in wartime soldiers' uniforms, while their parents can buy a Soviet-era military cap (*pilotka*) to wear for the day. Young children are present with their parents in both the town centre and in Myskhako, although lone teenagers are more common in the centre of Novorossiisk than in rural Myskhako. This is a probable reflection of the greater buzz and more dynamic activities in the town centre, where teenagers and young adults say they are are attracted by the Victory Day procession with its increasing quantities of military hardware, in a provincial replication of the impressive column of tanks and rockets that thunders over Moscow's Red Square, leading to a sense of nationalistic pride.

The most obvious participation of schoolchildren in rituals, however, is their standing on guard duty at war memorials – the so-called 'guard of memory' ('*vakhta pamiati*') – a nationwide tradition dating from the Soviet era.[36] While most monuments have their guard on Victory Day only, the eternal flame has a constant daytime squad of older pupils drawn from local schools. This tradition, dating from the height of the Brezhnev-era war cult, is known as 'Post No. 1', reflecting the special significance of the place where the tomb of the heroes of Malaia zemlia is located on Heroes' Square. This ritual was inaugurated in 1975, the year following Brezhnev's visit to Novorossiisk, by veteran naval captain Vitalii Lesik, with the support of the Communist Party and Komsomol Gorkom.[37] Nowadays, however, the tradition is facilitated and funded by the town council through its department of culture, which also provides uniforms for the young guards.

According to interviewees Elvira, Albina and Aleksei, some parents recall with nostalgia their own stints of guard duty from their youth and appreciate a constructive activity provided by the state for their children which replicates the values of the older generations. Welcoming this aspect of *vospitanie* for her children, Alisa proudly watches and photographs them. For different reasons, the young people themselves appear content to take part in this ritual, regarding selection for the duty as an honour. Nikita, in particular, was not unhappy to miss school for a few days and actively enjoyed the chance to strut around the square armed with an automatic rifle.

Composed originally from Komsomol or Young Pioneer members, the guard of 'living memory' is now fulfilled by 20 schoolchildren, ten boys and ten girls aged 14 to 16, who have a whole week off school for their turn in the duty roster, involving 1,900 young people annually drawn from most schools in the town. The tradition is so longstanding – the only one in the region to continue during the 1990s – that it now commemorates not only the heroes of Malaia zemlia, but also former *postovtsy* (the people who stand on military guard) who died in Afghanistan or Chechnia. In an almost unchanging continuation of the Soviet tradition, the young guards wear naval uniform and take a solemn oath, a reminder of that made by the *Malozemel'tsy* prior to the landings:

> As I start my guard duty at Post No. 1 by the flame of eternal glory, I solemnly swear to be worthy to the end of my days of the memory of the heroes who gave their lives in the battles for the fatherland!
>
> I swear to hold my weapons in my hands as firmly as did Tsezar' Kunikov and Nikolai Sipiagin, defenders of the Hero City of Novorossiisk![38]

Previous *postovtsy* include influential members of the local community, including the Deputy Director of the Maritime Academy and current town councillors, who have an inherent wish to retain the tradition. In this way a self-propagating mechanism for the intergenerational maintenance of memory is effected, which is endorsed by schools, parents and young people.

For decades Captain Lesik taught groups of young people how to march and hold their rifles, presenting the official face of the town to important visitors and foreign delegations as he patrolled his territory on Heroes' Square until well past his ninetieth birthday. Both the ritual and its leader have apparently built up their own myth over the years: Lesik is an honoured citizen of Novorossiisk and Post No. 1 appears in school lessons of patriotism, stimulating creative work by pupils, such as the acrostic poem composed collaboratively by a group of children for the sixty-fifth anniversary of Victory Day.[39] Praising Lesik for his *vospitanie* of *postovtsy*, the poem sites him at the centre of Heroes' Square. Although he is an integral part of Post No. 1, the local authorities recently felt the need to install two deputies to work alongside Lesik, to ensure provision for succession and the continuity of this tradition, which places the young generation at the heart of the memorial identity of the town.

Not all the activities for children are organised under the auspices of the school or family, however. Those without families live in social institutions, which are also included in the official memory campaign. Children from an orphanage near Myskhako are taken with veterans on trips to war monuments, led by the village youth worker and the head of the Veterans' Council. In a similar fashion, coachloads of children from sanatoria in Gelendzhik are taken to visit the main Malaia zemlia monument on the sea shore. Furthermore, Oleg, a man in his late sixties, organises hiking and orienteering tours for teenagers from other regions to sites of memorial interest in the rugged hinterland of Malaia zemlia. Although this may be seen by some as 'dark tourism' for children,[40] its proponents argue for increasing historical understanding in what may also be an emotional experience that promotes cross-generational empathy while offering days out in the fresh air.

Monumental tourism is nothing new: trips for children to famous war sites were led by the Red Pathfinders, an organisation founded by the Komsomol and the army in 1965. The *Vsesoiuznyi pokhod molodezhi dorogami otsov-geroev* (Pan-Union Youth March along the Routes of our Heroic Fathers) encouraged Komsomol ratification of young people's activities at sites of special wartime interest. According to Tumarkin, teenagers also took part in search activities, collecting military artefacts, while occasionally finding soldiers' remains.[41] Search work was started in a coordinated fashion in 1960 and children still seem to be interested in this type of activity, organised in Myskhako by School Number 27. The teenage searchers themselves sometimes take part in the re-interments of any human remains, marching alongside the coffins and giving a final rifle salute. This participation is apparently voluntary, as testified by a short film made by local schoolchildren of one such ceremony in 2008.[42] The continuation of both monumental tourism and search activities well into the twenty-first century demonstrates a further, if sometimes necessary, continuity with the Soviet past, while also indicative of the apparent need still to complete the perceived duty of exhumation, identification and re-interment of the fallen.

If the state, according to the Bekar School syllabus for patriotism, wishes to combat disaffection amongst youth, it is clearly successful judging by the actions of the pupils of School Number 27. The attitude they display to fallen soldiers in their amateur video appears very different from that of the young men in the opening scenes of the film *We are from the Future*, whose cynicism about human remains was highlighted as they searched the bodies for marketable items. These youths were portrayed as examples of the extreme right-wing nationalism which has surfaced in Russia over the last two decades, particularly among young people, sometimes skinheads, epitomised by the *Pamiat'* (Memory) group with its black shirts typical of a neo-fascist, often anti-Semitic ideology.[43]

Although five respondents pointed to the growth of neo-fascism in major cities, my research in Novorossiisk uncovered a little but no overwhelming evidence of disaffection in regard to the war myth on the part of young people. Indeed, seven respondents across the age spectrum declared that it was impossible for children in the hero city of Novorossiisk to question the need for patriotism. Even young adults Misha, Polina and Yuliya stated that, although disaffection may exist elsewhere, there could be no dissent or disrespect for remembrance in Novorossiisk, while Boris, a veteran of Afghanistan, declared that 'people like that could only exist on another planet'. Older respondents

Zinaida and Lyudmila felt that, if young people were not interested in the war, it was simply the result of poor teaching, shifting the responsibility for any apathy towards the war myth on the part of young people onto the education system. Elderly Leonid roundly blamed the parents for a poor upbringing, reminiscent of the verdict handed down by the judge in the case of the young twerkers of Malaia zemlia.

Some isolated incidents of vandalism around the war graves in Myskhako have also been observed. This, though, is definitely the exception rather than the rule. The notable lack of disaffection on the part of the young may partly be due to the efforts of families, educational institutions and the town council, largely members of Putin's United Russia party, which actively promotes the war cult. Young people are also the subject of a wider state campaign to mobilise youth in the cause of nationalism. For example, the pro-Kremlin nationalist youth movement, *Nashi* (Our People), was formed in time for Victory Day in 2005 to encourage patriotism, probably by no coincidence in the same year that the St George ribbon movement was first seen on the streets. These top-down intitiatives to mass produce patriotic young people were introduced partly as a response to the perceived threat of a potential rebellion in Russia similar to the 2004 Orange Revolution in Ukraine. By its very name, *Nashi* promoted unity of attitude to both the country and the state, whilst also provoking some feelings of xenophobia to those foreigners who were not 'ours'. In an attempt to foster model citizens of the future, young *Nashi* members were encouraged, just like their Komsomol predecessors in the Soviet Union, to engage in civil activities and projects, often validated by their link to the war, for example giving presents to veterans.[44]

If veterans are exploited by the state for their political capital, then the younger student generation appears also to be deployed strategically to drum the rest of the population into the desired quasi-military order, a tactic sometimes attributed to *Nashi* activists before this authoritarian, anti-Western movement was disbanded in 2012. The *Nashi* summer camp for young people aged from 18 to 30 organised annually at Lake Seliger continued to be run until 2014 by *Rosmolodezh*, the Federal Agency for Youth Affairs. Reminiscent of the Komsomol camps of the Soviet period, it promoted both patriotism and service in the armed forces in what appeared to be a training camp for the leaders of tomorrow. With its own eternal flame and links to elite regiments, it

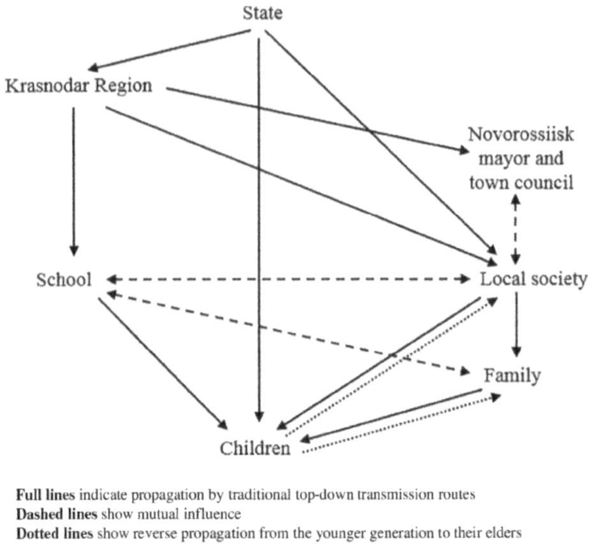

Figure 15.1 Hierarchical Diagram of Agencies Involved in the Propagation of the War Myth

reproduced in the twenty-first century the military-patriotic work prevalent in the Komsomol in the latter stages of the Soviet Union. This national initiative was replaced in 2015 by a series of regional gatherings around similar themes. One of the first took political advantage of a southern site in the sun in the newly-annexed Crimea, although the momentum of the original Seliger camp was somewhat diluted.[45]

Despite some evidence of local disaffection in Novorossiisk due perhaps to a lack of family interest or right-wing extremism, Councillor Andrievskii is optimistically convinced that, with the continuing conservative emphasis on *vospitanie* of the young citizens of Novorossiisk, the upcoming generation will continue to uphold and propagate the war myth. In general, my observations and responses from interviewees support the attitude that Novorossiisk has a special identity with respect to remembrance in comparison with other regional centres, which will probably override any potential disengagement among its young for years to come.

The cross-generational propagation of the war myth to the young depends on the mutual reinforcement of a complex and closed social network. The hierarchical diagram (Figure 15.1) shows the influence of the various agencies involved, highlighting the driving force of the state in its cultivation of the new war cult under the Putin regime, which feeds down directly via the mass media and indirectly via the regional and town authorities to the younger generation. Dating from the early years of the Beskozyrka ritual, young people have played a key role in the transmission of the war myth. Parents may even learn aspects of the war myth from their children through the largely unplanned mechanism of reverse propagation. This not only reinforces the traditional propagation mechanism, but also unifies the generations in commemorative practices. This is a tendency that may increasingly result in future mnemonic stagnation, apparently a desired product of the sponsors of the war cult today.

I have disclosed a mixture of top-down and bottom-up mechanisms for propagation of the war myth, where the state, school and family play the most important roles in socialisation of the young. Young people are subjected to a concerted mnemonic campaign which is successful in most cases, although resisted by some. The most ubiquitous means of transmission is the school, the nexus for other multiple influences, where propagation is most effective when it fosters the proactivity of students of all ages, and joins with the family to render lessons on local history more personal and geographically relevant for pupils. Attempts by some educational institutions to digitise memory appear also to make it more appealing to young people. Furthermore, my evidence suggests that the most effective methods of cross-generational transmission of memory are those that reduce the temporal and spatial distance between older and younger generations with the vividness of film or war reconstructions.

My interviews show that many modern citizens of Novorossiisk are avid consumers of television and newspaper revelations of the 'truth' about the war period, revealing a change in transmission mechanism from the oral propagation of the postwar years and the state-sponsored narrative of the Brezhnev and Putin war cults. Although access to information is changing, respondents indicate a continuing reliance on informal family discussions, although eye-witness testimony is now scarcely viable. For the moment both the state and the family remain guardians of memory, while the local authority takes responsibility for the custody of the many artefacts that will replace direct oral propagation in the future.

Through their youth policy, covering both formal education and special projects such as summer camps, the Putin and Medvedev governments have managed to unify many thousands of young people as a political force to project the state's desired nationalistic image. With a renewed emphasis on *vospitanie* and patriotism under the Putin regime, the youngest and the oldest generations are increasingly united in often contrived social meetings – a forum for the transmission of memory under the conditions of a new war cult that aims to revive the traditional moral values of the Brezhnev era. This includes the cultivation of an attitude which regards military service and patriotic courage in a positive light, where making war (successfully) is valued and those not willing actively to endorse the war myth are frowned upon by society.

CONCLUSION

LOOKING BACK TO THE FUTURE

> Many, many years may pass – decades, centuries, but memory of the exploit of the *Malozemel'tsy* will live on in the hearts of their descendants.[1]

A new war film hit Russian cinema screens in late 2016, strongly endorsed by President Putin. *28 panfilovtsev* (*Panfilov's 28*) tells the story of a handful of outnumbered Red Army soldiers who make a stand against a German tank battalion closing in on Moscow in November 1941.[2] In an heroic act of self-sacrifice, they destroy 18 tanks while paying the ultimate price. This is a new version of the 1967 film *Za nami Moskva* (*Moscow is Behind Us*), which appeared during the war cult of the Brezhnev years.[3] Still popular at the height of the Putin-era war cult, *Panfilov's 28* is overtly supportive of the national war myth, painted in black and white with its unquestionable heroes martyred in the defence of the Fatherland in the face of the fiendish enemy threatening its very existence.

The film retells the story of an exploit which was widely reported during the war to boost the morale of the population. Like Malaia zemlia, this local myth was so powerful that it was taught in school history lessons in the postwar years. Streets and towns were named after the heroic riflemen, monuments were erected to them and books written about them. Its heroes became a legend. This is the reason given by writer and director Andrei Shal'opa for wanting to make the film in the first place. However, during the lengthy filming process, archival evidence came to light suggesting that, although such a skirmish had indeed taken place, not all the Soviet soldiers had died. It appears that the encounter had been mythologised at the time thanks to an exaggerated report by *Krasnaia zvezda* war correspondent Vasilii Koroteev.[4] Although Koroteev was probably doing his duty within the unspoken guidelines of the times to seek out examples of Soviet heroism in order to boost public morale, an investigation in 1948 into the incident proved that the whole affair had been wildly over-inflated. The findings of the investigation were, however, suppressed by the authorities in order to maintain the popular myth that had by then developed.[5] The parallels with the hyped-up Soviet myth of Malaia zemlia are obvious.

Fast forward to today, when transparency is still apparently an issue. Shal'opa protested against mounting criticism of the resurrected myth by attacking those who seek to debunk instances of accepted national heroism, which in his view only serves 'to weaken the people's moral foundation'.[6] According to the director, it is dangerous to pull the carpet out from under this widespread myth, a mainstay of Russian cultural heritage and the nation's identity. Although Shal'opa recognises that the action is not strictly speaking historically true, he claims that the basic facts remain relevant: that the incident actually took place and real, heroic people definitely died.[7] Accordingly, he has creatively reworked this longstanding myth along the lines of a David and Goliath encounter, using it to explore the nature of idealised patriotism as the state currently wishes to see it disseminated.

Despite its much-vaunted discrepancies, many Russians still buy into this emotive myth. The film was funded in several ways, indicative of the appetite for this type of material across the board. A very successful crowd funding operation proved that the film resonates with those who are comfortable using the internet to consume their culture. Like *We are from the Future*, this blockbuster is aimed at younger viewers and also received funding from an internet gaming company. Finally, state sponsorship and endorsement by the president and minister of culture demonstrate its utility in developing Russian national pride today.[8]

The production of this film demonstrates that unashamed myth making still has a place in modern Russia, which is actively promoting the positive side of its history to motivate and cement its population in the present. Alongside the huge interest in patriotic films, a new statue to Vladimir the Great has appeared next to the Kremlin in Moscow.[9] As the new monument was unveiled, President Putin urged

Russians to unite against external threats, to become once again the victorious nation led by his namesake over a thousand years ago. State rhetoric has thus moved on from the Soviet era with a noticeable shift in emphasis in the twenty-first century from simply remembering the war, its heroes and victims, to a focus on the celebration of victory firmly linked to national pride. Under the current memorial climate, the war has become both an existential narrative of Russia's national identity and a metaphor for national unity as, more than ever, the state is once again staking a firm claim to ownership of the war cult.

In Novorossiisk, this state-centric grip on the war myth is much in evidence, backed up by the mayor and the local authorities who organise the cycle of annual rituals. Just as in the case of the crowd funders of *Panfilov's 28*, though, the myth of Malaia zemlia also belongs to the ordinary people of Novorossiisk – in their families and schools and at ceremonies of remembrance. This book has uncovered the distinctiveness of mythology in the Soviet Union and contemporary Russia and the true complexity at work in the construction and propagation of a local war myth by exposing the human perspective of remembrance in addition to the much-flaunted ideology of a superpower.

There has always been much genuine reinforcement between top-down and bottom-up memorial initiatives in Novorossiisk, although the war cult of the Brezhnev era still left some scope for individual remembrance and the local dimension. In the twenty-first century, however, there remains some tension between perceived 'genuine' and 'designer' memory, with some proactivity and spontaneity of remembrance activities confirming the significance of the bottom-up agency of small groups and individuals. Most divergence from the official myth or mode of remembrance is to be found on the edge of the town, on the periphery of accepted memory, where the authorities are sometimes challenged and the emphasis is on the individuals remembering and remembered rather than on passive acceptance of a myth propagated from above.

The myth of Malaia zemlia has had a chequered journey from its inception in 1943 through its heyday in the Brezhnev era to today. Following a series of complicated twists and turns, the identity of the hero city has developed within an evolving memorial environment. This has been rendered even more complex thanks to the dubious presence in and huge influence on the myth of Leonid Brezhnev. This inherited problem has been resolved for the moment with the erection and relocation of the Brezhnev statue, as the general secretary has found his new memorial niche. Novorossiisk seems more at ease with its own history now that it has been reclaimed from the shadow of Brezhnev's political ownership. While a few grey corners still await closer scrutiny, the accepted local myth remains as black and white as the film about Panfilov's regiment.

With this new sense of ownership of their town's identity, many citizens of Novorossiisk feel a responsibility for the propagation of a myth which is perceived to be good for the moral education of the younger generation. In comparison with war memory in the West it is perhaps surprising that so many young people buy into the myth. However, Russia has seen a campaign of patriotism in the twenty-first century, with a focus through the school curriculum on the younger generation who will, in the future, bear the responsibility for remembrance. In this way, perhaps, the Russian government has led the way where other Western states are only just starting to educate their children to follow.

Today's myth is a powerful social construction, founded under Stalinism and propagated under communism, while remaining strong in modern Russia. Virtually every living participant may be dead, and many of the postwar generation too, but the myth lives on successfully. This longevity is due to the undeniably positive narrative and proactive attempts to rejuvenate commemorative rituals. The sheer resonance of the myth with generations of citizens of Novorossiisk is clear from my research, underlined by the inter-connectedness in the hero city of a sense of historic place with the urban and political landscape.

Despite an element of legend, today's myth of Malaia zemlia is based largely on indisputable fact, supported by increasing quantities of historical minutiae. Novorossiisk is forging a successful relationship with its Soviet history, which is effective for the town by virtue of its largely unchallengeable nature. Thanks to its local significance and the unique Beskozyrka ritual, citizens seem content to adopt the myth and proud of their cultural and military heritage. In this respect, Novorossiisk represents an extreme case, where the desire for continued local war memory coincides with the national position on the transmission of memory, assuring the maintenance of the hero city's own special identity and status.

So what of the future? In contrast with Brezhnev's legacy, the war cult of the Putin era is not centred on the alleged exploits of one man, nor is

Putin as frail as the elderly Brezhnev in his final years. Both these facts render the contemporary war cult potentially more enduring than that of the Brezhnev era, particularly as the recent conflict in Ukraine and increased tension with the West have triggered a build-up of rhetoric referring to the Great Patriotic War in the Russian media. It is not possible to predict the future of the war myth in Novorossiisk precisely, but this book has uncovered sufficient evidence to make some informed speculation. There is no reason to suppose that popular opinion will change tack with a sudden wish to forget the local history evident in museums and libraries and on the streets of the hero city. Even with a new mayor, Beskozyrka is successfully continuing after the death of Konstantin Podyma and the town has made plans for the replacement of Captain Lesik on Heroes' Square. The end of direct transmission of war memory in Novorossiisk will conclude a tradition of intergenerational meetings, but this may equally result in fewer bored pupils as students are allowed to research local history more independently. Similarly, the new Immortal Regiment ceremony seems set to continue engaging children and their families. Even as the war myth gradually evolves into local history, it retains its relevance and utility for Novorossiisk: as long as it guarantees regional prestige and a stream of tourists, it will surely be supported by the local authorities and town council.

Propagation of the myth is not merely a local initiative and it is doubtful if remembrance would be so popular if maintained in its own bubble outside the national mnemonic environment generated under the Putin government. The state's war myth has been increasingly deployed since the turn of the century to imbue self-confidence amongst Russians sometimes criticised by the West. Similarly, political authoritarianism has been gradually ramped up by a government looking to forestall any potential internal revolution, such as those occurring in neighbouring Georgia (2003) and Ukraine (2004 and 2014). The strong element of state control and centralisation under the guise of a democratic society may not be evident or even matter to the ordinary resident of Novorossiisk, who takes it for granted and sees only the local result of the national war cult that has helped to fuel the popularity of the myth of Malaia zemlia.

The main proponent of the national meta-narrative of the war is the president and the longevity of the current war cult may depend on the length of his tenure. Vladimir Putin has developed a tight emotional hold on Russia with an increasingly powerful narrative of patriotism and militarism, both referring back to war victory.[10] Since the annexation of Crimea, Putin has personally promised to build up trade in the Novorossiisk area, including the formation of a new transport hub linking the two hero cities of Novorossiisk and Sevastopol', with the development of more modern infrastructure behind Novorossiisk.[11] A new bridge linking Russia to Ukraine is being built across the Kerch' Straits – Putin is succeeding in this expensive project, where Hitler's plans in early 1943 for a five-kilometre bridge for cars and trains came to nothing.[12] In conjunction with the growing naval base in Novorossiisk, these measures should boost the local economy considerably and probably stimulate not only the maintenance of monuments but also the budget devoted to remembrance.

For the moment, though, the Russian economy continues to struggle as a result of Western sanctions, conflict in the Middle East and a weak rouble. This disruption may exacerbate the unsustainability of a national economy facing lower oil prices, and the local economy will no doubt suffer as the national embargo on some imports reduces the flow of goods through the port of Novorossiisk. The consequences could be similar to those of the 1990s, when everyday financial concerns and decreasing official budgets displaced commemoration of the war from the political agenda nationwide. If state policies and President Putin become too unpopular, both he and his war cult may themselves be consigned to history. Whatever happens in the short to medium term, the myth of Malaia zemlia is strong and stable enough to live on in Novorossiisk in the longer term as it mutates into local history. The town is moving forward, comfortable in its own skin, as the shadows of Brezhnev and the Brezhnev-era monuments remain static in the background.

APPENDIX I

SOME COMMENTS FROM CITIZENS OF NOVOROSSIISK

'Do you know, [...] I have travelled a lot in the world, but nowhere have I come across a more patriotic town than our Novorossiisk.' (Konstantin Podyma)[1]

The following comments are listed in order of subjects' age, youngest first.

'I am proud of Novorossiisk and don't want to leave it. It has a splendid role in the history of the Great Patriotic War. People gave their lives for Novorossiisk and for our opportunity to live here. We, the children, are grateful.' (Veronika)

'People in Moscow don't know where Novorossiisk is, even today, so they don't know what happened here 65 years ago; maybe they don't want to know. Perhaps it wasn't as big a battle as Stalingrad, but it played a key role. Most people remember that Brezhnev fought here and that it's a hero city. It was strategic and significant.' (Nikita)

'This is an unusual town; it is important because it was defended by lots of people. Lots of heroes were here.' (Mikhail)

'I feel pride and responsibility for the memory of those who helped our generation. Pride in those who gave their blood for the town. They gave *us* life. We like the rituals and parades on special days; this reminds us to be grateful.' (Kolya)

'Malaia zemlia has become well known in the town. It is part of the town's organism, it's a natural matter of fact, it's like asking us how important it is to have feet.' (Alina)

'We know that Novorossiisk is a special town, compared with Krasnodar; Malaia zemlia is part of the town when we have celebrations.' (Polina)

'There is a bigger sense of patriotism here, in a hero city. The whole country suffered, but there is a special attitude to hero cities. Here it is underlined by remembrance events more than in other places. It's a super town, and it is especially good to look across from the Maritime Academy to the Malaia zemlia monument.' (Elvira)

'Novorossiisk is a very significant place. I lived elsewhere, but now I like living in a hero city.' (Diana)

'I am not from around here, but now I associate myself with this town, and feel really proud to live in a hero city. There is no other hero city nearby; even Krasnodar, which is twice as big, isn't a hero city. Now I call it my own and I like it more and more as the years pass.' (Anton)

'You walk on land soaked in blood.' (Stanislav)

'I like life in a hero city. I like its history. I think everything – monuments, nature, sea, and its history – are all linked with its mighty power. I want to transmit this to the next generation.' (Nikolai)

'Living in a hero city has little significance for life today, but I feel very proud of past events.' (Nadezhda)

'Living here brings responsibility and pride.' (Oksana)

'I like this town, with its historic past, and feel a sense of pride.' (Antonina)

'You have to think about what took place here, to know about it, to be sorry for the people.' (Nina)

'This may be a military town, but the people are ordinary. Novorossiisk is just one of many. Leningrad, Stalingrad and Moscow are genuine hero cities. But of course Malaia zemlia is part of my everyday life.' (Yurii)

'I was born in the former Soviet Union and I have always known that Novorossiisk was a hero city since my childhood. The attitude of people may have changed; it's not really in the press so much now. But now I just feel respect for the town which does not depend on the fact that it's a hero city; you don't need to live here to feel respect for the fallen.' (Boris)

'This is a living place and this one place is special because this little bit of land was held. I am very proud and my son, when he was little, when we went to relatives, to other places in Russia, he always told people he lived in a hero city.' (Lidiya)

'I got married and came here in my youth, and have a feeling of pride, but I may feel the same about any other town if I lived there. We live on the exact spot where the battles took place. On the anniversary of the landings, three-quarters of the people come to honour the heroes; everyone comes: civil servants, children, residents, old people, come, and it's really cold, but people come. They talk a lot about it then. It's better to talk than to forget.' (Irina)

'Friends from some way away come to Novorossiisk, as this is a centre where memory is concentrated.' (Vera)

'I feel a responsibility, living here, as if I am the visiting card of the town. I am very proud of the local heroes and the monuments.' (Svetlana)

'I have lived here for 14 years. This is an unusual town, not simple or ordinary. Everything reminds you of the war years. There is respect for the heroes, to whom the monuments are dedicated. Your heart beats, on the streets, and especially on Malaia zemlia, where people go to relax; it's attractive, and life goes on, but memory of the past is important. But I won't swim in the sea, because the ground is sacred; we are reminded of how much blood was shed. It is a responsibility for our children, to keep the town and its streets clean and to respect memory, look after the monuments and influence personal behaviour. Malaia zemlia is part of my everyday life, as you come across all these places all the time in our town.' (Elena)

'I feel pride in my town, where there was a big battle.' (Anastasiya)

'We take memory and death so seriously, more than any other town.' (Marina)

'I have always lived here in Novorossiisk and feel a sense of responsibility. This is my personal view; it may be a small town, but this is a hero city. It was a real battle, lots of metal dropped on everyone, 1,250 kilograms per square metre, the beach-head was held, they defended the strategic gateway to the Caucasus, and stopped the Germans before they took the oil. That's the reason it's a hero city. But Novorossiisk was so small, it did not get the historic recognition it deserved.' (Aleksei)

'I like the monuments but it's not important that this is a hero city.' (Anna)

'I don't really feel a sense of responsibility for memory here.' (Zinaida)

'Of course I feel a responsibility for memory, it's my own town, so we try to maintain memory, to teach our children, as best we can. But maybe Malaia zemlia isn't part of everyday life.' (Tatyana)

'I am proud of my hero city.' (Eduard)

'I have a sense of respect and honour and some responsibility. The town was made a hero city after the victory, and each inhabitant has a feeling of responsibility and pride. It may be a small town, but it saw important events.' (Natalya)

'Maybe this isn't a real hero city because the population was not involved in the defence and the fighting.' (Dmitrii)

APPENDIX II

DETAILS OF INTERVIEW SUBJECTS

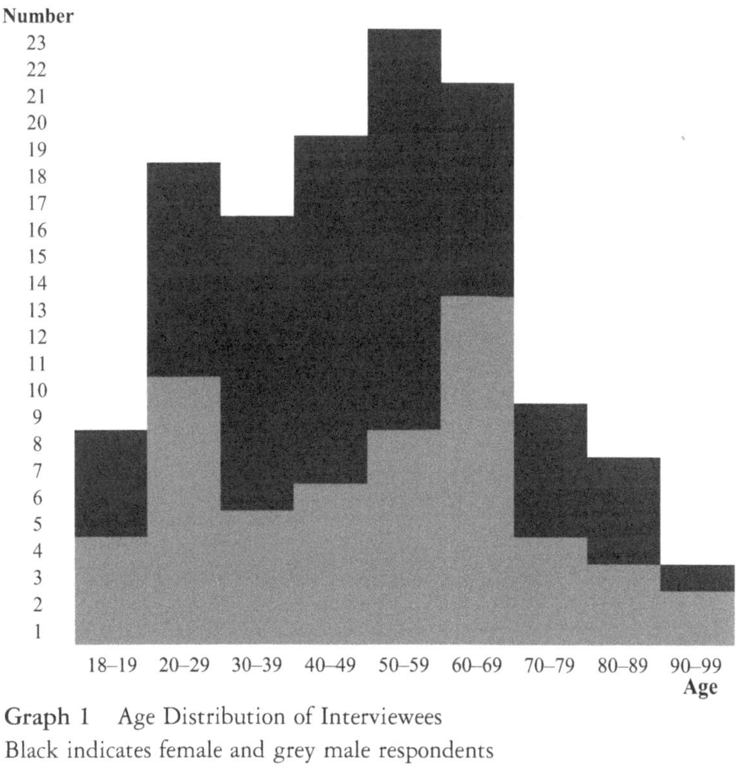

Graph 1 Age Distribution of Interviewees
Black indicates female and grey male respondents

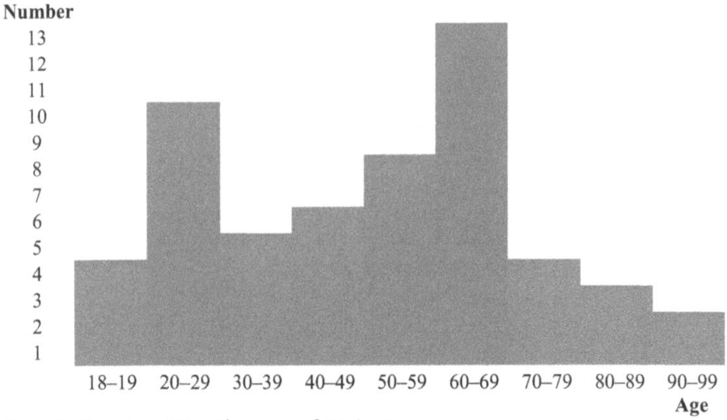

Graph 2 Age Distribution of Male Interviewees

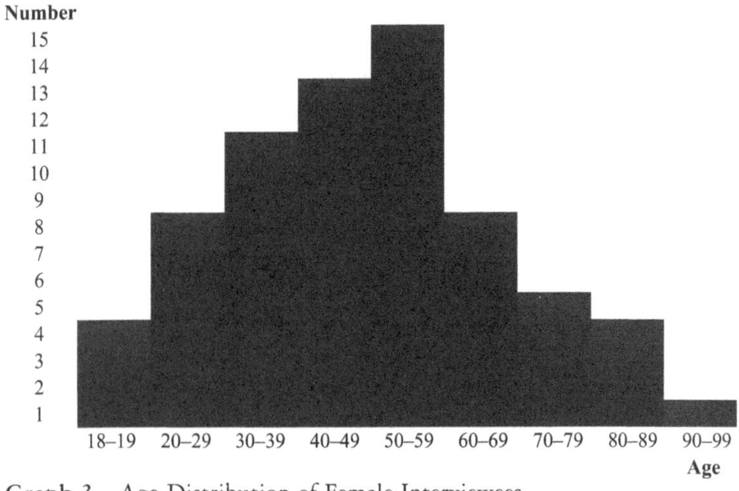

Graph 3 Age Distribution of Female Interviewees

Socio-Economic Classification of Interviewees

All 124 interviewees in Novorossiisk have been included in the statistics analysed throughout the book. During the interview process it was sometimes necessary to estimate the age of respondents. Some are mentioned by real name or position in the text. In the following list of those individual interviewees mentioned by pseudonym, socio-economic class is based on the National Readership Survey categories commonly used in market research, with an expansion of group E (the unemployed) to distinguish between students (E1), housewives (E2), and retired persons (E3). In this latter category the previous class, where known, is included in brackets.

A: higher managerial, administrative and professional occupations
B: intermediate managerial, administrative and professional occupations
C1: supervisory or clerical and junior managerial, administrative and professional occupations
C2: skilled manual occupations
D: semi-skilled and unskilled manual occupations
E1: students
E2: housewives
E3: retired persons

Table 1 Details of Interviewees Mentioned by Pseudonym

Pseudonym	Gender	Approximate age (years)	Socio-economic class
Veronika	female	18–19	E1
Nikita	male	18–19	E1
Mikhail	male	18–19	E1
Elizaveta	female	20–29	C1
Kolya	male	20–29	E1
Misha	male	20–29	C1
Maksim	male	20–29	C1
Alina	female	30–39	C1
Varvara	female	30–39	C1
Polina	female	30–39	D
Kristina	female	30–39	E2
Elvira	female	30–39	D
Diana	female	30–39	C1
Sofiya	female	30–39	C1
Yuliya	female	30–39	E2
Anton	male	30–39	B
Stanislav	male	30–39	C2
Nikolai	male	30–39	B
Erik	male	30–39	C2
Nadezhda	female	40–49	B
Albina	female	40–49	B
Alisa	female	40–49	C1

Table 1 *Continued*

Pseudonym	Gender	Approximate age (years)	Socio-economic class
Oksana	female	40–49	E2
Antonina	female	40–49	E2
Klavdiya	female	40–49	D
Nina	female	40–49	D
Kseniya	female	40–49	C1
Yurii	male	40–49	B
Boris	male	40–49	C2
Vladimir	male	40–49	C2
Lidiya	female	50–59	B
Irina	female	50–59	C1
Vera	female	50–59	A
Svetlana	female	50–59	A
Elena	female	50–59	C1
Anastasiya	female	50–59	C1
Marina	female	50–59	B
Artem	male	50–59	A
Anatolii	male	50–59	B
Aleksei	male	50–59	A
Alena	female	60–69	B
Anna	female	60–69	E3(D)
Zoya	female	60–69	E3(C1)
Zinaida	female	60–69	E3(D)
Tatyana	female	60–69	C2
Mariya	female	60–69	E3(D)
Klara	female	60–69	C1
Eduard	male	60–69	E3(D)
Viktor	male	60–69	B
Petr	male	60–69	B
Oleg	male	60–69	C1
Natalya	female	70–79	A
Lyudmila	female	70–79	C1
Sonia	female	70–79	E3(D)
Marta	female	70–79	E3
Lev	male	70–79	E3(C2)
Dmitrii	male	70–79	E3(A)
Leonid	male	70–79	E3(A)
Lyubov	female	80–89	E3(C1)
Darya	female	80–89	E3(D)
Vasilisa	female	80–89	E3(C1)
Stepan	male	90–99	E3(A)

NOTES

Notes on the Text

1. M.V. Erokhin, *Novorossiisk*, ed. D.A. Vasil'evich (Krasnodar: RIO, 2012), p. 4.
2. Vicky Davis, 'Time and tide: The Remembrance Ritual of "Beskozyrka" in Novorossiisk', *Cahiers du Monde Russe*/54 (2013), pp. 103–29; and Vicky Davis, 'Memory for Sale: Local and National Interpretations of Brezhnev's *Malaia zemlia*', in *Twentieth Century Wars in European Memory*, ed. Jozef Niznik (Frankfurt am Main: Peter Lang, 2013), pp. 135–49.

Introduction The Myth of Malaia zemlia

1. 'Lay wreaths on the sea./It is a human custom/in memory of troops who died in the sea,/lay wreaths on the sea. // Lay wreaths on the sea/to the sound of pipes and drums and sirens./Lay wreaths on the sea/made of jasmine, roses and lilacs. // Lay wreaths for Time,/we were consumed in this eternal flame./Lay wreaths on the flame/made of jasmine and white lilac.' From Andrei Voznesenskii, 'Rekviem' (1984), in Andrei Voznesenskii, *Ne otrekus'. Izbrannaia lirika* (Minsk: Beladi, 1996).
2. T.I. Iurina, *Novorossiiskoe protivostoianie: 1942–1943 gg.* (Krasnodar: Kniga, 2008), p. 230.
3. M.V. Erokhin, *Novorossiisk*, ed. D.A. Vasil'evich (Krasnodar: RIO, 2012), p. 55.
4. See notably Catherine Merridale, *Night of Stone: Death and Memory in Russia* (London: Granta Books, 2000); Amir Weiner, *Making Sense of War: The Second World War and the Fate of the Bolshevik Revolution* (Princeton, NJ: Princeton University Press, 2001); and Stephen Lovell, *The Shadow of War: Russia and the USSR, 1941 to the Present* (Chichester: Wiley-Blackwell, 2010).
5. See Zhores Medvedev, *Andropov* (Oxford: Blackwell, 1983), pp. 101–3; Nina Tumarkin, *The Living and the Dead: The Rise and Fall of the Cult of World War II*

in Russia (New York: BasicBooks, 1994), pp. 155–6; and Roi Medvedev, Politicheskie portrety (Moscow: Moskva, 2008), p. 219.

6. See notably on Kiev, Michael Ignatieff, 'Soviet War Memorials', *History Workshop Journal*/17 (1984), pp. 157–63; on Leningrad, Lisa A. Kirschenbaum, *The Legacy of the Siege of Leningrad, 1941–1995: Myth, Memories and Monuments* (Cambridge and New York: Cambridge University Press, 2006); and Alexis Peri, 'Revisiting the Past: History and Historical Memory during the Leningrad Blockade', *Soviet and Post-Soviet Review*/38 (2011), pp. 105–29; on Stalingrad, Scott Palmer, 'How Memory was Made: The Construction of the Memorial to the Heroes of the Battle of Stalingrad', *The Russian Review*/68 (2009), pp. 373–407; on Sevastopol, Karl Qualls, 'Who Makes Local Memories?: The Case of Sevastopol after World War II', *Soviet and Post-Soviet Review*/38 (2011), pp. 130–48; on Minsk and Brest, Bernhard Chiari and Robert Maier, 'Volkskrieg und Heldenstätte: Zum Mythos des Großen Vaterländischen Krieges in Weißrußland', in *Mythen der Nationen, Vol. 2. 1945: Arena der Erinnerung* (Mainz am Rhein: Philipp von Zabern, 2004), pp. 737–51; and on Moscow, Nina Tumarkin, 'Story of a War Memorial', in *World War 2 and the Soviet People*, eds John Garrard and Carol Garrard (New York: St Martin's, 1993), pp. 125–46.
7. I. Irwin-Zarecka, *Frames of Remembrance: The Dynamics of Collective Memory* (New Brunswick, NJ: Transaction Books, 1994); T.G. Ashplant, et al., 'The Politics of War Memory and Commemoration: Contexts, Structures and Dynamics', in *The Politics of War, Memory and Commemoration*, eds T.G. Ashplant, Graham Dawson and Michael Roper (London: Routledge, 2000), pp. 3–85; and Peter Carrier, 'Political and Ethical Contexts of Collective Memories of the Second World War', in *Recalling the Past–(Re)constructing the Past: Collective and Individual Memory of World War II in Russia and Germany*, eds Withold Bonner and Arja Rosenholm (Iyvaskyla, Finland: Gummerus, 2008), pp. 245–55.
8. Marianne Hirsch, 'Projected Memory: Holocaust Photographs in Personal and Public Fantasy', in *Acts of Memory: Cultural Recall in the Present*, eds Mieke Bal, Jonathan Crewe and Leo Spitzer (Hanover, NH and London: University Press of New England, 1999), pp. 3–23, p. 8; and Alison Landsberg, *The Transformation of American Remembrance in the Age of Mass Culture* (New York and Chichester: Columbia University Press, 2004), pp. 2, 19 and 24.
9. Similar methodological encounters are described by Bo Petersson in *National Self-Images and Regional Identities in Russia* (Aldershot: Ashgate, 2001). The difficulties of interpretation of interviews faced by the researcher are analysed particularly well in Anike Walke, *Pioneers and Partisans: An Oral History of Nazi Genocide in Belorussia* (Oxford: Oxford University Press, 2015), Chapter 1. Alistair Thomson discusses the pressures on veterans to alter their narratives in *Anzac Memories: Living with the Legend* (Clayton, Australia: Monash University Publishing, 2013).
10. The interested reader is referred to Michael Schudson, 'Dynamics of Distortion in Collective Memory', in *Memory Distortion: How Minds, Brains, and Societies*

Reconstruct the Past, ed. D.L. Schacter (Cambridge, MA and London: Harvard University Press, 1995), pp. 346–64; D.L. Schacter, *The Seven Sins of Memory: How the Mind Forgets and Remembers* (Boston, MA: Houghton Mifflin, 2001); and Paul Connerton, 'Seven Types of Forgetting', *Memory Studies*/1 (2008), pp. 59–71.

11. See Thomson, *Anzac Memories*.
12. See for example Merridale, *Night of Stone*; Jay Winter, 'Thinking about Silence', in *Shadows of War: A Social History of Silence in the Twentieth Century*, eds E. Ben-Ze'ev, R. Ginio and J. Winter (Cambridge: Cambridge University Press, 2010), pp. 3–31; and Walke, *Pioneers and Partisans*.

Chapter 1 What is a War Myth?

1. Iu. Ponomarenko, 'Bol'shaia slava Maloi zemli: Reportazh iz goroda-geroia Novorossiiska', *Izvestiia*, 6 September 1974, p. 1.
2. Maria Mavromataki, *Greek Mythology and Religion* (Athens: Haitalis, 1997), p. 231.
3. Mikhail Lermontov, 'Borodino', in *M. Iu. Lermontov: Stikhotvoreniia*, Vol. 1 (Moscow: Russkaia kniga, 1996), pp. 9–12.
4. See especially Maurice Halbwachs, *On Collective Memory*, trans. Lewis A. Coser (Chicago, IL and London: University of Chicago Press, 1992).
5. J.M. Winter, *Sites of Memory, Sites of Mourning: The Great War in European Cultural History* (Cambridge: Cambridge University Press, 1995).
6. John Ramsden, 'Myths and Realities of the "People's War" in Britain', in *Experience and Memory: The Second World War in Europe*, eds Jorg Echternkamp and Stefan Martens (New York and Oxford: Berghahn, 2010), pp. 40–52, p. 40.
7. Lisa A. Kirschenbaum, *The Legacy of the Siege of Leningrad, 1941–1995: Myth, Memories and Monuments* (Cambridge and New York: Cambridge University Press, 2006), p. 7.
8. Malcolm Smith, *Britain and 1940: History, Myth, and Popular Memory* (New York: Routledge, 2000), p. 2.
9. Barry Schwartz, Y. Zerubavel, and B. Bartlett, 'The Recovery of Masada', *Sociological Quarterly*/27 (1986), pp. 147–64.
10. Frederick C. Corney, *Telling October: Memory and the Making of the Bolshevik Revolution* (Ithaca, NY, and London: Cornell University Press, 2004), pp. 8–9; and 201–21.
11. Ibid., pp. 1–5.
12. Joseph Schull, 'What is Ideology? Theoretical Problems and Lessons from Soviet-type Societies', *Political Studies*/40 (1992), pp. 728–41; Neil Robinson, 'What was Soviet Ideology? A Comment on Joseph Schull and an Alternative', *Political Studies*/43 (1995), pp. 325–32; and Rachel Walker, 'Thinking about Ideology and Method: A Comment on Schull', *Political Studies*/43 (1995), pp. 333–42.
13. M.E. Urban and J. McClure, 'The Folklore of State Socialism: Semiotics and the Study of the Soviet State', *Soviet Studies*/35 (1983), pp. 471–86, p. 474.

14. Amir Weiner, *Making Sense of War: The Second World War and the Fate of the Bolshevik Revolution* (Princeton, NJ: Princeton University Press, 2001), p. 8; and Amir Weiner, 'The Making of a Dominant Myth: The Second World War and the Construction of Political Identities within the Soviet Polity', *Russian Review*/55 (1996), pp. 638–60, p. 658.
15. Vitaliia Kuz'mina, 'V Novorossiiske prem'er-ministr vozglavil kolonnu baikerov', *Vesti*, 30 August 2011, <http://www.vesti.ru/doc.html?id=553582> [accessed 31 August 2011].
16. E. Renan, 'What is a Nation?', in *Nation and Narration*, ed. H.K. Bhabha (London: Routledge, 1990), pp. 8–22, p. 19.
17. Clive Ponting, *1940: Myth and Reality* (London: Hamish Hamilton, 1990).
18. Angus Calder, *The Myth of the Blitz* (London: Pimlico, 1992); Malcolm Smith, *Britain and 1940*; and Mark Connelly, *We Can Take It! Britain and the Memory of the Second World War* (Harlow: Pearson Longman, 2004).
19. George Schöpflin, 'The Functions of Myth and a Taxonomy of Myths', in *Myths and Nationhood*, eds Geoffrey Hosking and George Schöpflin (London: Hurst, 1997), p. 19.
20. Nina Tumarkin, *The Living and the Dead: The Rise and Fall of the Cult of World War II in Russia* (New York: BasicBooks, 1994), p. 104; Thomas C. Wolfe, 'Past as Present, Myth, or History? Discourses of Time and the Great Fatherland War', in *The Politics of Memory in Postwar Europe*, eds Richard Ned Lebow, Wulf Kansteiner and Claudio Fogu (Durham, NC and London: Duke University Press, 2006), pp. 249–83, p. 262; and Mikhail Ivanovich Gorbyev and Anatolii Ivanovich Dokuchaev, *Goroda-geroi i goroda voinskoi slavy Rossii* (Moscow: Armpress, 2010).
21. Kathleen E. Smith, *Mythmaking in the New Russia: Politics and Memory during the Yeltsin Era* (Ithaca, NY and London: Cornell University Press, 2002), pp. 86–90.
22. 'Putin Hails Russian Military', *BBC News*, 9 May 2000, <http://news.bbc.co.uk/1/hi/world/europe/741415.stm> [accessed 30 May 2016].

Part I War Correspondence and Memoirs: The Construction of the War Myth through Literature

1. 'I have more memories than if I were a thousand years old./A heavy chest of drawers stuffed with bank statements,/Poems, love-letters, lawsuits, love-songs,/With heavy locks of hair wrapped in receipts,/Hides fewer secrets than my sad brain./It is a pyramid, a vast vault,/Which contains more corpses than the communal grave./I am a cemetery abhorred by the moon.' From Charles Baudelaire, 'Spleen', in *Les Fleurs du Mal* (Paris: Pocket, 2006), p. 91.
2. Samuel Hynes, 'Personal Narratives and Commemoration', in *War and Remembrance in the Twentieth Century*, eds Jay Winter and Emmanuel Sivan (Cambridge: Cambridge University Press, 2000), pp. 205–20, p. 207.

3. Glavlit: Glavnoe upravlenie po okhrane gosudarstvennykh tain v pechati pri SM SSSR; KGB: Komitet gosudarstvennoi bezopasnosti.
4. Soiuz pisatelei SSSR.
5. Jeffrey Brooks, *Thank You, Comrade Stalin! Soviet Public Culture from Revolution to Cold War* (Princeton, NJ: Princeton University Press, 2001), p. 108.
6. Katharine Hodgson, *Written with the Bayonet: Soviet Russian Poetry of World War Two* (Liverpool: Liverpool University Press, 1996), p. 134.
7. Orlando Figes, *Natasha's Dance: A Cultural History of Russia* (London: Allen Lane, 2002), p. 474.
8. Katerina Clark, *The Soviet Novel: History as Ritual* (Bloomington and Indianapolis, IN: Indiana University Press, 2000), pp. 183 and 253.
9. Brooks, *Thank You, Comrade Stalin!*, p. 109, citing Louis Fischer in Richard Crossman, ed., *The God that Failed* (New York: Harper, 1949), p. 205.
10. Wolfe, 'Past as Present, Myth, or History? Discourses of Time and the Great Fatherland War', in *The Politics of Memory in Postwar Europe*, eds Richard Ned Lebow, Wulf Kansteiner and Claudio Fogu (Durham, NC and London: Duke University Press, 2006), pp. 249–83, p. 258.
11. Clark, *The Soviet Novel*, p. 40.
12. 'Time ticks blank and busy on their wrists' ('Attack', 1918); 'chaps who work in peace with Time for friend' ('To any Dead Officer', 1918); 'Taking your peaceful share of Time, with joy to spare' ('Aftermath', 1919); and 'War was a fiend who stopped our clocks' ('Song-Books of the War', 1918): Siegfried Sassoon, *The Complete War Poems: Siegfried Sasson* (USA: Create Space Independent Publishing Platform, 2013), pp. 27, 41, 52 and 53.
13. Hodgson, *Written with the Bayonet*, p. 141, citing Mircea Eliade, *Myth and Reality*, trans. Willard R. Trask (Prospect Heights, IL: Waveland Press, 1998), p. 139.
14. Hodgson, *Written with the Bayonet*, p. 143.
15. Hynes, 'Personal narratives and commemoration', p. 208.
16. Lisa A. Kirschenbaum, *The Legacy of the Siege of Leningrad, 1941–1995: Myth, Memories and Monuments* (Cambridge and New York: Cambridge University Press, 2006), p. 232.

Chapter 2 A Myth is Born: War Correspondence from Malaia zemlia

1. 'The sea is always rough/And the shore alarmingly steep,/The dear little patch of land/Gleams like a star in the darkness./The waves splash and smash,/The nightly convoy is under fire./But the shore comes ever closer,/We are sailing doggedly towards it.//We are sailing, but that's not the last shell/To fall into the sea close to us,/To where, on the slopes of the foothills,/Our comrades do not sleep./Here is the shore, with moorings and path,/Our native trees in the dust,/The high proud hills are/The guardians of "Malaia zemlia".' (Lt. A. Petrov, 'My "Maluiu zemliu" rasshirim …', *Znamia Rodiny*, 7 September 1943).

2. Paul Carell, *Scorched Earth: Hitler's War on Russia*, trans. Ewald Osers (London: Harrap, 1970), p. 170.
3. N.V. Kolesov, *V pamiati i v serdtse – navsegda* (Moscow: Izdatel'stvo politicheskoi literatury, 1975), pp. 37–8.
4. Samuel Hynes, *The Soldiers' Tale: Bearing Witness to Modern War* (London: Pimlico, 1998), pp. 178–9 and 212.
5. Malcolm Smith, *Britain and 1940: History, Myth, and Popular Memory* (New York: Routledge, 2000), p. 29.
6. Jeffrey Brooks, *Thank You, Comrade Stalin! Soviet Public Culture from Revolution to Cold War* (Princeton, NJ: Princeton University Press, 2001), pp. 159–60.
7. Louise McReynolds, 'Dateline Stalingrad: Newspaper Correspondents at the Front', in *Culture and Entertainment in Wartime Russia*, ed. Richard Stites (Bloomington and Indianapolis, IN: Indiana University Press, 1995), pp. 28–43, pp. 29–30.
8. Karel C. Berkhoff, *Motherland in Danger: Soviet Propaganda during World War II* (Cambridge, MA: Harvard University Press, 2012), p. 13.
9. Brooks, *Thank You, Comrade Stalin!*, pp. 161–2; James von Geldern, 'Radio Moscow: The Voice from the Center', in *Culture and Entertainment in Wartime Russia*, ed. Richard Stites (Bloomington and Indianapolis, IN: Indiana University Press), 1995, pp. 44–61, pp. 48–9; and Rodric Braithwaite, *Moscow 1941: A City and its People at War* (New York: Knopf, 2006), p. 93.
10. L.I. Lazarev, *Konstantin Simonov: Ocherk zhizni i tvorchestva* (Moscow: Khudozhestvennaia literatura, 1985), p. 82.
11. Berkhoff, *Motherland in Danger*, pp. 59–67.
12. McReynolds, 'Dateline Stalingrad', p. 28.
13. Berkhoff, *Motherland in Danger*, pp. 38, 42, 43, 46 and 55.
14. Katerina Clark, *The Soviet Novel: History as Ritual* (Bloomington and Indianapolis, IN: Indiana University Press, 2000), p. 178.
15. McReynolds, 'Dateline Stalingrad', p. 31.
16. Brooks, *Thank You, Comrade Stalin!*, pp. 160 and 167.
17. Borzenko's postwar works include: S. Borzenko, *Zhizn' na voine: Zapiski voennogo korrespondenta* (Moscow: Voennoe izdatel'stvo Ministerstva oborony Soiuza SSR, 1958); S. Borzenko, *Na avanpostakh* (Moscow: Voennoe izdatel'stvo Ministerstva oborony SSSR, 1964); S. Borzenko, *Ogni Novorossiiska: Podvig, rasskazy, ocherki* (Elitsa: Kalmytskoe knizhnoe izdatel'stvo, 1975); and Sergei Borzenko, *Piat'desiat ognennykh strok* (Moscow: DOSAAF SSSR, 1982).
18. A. Sofronov, 'V Novorossiiske, posle boiia . . .', *Izvestiia*, 18 September 1943, p. 3.
19. Georgii Sokolov, *Malaia zemlia: Rasskazy i ocherki* (Krasnodar: Krasnodarskoe knizhnoe izdatel'stvo, 1967), p. 57; and G.P. Bondar', *Uroki muzhestva* (Krasnodar: Krasnodarskoe knizhnoe izdatel'stvo, 1982), p. 13.
20. A.F. Galatenko, *Katera idut k Myskhako* (Krasnodar: Krasnodarskoe knizhnoe izdatel'stvo, 1979), p. 8.
21. 'Struggle on the Kuban', *The Times*, 20 April 1943, p. 4.

22. L.V. Puseva, 'Frontovye pis'ma kak istoricheskii istochnik', in *Novorossiisk: Pamiat' i Pravda o Velikoi Otechestvennoi voine. K istoricheskoi istine cherez istochnik*, eds L.A. Kolbasina, S.G. Novikov, L.A. Stepko, B.A. Trekhbratov, V.S. Shikin and T.I. Iurina (Novorossiisk: Departament kul'tury Krasnodarskogo kraia, 2005), pp. 99–102, p. 102.
23. Sokolov, *Malaia zemlia*, 1967, pp. 322–35.
24. A. Svetov and B. Milianskii, 'Segodnia na "Maloi zemle"', *Znamia Rodiny*, 30 June 1943.
25. Mark Kolosov, 'Myskhako', *Pravda*, 18 September 1943, p. 3.
26. Angus Calder, *The Myth of the Blitz* (London: Pimlico, 1992), p. 2; and Mark Connelly, *We Can Take It! Britain and the Memory of the Second World War* (Harlow: Pearson Longman, 2004), p. 1.
27. *Morskaia pekhota*; I am grateful to Antony Beevor for this terminology.
28. Kolosov, 'Myskhako'.
29. Lisa A. Kirschenbaum, *The Legacy of the Siege of Leningrad, 1941–1995: Myth, Memories and Monuments* (Cambridge and New York: Cambridge University Press, 2006), pp. 42–76.
30. von Geldern, 'Radio Moscow', pp. 44–5; and Kirschenbaum, *The Legacy of the Siege of Leningrad*, pp. 42–76.
31. Leonid Il'ich Brezhnev, 'Malaia zemlia', in *Malaia zemlia. Vozrozhdenie* (Moscow: Prosveshchenie, 1979), pp. 1–45, p. 28; G. Sokolov, *My s Maloi zemli* (Moscow: Sovetskaia Rossiia, 1979), p. 289; and S.T. Grigor'ev, *Tak srazhalis' kommunisty* (Krasnodar: Krasnodarskoe knizhnoe izdatel'stvo, 1982), p. 61.
32. I.S. Shiian, *Novorossiisk – gorod-geroi* (Moscow: Voennoe izdatel'stvo Ministerstva oborony SSSR, 1982), p. 63; A. Eremenko and K. Podyma, eds, *Imenem Rossii narechennyi* (Moscow: Sovetskaia Rossiia, 1988), p. 231; and T.N. Shubnikova, 'Partizanskaia gazeta', in *Novorossiisk: Pamiat' i Pravda o Velikoi Otechestvennoi voine* (2005), pp. 117–9.
33. 'Vse sily – na razgrom vraga', *Leningradskaia pravda*, 2 July 1943, p. 1.
34. Svetov and Miliavskii, 'Segodnia na Maloi zemle'.
35. Clark, *The Soviet Novel*, p. 40.
36. 'Byt' dostoinymi vysokoi nagrady!', *LP*, 4 June 1943, p. 1.
37. 'Vse sily – na razgrom vraga'. See also L. Govorov, 'V boiakh za gorod Lenina: Predstoiat tiazhelye, napriazhennye boi', *LP*, 1 May 1943, p. 2.
38. 'Shkolniki nashego goroda', *LP*, 1 June 1943, p. 3.
39. 'Kollektivnyi podvig goroda-geroia', *LP*, 2 July 1943, p. 3.
40. A. Svetov and B. Miliavskii, 'I pesnia i stikh – eto bomba', *ZR*, 12 July 1943.
41. McReynolds, 'Dateline Stalingrad', p. 32; and Brooks, *Thank You, Comrade Stalin!*, pp. 160–83.
42. See Hodgson, *Written with the Bayonet: Soviet Russian Poetry of World War Two* (Liverpool: Liverpool University Press, 1996), p. 130; Brooks, *Thank You, Comrade Stalin!*, pp. 167, 169, 175, and 185–7; Orlando Figes, *The Whisperers: Private Life in Stalin's Russia* (London: Allen Lane, 2007), p. 383; and Berkhoff, *Motherland in Danger*, pp. 30–4.

43. 'Kollektivnyi podvig goroda-geroia'.
44. Svetov and Miliavskii, 'I pesnia i stikh – eto bomba'.
45. Ibid.; and Kolosov, 'Myskhako'.
46. Svetov and Miliavskii, 'I pesnia i stikh – eto bomba'.
47. For example: S. Borzenko, 'Rytsar' "Maloi zemli"', *ZR*, 14 July 1943; and B. Galanov, 'Geroi "Maloi zemli": Doch' Kubani', *ZR*, 5 August 1943. Quotation from Svetov and Miliavskii, 'I pesnia i stikh – eto bomba'.
48. B. Borisov, 'Voiny sevastopol'skoi zakalki', *ZR*, 27 August 1943.
49. Puseva, 'Frontovye pis'ma kak istoricheskii istochnik', p. 102.
50. Svetov and Milianskii, 'Segodnia na "Maloi zemle"'.
51. S. Borzenko and I. Semiokhin, 'Zavershenie geroicheskoi epopei', *ZR*, 17 September 1943. The statue of Lenin in the centre of Novorossiisk was remarkably still standing at the end of the battle.
52. See Borzenko, *Zhizn' na voine*, p. 166; and Brezhnev, 'Malaia zemlia', 1979, p. 18. For an extended discussion of frontline entertainment, see Richard Stites, 'Frontline Entertainment', in *Culture and Entertainment in Wartime Russia*, ed. Richard Stites (Bloomington and Indianapolis, IN: Indiana University Press, 1995), pp. 126–40.
53. Svetov and Miliavskii, 'I pesnia i stikh – eto bomba'.
54. A.S. Pushkin, *A.S. Pushkin: Sobranie sochinenii v shesti tomakh*, Vol. 1 (Moscow: Pravda, 1969), p. 425; G.R. Derzhavin, *G.R. Derzhavin: Stikhotvoreniia* (Leningrad: Sovetskii pisatel', 1957), p. 233; and Jeffrey H. Kaimowitz (trans.), *The Odes of Horace* (Baltimore, MD: The John Hopkins University Press, 2008), p. 142.
55. Horace's 'Exegi monumentum' is the conclusion of a cycle of odes (Book 3, ode XXX), see John Kevin Newman, 'Pushkin and Horace: Remarks on "Exegi monumentum" and "Pamyatnik"', *Neohelicon*/3 (1975), p. 333.
56. 'Likuet ves' narod', *Novorossiiskii rabochii*, 11 May 1945, p. 3.

Chapter 3 Early Memoir Literature

1. 'Yes, there were people in our time,/A mighty, spirited tribe.' From the final stanza of Lermontov's poem 'Borodino' (1837) in *M.Iu. Lermontov: Stikhotvoreniia*, Vol. 1 (Moscow: Russkaia kniga, 1996), pp. 9–12. This quotation is cited in Georgii Sokolov, *Malaia zemlia: Rasskazy i ocherki* (Krasnodar: Krasnodarskoe knizhnoe izdatel'stvo, 1967), p. 351.
2. V.N. Kaida, *Atakuet morskaia pekhota* (Krasnodar: Krasnodarskoe knizhnoe izdatel'stvo, 1980), p. 59.
3. Elena Zubkova, *Russia after the War: Hopes, Illusions, and Disappointments, 1945–1957*, trans. Hugh Ragsdale (Armonk, NY and London: Sharpe, 1998), pp. 27–8; and Beate Fizeler, '"Nishchie pobediteli": Invalidy Velikoi Otechestvennoi voiny v Sovetskom Soiuze', *Neprikosovennyi zapas*/40–1 (2005), para. 24. See also Sokolov, *Malaia zemlia*, 1967, p. 383.
4. M.V. Erokhin, *Novorossiisk*, ed. D.A. Vasil'evich (Krasnodar: RIO, 2012), p. 70.

5. Catherine Merridale, *Night of Stone: Death and Memory in Russia* (London: Granta Books, 2000), p. 253; and Lisa A. Kirschenbaum, *The Legacy of the Siege of Leningrad, 1941–1995: Myth, Memories and Monuments* (Cambridge and New York: Cambridge University Press, 2006), pp. 115–16.
6. Jay Winter, *Sites of Memory, Sites of Mourning: The Great War in European Cultural History* (Cambridge: Cambridge University Press, 1995), pp. 30 and 98.
7. Lazar Lazarev, 'Russian Literature on the War and Historical Truth', in *World War 2 and the Soviet People*, eds John Garrard and Carol Garrard (New York: St Martin's, 1993), pp. 28–37, p. 31; and Nina Tumarkin, *The Living and the Dead: The Rise and Fall of the Cult of World War II in Russia* (New York: BasicBooks, 1994), p. 103.
8. Merridale, *Night of Stone*.
9. Sergei Kudryashov, 'Remembering and Researching the War: The Soviet and Russian Experience', in *Experience and Memory: The Second World War in Europe*, eds Jorg Echternkamp and Stefan Martens (New York and Oxford: Berghahn, 2010), pp. 86–115, p. 98; and Geoffrey Hosking, 'The Second World War and Russian National Consciousness', *Past and Present*/175 (2002), pp. 162–87, pp. 179 and 180–6.
10. Lazarev, 'Russian Literature on the War and Historical Truth', p. 31, citing Marshal Vasilevskii.
11. Kristin Roth-Ey, *Moscow Prime Time: How the Soviet Union Built the Media Empire that Lost the Cultural Cold War* (Ithaca, NY and London: Cornell University Press, 2011), p. 52.
12. For 'V poiskakh geroev Brestskoi kreposti', see: *TVmuseum.ru*, <http://www.tvmuseum.ru/search.asp?cat_ob_no=17&ob_no=17&a=1&pg=12> [accessed 1 May 2013]; and for 'Rasskazy o geroizme', see: *TVmuseum.ru*, <http://www.tvmuseum.ru/search.asp?cat_ob_no=17&ob_no=17&a=1&pg=14> [accessed 1 May 2013].
13. Roth-Ey, *Moscow Prime Time*, pp. 266 and 271–2; and 'Smirnov povedal tainu neizvestnoi voiny', *Newsland*, 21 February 2012, <http://newsland.com/news/detail/id/894387/> [accessed 30 April 2013]. Sergei Smirnov, *Rasskazy o neizvestnykh geroiakh* (Moscow: Molodaia gvardiia, 1963), p. 85.
14. Kudryashov, 'Remembering and Researching the War', pp. 98, 105 and 113.
15. Kirschenbaum, *The Legacy of the Siege of Leningrad*, pp. 160–1. For example, A.V. Karasev, *Leningradtsy v gody blokady 1941–1943* (Moscow, 1959).
16. A.V. Fadeev, *Geroi Maloi zemli* (Moscow: Gospolitizdat, 1959); G.N. Gaidovskii and A.A. Uzlian, *S 'leikoi' i bloknotom: Vospominaniia voennykh let* (Moscow: Voenizdat, 1961); Fedor Vasil'evich Monastyrskii, *Zemlia, omytaia krov'iu* (Moscow: Voenizdat, 1961) (See I.V. Efebovskii, et al., eds, *Velikaia Otechestvennaia voina Sovetskogo Soiuza 1941–1945: Rekomendatel'nyi ukazatel' literatury* (Moscow: Kniga, 1965), pp. 52–3).
17. Kudryashov, 'Remembering and Researching the War', pp. 98–9.
18. Introduction by Vice Admiral G.N. Kholostiakov to Georgii Sokolov, *My s Maloi zemli* (Moscow: Sovetskaia Rossiia, 1979), p. 8; N.F. Zavorotniak,

'Proizvedeniia literatov vo frontovoi pechati', in *Novorossiisk: Pamiat' i Pravda o Velikoi Otechestvennoi voine* (2005), pp. 95–8, p. 96; and Evgenii Lapin, 'Malaia zemlia Georgiia Sokolova', *Novorossiiskii rabochii*, 3 November 2011, <http://www.novorab.ru/ArticleSection/Details/4249/1> [accessed 12 November 2011].

19. Sokolov, *My s Maloi zemli*, 1979, p. 370; and Aleksandr Maisurian, *Drugoi Brezhnev* (Moscow: Vagrius, 2004), p. 540.
20. Sokolov, *Malaia zemlia*, 1967, p. 383.
21. Ibid.
22. Leonid I. Brezhnev, *The Great Victory of the Soviet People* (Moscow: Novosti Press Agency, 1965). On the minute's silence, see Tumarkin, *The Living and the Dead*, p. 41; and 'Minuta molchaniia', *TVmuseum.ru*, <http://www.tvmuseum.ru/catalog.asp?ob_no=12899> [accessed 24 October 2014].
23. S. Kolosovii, *Vyzyvaem ogon' na sebia* (USSR: Mossfil'm, 1964–5); *Podvig* (USSR: Tsentral'nyi televidenie SSSR, 1965).
24. Polly Jones, ed., *The Dilemmas of De-Stalinization: Negotiating Cultural and Social Change in the Khrushchev Era* (New York: Routledge Curzon, 2005); and Polly Jones, *Myth, Memory, Trauma: Rethinking the Stalinist Past in the Soviet Union, 1953–70* (New Haven, CT: Yale University Press, 2013).
25. Lazarev, 'Russian Literature on the War and Historical Truth', p. 35.
26. Tumarkin, *The Living and the Dead*, pp. 134–5. For details of the mechanism of publication in the light of censorship, see: Kudryashov, 'Remembering and Researching the War', p. 105.
27. Lapin, 'Malaia zemlia Georgiia Sokolova'. Sokolov's other works include: G. Sokolov, *Malaia zemlia* (Moscow: Sovetskaia Rossiia, 1971); G. Sokolov, *My s Maloi zemli* (Moscow: Sovetskaia Rossiia, 1979); and G. Sokolov, *My s Maloi zemli: Dokumental'nye rasskazy* (Krasnodar: Krasnodarskoe knizhnoe izdatel'stvo, 1985).
28. A. Ryzhov, 'Pamiat' serdtse', in Sokolov, *Malaia zemlia*, 1967, pp. 404–6, p. 406.
29. 'Klavochka', in Sokolov, *Malaia zemlia*, 1967, pp. 218–25.
30. G. Sokolov, *My s Maloi zemli*, 1979, p. 371.
31. Sokolov, *Malaia zemlia*, 1967, pp. 98–112.
32. P.N. Pospelov, et al., eds, *Istoriia Velikoi Otechestvennoi voiny Sovetskogo Soiuza, 1941–1945*, Vol. 3 (Moscow, Voennoe izdatel'stvo Ministerstva oborony Soiuza SSR, 1961), pp. 94–5.
33. Deming Brown, *Soviet Russian Literature since Stalin* (Cambridge: Cambridge University Press, 1978), pp. 171–2.
34. Sokolov, *Malaia zemlia*, 1967, p. 111.
35. 'Vitia Chalenko. V pamiat' o geroiakh: ob ul. V. Chalenko', *NR*, 15 October 1968.
36. For example, the poetry of Wilfred Owen and Siegfried Sassoon; Henri Barbusse, *Le Feu: Journal d'une Escouade* (1916); C.E. Montague, *Disenchantment* (1922); Herbert Read, *In Retreat* (1925); Erich Maria Remarque, *Im Westen nichts Neues* (1928); E. Blunden, *Undertones of War* (1929); and Robert Graves, *Goodbye to All That* (1929).

37. 'Tsvetok Korei', in Sokolov, *Malaia zemlia*, 1967, pp. 355–64.
38. A. Svetov and B. Milianskii, 'Segodnia na "Maloi zemle"', *Znamia Rodiny*, 30 June 1943.
39. Katerina Clark, *The Soviet Novel: History as Ritual* (Bloomington and Indianapolis, IN: Indiana University Press, 2000), pp. 40 and 175.
40. Lapin, 'Malaia zemlia Georgiia Sokolova'.
41. 'Davdtsat' let spustia', in Sokolov, *Malaia zemlia*, 1967, pp. 382–403.
42. Jörg Ganzenmüller, *Das belagerte Leningrad 1941–1944: Die Stadt in den Strategien von Angreifern und Verteidigern* (Paderborn: Ferdinand Schöningh, 2005), p. 340, cited in Ivo Mijnssen, *Memorial Landscapes in the Postwar Generation: The Soviet Hero-Cities of Tula and Novorossiysk in the Brezhnev era*, PhD thesis (University of Basel, Switzerland, 2015), pp. 84–5.
43. See Ol'ga Berggol'ts, V.N. Druzhinin, A.L. Dymshits, A.G. Rosen and N.S. Tikhonov, eds, *900 dnei* (Leningrad: Lenizdat, 1957); Ales Adamovich and Daniil Granin, *Blokadnaia kniga* (Moscow: Sovetskii pisatel', 1982); Cynthia Simmons and Nina Perlina, *Writing the Siege of Leningrad: Women's Diaries, Memoirs, and Documentary Prose* (Pittsburgh, PA: University of Pittsburgh Press, 2002, p. xxx; and Kirschenbaum, *The Legacy of the Siege of Leningrad*, pp. 152, 163 and 166–7.
44. Kirschenbaum, *The Legacy of the Siege of Leningrad*, p. 166.
45. Ibid., pp. 181–2; and Sokolov, *Malaia zemlia*, 1967, pp. 405–6.
46. Clark, *The Soviet Novel*, p. 198.
47. Sokolov, *Malaia zemlia*, 1967, pp. 5, 9, 403 and 405.
48. Susan A. Crane, 'Writing the Individual Back into Collective Memory', *The American Historical Review*/102 (1997), pp. 1372–85, p. 1383; James V. Wertsch, *Voices of Collective Remembering* (Cambridge: Cambridge University Press, 2002), pp. 6–7 and 21–5; and Jerome Bruner and Carol Fleischer Feldman, 'Group Narrative as a Cultural Context of Autobiography', in *Remembering Our Past: Studies in Autobiographical Memory*, ed. David C. Rubin (Cambridge: Cambridge University Press, 2005), pp. 291–317. See also Donald Campbell, *Methodology and Epistemology for Social Sciences: Selected Papers of Donald T. Campbell*, ed. E. Samuel Overman (Chicago, IL: University of Chicago Press, 1988); and Edwin Hutchins, *Cognition in the Wild* (Cambridge, MA: MIT Press, 1995), both arguing for the building of collective memory from complementary personal perspectives.
49. Deming Brown observes that anything defeatist would automatically be censored: Brown, *Soviet Russian Literature since Stalin*, p. 170.

Chapter 4 Brezhnev's War Memoirs

1. William Shakespeare, *Henry V*, Act IV, scene iii.
2. See TVmuseum.ru, <http://www.tvmuseum.ru/search.asp?cat_ob_no=17&ob_no = 17&a = 1&pg = 18> [accessed 3 May 2013]. Moreover, the radio

programme 'V etot den' 30 let nazad' (1974–5) focused on memory of the final stages of the war, see *TVmuseum.ru*, <http://www.tvmuseum.ru> [accessed 1 May 2013]. See also Kristin Roth-Ey, *Moscow Prime Time: How the Soviet Union Built the Media Empire that Lost the Cultural Cold War* (Ithaca, NY and London: Cornell University Press, 2011), pp. 275–7.

3. Denis Kozlov, 'The Historical Turn in Late Soviet Culture: Retrospectivism, Factography, Doubt, 1953–91', *Kritika: Explorations in Russian and Eurasian History*/2 (2001), pp. 577–600, pp. 578, 585 and 599.
4. William Tompson, *The Soviet Union under Brezhnev* (Harlow: Pearson Education, 2003), p. 102. The successful series of biographies of historical figures 'Plamennye revoliutsionery' was published from 1964 to 1990; see Polly Jones, 'The Fire Burns On? The "Fiery Revolutionaries" Biographical Series and the Rethinking of Propaganda in the Brezhnev Era', *Slavic Review*/74 (2015), pp. 32–56.
5. A. Svetov and B. Milianskii, 'Segodnia na "Maloi zemle"', *Znamia Rodiny*, 30 June 1943; and 'Tsvetok Korei' in Georgii Sokolov, *Malaia zemlia: Rasskazy i ocherki* (Krasnodar: Krasnodarskoe knizhnoe izdatel'stvo, 1967), pp. 355–64.
6. Hedrick Smith, *The Russians* (New York: Quadrangle and The New York Times Book Company, 1976), p. 316.
7. See Leonid I. Brezhnev, *The Great Victory of the Soviet People* (Moscow: Novosti Press Agency, 1965); Nina Tumarkin, *The Living and the Dead: The Rise and Fall of the Cult of World War II in Russia* (New York: BasicBooks, 1994), pp. 132–4; Lisa A. Kirschenbaum, *The Legacy of the Siege of Leningrad, 1941–1995: Myth, Memories and Monuments* (Cambridge and New York: Cambridge University Press, 2006), p. 180; and Catherine Merridale, *Ivan's War: Life and Death in the Red Army, 1939–1945* (New York: Picador, 2006), pp. 374–5.
8. Tumarkin, *The Living and the Dead*, 1994, pp. 155–6.
9. A. Khinshtein, *Skazka o poteriannom vremeni: Pochemu Brezhnev ne smog stat' Putinym* (Moscow: OLMA, 2011), pp. 628–30.
10. Kirschenbaum, *The Legacy of the Siege of Leningrad*, pp. 153 and 163.
11. S. Borzenko, *Zhizn' na voine: Zapiski voennogo korrespondenta* (Moscow: Voennoe izdatel'stvo Ministerstva oborony Soiuza SSR, 1958), p. 167.
12. S. Borzenko, *Na avanpostakh* (Moscow: Voennoe izdatel'stvo Ministerstva oborony SSSR, 1964), pp. 40–1; and Sergei Borzenko, '225 dnei muzhestva i otvagi', in *Podvig Novorossiiska*, ed. A.I. Makarenko (Krasnodar: Krasnodarskoe knizhnoe izdatel'stvo, 1978), pp. 76–84, p. 82.
13. Roger D. Markwick, *Rewriting History in Soviet Russia: The Politics of Revisionist Historiography 1956–1974* (Basingstoke: Palgrave, 2001), p. 5; and Pospelov, et al., *Istoriia Velikoi Otechestvennoi voiny Sovetskogo Soiuza, 1941–1945*, Vol. 3 (Moscow, Voennoe izdatel'stvo Ministerstva oborony Soiuza SSR, 1961), p. 95.
14. R.W. Davies, *Soviet History in the Gorbachev Revolution* (London: Macmillan, 1989), p. 101, cited in Merridale, *Ivan's War*, p. 375.
15. Lazar Lazarev, 'Russian Literature on the War and Historical Truth', in *World War 2 and the Soviet People*, ed. John Garrard and Carol Garrard (New York: St Martin's, 1993), pp. 28–37, p. 34.

16. Denis Kozlov, 'The Historical Turn in Late Soviet Culture: Retrospectivism, Factography, Doubt, 1953–91', *Kritika: Explorations in Russian and Eurasian History*/2 (2001), pp. 577–600, p. 153.
17. Hedrick Smith, *The Russians*, p. 314.
18. K.K. Rokossovskii, *Soldatskii dolg* (Moscow: Voenizdat, 1968); G.K. Zhukov, *Vospominaniia i razmyshleniia* (Moscow: Voenizdat, 1969); and I.S. Konev, *Sorok piatyi* (Moscow: Voenizdat, 1970) and *Zapiski komanduiushchego frontom* (Moscow: Voenizdat, 1972). William Taubman, *Khrushchev: The Man, his Era* (London: Simon and Schuster, 2005), p. 631.
19. G. Zhukov, *Reminiscences and Reflections*, Vol. 2 (Moscow: Progress, 1985), p. 162.
20. M.G. Zhukova, 'G.K. Zhukov: Korotko o Staline', *Pravda*, 20 January 1989, p. 3; Roi Medvedev, *Lichnost' i epokha: Politicheskii portret L.I. Brezhneva (kniga 1)* (Moscow: Novosti, 1991), p. 43; and Roi Medvedev, *Politicheskie portrety* (Moscow: Moskva, 2008), p. 219.
21. Khinshtein, *Skazka o poteriannom vremeni*, pp. 83–96.
22. Orlando Figes, *The Whisperers: Private Life in Stalin's Russia* (London: Allen Lane, 2007), pp. 620–1.
23. Khinshtein, *Skazka o poteriannom vremeni*, pp. 94–5; A.A. Grechko, *Bitva za Kavkaz* (Moscow: Voenizdat, 1967); and G.N. Kholostiakov, *Vechnyi ogon'* (Moscow: Voenizdat, 1976).
24. I.S. Shiian, *Na Maloi zemle* (Moscow: Voennoe izdatel'stvo Ministerstva oborony SSSR, 1971) (with a fuller and more expensive edition in 1974); and I.S. Shiian, *Ratnyi podvig Novorossiiska* (Moscow: Voennoe izdatel'stvo Ministerstva oborony SSSR, 1977).
25. Sergei Borzenko, 'Prazdnichnyi saliut nad Novorossiiskom', *Pravda*, 16 September 1968.
26. SSSR TV, *Leonid Il'ich Brezhnev: Zhiznennyi put'* (USSR: Televidenie SSSR, 1973), <http://www.youtube.com/watch?v=ulNLcid4sho> [accessed 29 April 2013]; and Nostal'giia, *General'nyi sekretar': Leonid Il'ich Brezhnev* (USSR: Televidenie SSSR, 1976), <http://www.youtube.com/watch?v=fect9ejZhig> [accessed 29 April 2013].
27. James V. Wertsch, *Voices of Collective Remembering* (Cambridge: Cambridge University Press, 2002), p. 80.
28. A.V. Sofronov, 'Deviatyi val: Geroicheskaia drama v dvukh chastiakh', in *Uragan: P'esy poslednykh let* (Moscow: Sovetskii pisiatel', 1975), pp. 5–62.
29. B. Privalov, 'Deviatyi val', *Pravda vostoka*, 15 September 1975, p. 3.
30. *Al'bom o Maloi zemle*, see D. Rezaev, 'Rasskazyvaiut veterany', *Novorossiiskii rabochii*, 13 September 1974, p. 3.
31. Katerina Clark, *The Soviet Novel: History as Ritual* (Bloomington and Indianapolis, IN: Indiana University Press, 2000), pp. 237–8.
32. Nostal'giia, *General'nyi sekretar'*; and Igor' V. Bessarabov, *Povest' o kommuniste* (USSR: 1976).
33. Valerii Drannikov, 'Zemlia byla malaia, no gonorary ochen' bol'shie', *Kommersant' Vlast'*/12 (363), 28 March 2000, <http://kommersant.ru/doc/16688>

[accessed 21 March 2013]; '"Memuary" za Brezhneva pisali literaturnye raby', *Argumenty i fakty*, 31 March 2010, <http://www.aif.ru/politics/article/33698> [accessed 21 March 2013]; Roi Medvedev, '"Malaia zemlia": istoriia literaturnogo podloga', *RIA "Novosti"*, 8 October 2010, <http://ria.ru/online/282083202.html> [accessed 12 November 2011]; the documentary film *'Malaia zemlia' Leonida Brezhneva* (Russia: Galakon Studio, 2010); and Nikolaus Katzer, 'Dans la Matrice Discursive du Socialisme Tardif: Les "Mémoires" de Leonid Il'ič Brežnev', *Cahiers du Monde Russe*/54 (2013), pp. 73–101.

34. *'Malaia zemlia' Leonida Brezhneva*; and Leonid Mlechin, *Brezhnev* (Moscow: Molodaia gvardiia, 2011), pp. 592–3.
35. Tompson, *The Soviet Union under Brezhnev*, p. 115.
36. Notably T.I. Iurina, 'Novorossiiskoe protivostoianie 1942–1943 gg.: Istoriografiia problemy', in *Istoricheskie zapiski: Issledovaniia i materialy*, Vol. 4, eds S.G. Novikov and T.V. Raskatova (Novorossiisk: Kubanskoe knizhnoe izdalel'stvo, 2003), pp. 214–35, p. 220; Sergei Semanov, *Dorogoi Leonid Il'ich* (Moscow: Algoritm, 2007), pp. 69–70; '"Memuary" za Brezhneva pisali literaturnye raby'; Roi Medvedev, '"Malaia zemlia": istoriia literaturnogo podloga'; and Aleksandr V. Filippov, 'Zhivopistsy "Maloi zemli": Kak sozdavalis' vospominaniia L.I. Brezhneva', *lenta.ru,* 7 February 2015, <http://m.lenta.ru/articles/2015/02/07/brezhnev> [accessed 10 February 2015].
37. Mlechin, *Brezhnev*, p. 593; and Taubman, *Khrushchev*, pp. 633–9.
38. Drannikov, 'Zemlia byla malaia, no gonorary ochen' bol'shie'.
39. *Novyi mir*, 2, February 1978; *Literaturnaia gazeta*, 8 February 1978, pp. 2–4; and *NR*, 7 and 8 February 1978.
40. The first was a volume of 48 pages: L.I. Brezhnev, *Malaia zemlia* (Moscow, Politizdat, 1978).
41. Leonid Il'ich Brezhnev, *Malaia zemlia. Vozrozhdenie* (Moscow: Prosveshchenie, 1979).
42. '"Memuary" za Brezhneva pisali literaturnye raby'; and Katzer, 'Dans la Matrice Discursive du Socialisme Tardif', p. 84.
43. Michael Binyon, 'Mr Brezhnev Joins Ranks of the Military Great', *The Times*, 21 February 1978, p. 6.
44. Leonid Il'ich Brezhnev, *Malaia zemlia* (Moscow and Krasnodar: Politizdat and Krasnodarskoe knizhnoe izdatel'stvo, 1978).
45. Brezhnev, *Malaia zemlia. Vozrozhdenie*, pp. 20–1.
46. Sokolov, *Malaia zemlia*, 1967, p. 10.
47. Brezhnev, *Malaia zemlia. Vozrozhdenie*, p. 7.
48. Ibid., p. 21.
49. Sokolov, *Malaia zemlia*, 1967, p. 10.
50. Brezhnev, *Malaia zemlia. Vozrozhdenie*, p. 9.
51. Sokolov, *Malaia zemlia*, 1967, pp. 327–35.
52. Brezhnev cites Konstantin Simonov's poem, 'Smert' druga' (1942): Brezhnev, *Malaia zemlia. Vozrozhdenie*, p. 34.
53. Mlechin, *Brezhnev*, p. 593.

54. 'Geroi velikikh stroek nashego vremeni i sovetskaia literatura', *Literaturnaia gazeta*, 7 February 1978, p. 5.
55. Anatolii Anan'ev, 'Zemlia malaia i bol'shaia', *Pravda*, 16 February 1978, p. 2; and 'Knigi-boitsy, knigi-sozidateli', *LG*, 17 May 1978, p. 3.
56. M.E. Teslia, N.I. Semeniuta and E.V. Malnach, eds, *Ne pomerknet nikogda* (Rostov-on-Don: Rostovskoe knizhnoe izdatel'stvo, 1978).
57. Ibid., p. 3.
58. 'Knigi-boitsy, knigi-sozidateli', p. 3; A.S. Kliunenko, 'Skarbnitsia lenins'kogo stiliu roboti (Do vikhodu knig L.I. Brezhneva "Mala zemlia" i "Vidrodzhennia")', *Ukrainskii istorichnii zhurnal*/8, 1978, pp. 5–13; O.M. Verbilo, 'Itogi Vtoroi mirovoi voiny i ee uroki v proizvedeniikh L.I. Brezhneva', *Ukrainskii istorichnii zhurnal*/10, 1979, pp. 7–16; and Mlechin, *Brezhnev*, p. 595.
59. Clark, *The Soviet Novel*, p. 237; Iain D. Thatcher, 'Brezhnev as Leader', in *Brezhnev Reconsidered*, eds Edwin Bacon and Mark Sandle (Basingstoke: Palgrave MacMillan, 2002), pp. 22–37; Tompson, *The Soviet Union under Brezhnev*, p. xvi; and Khinshtein, *Skazka o poteriannom vremeni*, p. 630.
60. *The Times*, 5 November 1980, p. 7.
61. *'Malaia zemlia' Leonida Brezhneva.*
62. Mlechin, *Brezhnev*, p. 595.
63. This is the joke most frequently heard in the context of Brezhnev's memoirs. Versions of this joke were related to me in Novorossiisk and Moscow. See also Maisurian, *Drugoi Brezhnev*, p. 499; and David Priestland, *The Red Flag: A History of Communism* (New York: Grove Press, 2009), p. 430.
64. Sokolov, *Malaia zemlia*, 1967, p. 10.
65. Roi Medvedev agrees: Roi Medvedev, '"Malaia zemlia": istoriia literaturnogo podloga'.
66. Sokolov, *Malaia zemlia*, 1967, p. 384; and *My s Maloi zemli*, 1979, p. 366.
67. Mlechin, *Brezhnev*, p. 596.
68. Roi Medvedev, *Lichnost' i epokha: Politicheskii portret L.I. Brezhneva (kniga 1)* (Moscow: Novosti, 1991), p. 41; and T.I. Iurina, *Novorossiiskoe protivostoianie: 1942–1943 gg.* (Krasnodar: Kniga, 2008), p. 270.
69. Brezhnev, *Malaia zemlia. Vozrozhdenie*, p. 21.
70. E.Ia. Savitskii, *V nebe nad Maloi zemlei* (Krasnodar: Krasnodarskoe knizhnoe izdatel'stvo, 1980), p. 154.

Chapter 5 Beyond Brezhnev and Brezhnevism

1. James Young, *The Texture of Memory: Holocaust Memorials and Meaning* (New Haven, CT and London: Yale University Press, 1993), p. 2.
2. Roi Medvedev, '"Malaia zemlia": istoriia literaturnogo podloga', *RIA "Novosti"*, 8 October 2010, <http://ria.ru/online/282083202.html> [accessed 12 November 2011].
3. 'Ob izuchenii v obshcheobrazovatel'nykh shkolakh knig general'nogo sekretaria TsK KPSS, predsedatelia prezidiuma verkhovnogo soveta SSSR

tovarishcha L.I. Brezhneva "Malaia zemlia" i "Vozrozhdenie"', *Prepodavanie istorii v shkole*/5 (1978), pp. 17–23; and A.F. Vovchik and M.O. Nemchenko, 'Vikoristannia prats' tovarisha L.I. Brezhneva "Mala zemlia", "Vidrodzhennia" i "Tselina" u vuzivs'komy kursy istorii KPRS', *Ukrainskii istorichnii zhurnal*/7 (1979), pp. 113–25.

4. M.E. Teslia, N.I. Semeniuta, and E.V. Malnach, eds, *Ne pomerknet nikogda* (Rostov-on-Don: Rostovskoe knizhnoe izdatel'stvo, 1978).
5. According to two retired teachers.
6. Roi Medvedev, '"Malaia zemlia": istoriia literaturnogo podloga'.
7. Michael Schudson, 'The Past in the Present versus the Present in the Past', in *The Collective Memory Reader*, eds Jeffrey K. Olick, Vered Vinitzky-Seroussi and Daniel Levy (Oxford: Oxford University Press, 2011), pp. 287–90, p. 288.
8. Dmitrii Aleksandrovich, *Malaia zemlia* (USSR: 1979); Leonid Mlechin, *Brezhnev* (Moscow: Molodaia gvardiia, 2011), p. 594; and Jutta Scherrer, Sowjetunion/Rußland: Siegesmythos versus Vergangenheitsaufarbeitung', in *Mythen der Nationen, Vol. 2. 1945: Arena der Erinnerung*, ed. Monika Flacke (Mainz am Rhein: Philipp von Zabern, 2004), pp. 619–57, p. 645.
9. Notably 'Malaia zemlia' (1974), words by N. Dobronravev, music by A. Pakhmutova.
10. *Malaia zemlia*, composer Iurii Abramovich Levitin, lyricists E. Dolmatovskii and Iu. Miliutin, 1979. Levitin's musical score for *Malaia zemlia* is to be found in RGALI, f. 3313, op. 1, d. 96, with the libretto at d. 137.
11. Vera Ukharova, 'Oratoriia o Maloi zemle', *Izvestiia*, 20 December 1981, p. 6.
12. Konstantin Podyma, *"Beskozyrka": Cherez gody i stoletiia: Dokumental'naia povest'* (Novorossiisk and Moscow: 2008), p. 7.
13. Katerina Clark, *The Soviet Novel: History as Ritual* (Bloomington and Indianapolis, IN: Indiana University Press, 2000), p. 183.
14. Leonid Il'ich Brezhnev, *Malaia zemlia. Vozrozhdenie* (Moscow: Prosveshchenie, 1979), pp. 27–8; Mariia Pedenko, *"Polundra, Krasnoflottsy!": Povest'* (Kiev: Molod', 1980), pp. 140–1; and N.N. Ivanova, 'Obraz zhenshchiny v proizvedeniikh frontovykh khudozhnikov', in *Novorossiisk: Pamiat' i Pravda o Velikoi Otechestvennoi voine* (2005), pp. 91–4, p. 94.
15. Mariia Petrovna Pedenko, *Frontovoi dnevnik* (Krasnodar: Krasnodarskoe knizhnoe izdatel'stvo, 1981) (first published in 1945; re-published in 1965 and 1979 in Kiev).
16. Georgii Sokolov, *My s Maloi zemli* (Moscow: Sovetskaia Rossiia, 1979), p. 159, repeated verbatim in Sokolov's afterword to Pedenko, *Frontovoi dnevnik*, p. 77.
17. Sokolov, *My s Maloi zemli*, 1979, pp. 149–59.
18. Ibid., pp. 8 and 379.
19. V.F. Mol'chenko, 'Geroinia "Maloi zemli"', *Ukrainskii istorichnii zhurnal*/6 (1980), pp. 118–23.
20. Mariia Pedenko, *"Polundra, Krasnoflottsy!"*.

21. Susanne Conze and Beate Fieseler, 'Soviet Women as Comrades-in-Arms: A Blind Spot in the History of the War', in *The People's War: Responses to World War II in the Soviet Union*, eds Robert W. Thurston and Bernd Bonwetsch (Urbana and Chicago, IL: University of Illinois Press, 2000), pp. 211–34, p. 227; Roger D. Markwick, '"A Sacred Duty": Red Army Women Veterans Remembering the Great Fatherland War, 1941–45', in *Recalling the Past–(Re) constructing the Past: Collective and Individual Memory of World War II in Russia and Germany*, eds Withold Bonner and Arja Rosenholm (Iyvaskyla, Finland: Gummerus, 2008), pp. 315–26, pp. 322–3; and Svetlana Alexievich, *U voiny – ne zhenskoe litso* (Moscow: Palmira, 1985). See also V.S. Murmantseva, 'Zhenshchiny-voiny Maloi zemli', *Voprosy istorii*/2 (1981), pp. 177–9, p. 179.
22. Boris Avksent'evich Privalov, *Novorossiisk* (Moscow: Planeta, 1978).
23. *Rubezhi Velikoi Epokhi: Fotoal'bom po motivam proisvedenii L.I. Brezhneva. Malaia zemlia; Vozrozhdenie; Tselina* (Moscow: Planeta, 1980).
24. A.P. Marfin, *Geroicheskii shturm* (Krasnodar: Krasnodarskoe knizhnoe izdatel'stvo, 1985), p. 203.
25. A.F. Galatenko, *Katera idut k Myskhako* (Krasnodar: Krasnodarskoe knizhnoe izdatel'stvo, 1979); V.I. Minakov, *Pod krylom – Tsemesskaia bukhta: Zapiski morskogo letchika* (Krasnodar: Krasnodarskoe knizhnoe izdatel'stvo, 1979); V. N. Kaida, *Atakuet morskaia pekhota* (Krasnodar: Krasnodarskoe knizhnoe izdatel'stvo, 1980); I.V. Zhernovoi, *Dal'she vrag ne proshel* (Krasnodar: Krasnodarskoe knizhnoe izdatel'stvo, 1980); Pedenko, *Frontovoi dnevnik*; V. T. Protsenko, *Ognennye mili* (Krasnodar: Krasnodarskoe knizhnoe izdatel'stvo, 1981); G.A. Pshenianik, *Novorossiiskii istrebitel'nyi* (Krasnodar: Krasnodarsko knizhnoe isdatel'stvo, 1981); G.P. Bondar', *Uroki muzhestva* (Krasnodar: Krasnodarskoe knizhnoe izdatel'stvo, 1982); V.I. Grezin, *Narodnye mstiteli* (Krasnodar: Krasnodarskoe knizhnoe izdatel'stvo, 1982); S. T. Grigor'ev, *Tak srazhalis' kommunisty* (Krasnodar: Krasnodarskoe knizhnoe izdatel'stvo, 1982); N.M. Voronkin and K.G. Lavrent'ev, *Artilleristy Maloi zemli* (Krasnodar: Krasnodarskoe knizhnoe izdatel'stvo, 1982); A.V. Raikunov, *Rota, za mnoi!* (Krasnodar: Krasnodarskoe knizhnoe izdatel'stvo, 1984); and Marfin, *Geroicheskii shturm*.
26. Sergei Kudryashov, 'Remembering and Researching the War: The Soviet and Russian Experience', in *Experience and Memory: The Second World War in Europe*, ed. Jorg Echternkamp and Stefan Martens (New York and Oxford: Berghahn, 2010), pp. 86–115, p. 104.
27. For example, Kaida, *Atakuet morskaia pekhota*, pp. 37–8; Bondar', *Uroki muzhestva*, p. 11; and Grigor'ev, *Tak srazhalis' kommunisty*, pp. 14, 25 and 30.
28. Bondar', *Uroki muzhestva*, pp. 23 and 31.
29. Ibid., p. 98.
30. Ibid., pp. 57–64.
31. Ibid., pp. 133–6.
32. Ibid., pp. 49–52.

33. Galatenko, *Katera idut k Myskhako*, pp. 20–30.
34. Kaida, *Atakuet morskaia pekhota*, p. 34.
35. Bondar', *Uroki muzhestva*, p. 133.
36. Ibid., pp. 130–1; and Galatenko, *Katera idut k Myskhako*, p. 66.
37. Bondar', *Uroki muzhestva*, pp. 104–5 and 124–32. See also Murmantseva, '*Zhenshchiny-voiny Maloi zemli*', pp. 177–9.
38. Grigor'ev, *Tak srazhalis' kommunisty*, p. 61.
39. Savitskii, *V nebe nad Maloi zemlei*, p. 154.
40. Vladimir Fomenko and Il'ia Khomenko, 'Svideteli i sud'i', *Zerkolo nedeli*, 13–19 June 2002, <http://www.zn.ua/3000/3150/35385> [accessed 23 November 2014].
41. Galatenko, *Katera idut k Myskhako*, p. 79.
42. Kaida, *Atakuet morskaia pekhota*, p. 41.
43. Grigor'ev, *Tak srazhalis' kommunisty*, pp. 50–1.
44. Bondar', *Uroki muzhestva*, pp. 53–5; Grigor'ev, *Tak srazhalis' kommunisty*, pp. 108–9; and Kaida, *Atakuet morskaia pekhota*, p. 60.
45. Lisa A. Kirschenbaum, *The Legacy of the Siege of Leningrad, 1941–1995: Myth, Memories and Monuments* (Cambridge and New York: Cambridge University Press, 2006), p. 185.
46. Malcolm Smith, *Britain and 1940: History, Myth, and Popular Memory* (New York: Routledge, 2000), pp. 85–6; and Mark Connelly, '"We Can Take It!" Britain and the Memory of the Home Front in the Second World War', in *Experience and Memory: The Second World War in Europe*, ed. Jorg Echternkamp and Stefan Martens (New York and Oxford: Berghahn, 2010), pp. 53–69, p. 59.
47. For example, Nina Tumarkin, *Moscow's War Memorial: The Story of a National Symbol* (Wellesley, MA: Wellesley College, 1988), p. 50.
48. Michael Ignatieff, 'Soviet War Memorials', *History Workshop Journal*/17 (1984), pp. 157–63, p. 158.
49. Zhores Medvedev, *Andropov* (Oxford: Blackwell, 1983), p. 101.
50. Roi Medvedev, '"Malaia zemlia": istoriia literaturnogo podloga'; and Lazar Lazarev, 'Russian Literature on the War and Historical Truth', in *World War 2 and the Soviet People*, eds John Garrard and Carol Garrard (New York: St Martin's, 1993), pp. 28–37, p. 34.
51. Sergei Borzenko, 'Malaia zemlia', in *Ot Sovetskogo informbiuro 1943–45*, ed. L. Lazarev (Moscow: Agentstvo pechati Novosti, 1982), pp. 119–27.
52. Georgii Sokolov, *Malaia zemlia: Rasskazy i ocherki* (Krasnodar: Krasnodarskoe knizhnoe izdatel'stvo, 1967), pp. 157–8.
53. This was on 15 September 1963 (Sokolov, *Malaia zemlia*, 1967, p. 386).
54. Georgii Sokolov, *Malaia zemlia* (Moscow: Sovetskaia Rossiia, 1971).
55. Georgii Sokolov, *My s Maloi zemli* (Moscow: Sovetskaia Rossiia, 1979), pp. 7–9.
56. Sokolov, *My s Maloi zemli*, 1979, pp. 369–70.
57. James V. Wertsch, *Voices of Collective Remembering* (Cambridge: Cambridge University Press, 2002), p. 35.
58. Ibid., pp. 14–5.

59. Raikunov, *Rota, za mnoi!*; and Marfin, *Geroicheskii shturm*.
60. Roi Medvedev, '"Malaia zemlia": istoriia literaturnogo podloga'.
61. Philip Taubman, *New York Times*, 8 February 1988, <http://www.nytimes.com/1988/02/08/world/across-soviet-brezhnev-s-name-falls.html?src=pm> [accessed 29 January 2013]; 'Minuta molchaniia', *TVmuseum.ru*, <http://www.tvmuseum.ru/catalog.asp?ob_no=12899> [accessed 28 April 2013]; and documentary film *'Malaia zemlia' Leonida Brezhneva* (Russia: Galakon Studio, 2010).

Part II Leonid Brezhnev: Local Legend or National Statesman?

1. Thomas Lahusen, *How Life Writes the Book: Real Socialism and Socialist Realism in Stalin's Russia* (Ithaca, NY: Cornell University Press, 1997), p. 2.
2. Alon Confino, *The Nation as a Local Metaphor: Württemberg, Imperial Germany, and National Memory, 1871–1918* (London and Chapel Hill, NC: University of Carolina Press, 1997); and Alon Confino, *Germany as a Culture of Remembrance: Promises and Limits of Writing History* (Chapel Hill, NC: University of North Carolina Press, 2006).
3. See, however, K. Qualls, *From Ruins to Reconstruction: Urban Identity in Soviet Sevastopol after World War II* (Ithaca, NY: Cornell University Press, 2009); Stephen Lovell, *The Shadow of War: Russia and the USSR, 1941 to the Present* (Chichester: Wiley-Blackwell, 2010), Chapter 6; and K. Qualls, 'Who Makes Local Memories?: The Case of Sevastopol after World War II', *Soviet and Post-Soviet Review*/38 (2011), pp. 130–48. See also Kirschenbaum's excellent case study of Leningrad, which substantially transcends the local in its scope (Lisa A. Kirschenbaum, *The Legacy of the Siege of Leningrad, 1941–1995: Myth, Memories and Monuments* (Cambridge and New York: Cambridge University Press, 2006).
4. 'Those serving on Malaia zemlia fostered a cherished dream to unite the Small with the Large' (Georgii Sokolov, *Malaia zemlia: Rasskazy i ocherki* (Krasnodar: Krasnodarskoe knizhnoe izdatel'stvo, 1967), p. 10).
5. Alexander Etkind, 'Mapping Memory Events in the East European Space', *East European Memory Studies* (2010), pp. 4–5, p. 4.
6. On nostalgia in Russia, see Svetlana Boym, 'From the Russian Soul to Post-Communist Nostalgia', *Representations*/49 (1995), pp. 133–66; Svetlana Boym, *The Future of Nostalgia* (New York: BasicBooks, 2001); Maya Nadkarni and Olga Shevchenko, 'The Death of Socialism and the Afterlife of its Monuments: Making and Marketing the Past in Budapest's Statue Park Museum', in *Contested Pasts: The Politics of Memory*, eds Katharine Hodgkin and Susannah Radstone (London and New York: Routledge, 2003), pp. 193–207; Svetlana Boym, 'Nostalgia and its Discontents', *Hedgehog Review*/9 (2007), pp. 7–18; and Serguei A. Oushakine, 'We're Nostalgic but We're not Crazy: Retrofitting the Past in Russia', *The Russian Review*/66 (2007), pp. 451–82.

Chapter 6 Brezhnev Comes to Town

1. Georgii Sokolov, 'O dniakh geroicheskikh, o liudiakh-geroiakh', *Novorossiiskii rabochii*, 13 September 1973, p. 3; 'Torzhestva v gorodakh-geroiakh', *Pravda*, 16 September 1973, p. 1; Captain A. Basov and Colonel V. Morozov, 'Nezabyvaemyi podvig: K 30-letiiu osvobozhdeniia goroda Novorossiiska', *Pravda*, 16 September 1973, p. 3; and TASS, 'Podvig i trud chernomortsev', *Izvestiia*, 17 September 1973, p. 1.
2. Nina Tumarkin, *Moscow's War Memorial: The Story of a National Symbol* (Wellesley, MA: Wellesley College, 1988), p. 50.
3. 'Torzhestva v gorodakh-geroiakh'.
4. Reprinted in Konstantin Podyma, 'Viktor Golikov: "Ia veriu i nadeius'...": poslednee interv'iu', *Novorossiiskie izvestiia*, 3 May 2012, <http://novodar.ru/index.php/novohistory-punkt/5683-vgpi-05-2012> [accessed 22 March 2016].
5. Sokolov, 'O dniakh geroicheskikh, o liudiakh-geroiakh'; and TASS, 'Podvig i trud chernomortsev'.
6. S. Borzenko, 'Vstrecha odnopolchan', *Ogonek*, June 1970, pp. 4–5.
7. TASS, 'Ot"ezd tovarishcha L.I. Brezhneva v Novorossiisk', *Izvestiia*, 6 September 1974, p. 1. This was repeated in *Pravda* the following day: 'Ot"ezd tovarishcha L.I. Brezhneva v Novorossiisk', *Pravda*, 7 September 1974, p. 1.
8. Iu. Ponomarenko, 'Bol'shaia slava Maloi zemli: Reportazh iz goroda-geroia Novorossiiska', *Izvestiia*, 6 September 1974, p. 1.
9. V. Belov, 'Novorossiisk, gorod-geroi', *Izvestiia*, 5 September 1974, p. 4.
10. TASS, 'Serdechnaia vstrecha v gorode-geroe: Pribytie tovarishcha L.I. Brezhneva v Novorossiisk', *Pravda*, 7 September 1974, p. 1. See also Georgii Sokolov, *My s Maloi zemli* (Moscow: Sovetskaia Rossiia, 1979), p. 365.
11. TASS, 'Serdechnaia vstrecha v gorode-geroe'; Iu. Alenchenko, 'Slava Novorossiiska', *Pravda*, 7 September 1974, p. 2; Ponomarenko, 'Bol'shaia slava Maloi zemli'; and TASS, 'Serdechnaia vstrecha', *Izvestiia*, 7 September 1974, p. 2.
12. TASS, 'Serdechnaia vstrecha', also in *NR*, 7 September 1974, p. 1; and Konstantin Podyma, 'Postoite u kamennykh listov', *NR*, 7 September 1974, p. 4.
13. TASS, 'Rodina slavit gorod-geroi!', *Izvestiia*, 7 September 1974, p. 1; and B. Galatenko, 'Zvezda Pobedy', *Literaturnaia gazeta*, 11 September 1974, p. 1.
14. Brezhnev's speech is reported in full in TASS, 'Rech' tovarishcha L.I. Brezhneva', *Izvestiia*, 7 September 1974, pp. 1–2.
15. Now available on the CD: L.I. Brezhnev: *'Budet khleb, budet i pesnia'* (Russia: Kapel'meister, 2005).
16. TASS, 'Rech' tovarishcha L.I. Brezhneva'.
17. P. Kostin, 'Rodina slavit gorod-geroi', *NR*, 11 September 1974, p. 3; and D. Rezaev, 'Fil'my o Novorossiiske', *NR*, 11 September 1974, p. 2.
18. TASS, 'Na zemle boevoi i trudovoi slavy', *Pravda*, 8 September 1974, p. 3; 'Na zemle, oveiannoi slavoi', *Izvestiia*, 9 September 1974, pp. 1 and 3; Ponomarenko, 'Bol'shaia slava Maloi zemli'; and Galatenko, 'Zvezda Pobedy'.

19. 'Znamenatel'naia data', *NR*, 14 September 1974, p. 1.
20. P. Belen'kin, 'Nash otvet – udarnyi trud', *NR*, 13 September 1974, p. 3.
21. 'Na zemle boevoi i trudovoi slavy', *NR*, 10 September 1974, p. 1. See also Valerie Bunce, 'The Political Economy of the Brezhnev Era: The Rise and Fall of Corporatism', *British Journal of Political Science*/13 (1983), pp. 129–58, pp. 131, 145 and 148.
22. Tat'iana Besedina, 'Brezhnev i Novorossiisk: o chem zhurnalisty "*NR*" ne napisali 25 let nazad', *NR*, 3 February 1999, pp. 4–5.
23. N.V. Kolesov, *V pamiati i v serdtse – navsegda* (Moscow: Izdatel'stvo politicheskoi literatury, 1975).
24. Sokolov, *My s Maloi zemli*, 1979, pp. 365–6.
25. E.Ia. Savitskii, *V nebe nad Maloi zemlei* (Krasnodar: Krasnodarskoe knizhnoe izdatel'stvo, 1980), p. 154; S.T. Grigor'ev, *Tak srazhalis' kommunisty* (Krasnodar: Krasnodarskoe knizhnoe izdatel'stvo, 1982), p. 108; and V.I. Grezin, *Narodnye mstiteli* (Krasnodar: Krasnodarskoe knizhnoe izdatel'stvo, 1982), p. 107.
26. Grigor'ev, *Tak srazhalis' kommunisty*, p. 108.
27. Sergei Kudryashov, 'Remembering and Researching the War: The Soviet and Russian Experience', in *Experience and Memory: The Second World War in Europe*, ed. Jorg Echternkamp and Stefan Martens (New York and Oxford: Berghahn, 2010), pp. 86–115, p. 89.
28. G. Sokolov, *My s Maloi zemli: Dokumental'nye rasskazy* (Krasnodar: Krasnodarskoe knizhnoe izdatel'stvo, 1985), p. 376.

Chapter 7 The Godfather

1. T.I. Iurina, *Novorossiiskoe protivostoianie: 1942–1943 gg.* (Krasnodar: Kniga, 2008).
2. 'Malaia zemlia', *Izvestiia*, 14 September 1995, p. 5.
3. Tat'iana Besedina, 'Brezhnev i Novorossiisk: o chem zhurnalisty "*NR*" ne napisali 25 let nazad', *Novorossiiskii rabochii*, 3 February 1999, pp. 4–5.
4. Sergei Kudryashov, 'Remembering and Researching the War: The Soviet and Russian Experience', in *Experience and Memory: The Second World War in Europe*, eds Jorg Echternkamp and Stefan Martens (New York and Oxford: Berghahn, 2010), pp. 86–115, p. 89.
5. V.A. Golikov, ed., *Novorossiisk* (Moscow: Planeta, 1978), p. 54.
6. Marianne Hirsch, 'Projected Memory: Holocaust Photographs in Personal and Public Fantasy', in *Acts of Memory: Cultural Recall in the Present*, eds Mieke Bal, Jonathan Crewe and Leo Spitzer (Hanover, NH and London: University Press of New England, 1999), pp. 3–23, p. 8.
7. Maria Bucur, *Heroes and Victims: Remembering War in Twentieth-Century Romania* (Bloomington, IN: Indiana University Press, 2009), p. 248.
8. E.D. Prialkina, 'V zhizni est' minuty, kotorye ne zabyvaiutsia . . .', in *Istoricheskie zapiski: Issledovaniia i materialy, vypusk 4*, eds S.G. Novikov and T.V. Raskatova

(Krasnodar: Kubanskoe knizhnoe izdatel'stvo, 2003), pp. 294–9, p. 296; Besedina, 'Brezhnev i Novorossiisk'; and 'Brezhnev v vospominaniiakh Novorossiitsev', *Kuban' TV*, 19 December 2012, <http://kubantv.ru/rossija/23512-leonid-ilich-brezhnev-v-vospominanijakh–novorossijjtsev/> [accessed 6 August 2013].

9. *Novorostsement: 1882–2012* (Krasnodar: Hyppogrifon, 2012), p. 31.
10. A. Eremenko and K. Podyma, *Imenem Rossii narechennyi* (Moscow: Sovetskaia Rossiia, 1988), p. 269.
11. Bunce, 'The Political Economy of the Brezhnev Era', pp. 130 and 137; and M.V. Erokhin, *Novorossiisk*, ed. D.A. Vasil'evich (Krasnodar: RIO, 2012), pp. 72–3.
12. Ivo Mijnssen, *Memorial Landscapes in the Postwar Generation: The Soviet Hero-Cities of Tula and Novorossiysk in the Brezhnev era*, PhD thesis (University of Basel, Switzerland, 2015), pp. 300–1.
13. Ibid., p. 318.
14. Ibid., p. 290.
15. Yoram Gorlizki, 'Too Much Trust: Regional Party Leaders and Local Political Networks under Brezhnev', *Slavic Review*/69 (2010), pp. 676–700, p. 693.
16. See also Evgenii Lapin, 'Vspomnim prezhnego Leonida Brezhneva', *NR*, 19 December 2006, p. 4.
17. Evgenii Rozhanskii, 'Bez dozhdia i vody ne budet', *NR*, 19 June 2013, <http://www.novorab.ru/ArticleSection/Index/40> [accessed 19 June 2013]; and Ol'ga Ovcharnko, 'Posledniaia kaplia?', *NR*, 8 February 2013, pp. 1–2.
18. I.S. Shiian, *Novorossiisk – gorod-geroi* (Moscow: Voennoe izdatel'stvo Ministerstva oborony SSSR, 1982); Besedina, 'Brezhnev i Novorossiisk'; Erokhin, *Novorossiisk*, p. 73; and Sergei Novikov, 'Bol'shaia voda', 28 January 2011, <http://novorosforum.ru/threads/antologija-gorodskoj-istorii-ot-sergeja-novikova.1421> [accessed 22 March 2016].
19. *PepsiCo*, 7 June 2009, <http://www.pepsico.com/PressRelease/PepsiCo-and-Pepsi-Bottling-Group-to-Invest-1-Billion-In-Russia-50-Years-After-Ru-07062009.html> [accessed 17 June 2013]; Leonid Mlechin, *Brezhnev* (Moscow: Molodaia gvardiia, 2011), p. 496; and Sergei Novikov, 'Kak "Stolichnuiu" na "Pepsi" meniali …', 7 February 2011, <http://novorosforum.ru/threads/antologija-gorodskoj-istorii-ot-sergeja-novikova.1421/page-2> [accessed 22 March 2016].
20. Georgii Sokolov, *Malaia zemlia: Rasskazy i ocherki* (Krasnodar: Krasnodarskoe knizhnoe izdatel'stvo, 1967), pp. 104–11; TASS, 'Serdechnaia vstrecha v gorode-geroe: Pribytie tovarishcha L.I. Brezhneva v Novorossiisk', *Pravda*, 7 September 1974, p. 1; and Aleksandr Maisurian, *Drugoi Brezhnev* (Moscow: Vagrius, 2004), p. 84.
21. The Holy Bible: The Gospel according to John 4, vv. 4–26; and Evgenii Matveev, *Sud'ba po-russki* (Moscow: Vagrius, 2000), p. 197.
22. Sergei Novikov, *Novorossiisk: Istoriia dlia vsekh* (Stavropol': Kniga, 2007), p. 38.

23. *Tsentral'naia gorodskaia biblioteka im. Gor'kogo*, <http://www.ballion.ru/skulptura_daryashhaya_vodu.html> [accessed 18 June 2013].
24. V.A. Golikov, *Novorossiisk*; Igor' Platonov, ed., *Novorossiisk: 1838–1998* (Tula: Lev Tolstoi, 1998); and Erokhin, *Novorossiisk*, pp. 74–5.
25. Prialkina, 'V zhizni est' minuty, kotorye ne zabyvaiutsia …', p. 299.

Chapter 8 The Making of a Modern Legend

1. 'Enough of talking and arguing,/And love of weary eyes … /Away on the pirate's sea/The brigantine unfurls her sails.' From 'Brigantina' (1937) by Pavel Kogan, cited in T.I. Iurina, *Novorossiiskoe protivostoianie: 1942–1943 gg.* (Krasnodar: Kniga, 2008), p. 339.
2. Philip Taubman, *New York Times*, 8 February 1988, <http://www.nytimes.com/1988/02/08/world/across-soviet-brezhnev-s-name-falls.html?src=pm> [accessed 29 January 2013].
3. Otto Boele, 'Remembering Brezhnev in the New Millennium: Post-Soviet Nostalgia and Local Identity in the City of Novorossiisk', *The Soviet and Post-Soviet Review*/38 (2011), pp. 3–29, pp. 7–8.
4. See Maya Nadkarni, 'The Death of Socialism and the Afterlife of its Monuments: Making and Marketing the Past in Budapest's Statue Park Museum', in *Contested Pasts: The Politics of Memory*, ed. Katharine Hodgkin and Susannah Radstone (London and New York: Routledge, 2003), pp. 193–207, p. 195.
5. Evgenii Kharchenko, 'Iz zhizni pamiatnikov: Brezhnev vernulsia na Maluiu zemliu', *Komsomol'skaia pravda*, 18 September 2004, p. 3.
6. 'Struktura Administratsii', *Ofitsial'nyi sait administratsii* <www.admnvrsk.ru/administratsiya/struktura-administratsii> [accessed 22 February 2017].
7. Svetlana Tur'ialai, 'Leonid Brezhnev vernetsia na Maluiu Zemliu', *Kommersant'*, 26 August 2004, <http://www.kommersant.ru/doc/500605> [accessed 24 June 2013].
8. 'Pamiatnik sovetskomu lideru 1964–1982 godov Leonidu Brezhnevu reshili ustanovit' vlasti Novorossiiska', *Ural.ru*, 25 August 2004, <www.ural.ru/news/life/news-42314> [accessed 23 June 2013].
9. Mikhail Prorok, 'Ne trat'tes' na Brezhneva!', *Novorossiiskii rabochii*, 12 February 2004, p. 5.
10. 'Brezhnev zhil. Brezhnev zhiv?', *NR*, 26 February 2004, p. 5.
11. Sergei Karamaev, 'I Brezhnev takoi molodoi', *lenta.ru*, 17 September 2004, <http://lenta.ru/articles/2004/09/17/brezhnev> [accessed 3 September 2011].
12. Notably Evgenii Kozyrenov, see Mariia Anan'eva, 'Svoi sredi svoikh', *NR*, 17 September 2004, p. 1.
13. Mariia Anan'eva, 'Brezhnev ostanetsia v gorode vechno molodym', *NR*, 24 August 2003, p. 1.
14. Tur'ialai, 'Leonid Brezhnev vernetsia na Maluiu Zemliu'; Mariia Aleksandrova, 'Pamiat' v bronze: Brezhnev vernulsia na Maluiu zemliu', *Gazeta*, 17 September

2004, p. 4; Kharchenko, 'Iz zhizni pamiatnikov'; and Anan'eva, 'Brezhnev ostanetsia v gorode vechno molodym'.

15. Tur'ialai, 'Leonid Brezhnev vernetsia na Maluiu Zemliu'.
16. 'Svoi sredi svoikh'.
17. Anan'eva, 'Brezhnev ostanetsia v gorode vechno molodym'. See also Aleksandrova, 'Pamiat' v bronze'; and Kharchenko, 'Iz zhizni pamiatnikov'.
18. Evgenii Lapin, 'Vspomnim prezhnego Leonida Brezhneva', *NR*, 19 December 2006, p. 4.
19. 'Il'icha perenesut, esli na to budet volia zhitelei Novorossiiska', *Munitsipal'naia novostnaia lenta*, 26 February 2009, <http://nrnews.ru/33912.html> [accessed 23 June 2013].
20. See particularly Tur'ialai, 'Leonid Brezhnev vernetsia na Maluiu Zemliu'.
21. Notably Sergei Borzenko, *Na avanpostakh* (Moscow: Voennoe izdatel'stvo Ministerstva oborony SSSR, 1964), p. 41; Sergei Borzenko, '225 dnei muzhestva i otvagi', in *Podvig Novorossiiska*, ed. A.I. Makarenko (Krasnodar: Krasnodarskoe knizhnoe izdatel'stvo, 1978), pp. 76–84, p. 82; R.Ia. Kirpichev, *225 dnei muzhestva: Novorossiiskii desant 1943* (Krasnodar: Krasnodarskoe knizhnoe izdatel'stvo, 1978), p. 9; G. Sokolov, *My s Maloi zemli* (Moscow: Sovetskaia Rossiia, 1979), pp. 365–6; Mariia Pedenko, *"Polundra, Krasnoflottsy!": Povest'* (Kiev: Molod', 1980), pp. 5–6; Mariia Petrovna Pedenko, *Frontovoi dnevnik* (Krasnodar: Krasnodarskoe knizhnoe izdatel'stvo, 1981), p. 77; and S.T. Grigor'ev, *Tak srazhalis' kommunisty* (Krasnodar: Krasnodarskoe knizhnoe izdatel'stvo, 1982), p. 108.
22. William Tompson, *The Soviet Union under Brezhnev* (Harlow: Pearson Education, 2003), pp. 20–2; Edwin Bacon and Mark Sandle, 'Brezhnev Reconsidered', in *Brezhnev Reconsidered*, eds Edwin Bacon and Mark Sandle (Basingstoke: Palgrave, 2002), pp. 203–17, p. 208.
23. Sergei Semanov, 'Leonid Neodnoznachnyi', *Literaturnaia gazeta*/48 (2006), p. 3. For a portrait of the young Brezhnev, proving his organisational skills and leadership, see Aleksandr Kuznetsov, 'I Brezhnev takoi molodoi ...', *LG*/50 (2006), p. 4.
24. See discussions in *Literaturnaia gazeta*, Nos. 39–40, 42, 44, 46, 47, 48 and 50 (2006).
25. Zhores Medvedev, *Andropov* (Oxford: Blackwell, 1983); Roi Medvedev, *Lichnost' i epokha: Politicheskii portret L.I. Brezhneva (kniga 1)* (Moscow: Novosti, 1991); Roi Medvedev, *Politicheskie portrety* (Moscow: Moskva, 2008); and Leonid Mlechin, *Brezhnev* (Moscow: Molodaia gvardiia, 2011).
26. For example, Aleksandr Maisurian, *Drugoi Brezhnev* (Moscow: Vagrius, 2004) with its Brezhnev jokes; and Sergei Semanov, *Dorogoi Leonid Il'ich* (Moscow: Algoritm, 2007).
27. A. Khinshtein, *Skazka o poteriannom vremeni: Pochemu Brezhnev ne smog stat' Putinym* (Moscow: OLMA, 2011). See also Sergei Kara-Murza, 'Zolotoi "zastoi"?', *LG*/44 (2006), p. 4; Dimitrii Karalis, 'Natsional'nyi geroi?', *LG*/46 (2006), p. 4; Sergei Kurginian, *LG*/47 (2006), p. 4; and Semanov, 'Leonid Neodnoznachnyi'.

28. Edwin Bacon, 'Reconsidering Brezhnev', in *Brezhnev Reconsidered*, eds Edwin Bacon and Mark Sandle (Basingstoke: Palgrave, 2002), pp. 1–21, pp. 4–6; Press Release No. 359, *VTsIOM*, 15 December 2005, <http://wciom.ru/index.php?id=268&uid=2113> [accessed 28 June 2013]; Kurginian, *LG*/47; and Boris Kagarlitskii, 'Dorogaia stabil'nost'', *LG*/47 (2006), p. 4.
29. Press Release No. 359, *VTsIOM*.
30. Serafima Prorocheskaia, 'Ia gorzhus', chto zhila v SSSR', *NR*, 26 February 2004, p. 5.
31. Boele, 'Remembering Brezhnev in the New Millennium'.
32. Iurina, *Novorossiiskoe protivostoianie*, p. 272.
33. Jan Assmann, 'Collective Memory and Cultural Identity', *New German Critique*/65 (1995), pp. 125–33; and Mikhail Yampolsky, 'In the Shadow of Monuments: Notes on Iconoclasm and Time', in *Soviet Hieroglyphics: Visual Culture in Late Twentieth-Century Russia*, ed. Nancy Condee (Bloomington, IA and London: Indiana University Press and BFI, 1995), pp. 93–112.
34. Paul Connerton, *How Modernity Forgets* (Cambridge: Cambridge University Press, 2009), p. 122.
35. Ibid., pp. 99–131.
36. I. Krivosheina, 'Ulitsa smotrit v budushchee', *NR*, 11 October 1980.
37. 'Il'icha perenesut, esli na to budet volia zhitelei Novorossiiska', *NR*, 26 February 2009.
38. Katharine Hodgkin and Susannah Radstone, 'Introduction: Contested Pasts', in *Contested Pasts: The Politics of Memory*, eds Katharine Hodgkin and Susannah Radstone (London and New York: Routledge, 2003), pp. 1–21, pp. 1 and 11–12.
39. 'Sud'bu pamiatnika reshat publichno', *NR*, 28 February 2009, p. 2.
40. 'Genseka podvinut', *NR*, 19 February 2009, p. 5; and Boele, 'Remembering Brezhnev in the New Millennium'.
41. 'Genseka podvinut'.
42. Information from the former director of the Hotel Brigantina, Boris Timchenko, in Tat'iana Besedina, 'Brezhnev i Novorossiisk: o chem zhurnalisty "*NR*" ne napisali 25 let nazad', *NR*, 3 February 1999, pp. 4–5.
43. Besedina, 'Brezhnev i Novorossiisk'; Sergei Novikov, 'Chelovek proshel po gorodu', *Novorossiiskie vesti*, 7 November 2009, p. 4.
44. Lapin, 'Vspomnim prezhnego Leonida Brezhneva'.
45. Novikov, 'Chelovek proshel po gorodu'.
46. Walter Scott, *Ivanhoe* (1820); and Bradford B. Broughton, *The Legends of King Richard I, Coeur de Lion* (The Hague and Paris: Mouton, 1966).
47. Jeffrey Olick, 'Introduction', in *The Collective Memory Reader*, eds Jeffrey K. Olick, Vered Vinitzky-Seroussi and Daniel Levy (Oxford: Oxford University Press, 2011), pp. 3–62.
48. Gillian Bennett and Paul Smith, 'Introduction', in *Contemporary Legend: A Reader*, eds Gillian Bennett and Paul Smith (New York and London: Garland, 1996), pp. xxi–xxxix, pp. xxii–xxiv.
49. Novikov, 'Chelovek proshel po gorodu'; and Novikov, 'Genseka podvinut'.

50. Eleonora Kivachitskaia, 'Sprosite narod!'; Igor' Sergeevich, 'Vy kogo guliat' ne puskaete?'; V. Vasil'ev, 'Teper' ochered' Novorossiiska povoevat' za Brezhneva', and V. Rudik, 'Zamakhnulis' eshche na odnogo russkogo soldata', *NR*, 19 February 2009, p. 5; Riazanovy Ivanenko, 'Milosti prosim k nam!'; V.A. Rodchenko, 'Uvidit vsia strana'; Irina Zinchuk, '"Propisku" pamiatnikam – podbirat' ne naspekh'; and Sergei Novikov, 'Ubezhat' ot eklektiki', *NR*, 21 February 2009, p. 2; Evgenii Kofman, Viktoriia Zhdanova, Tat'iana Kulakova, Anatolii Chernenko and El'vira Skliarova, 'Pochemu liudi voiuiut s pamiatnikami?', *NR*, 4 April 2009, p. 5.
51. Novikov, 'Chelovek proshel po gorodu'.
52. *Postanovlenie* No. 3525 of 12 October 2009, *NV*, 20 October 2009, p. 7.
53. *Postanovlenie* No. 3920 of 13 November 2009. See 'Leonida Il'icha v Novorossiiske resheno ostavit' v pokoe', *MNL*, 19 November 2009, <http://nrnews.ru/38470-.html> [accessed 23 June 2013].
54. Vitalii Chaika, 'Brezhnev "poidet" k moriu', *NR*, 29 June 2010.
55. Oksana Mashkarova, 'K glave – kak v posledniuiu instantsiiu', *NR*, 29 December 2010, <http://www.novorab.ru/ArticleSection/Details/1945/1> [accessed 5 September 2011].
56. The expression is from Ashplant, et al., 'The Politics of War Memory and Commemoration: Contexts, Structures and Dynamics', in *The Politics of War, Memory and Commemoration*, eds T.G. Ashplant, Graham Dawson and Michael Roper (London: Routledge, 2000), pp. 3–85, p. 43.
57. 'Leonid Il'ich obretet novuiu propisku', *MNL*, 21 October 2009, <http://nrnews.ru/38024-.html> [accessed 23 June 2013]. See also 'Leonida Il'icha v Novorossiiske resheno ostavit' v pokoe'; V. Rudik, 'Zamakhnulis' eshche na odnogo russkogo soldata', *NR*, 19 February 2009, p. 5; and Boele, 'Remembering Brezhnev in the New Millennium', p. 27.
58. Connerton, *How Modernity Forgets*, pp. 99–131.
59. 'Leonid Il'ich obretet novuiu propisku'.
60. Cruise Manager at 'Voyages of Discovery'.
61. 'Leonid Brezhnev vernetsia na Maluiu Zemliu'.

Chapter 9 The State Comes to Town Again

1. 'Na "Maloi zemle" Brezhneva postroiat elitnye kottedzhi i torgovye tsentry', *RBK Nedvizhimost'*, 19 November 2012, <http://realty.rbc.ru/articles/19/11/2012/562949986403022.shtml> [accessed 22 March 2016].
2. See, for example, Lisa A. Kirschenbaum, *The Legacy of the Siege of Leningrad, 1941–1995: Myth, Memories and Monuments* (Cambridge and New York: Cambridge University Press, 2006); K. Qualls, *From Ruins to Reconstruction: Urban Identity in Soviet Sevastopol after World War II* (Ithaca, NY: Cornell University Press, 2009); and K. Qualls, 'Who Makes Local Memories?: The Case of Sevastopol after World War II', *Soviet and Post-Soviet Review*/38 (2011), pp. 130–48.

3. The Putin era war cult has been well documented in, for example, Scherrer, 'Sowjetunion/Rußland: Siegesmythos versus Vergangenheitsaufarbeitung', in *Mythen der Nationen, Volume 2. 1945: Arena der Erinnerung*, ed. Monika Flacke (Mainz am Rhein: Philipp von Zabern, 2004), pp. 619–57; I. Kurilla, 'The Symbolic Politics of the Putin Administration', in *Identities and Politics during the Putin Presidency*, eds Philipp Casula and Jeronim Perovic (Stuttgart: Ibidem, 2009), pp. 255–69; Stephen Lovell, *The Shadow of War: Russia and the USSR, 1941 to the Present* (Chichester: Wiley-Blackwell, 2010); Ivo Mijnssen, 'The Victory Myth and Russia's Identity', *Russian Analytical Digest*/72 (2010), pp. 6–9; Myriam Désert, 'Comment sont Regardés les Films sur la Grande Guerre Patriotique dans la Russie Actuelle?', *The Journal of Power Institutions in Post-Soviet Societies*/12 (2011); Lisa Kirschenbaum, 'World War II in Soviet and Post-Soviet Memory', *Soviet and Post-Soviet Review*/38 (2011), pp. 97–103; N.E. Koposov, *Pamiat' strogogo rezhima: istoriia politika v Rossii* (Moscow: Novoe literaturnoe obozrenie, 2011); Olga Kucherenko, 'That'll Teach'em to Love Their Motherland!: Russian Youth Revisit the Battles of World War II', *The Journal of Power Institutions in Post-Soviet Societies*/12 (2011); Stephen M. Norris, 'Memory for Sale: Victory Day 2010 and Russian Remembrance', *Soviet and Post-Soviet Review*/38 (2011), pp. 201–29; and Elizabeth A. Wood, 'Performing Memory: Vladimir Putin and the Celebration of World War II in Russia', *Soviet and Post-Soviet Review*/38 (2011), pp. 172–200.
4. Bo Petersson, *National Self-Images and Regional Identities in Russia* (Aldershot: Ashgate, 2001), p. 60.
5. For example, Eric Hobsbawm, 'Introduction: Inventing Traditions', in *The Invention of Tradition*, eds Eric Hobsbawm and Terence Ranger (Cambridge: Cambridge University Press, 2008), pp. 1–14; and John Bodnar, 'Remaking America: Public Memory, Commemoration and Patriotism in the Twentieth Century', in *The Collective Memory Reader*, eds Jeffrey K. Olick, Vered Vinitzky-Seroussi and Daniel Levy (Oxford: Oxford University Press, 2011), pp. 265–8, p. 266.
6. Bacon and Sandle, 'Brezhnev Reconsidered', in *Brezhnev Reconsidered*, eds Edwin Bacon and Mark Sandle (Basingstoke: Palgrave, 2002), pp. 203–17, p. 206.
7. From Putin's annual address to parliament (25 April 2005).
8. Bacon and Sandle, 'Brezhnev Reconsidered', p. 205.
9. A. Khinshtein, *Skazka o poteriannom vremeni: Pochemu Brezhnev ne smog stat' Putinym* (Moscow: OLMA, 2011).
10. Lina Gritsenko, 'Vladimir Putin priznaet dvizhenie tol'ko vpered', *Novorossiiskii rabochii*, 30 August 2011, <http://novorab.ru/ArticleSection/Details/3731> [accessed 30 August 2011]; and Tom Parfitt, 'Putin's Outrider: "The Surgeon" Vows to Quell Anti-Kremlin Dissent', *The Telegraph*, 24 March 2015, <http://www.telegraph.co.uk/news/worldnews/europe/russia/11492898/Putins-outrider-The-Surgeon-vows-to-quell-anti-Kremlin-dissent.html> [accessed 13 April 2016].

11. Gritsenko, 'Vladimir Putin priznaet dvizhenie tol'ko vpered'; and 'Vladimir Putin pribyl v Novorossiisk, gde primet uchastie v mezhdunarodnom baik-shou', *Pervyi kanal*, 29 August 2011, <http://www.1tv.ru/news/print/183762> [accessed 21 July 2013].
12. Kuz'mina, 'V Novorossiiske prem'er-ministr vozglavil kolonnu baikerov', 30 August 2011; and 'Vladimir Putin pribyl v Novorossiisk'.
13. Marina Rybkina and Sergei Mukhtarov, 'Putin v nov' chaeval s frontovnikami', *NR*, 8 May 2010, p. 1; and 'VIP-vizit', *Novorossiiskie vesti*, 11 May 2010, p. 2.
14. Dmitrii Medvedev, 'Velikaia Otechestvennaia voina nikogda ne budet dlia nashego naroda istoricheskoi abstraktsiei', *Prezident Rossii*, 08 May 2010, <http://www.kremlin.ru/news/7681> [accessed 20 May 2010].
15. <http://medvedev.kremlin.ru/biography> [accessed 20 May 2010].
16. 'Presidentskii desant', *Rossiiskaia gazeta*, 15 July 2009 <http://www.rg.ru/2009/07/15/medvedev.html> [accessed 26 July 2013].
17. Cynthia Simmons and Nina Perlina, *Writing the Siege of Leningrad: Women's Diaries, Memoirs, and Documentary Prose* (Pittsburgh, PA: University of Pittsburgh Press, 2002), p. xviii; and Richard Sakwa, *Putin: Russia's Choice* (London and New York: Routledge, 2004), pp. 2–3. See also Wood, 'Performing memory', pp. 176 and 198.

Part III Respect for the Dead: Ritual and Monumental Remembrance

1. 'In the silence everyone has stopped still:/The chimes beat regularly in the quiet air,/And the Eternal Flame burns up to heaven. // We lit it in memory of all those/Who gave their lives for the Motherland./These heroic deeds/Live on in our hearts.' Text from the Shostakovich Museum by G. Bel'kind, Headmaster of School Number Three (1964), written as words for the 'Novorossiisk Chimes'.
2. All dates pertaining to monuments are from records held in the Novorossiisk Museum archives.
3. 'Novorossiiskie kuranty', Shostakovich opus 111b; K. Mikhailov, 'Dmitrii Shostakovich v Novorossiiske', in *Istoricheskie zapiski: Issledovaniia i materialy, vypusk 3* (Krasnodar: Severnyi Kavkaz, 1999), pp. 268–78.
4. Nina Tumarkin, *The Living and the Dead: The Rise and Fall of the Cult of World War II in Russia* (New York: BasicBooks, 1994), p. 41; Geoffrey Hosking, *Russia and the Russians: A History from Rus to the Russian Federation* (London: Allen Lane, Penguin, 2001), p. 492.

Chapter 10 Hats off to Heroes: The Beskozyrka Ritual

1. G. Sokolov, *My s Maloi zemli* (Moscow: Sovetskaia Rossiia, 1979), pp. 367–8.
2. Discussed in Jonathan Brunstedt, 'Building a Pan-Soviet Past: The Soviet War Cult and the Turn Away from Ethnic Particularism', *Soviet and Post-Soviet Review*/38 (2011), pp. 149–71.

3. Eric Hobsbawm, 'Introduction: Inventing Traditions', in *The Invention of Tradition*, eds Eric Hobsbawm and Terence Ranger (Cambridge: Cambridge University Press, 2008), pp. 1–14, p. 1.
4. Catherine Merridale, 'War, death and remembrance in Soviet Russia', in *War and Remembrance in the Twentieth Century*, eds Jay Winter and Emmanuel Sivan (Cambridge: Cambridge University Press, 2000), pp. 61–83, pp. 62 and 77.
5. Captain M. Shiriamov, 'Zavtra – Prazdnik Pobedy', *Novorossiiskii rabochii*, 8 May 1963, p. 2; and *NR*, 9 May 1965.
6. 'Operatsiia "Beskozyrka"', *NR*, 12 January 1968, p. 4.
7. Konstantin Podyma, *Vechnyi ogon': ty gori, ne sgorai* ... (Moscow: Pilotnoe izdanie, 2008), p. 8.
8. Sergei I. Zhuk, 'Religion, "Westernization", and Youth in the "Closed City" of Soviet Ukraine, 1964–84', *Russian Review*/67 (2008), pp. 661–79, p. 672.
9. L. Lysenko, 'Schastlivogo plavaniia, "Seskor"', *Iunost'*/3 (1966), p. 142.
10. Konstantin Podyma, *Schastlivogo plavaniia, 'Shkhuna Rovesnikov'!* (Moscow: Detskaia literatura, 1975), pp. 5–6.
11. Raisa Sokolova, *Beskozyrka* (Novorossiisk: Departament kul'tury Krasnodarskogo kraia, *c.* 2005), pp. 8–9.
12. Gleb Tsipursky, 'Conformism and Agency: Model Young Communists and the Komsomol Press in the Later Khrushchev Years', *Europe-Asia Studies*/7 (2013), pp. 1396–416; and Jeffrey Brooks, *Thank You, Comrade Stalin! Soviet Public Culture from Revolution to Cold War* (Princeton, NJ: Princeton University Press, 2001), p. 241.
13. Konstantin Podyma, ... *chtob ikh ne zabyvali my: Dokumental'nye ocherki* (Novorossiisk and Moscow: 2009), p. 28; and T.I. Iurina, *Novorossiiskoe protivostoianie: 1942–1943 gg.* (Krasnodar: Kniga, 2008), p. 163.
14. Inna Sokolova, 'Bardic Song: From Exotica to Utopia', *Russian Studies in Literature*/41 (2005), pp. 83–100, pp. 84–5.
15. Ludmilla Alexeyeva, and Paul Goldberg, *The Thaw Generation: Coming of Age in the Post-Stalin Era* (Boston, MA: Little, Brown, 1990), p. 30.
16. Nikolai Mitrokhin, *Russkaia partiia: dvizhenie russkikh natsionalistov v SSSR, 1953–1985 gody* (Moscow: Novoe literaturnoe obozrenie, 2003), pp. 114–6 and 277; A. Yurchak, *Everything was Forever Until It Was No More: The Last Soviet Generation* (Princeton, NJ and Oxford: Princeton University Press, 2006), ch. 3; and Brunstedt, 'Building a Pan-Soviet Past', pp. 163–6.
17. Podyma, *Vechnyi ogon'*, p. 19; and 'Mify – ne rify, no v farvatere "Beskozyrki" – ni k chemu!', *Novorossiiskie izvestiia*, 16 February 2011, <http://novodar.ru/index.php/novohistory-punkt/2148-mnrnvfbnkch-02-2011> [accessed 21 December 2011].
18. V. Saloshenko, *Obiazan skazat'* (Krasnodar: Severnyi Kavkaz, 1998), p. 11.
19. Mark Edele, 'Collective Action in Soviet Society: The Case of War Veterans', in *Writing the Stalin Era: Sheila Fitzpatrick and Soviet Historiography*, eds Golfo Alexopoulos, Julie Hessler and Kiril Tomoff (New York: Palgrave Macmillan, 2011), pp. 117–32, pp. 117, and 124–8.

20. 'Mify – ne rify!'.
21. A. Eremenko and K. Podyma, *Imenem Rossii narechennyi* (Moscow: Sovetskaia Rossiia, 1988), p. 349.
22. V.D. Starikova, 'Veteranskoe dvizhenie v Novorossiiske', in *Istoricheskie zapiski: Issledovanniia i materialy, vypusk 4*, eds S.G. Novikov and T.V. Raskatova (Krasnodar: Kubanskoe knizhnoe izdatel'stvo, 2003), pp. 261–73.
23. Ibid.; and Konstantin Podyma, *"Beskozyrka": Cherez gody i stoletiia: Dokumental'naia povest'* (Novorossiisk and Moscow: 2008), pp. 41–2.
24. 'Mify – ne rify!'.
25. Podyma, *"Beskozyrka"*, pp. 41 and 47; and Konstantin Podyma, 'Plyvi, beskozyrka', *NR*, 7 February 1973, p. 3.
26. Sokolov, *My s Maloi zemli*, 1979, pp. 367–8.
27. Podyma, *"Beskozyrka"*, pp. 11–34.
28. Brunstedt, 'Building a Pan-Soviet Past', p. 163; and Polly Jones, 'The Fire Burns On? The "Fiery Revolutionaries" Biographical Series and the Rethinking of Propaganda in the Brezhnev Era', *Slavic Review*/74 (2015), pp. 32–56.
29. Hobsbawm, 'Introduction: Inventing Traditions'.
30. Edward Shils, *Tradition* (Chicago, IL: University of Chicago Press, 1981), p. 25.
31. Paul Connerton, *How Societies Remember* (Cambridge: Cambridge University Press, 1989), p. 23.
32. Maurice Halbwachs, *On Collective Memory*, trans. Lewis A. Coser (Chicago IL and London: University of Chicago Press, 1992) (originally published 1925).
33. Connerton, *How Societies Remember*, p. 23.
34. Sokolova, *Beskozyrka*, pp. 16–7.
35. Georgii Sokolov, *Malaia zemlia: Rasskazy i ocherki* (Krasnodar: Krasnodarskoe knizhnoe izdatel'stvo, 1967), p. 10; and V.S. Murmantseva, 'Zhenshchiny-voiny Maloi zemli', *Voprosy istorii*/2 (1981), pp. 177–9, p. 177.
36. Ibid., p. 8, reproduced in A.A. Grechko, *Bitva za Kavkaz* (Moscow: Voenizdat, 1967), pp. 279–80.
37. Sokolova, *Beskozyrka*, pp. 16–7; and leaflet held in the archives of Novorossiiskii istoricheskii muzei-zapovednik: 'Operatsiia "Beskozyrka–80"', 21 January 1980, MA 15049, Novorossiiskoe PPO, zak. No. 334.
38. Merridale, 'War, Death and Remembrance in Soviet Russia', p. 79; and Stephen Lovell, *The Shadow of War: Russia and the USSR, 1941 to the Present* (Chichester: Wiley-Blackwell, 2010), pp. 9–10.
39. Starikova, 'Veteranskoe dvizhenie v Novorossiiske', p. 268; and '... Beskozyrka na volne', *NR*, 4 February 1998, p. 1.
40. See also Stephen Norris, 'Memory for Sale: Victory Day 2010 and Russian Remembrance', *Soviet and Post-Soviet Review*/38 (2011), pp. 201–29; and Elizabeth A. Wood, 'Performing Memory: Vladimir Putin and the Celebration of World War II in Russia', *Soviet and Post-Soviet Review*/38 (2011), pp. 172–200.
41. Oksana Mashkarova, 'Vakhtu pamiati budut nesti i deti', *NR*, 18 January 2013, p. 2; Lina Gritsenko, 'Detiam pokazali, kto nastoiashchii supergeroi', *NR*, 5 February 2013), p. 2.

42. '"Belye chaiki" vzmyli nad Maloi zemlei', *Ofitsial'nyi sait administratsii i Dumy munitsipal'nogo obrazovaniia gorod-geroi Novorossiisk*, 3 February 2017, <http://admnvrsk.ru/o-gorode/novosti/glavnye-novosti/news-20170203145257-234523/> [accessed 8 February 2017].
43. Norris, 'Memory for Sale', p. 217; and Julie Buckler, 'Taking and Retaking the Field: Borodino as a Site of Collective Memory', in *Rites of Place: Public Commemoration in Russia and Eastern Europe*, eds Julie Buckler and Emily D. Johnson (Evanston, IL: Northwestern University Press, 2013), pp. 203–23, p. 218.
44. Ol'ga Gailesh, 'Novorossiisk "Beskozyrka 2011"', *Munitsipal'naia novostnaia lenta*, 4 February 2011, <http://www.nrnews.ru/news/?id=42581> [accessed 9 February 2011].
45. Ibid., online responses.
46. Evgeniia Simanovich, '"Svechu v okne" mozhet zazhech' kazhdyi', *NR*, 23 January 2012, <http://www.novorab.ru/> [accessed 23 January 2012].
47. Sokolova, *Beskozyrka*, pp. 17–9.
48. Podyma, *Vechnyi ogon'*, p. 5. Other works on memory by Podyma include: *Na volne pamiati* (Moscow and Novorossiisk: Sentiabr', 2008); *'Beskozyrka'*; and *... chtob ikh ne zabyvali my*.
49. Podyma, *Vechnyi ogon'*, p. 5.
50. Sokolova, *Beskozyrka*; and Tamara Iurina, *Teleurok grazhdanstvennosti, posviashchennyi 40-letiiu operatsii 'Beskozyrka'* (Russia: Novaia Rossiia, 3 February 2008).
51. Catherine Merridale, 'Russia', in Glennys Howarth and Oliver Leaman, eds, *Encyclopedia of Death and Dying* (London: Routledge, 2001), pp. 390–1.
52. Barbara Misztal, 'Durkheim on Collective Memory', *Journal of Classical Sociology*/3 (2003), pp. 123–43, p. 139; Catherine Merridale, *Ivan's War: Life and Death in the Red Army, 1939–1945* (New York: Picador, 2006), p. 378; and Evgenii Rozhanskii, 'Zashchitnikam tvoim, podvigu tvoemu, Novorossiisk', *NR*, 5 February 2014, <http://www.novorab.ru/ArticleSection/Details/11327> [accessed 7 February 2014].
53. Merridale, *Ivan's War*, pp. 378–9.
54. 'Soldaty obreli pokoi', *NR*, 17 September 2012, <http://www.novorab.ru/ArticleSection/Details/6564/3> [accessed 7 October 2012].
55. John Bodnar, 'Public Memory in an American City: Commemoration in Cleveland', in *Commemorations: The Politics of National Identity*, ed. J.R. Gillis (Princeton, NJ: Princeton University Press, 1994), pp. 74–89, p. 75.
56. 'Fevral'skii poryv', *NR*, 29 January 2011, p. 3; and Tat'iana Staroverova, 'Galina Krympokha: Snova rvu na sebe tel'niashku', *NR*, 30 November 2010, <http://www.novorab.ru/ArticleSection/Details/1733> [accessed 2 September 2011].
57. Shils, *Tradition*, p. 236.
58. 'V Novorossiiske proshla Vserossiiskaia vakhta pamiati "Beskozyrka–2011"', *OSA*, 4 February 2011, <http://www.admnvrsk.ru/index.php/2010-02-26-12-44-41/4277--l-2011r> [accessed 9 February 2011]; and Gailesh, 'Novorossiisk "Beskozyrka 2011"'.

59. 'Segodnia v Tsemesskoi bukhte gremeli vzryvy snariadov i avtomatnye ocheredi', *OSA*, 3 February 2017, <http://admnvrsk.ru/o-gorode/novosti/glavnye-novosti/news-20170203231527-728465/> [accessed 7 February 2017].
60. Podyma, *'Beskozyrka'*, p. 47; and Oksana Mashkarova, 'Novorossiisk pomnit!', *NR*, 5 February 2013, p. 1.
61. 'Novosti', *Pervyi kanal*, 0900, 4 February 2011), <http://www.1tv.ru/newsvideoarchive/pd=04.02.2011> [accessed 8 July 2012].
62. 'Community of memory' is the term adopted in Robert Bellah, Richard Madsen, William M. Sullivan, Ann Swidler and Steven M. Tipton, *Habits of the Heart: Individualism and Commitment in American Life* (Berkeley, CA: University of California Press, 1985).
63. John E. Bodnar, *Remaking America: Public Memory, Commemoration, and Patriotism in the Twentieth Century* (Princeton, NJ: Princeton University Press, 1992).
64. Thomas C. Wolfe, 'Past as Present, Myth, or History? Discourses of Time and the Great Fatherland War', in *The Politics of Memory in Postwar Europe*, ed. Richard Ned Lebow, Wulf Kansteiner and Claudio Fogu (Durham, NC and London: Duke University Press, 2006), pp. 249–83, p. 266.
65. Mikhail Yampolsky, 'In the Shadow of Monuments: Notes on Iconoclasm and Time', in *Soviet Hieroglyphics: Visual Culture in Late Twentieth-Century Russia*, ed. Nancy Condee (Bloomington, IA and London: Indiana University Press and BFI, 1995), pp. 93–112, p. 96.
66. Katerina Clark, *The Soviet Novel: History as Ritual* (Bloomington and Indianapolis, IN: Indiana University Press, 2000), p. 40.
67. Sokolov, *My s Maloi zemli*, 1979, p. 368.
68. Sokolova, *Beskozyrka*, p. 14.
69. 'Fevral'skii poryv'.
70. Viktoriia Nikolaenko, '"Beskozyrka" vskolykhnula volny nashei pamiati', *NR*, 4 February 2011, p. 1.
71. Evgenii Rozhanskii, 'Zashchitnikam tvoim, podvigu tvoemu, Novorossiisk', *NR*, 5 February 2014, <http://www.novorab.ru/ArticleSection/Details/11327> [accessed 7 February 2014].
72. Podyma, *Schastlivogo plavaniia, 'Shkhuna Rovesnikov'!*, pp. 67–8.
73. 'V Novorossiiske sostoialas' sorok chetvertaia operatsiia "Beskozyrka"', *NR*, 3 February 2012, <http://www.nrnews.ru/news/?id=47939> [accessed 4 February 2012].
74. E. Zerubavel, *Hidden Rhythms: Schedules and Calendars in Social Life* (Chicago, IL: University of Chicago Press, 1981).
75. 'Kalendar' znamenatel'nykh i pamiatnykh dat goroda-geroia Novorossiiska na 2012 god: A u nas vse daty – kruglye', *NR*, 25 January 2012, <http://www.novorab.ru/ArticleSection/Details/4847> [accessed 26 January 2012].
76. Sokolova, *Beskozyrka*, p. 15.
77. 'Galina Krympokha prochitala lektsiiu o vysadke desanta na Maluiu zemliu starsheklassnikam shkoly No. 30', *MNL*, 1 February 2007, <http://nrnews.ru/news/?id=2729> [accessed 2 September 2011].

78. Jan Assmann, 'Collective Memory and Cultural Identity', *New German Critique*/65 (1995), pp. 125–33, p. 128; Eviatar Zerubavel, 'Calendars and History: A Comparative Study of the Social Organization of National Memory', in *States of Memory: Continuities, Conflicts, and Transformations in National Retrospection*, ed. Jeffrey K. Olick (Durham, NC and London: Duke University Press, 2003), pp. 315–37; and M. Christine Boyer, 'The City of Collective Memory: Its Historical Imagery and Architectural Entertainments', in *The Collective Memory Reader*, ed. Jeffrey K. Olick, Vered Vinitzky-Seroussi and Daniel Levy (Oxford: Oxford University Press, 2011), pp. 378–81, p. 381.

Chapter 11 Myth and Monuments: The Place of the Dead

1. 'We were as big as time./We were as alive as time./Now we are found in legends of those renowned days./Now we are found in epic poems and prose./Now we are found in granite and bronze./Now we are found in the silence of gravestones.' Robert Rozhdestvenskii, 'Pesnia pavshikh v boiu' (1971), *Robert Rozhdestvenskii: Sobranie sochinenii v trekh tomakh*, Vol. 2 (Moscow: Khudozhestvennaia literatura, 1985), p. 496.
2. Leonid Il'ich Brezhnev, 'Malaia zemlia', in *Malaia zemlia. Vozrozhdenie* (Moscow: Prosveshchenie, 1979), pp. 1–45, p. 12.
3. More scientifically, entropy, S, is equated to klnW, where k is the Boltzmann constant, and W the number of possible molecular arrangements.
4. This is one implication of the Second Law of Thermodynamics.
5. A. Eremenko and K. Podyma, *Imenem Rossii narechennyi* (Moscow: Sovetskaia Rossiia, 1988), p. 269.
6. M.V. Erokhin, *Novorossiisk*, ed. D.A. Vasil'evich (Krasnodar: RIO, 2012), pp. 70–1.
7. Evgenii Lapin, 'Na chertezhakh Iofana Novorossiisk predstaval grandioznym', *Novorossiiskii rabochii*, 20 February 2012, <http://novorab.ru/ArticleSection/Details/4993> [accessed 9 June 2016].
8. Eremenko and Podyma, *Imenem Rossii narechennyi*, p. 270.
9. V.N. Kaida, *Atakuet morskaia pekhota* (Krasnodar: Krasnodarskoe knizhnoe izdatel'stvo, 1980), p. 59.
10. All dates pertaining to monuments are from records held in the Novorossiisk Museum archives.
11. Ivo Mijnssen, *Memorial Landscapes in the Postwar Generation: The Soviet Hero-Cities of Tula and Novorossiysk in the Brezhnev era*, PhD thesis (University of Basel, Switzerland, 2015), p. 256.
12. Ibid., p. 266; and information from the regional manager in charge of maintenance and planning of monuments in Novorossiisk.
13. 'Monument to Mark Brezhnev Battle Site', *The Times*, 5 November 1980, p. 7.
14. Nina Tumarkin, 'Story of a War Memorial', in *World War 2 and the Soviet People*, eds John Garrard and Carol Garrard (New York: St Martin's, 1993), pp. 125–

46, p. 126; Scott W. Palmer, 'How Memory was Made: The Construction of the Memorial to the Heroes of the Battle of Stalingrad', *The Russian Review*/68 (2009), pp. 373–407, p. 378; and Jutta Scherrer, 'Sowjetunion/Rußland: Siegesmythos versus Vergangenheitsaufarbeitung', in *Mythen der Nationen, Volume 2. 1945: Arena der Erinnerung*, ed. Monika Flacke (Mainz am Rhein: Philipp von Zabern, 2004), pp. 619–57, p. 643.

15. Evgenii Rozhanskii, 'Zashchitnikam tvoim, podvigu tvoemu, Novorossiisk', *NR*, 5 February 2014, <http://www.novorab.ru/ArticleSection/Details/11327> [accessed 7 February 2014].
16. Viktoriia Nikolaenko, 'Nemetskie iaseni budut derzhat' oboronu na Maloi zemle', *NR*, 5 November 2010.
17. Catherine Merridale, 'Russia', in Glennys Howarth and Oliver Leaman, eds, *Encyclopedia of Death and Dying* (London: Routledge, 2001), pp. 390–1, p. 390.
18. Jennifer Iles, 'Recalling the Ghosts of War: Performing Tourism on the Battlefields of the Western Front', *Text and Performance Quarterly*/26 (2006), pp. 162–180, p. 170.
19. C. Winter, 'Tourism, Social Memory and the Great War', *Annals of Tourism Research*/36 (2009), pp. 607–26, p. 611.
20. Georgii Sokolov, *Malaia zemlia: Rasskazy i ocherki* (Krasnodar: Krasnodarskoe knizhnoe izdatel'stvo, 1967), pp. 348 and 354.
21. A. Pakhmutova and N. Dobronravov, 'Malaia zemlia' (1974); and E.D. Prialkina, 'Novorossiitsy chtiat i pomniat', in *Novorossiisk: Pamiat' i Pravda o Velikoi Otechestvennoi voine* (2005), pp. 150–3, p. 150.
22. I.S. Shiian, *Novorossiisk – gorod-geroi* (Moscow: Voennoe izdatel'stvo Ministerstva oborony SSSR, 1982), p. 170.
23. 'V Novorossiiske zhiteli zapisali videoobrashchenie V.V. Putinu protiv stroitel'stva khrama', *YouTube*, 8 January 2016, <https://www.youtube.com/watch?v=wMe-ursBqNI> [accessed 14 August 2016].
24. Paul Connerton, *How Modernity Forgets* (Cambridge: Cambridge University Press, 2009), p. 29.
25. E.D. Prialkina, 'Novorossiitsy chtiat i pomniat', p. 151; also the constantly updated collection of newspaper articles in the Novorossiisk Central Library: *Ikh imenami nazvany ulitsy.*
26. P.B. Shelley, *Percy Bysshe Shelley: The Major Works*, ed. Zachary Leader and Michael O'Neill (Oxford and New York: Oxford University Press, 2003), p. 198.
27. A. Gorognichenko, 'Zdanie-pamiatnik', *NR*, 13 September 1973, p. 3.
28. See Evgeniia Simanovich, 'Pamiatniki – v pochinku', *NR*, 31 August 2011, <http://www.novorab.ru/ArticleSection/Details/3753> [accessed 5 September 2011]; and 'V Novorossiiske prodolzhaetsia konkurs na luchshee soderzhanie pamiatnikov i monumentov', *Munitsipal'naia novostnaia lenta*, 11 August 2009, <http://nrnews.ru/news/?id=37149> [accessed 4 September 2011].
29. Matvei Prokorenko, 'Initsiativa nakazuema?', *Nash Novorossiisk*, 25 September 2008, <http://www.nnvrsk.ru/?article=1891&fullarticle=print> [accessed 16 November 2011]; and Matvei Prokorenko, 'Kampera ne tol'ko zametili, no i

priznali', *NN*, 23 April 2009, <http://www.nnvrsk.ru/?article=2519&fullarticle=print> [accessed 16 November 2011].

30. Simon Richmond, *Russia* (China: Lonely Planet, 2012), p. 414.
31. 'Inostrannye turisty spliasali pod "dubinushku"', *NR*, 20 September 2012, <http://www.novorab.ru/ArticleSection/Details/6594> [accessed 14 October 2014]; *Voyages of Discovery*, <http://www.voyagesofdiscovery.co.uk/excursion_calendar.php?port_id=18474&cruise_id = 18561&date_port = 2012-10-24> [accessed 9 October 2012]; *Sea Dream Yacht Club*, <http://www.seadream.com/voyages/11322> [accessed 14 October 2014].
32. Karen Oganesian, *Marafon* (Russia: 2013).
33. Liudmila Shalagina, 'Granitnyi dozor Novorossiiska', *NR*, 10 May 2012, <http://novorab.ru/ArticleSection/Details/5589> [accessed 22 March 2016].
34. A. Svetov and B. Miliavskii, 'I pesnia i stikh – eto bomba', *Znamia Rodiny*, 12 July 1943.

Chapter 12 People on the Periphery

1. 'No monuments stand above Babii Iar./The steep precipice is like a crude headstone./I am horrified.' Evgenii Evtushenko, 'Babii Iar' (1961), *Proza.ru*, <https://www.proza.ru/2012/08/17/363> [accessed 17 February 2017].
2. Evgenii Aleksandrov, 'Bratskaia mogila', *Novorossiiskii rabochii*, 24 September 2010.
3. 'Otkryt dlia poseshcheniia monument na Myskhakskom shosse', *Novorossiiskie vesti*, 11 May 2010, p. 2.
4. Matvei Prokorenko, 'Plity – na lom?', *Nash Novorossiisk*, 8 October 2008.
5. Karen Petrone, *The Great War in Russian Memory* (Bloomington, IN: Indiana University Press, 2011), pp. 41–2. See also Catherine Merridale, 'War, death and remembrance in Soviet Russia', in *War and Remembrance in the Twentieth Century*, ed. Jay Winter and Emmanuel Sivan (Cambridge: Cambridge University Press, 2000), pp. 61–83; and Catherine Merridale, 'Russia', in Glennys Howarth and Oliver Leaman, eds, *Encyclopedia of Death and Dying* (London: Routledge, 2001), pp. 390–1, p. 390.
6. Evgenii Lapin, 'Novorossiisk pomnit', *NR*, 18 September 2013, <http://www.novorab.ru/ArticleSection/Details/10115> [accessed 13 December 2013].
7. Denis Kurov, 'Nikto ne zabyt? … ', *7 dnei Kubani*, 18 May 2003, p. 2.
8. Evgenii Rozhanskii, 'Bratskaia mogila imen ne sokhranila', *NR*, 3 October 2013, <http://www.novorab.ru/ArticleSection/Details/10267> [accessed 13 December 2013].
9. Thomas C. Wolfe, 'Past as Present, Myth, or History? Discourses of Time and the Great Fatherland War', in *The Politics of Memory in Postwar Europe*, ed. Richard Ned Lebow, Wulf Kansteiner and Claudio Fogu (Durham, NC and London: Duke University Press, 2006), pp. 249–83, p. 267.
10. Voprosy uvekovecheniia pamiati pogibshikh pri zashchite Otechestva, 2006; Zakon Krasnodarskogo kraia o poiskovoi rabote, 1997; and Protokol eksgumatsii odinochnogo zakhoroneniia.

11. L. Ash, *Russia: Digging up the Dead* (United Kingdom: BBC Radio 4, 13 January 2014).
12. E.V. Romanov, 'Krovotochashchie rany voiny', in *Novorossiisk: Pamiat' i Pravda o Velikoi Otechestvennoi voine* (2005), pp. 158–61, p. 160.
13. Aleksandrov, 'Bratskaia mogila'; 'Soldaty obreli pokoi', *NR*, 17 September 2012, <http://www.novorab.ru/ArticleSection/Details/6564/3> [accessed 7 October 2012]; and Lapin, 'Novorossiisk pomnit'.
14. Raisa Sokolova, *Memorial'nyi kompleks v gorode-geroe Novorossiiske* (Novorossiisk: KADO, 2006), pp. 8–9.
15. 'Iubilei pamiatnika otmenili ritualom "Pamiat'"', *NR*, 18 September 2012, <http://www.novorab.ru/ArticleSection/Details/6565/2> [accessed 7 October 2012]; and Evgenii Lapin, 'Kapsula pamiati popolnilas' imenami pavshikh', *NR*, 4 May 2017, <www.novorab.ru/ArticleSection/Details/15119> [accessed 10 May 2017].
16. 'V Rossii otmechaiut Den' Neizvestnogo soldata', *Argumenty i fakty*, 3 December 2014, <http://www.aif.ru/society/history/1396958> [accessed 5 December 2014].
17. Robert Gold, *Du Sollst Nicht Töten!* (Germany: 2010).
18. *Volksbund*, <http://www.volksbund.de> [accessed 25 February 2012].
19. <http://www.volksbund.de/kriegsgraeberstaetten.html> [accessed 9 July 2016]. See also Anna Lebedeva, 'Krasnodarskii krai. V Apsheronske ofitsial'no otkryto nemetskoe kladbishche', *Novaia gazeta*, 8 September 2008, <http://www.novayagazeta.ru/news/38745.html> [accessed 25 February 2012].
20. Mark Donskoi, *Nepokorennye* (Kiev: Kiev Studios, 1945).
21. 'Pis'mo drugu', *NR*, 15 September 1963, p. 1; 'Nepokorennye', *NR*, 24 September 1963, p. 2; and 'Vechnaia pamiat' geroiam', *NR*, 24 September 1963, p. 2.
22. 'Zhertvam massovogo rasstrelia', in 'Nepokorennye'.
23. Nina Tumarkin, *The Living and the Dead: The Rise and Fall of the Cult of World War II in Russia* (New York: BasicBooks, 1994), p. 124; and Zvi Gitelman, 'Politics and Historiography of the Holocaust in the Soviet Union', in *Bitter Legacy: Confronting the Holocaust in the USSR*, ed. Zvi Gitelman (Bloomington and Indianapolis, IN: Indiana University Press, 1997), pp. 14–42, p. 20.
24. A. Eremenko and K. Podyma, *Imenem Rossii narechennyi* (Moscow: Sovetskaia Rossiia, 1988), p. 219.
25. Scholarship relevant to the situation of Jewish citizens in the Soviet Union includes: Petr Vail' and Aleksandr Genis, *60-e: Mir sovetskogo cheloveka* (Ann Arbor, MI: Ardis, 1988), pp. 269–79; Ludmilla Alexeyeva and Paul Goldberg, *The Thaw Generation: Coming of Age in the Post-Stalin Era* (Boston, MA: Little, Brown, 1990), pp. 43–67; Gitelman, 'Politics and Historiography of the Holocaust in the Soviet Union', p. 18; Jeffrey Brooks, *Thank You, Comrade Stalin! Soviet Public Culture from Revolution to Cold War* (Princeton, NJ: Princeton University Press, 2001), p. 215; Zvi Gitelman, 'Remembrance of Things Past:

Soviet Histories and Jewish Memories', in *Recalling the Past – (Re)constructing the Past: Collective and Individual Memory of World War II in Russia and Germany*, eds Withold Bonner and Arja Rosenholm (Iyvaskyla, Finland: Gummerus, 2008), pp. 289–302; Jeremy Hicks, 'Confronting the Holocaust: Mark Donskoi's "The Unvanquished"', *Studies in Russian and Soviet Cinema*/3 (2009), pp. 33–51, pp. 35 and 45; Olga Gershenson and David Shneer, 'Soviet Jewishness and Cultural Studies', *Journal of Jewish Identities*/1 (2011); Karel C. Berkhoff, *Motherland in Danger: Soviet Propaganda during World War II* (Cambridge, MA: Harvard University Press, 2012), Chapters 6–8; and Anika Walke, *Pioneers and Partisans: An Oral History of Nazi Genocide in Belorussia* (Oxford: Oxford University Press, 2015).

26. Elie Wiesel, *The Jews of Silence: A Personal Report on Soviet Jewry*, trans. Neal Kozodoy (Philadelphia, PA: Jewish Publication Society of America, 1967), pp. 12–4; Gershenson and Shneer, 'Soviet Jewishness and Cultural Studies'; and Arkadi Zeltser, 'Differing Views among Red Army Personnel about the Nazi Mass Murder of Jews', *Kritika: Explorations in Russian and Eurasian History*/15 (2014), pp. 563–90.
27. See Alexander Yanov, *The Russian New Right: Right-Wing Ideologies in the Contemporary USSR* (Berkeley, CA: Institute of International Studies, University of California, 1978); Nikolai Mitrokhin, *Russkaia partiia: dvizhenie russkikh natsionalistov v SSSR, 1953–1985 gody* (Moscow: Novoe literaturnoe obozrenie, 2003); and Charles Clover, *Black Wind, White Snow: The Rise of Russia's New Nationalism* (New Haven, CT: Yale University Press, 2016).
28. David Shneer, 'Picturing Grief: Soviet Holocaust Photography at the Intersection of History and Memory', *American Historical Review*/115 (2010), pp. 28–52.
29. 'Uroki Kholokosta v Novorossiiske', *Federatsiia evreiskikh obshchin Rossii*, 18 January 2006, <http://www.feor.ru/news/index.php?newsid=1861> [accessed 15 January 2014].
30. Il'ia Altman, *Kholokost na territorii SSSR: Entsiklopediia* (Moscow: Rosspen, 2009), pp. 474–5 and 661; and 'Krasnodarskii krai', *Bab'i Iary Rossii*, <http://www.holomemory.ru/?region=35> [accessed 18 February 2017].
31. Ilya Ehrenburg and Vasily Grossman, *The Black Book: The Ruthless Murder of Jews by German-Fascist Invaders Throughout the Temporarily-Occupied Regions of the Soviet Union and in the Death Camps of Poland During the War of 1941–1945*, trans. John Glad and James S. Levine (New York: Holocaust Library, 1981); I.S. Shiian, *Novorossiisk – gorod-geroi* (Moscow: Voennoe izdatel'stvo Ministerstva oborony SSSR, 1982); A. Eremenko and K. Podyma, *Imenem Rossii narechennyi* (Moscow: Sovetskaia Rossiia, 1988); T.I. Iurina, *Novorossiiskoe protivostoianie: 1942–1943 gg.* (Krasnodar: Kniga, 2008); and M.V. Erokhin, *Novorossiisk*, ed. D.A. Vasil'evich (Krasnodar: RIO, 2012).
32. 'Pamiatnik "Nepokorennye"', *Tsentral'naia gorodskaia biblioteka im. Gor'kogo*, <http://www.ballion.ru/pamyatnik_nepokorennye.html> [accessed 15 January 2014]; and 'Krasnodarskii krai', *Bab'i Iary Rossii: Memorialy zhertv kholokost*,

< http://webcache.googleusercontent.com/search?q=cache:8fsudwzl1qUJ:www.holomemory.ru/place/89%3Fregion%3D35+&cd=4&hl=en&ct=clnk&gl=uk> [accessed 15 January 2014].

33. Erokhin, *Novorossiisk*, p. 55.
34. 'Krasnodarskii krai', *Bab'i Iary Rossii: Memorialy zhertv kholokost.*
35. 'Nepokorennye', *NR*, 14 September 2013, p. 9.
36. Evgenii Rozhanskii, 'Nepokorennye', *Vol'naia Kuban'*, 22 January 2005, p. 6.
37. Mark Connelly, '"We Can Take It!" Britain and the Memory of the Home Front in the Second World War', in *Experience and Memory: The Second World War in Europe*, ed. Jorg Echternkamp and Stefan Martens (New York and Oxford: Berghahn, 2010), pp. 53–69, p. 61.
38. 'Dve vystavki v Novorossiiske', *Federatsiia Evreiskikh Obshchin Rossii*, 15 September 2005, <http://www.feor.ru/news/index.php?newsid=833> [accessed 8 March 2014]; and 'Vystavka evreiskoi obshchiny v Novorossiiske', *Federatsiia Evreiskikh Obshchin Rossii*, 26 September 2008, <http://www.feor.ru/news/index.php?newsid=6414> [accessed 8 March 2014].
39. 'V Novorossiiske antisemity oskvernili pamiatnik, ustanovlennyi na meste rasstrela natsistami evreev', *Sem40: Tsentral'nyi evreiskii resurs*, 30 July 2003, < http://www.sem40.ru/index.php?newsid=53590>, [accessed 15 January 2014].
40. 'Nepokorennye'.
41. Stephen Lovell, *The Shadow of War: Russia and the USSR, 1941 to the Present* (Chichester: Wiley-Blackwell, 2010), p. 321.
42. See, for example, Martin Dean, *Collaboration in the Holocaust: Crimes of the Local Police in Belorussia and Ukraine, 1941–44* (Basingstoke: Macmillan, 2000); Amir Weiner, *Making Sense of War: The Second World War and the Fate of the Bolshevik Revolution* (Princeton, NJ: Princeton University Press, 2001); Karel C. Berkhoff, *Harvest of Despair: Life and Death in Ukraine under Nazi Rule* (Cambridge, MA and London: Belknap, Harvard University Press, 2004), p. 77; Jeffrey W. Jones, '"Every Family Has Its Freak": Perceptions of Collaboration in Occupied Soviet Russia, 1943–1948', *Slavic Review*/64 (2005), pp. 747–70; Wendy Lower, *Nazi Empire-Building and the Holocaust in Ukraine* (USA: University of North Carolina Press, 2005); Olga Baranova, 'Collaboration by the Soviet Citizens with the Nazi Occupation Authorities during the Great Patriotic War: How the Issue was Represented and Treated in Soviet, Western and Post-Soviet Russian and Belarusian Historiography', in *Recalling the Past–(Re)constructing the Past: Collective and Individual Memory of World War II in Russia and Germany*, ed. Withold Bonner and Arja Rosenholm (Iyvaskyla, Finland: Gummerus, 2008), pp. 267–76; Ray Brandon and Wendy Lower, eds, *The Shoah in Ukraine: History, Testimony, Memorialisation* (Bloomington, IN: Indiana University Press, 2008); and Berkhoff, *Motherland in Danger*, pp. 223–43. See also Gitelman, 'Politics and Historiography of the Holocaust in the Soviet Union', pp. 33–4.
43. Arieh J. Kochavi, *Prelude to Nuremberg: Allied War Crimes Policy and the Question of Punishment* (Chapel Hill, NC and London: University of North Carolina Press,

1998); and Ilya Bourtman, '"Blood for Blood, Death for Death": The Soviet Military Tribunal in Krasnodar, 1943', *Holocaust and Genocide Studies*/22 (2008), pp. 246–65.

44. Evgenii Lapin, 'Byl li predan otchaiannyi desant?', *NR*, 3 February 2001, p. 3; and Petr Iliushkin, 'Poisk vedet pogranichnik', *Stavropol'skie gubernskie Vedomosti*, 11–18 July 2007, <http://www.guberniya.ru> [accessed 19 November 2014].
45. On the negative aspects of Kubanocentrism, see S.G. Novikov, 'Istoricheskoe kraevedenie v svete kontseptual'nogo osmysleniia mestnoi istorii', in *Istoricheskie zapiski: Issledovanniia i materialy, vypusk 4*, eds S.G. Novikov and T.V. Raskatova (Krasnodar: Kubanskoe knizhnoe izdatel'stvo, 2003), pp. 300–9, p. 307. See also Barbara Skinner, 'Identity Formation in the Russian Cossack Revival', *Europe-Asia Studies*/46 (1994), pp. 1017–37; Georgi M. Derluguian and Serge Cipko, 'The Politics of Identity in a Russian Borderland Province: The Kuban Neo-Cossack Movement, 1989–1996', *Europe-Asia Studies*/49 (1997), pp. 1485–500; Hege Toje, 'Cossack Identity in the New Russia: Kuban Cossack Revival and Local Politics', *Europe-Asia Studies*/58 (2006), pp. 1057–77; Marie Jego, 'Cossack Cadets Fill a Gap in Russia's Sense of Security and Patriotism', *Guardian Weekly*, 26 February 2013, <http://www.theguardian.com/world/2013/feb/26/russia-cossacks-cadets-volgograd> [accessed 19 January 2015]; and Courtney Weaver, 'Cossacks Ride Again as Russia Seeks to Fill Ideological Void', *Financial Times*, 4 August 2013, <https://www.ft.com/search?q=Cossacks+Ride+Again> [accessed 20 November 2013].
46. Online response to Ol'ga Gailesh, 'Novorossiisk "Beskozyrka 2011"', *Munitsipal'naia novostnaia lenta*, 4 February 2011, <http://www.nrnews.ru/news/?id=42581> [accessed 9 February 2011].
47. Marina Rybkina, 'Kuda vedet ulitsa Generala Shkuro?', *NR*, 5 December 2015, <www.novorab.ru/ArticleSection/Details/13959> [accessed 22 March 2016]; and Marina Rybkina, 'Ulitse naidut drugoe imia', *NR*, 16 December 2015, <www.novorab.ru/ArticleSection/Details/13982> [accessed 22 March 2016].
48. See further Julie Buckler and Emily D. Johnson, 'Introduction', in *Rites of Place: Public Commemoration in Russia and Eastern Europe*, eds Julie Buckler and Emily D. Johnson (Evanston, IL: Northwestern University Press, 2013), pp. 3–12, p. 6.

Part IV Meetings of Generations: Teaching the Young to Remember

1. 'Remember!/Across the centuries, across the years, –/remember!/About those who will never return, –/remember!' From Robert Rozhdestvenskii's 'Rekviem' (1960): *Robert Rozhdestvenskii: Sobranie sochinenii v trekh tomakh*, Vol. 2 (Moscow: Khudozhestvennaia literatura, 1985), pp. 205–18.
2. Andrei Maliukov, *My iz budushchego* (Russia: 2008), the first of a trilogy of films.
3. I. Irwin-Zarecka, *Frames of Remembrance: The Dynamics of Collective Memory* (New Brunswick, NJ: Transaction Books, 1994); T.G. Ashplant, et al., 'The Politics of

War Memory and Commemoration: Contexts, Structures and Dynamics', in *The Politics of War, Memory and Commemoration*, eds T.G. Ashplant, Graham Dawson and Michael Roper (London: Routledge, 2000), pp. 3–85; and Peter Carrier, 'Political and Ethical Contexts of Collective Memories of the Second World War', in *Recalling the Past–(Re)constructing the Past: Collective and Individual Memory of World War II in Russia and Germany*, eds Withold Bonner and Arja Rosenholm (Iyvaskyla, Finland: Gummerus, 2008), pp. 245–55.

4. For example Maurice Halbachs: 'Often we deem ourselves the originators of thoughts and ideas, feelings and passions, actually inspired by some group.' (Maurice Halbwachs, *On Collective Memory*, trans. Lewis A. Coser (Chicago IL and London: University of Chicago Press, 1992) (originally published 1925), cited in Jeffrey K. Olick, Vered Vinitzky-Seroussi and Daniel Levy, eds, *The Collective Memory Reader* (Oxford: Oxford University Press, 2011), p. 139.
5. See Emile Durkheim, *Moral Education*, trans. E.K. Wilson (New York: Free Press, 1961) (first published 1925); Marc Bloch, 'Mémoire Collective, Tradition et Coutume: A propos d'un Livre Récent', *Revue de Synthèse Historique*/40 (1925), pp. 73–83; Halbwachs, *On Collective Memory*, 1992; and Edward Shils, *Tradition* (Chicago, IL: University of Chicago Press, 1981).
6. Nina Tumarkin, *The Living and the Dead: The Rise and Fall of the Cult of World War II in Russia* (New York: BasicBooks, 1994), p. 133.

Chapter 13 Genes and Generations: Informal Transmission of Memory in the Family

1. George Steiner, *In Bluebeard's Castle: Some Notes towards the Re-definition of Culture* (London: Faber and Faber, 1971), p. 13.
2. A. Eremenko and K. Podyma, *Imenem Rossii narechennyi* (Moscow: Sovetskaia Rossiia, 1988), pp. 352–8; V. Saloshenko, *Obiazan skazat'* (Krasnodar: Severnyi Kavkaz, 1998), p. 16; and Raisa Sokolova, *Beskozyrka* (Novorossiisk: Departament kul'tury Krasnodarskogo kraia, *c*. 2005), p. 10.
3. Evgenii Lapin, 'Novorossiisk pomnit', *NR*, 18 September 2013, <http://www.novorab.ru/ArticleSection/Details/10115> [accessed 13 December 2013].
4. '"Belye chaiki" vzmyli nad Maloi zemlei', *Ofitsial'nyi sait administratsii i Dumy munitsipal'nogo obrazovaniia gorod-geroi Novorossiisk*, 3 February 2017, <http://admnvrsk.ru/o-gorode/novosti/glavnye-novosti/news-20170203145257-234523/> [accessed 8 February 2017].
5. From the final stanza of Lermontov's 'Borodino' (1837) in *M.Iu Lermontov: Stikhotvoreniia*, Vol. 1 (Moscow: Russkaia kniga, 1996), pp. 9–12.
6. 'Putin Hails Russian Military', *BBC News*, 9 May 2000, <news.bbc.co.uk/1/hi/world/europe/741415.stm> [accessed 30 May 2016].
7. 'Miting v podderzhku kandidata v Prezidenty RF Vladimir Putina sobral 130 tysiach chelovek', *Pervyi kanal*, 23 December 12, <www.1tv.ru/news/election/199798> [accessed 21 March 2014].

8. Serguei Oushakine, *The Patriotism of Despair: Nation, War and Loss in Russia* (Ithaca, NY and London: Cornell University Press, 2009), p. 6.
9. 'The harsh weather reminded their descendants of the conditions in which Kunikov's troops landed in the icy waves of the Black Sea': Evgenii Rozhanskii, 'Zashchitnikam tvoim, podvigu tvoemu, Novorossiisk', *NR*, 5 February 2014, <http://www.novorab.ru/ArticleSection/Details/11327> [accessed 7 February 2014].
10. Katharine Hodgkin and Susannah Radstone, eds, *Contested Pasts: The Politics of Memory* (London: Routledge, 2003), pp. 135 and 153.
11. See Nina Tumarkin, *The Living and the Dead: The Rise and Fall of the Cult of World War II in Russia* (New York: BasicBooks, 1994), p. 144.
12. Prialkina, 'Novorossiitsy chtiat i pomniat', in *Novorossiisk: Pamiat' i Pravda o Velikoi Otechestvennoi voine* (2005), pp. 150–3.
13. Tumarkin, *The Living and the Dead*, p. 144.
14. Prialkina, 'Novorossiitsy chtiat i pomniat', p. 151.
15. J.M. Winter, *Sites of Memory, Sites of Mourning: The Great War in European Cultural History* (Cambridge: Cambridge University Press, 1995), pp. 94 and 98.
16. Alec Luhn, 'Three Jailed in Russia for Dance Video Filmed at Novorossiysk War Memorial', *Guardian*, 26 April 2015, <https://www.theguardian.com/world/2015/apr/26/three-jailed-in-russia-dance-video-novorossiysk> [accessed 13 July 2016]; and 'Gruppu devushek, stantsevavshikh tverk na fone memorial Malaia zemlia v Novorossiiske mogut privlech' za khuliganstvo', *Pravda*, 25 April 2015, <http://www.pravda.ru/news/society/fashion/25-04-2015/1257920-0/> [accessed 13 July 2016].
17. Harald Welzer, 'Re-narrations: How Pasts Change in Conversational Remembering', *Memory Studies*/3 (2010), p. 15.
18. Raphael Samuel and Paul Thompson, 'Introduction', in *The Myths We Live By*, eds R. Samuel and P. Thompson (London and New York: Routledge, 1990), pp. 1–22.
19. Lisa A. Kirschenbaum, *The Legacy of the Siege of Leningrad, 1941–1995: Myth, Memories and Monuments* (Cambridge and New York: Cambridge University Press, 2006), p. 5.
20. Welzer, 'Re-narrations', p. 15.
21. Jerome Bruner and Carol Fleischer Feldman, 'Group Narrative as a Cultural Context of Autobiography', in *Remembering Our Past: Studies in Autobiographical Memory*, ed. David C. Rubin (Cambridge: Cambridge University Press, 2005), pp. 291–317.
22. Catherine Merridale, *Night of Stone: Death and Memory in Russia* (London: Granta Books, 2000). For a non-Russian examination of the meaning of oppressive popular memory for individuals, see Roy Rosenzweig and David Thelen, 'The Presence of the Past: Popular Uses of History in American Life', in *The Collective Memory Reader*, eds Jeffrey K. Olick, Vered Vinitzky-Seroussi and Daniel Levy (Oxford: Oxford University Press, 2011), pp. 269–70.

23. Tumarkin, *The Living and the Dead*. The 'complicated interweaving of the political and the personal' is also recognised in Kirschenbaum, *The Legacy of the Siege of Leningrad*, p. 5.
24. G. Sokolov, *My s Maloi zemli* (Moscow: Sovetskaia Rossiia, 1979), p. 157.
25. Alistair Thomson, *Anzac Memories: Living with the Legend* (Clayton, Australia: Monash University Publishing, 2013), pp. 11–2.
26. Michael Schudson, 'Dynamics of Distortion in Collective Memory', in *Memory Distortion: How Minds, Brains, and Societies Reconstruct the Past*, ed. Daniel Schacter (Cambridge, MA and London: Harvard University Press, 1995), pp. 346–64, pp. 59–71.
27. Tumarkin, *The Living and the Dead*; Merridale, *Night of Stone*; and Kirschenbaum, *The Legacy of the Siege of Leningrad*, p. 5.
28. Thomson, *Anzac Memories*.
29. Graham Carr, 'War, History, and the Education of (Canadian) Memory', in *Contested Pasts: The Politics of Memory*, eds Katharine Hodgkin and Susannah Radstone (London and New York: Routledge, 2003), pp. 57–78.
30. The necessity for the active role of key generations in the transmission of the past is discussed in Elizabeth Jelin and Susana G. Kaufman, 'Layers of Memories: Twenty Years After in Argentina', in *The Politics of War, Memory and Commemoration*, ed. T.G. Ashplant, Graham Dawson and Michael Roper (London: Routledge, 2000), pp. 89–110.
31. Nikolai Kambulov, *Gorod-geroi Novorossiisk* (Moscow: Malysh, 1979).
32. J. Fentress and C. Wickham, *Social Memory* (Oxford: Blackwell, 1992), pp. 140–2.
33. Catherine Merridale, 'War, death and remembrance in Soviet Russia', in *War and Remembrance in the Twentieth Century*, eds Jay Winter and Emmanuel Sivan (Cambridge: Cambridge University Press, 2000), pp. 61–83.
34. Artemi Romanov, 'Russian Grandparent–Grandchild Communications: Stories about the Past and Current Events', *Russian Journal of Communication*/5 (2013), pp. 141–60.
35. Rozhanskii, 'Zashchitnikam tvoim, podvigu tvoemu, Novorossiisk'; and Oksana Mashkarova 'Lentochka Pobedy', *Novorossiiskii rabochii*, 5 May 2011, <www.novorab.ru/ArticleSection/Details/2779> [accessed 9 May 2011].
36. Barbie Zelizer, 'Why Memory's Work on Journalism does not Reflect Journalism's Work on Memory', *Memory Studies*/1 (2008), pp. 79–87; and Carolyn Kitch, 'Placing Journalism inside Memory – and Memory Studies', *Memory Studies*/1 (2008), pp. 311–20.
37. See also Stephen M. Norris, 'Memory for Sale: Victory Day 2010 and Russian Remembrance', *Soviet and Post-Soviet Review*/38 (2011), pp. 201–29, pp. 215–9.
38. *NR*, 10 May 2013, pp. 5–12.
39. Steven Spielberg, *Saving Private Ryan* (USA: 1998).
40. Stephen M. Norris, *Blockbuster History in the New Russia: Movies, Memory and Patriotism* (Bloomington, IN: Indiana University Press, 2012).

41. Olga Kucherenko, 'That'll Teach'em to Love Their Motherland!: Russian Youth Revisit the Battles of World War II', *The Journal of Power Institutions in Post-Soviet Societies*/12 (2011), paragraph 16.
42. Alison Landsberg, *The Transformation of American Remembrance in the Age of Mass Culture* (New York and Chichester: Columbia University Press, 2004), pp. 2, 19 and 24.
43. *Bessmertnyi polk*, <http://www.moypolk.ru/novorossiysk> [accessed 27 April 2016]; and Igor' Zakharov, 'Zapisat' dedushku v "Bessmertnyi polk"', *NR*, 8 May 2013, <http://www.novorab.ru/ArticleSection/Details/8665> [accessed 27 April 2016].
44. V.I. Kondrat'ev, 'S prazdnikom, s Dnem Pobedy!', *NR*, 8 May 2016, <http://www.novorab.ru/ArticleSection/Details/14328> [accessed 9 May 2016].

Chapter 14 The Educational Role of Veterans

1. John McCrae, 'In Flanders Fields' (1915), in *In Flanders Fields and Other Poems of the First World War* (London: Arcturus, 2009), p. 128.
2. Marina Rybkina and Sergei Mukhtarov, 'Putin v Novorossiiske chaevnichal s frontovnikami', *Novorossiiskii rabochii*, 8 May 2010, p. 1.
3. G. Sokolov, *My s Maloi zemli* (Moscow: Sovetskaia Rossiia, 1979), p. 365.
4. V.A. Golikov, ed., *Novorossiisk* (Moscow: Planeta, 1978), p. 88.
5. Natalia Danilova, 'Veterans' Policy in Russia: A Puzzle of Creation', in *The Journal of Power Institutions in Post-Soviet Societies* (2007), p. 3.
6. Mark Edele, 'Collective Action in Soviet Society: The Case of War Veterans', in *Writing the Stalin Era: Sheila Fitzpatrick and Soviet Historiography*, eds Golfo Alexopoulos, Julie Hessler and Kiril Tomoff (New York: Palgrave Macmillan, 2011), pp. 117–32, pp. 123–4.
7. V.D. Starikova, 'Veteranskoe dvizhenie v Novorossiiske', in *Istoricheskie zapiski: Issledovanniia i materialy, vypusk 4*, eds S.G. Novikov and T.V. Raskatova (Krasnodar: Kubanskoe knizhnoe izdatel'stvo, 2003), pp. 261–73, pp. 266–7.
8. Danilova, 'Veterans' Policy in Russia'; and Serguei Oushakine, *The Patriotism of Despair: Nation, War and Loss in Russia* (Ithaca, NY and London: Cornell University Press, 2009).
9. Starikova, 'Veteranskoe dvizhenie v Novorossiiske', pp. 269–70. See also Svetlana Aleksievich, *U voiny – ne zhenskoe litso* (Moscow: Palmira, 1985); and Roger D. Markwick, '"A Sacred Duty": Red Army Women Veterans Remembering the Great Fatherland War, 1941–45', in *Recalling the Past–(Re)constructing the Past: Collective and Individual Memory of World War II in Russia and Germany*, eds Withold Bonner and Arja Rosenholm (Iyvaskyla, Finland: Gummerus, 2008), pp. 315–26, pp. 315–16.
10. Danilova, 'Veterans' Policy in Russia', pp. 6–7; and Starikova, 'Veteranskoe dvizhenie v Novorossiiske', p. 271.

11. *Pochta Rossii*, <http://www.russianpost.ru/rp/company/ru/home/creativ/arhive/thank_fellow> [accessed 13 April 2014].
12. Danilova, 'Veterans' Policy in Russia', p. 7.
13. Oushakine, *The Patriotism of Despair*, p. 165.
14. Interviews with the Krasnodar veterans' councils representative and Councillor Andrievskii.
15. J.M. Winter, *Sites of Memory, Sites of Mourning: The Great War in European Cultural History* (Cambridge: Cambridge University Press, 1995), pp. 40–54; and Jay Winter, *Remembering War: The Great War between Memory and History in the Twentieth Century* (New Haven, CT and London: Yale University Press, 2006), p. 136.
16. In 2010 a poster advertised the following old favourites: *In August 1944*; *The Ballad of the Soldier*; *The Second Front*; *The Cranes are Flying*; *Romance in the Field*; and *The Fall of the Third Reich*.
17. Catherine Merridale, *Ivan's War: Life and Death in the Red Army, 1939–1945* (New York: Picador, 2006), pp. 374–5.
18. See Stephen M. Norris, 'Memory for Sale: Victory Day 2010 and Russian Remembrance', *Soviet and Post-Soviet Review*/38 (2011), pp. 201–29.
19. Clément Marcel, 'Pourquoi les Français Portent-ils des Bleuets le 11 Novembre et les Britanniques des Coquelicots?', *Le Monde*, 11 November 2014, <http://www.lemonde.fr/les-decodeurs/article/2014/11/11/pourquoi-les-francais-portent-ils-des-bleuets-le-11-novembre-et-les-britanniques-des-coquelicots_4521931_4355770.html> [accessed 23 May 2016].
20. 'Georgievskaia lentochka', *9may.ru*, <http://gl.9may.ru> [accessed 26 June 2012]; and Jennifer Iles, 'In Remembrance: The Flanders Poppy', *Mortality*/13 (2008), pp. 201–21.
21. Benedict Anderson, *Imagined Communities* (London: Verso, 1983).
22. *9may.ru*, <http://gl.9may.ru> [accessed 26 June 2012]. On commercialisation, see Norris, 'Memory for Sale'.
23. Norris, 'Memory for Sale', pp. 225–6.
24. Oksana Mashkarova 'Lentochka Pobedy', *Novorossiiskii rabochii*, 5 May 2011, <www.novorab.ru/ArticleSection/Details/2779> [accessed 9 May 2011].
25. Katherine Verdery, *The Political Lives of Dead Bodies* (Columbia University Press: New York, 1999), p. 29.

Chapter 15 Formal Education of the Younger Generation

1. 'Tell your children about them [the war heroes],/so that they remember!/Tell your children's children about them,/so that they also remember!' From Robert Rozhdestvenskii's 'Rekviem' (1960): *Robert Rozhdestvenskii: Sobranie sochinenii v trekh tomakh*, Vol. 2 (Moscow: Khudozhestvennaia literatura, 1985), pp. 205–18.

2. For a nuanced study of patriotism amongst the young, comparing state and non-official values, see Anne Le Huérou, 'Where Does the Motherland Begin? Private and Public Dimensions of Contemporary Russian Patriotism in Schools and Youth Organisations: A View from the Field', *Europe-Asia Studies*/67 (2015), pp. 28–48.
3. All references are from the 55-page Bekar School syllabus for patriotic work in the academic year 2010–11 (*Patrioticheskaia rabota: rabota s uchashchimsia, 2010–2011 uchebnyi god*).
4. Catherine Merridale, 'Amnesiac Nation', *Index on Censorship*/34 (2005), pp. 76–82.
5. Anna Colin Lebedev, *Le Coeur Politique des Mères: Analyse du Mouvement des Mères de Soldats en Russie* (Paris: EHESS, 2013).
6. For a study of the fragmentation and collapse of the intergenerational chain of memory, see Danièle Hervieu-Leger, *Religion as a Chain of Memory* (Piscataway, NJ: Rutgers University Press, 2000).
7. The role of the school in the transmission of memory is explored in J. Fentress and C. Wickham, *Social Memory* (Oxford: Blackwell, 1992). The transmission of war memory in Canadian schools, linking public history to private memory through the use of 'retrospective identification' of successive generations is discussed in Graham Carr, 'War, History, and the Education of (Canadian) Memory', in *Contested Pasts: The Politics of Memory*, eds Katharine Hodgkin and Susannah Radstone (London and New York: Routledge, 2003), pp. 57–78. Narrated through the prism of the family, idealised memory may cause tension in cases where the original event may have been ethically controversial, see Harald Welzer, 'Re-narrations: How Pasts Change in Conversational Remembering', *Memory Studies*/3 (2010). A new syllabus for Soviet history in Georgia is treated by Jay Winter, 'Thinking about Silence', in *Shadows of War: A Social History of Silence in the Twentieth Century*, eds E. Ben-Ze'ev, R. Ginio and J. Winter (Cambridge: Cambridge University Press, 2010), pp. 3–31, p. 29. For an analysis of reforms in school and university teaching of history in Russia, see Catherine Merridale, 'Redesigning History in Contemporary Russia', *Journal of Contemporary History*/38 (2003), pp. 13–28. For a thorough analysis of the school history curriculum, see Thomas Sherlock, *Historical Narratives in the Soviet Union and Post-Soviet Russia: Destroying the Settled Past, Creating an Uncertain Future* (New York and Basingstoke: Palgrave Macmillan, 2007), pp. 168–73. For recent history texts see David Wedgwood Benn, 'The Teaching of History in Putin's Russia', *International Affairs*/84 (2008), pp. 365–70.
8. M. Gallagher, *The Soviet History of World War II: Myths, Memories and Realities* (New York: Praeger, 1963).
9. Graham Lyons, ed., *The Russian Version of the Second World War* (London: Leo Cooper, 1976), p. 52.
10. R.W. Davies, *Soviet History in the Gorbachev Revolution* (London: Macmillan, 1989), pp. 34, 37 and 229.

11. Stephen F. Jones, 'Old Ghosts and New Chains: Ethnicity and Memory in the Georgian Republic', in *Memory, History, and Opposition under State Socialism*, ed. Rubie S. Watson (Santa Fe, NM: School of American Research, 1994), pp. 149–65, p. 153. The place of the individual with respect to history is also discussed in Merridale, 'Redesigning History in Contemporary Russia'. For the case with respect to the Vietnam War, see Marita Sturken, *Tangled Memories: The Vietnam War, the AIDS Epidemic and the Politics of Remembering* (Berkeley, CA: University of California Press, 1997).
12. Davies, *Soviet History in the Gorbachev Revolution*, pp. 9–10; Merridale, 'Redesigning History in Contemporary Russia', p. 16; and Sherlock, *Historical Narratives in the Soviet Union and Post-Soviet Russia*, pp. 2, 17 and 22.
13. *Pravda*, 13 January 1988, p. 3.
14. Sherlock, *Historical Narratives in the Soviet Union and Post-Soviet Russia*, pp. 168–74.
15. N.V. Zagladin, S.I. Kozlenko, S.T. Minakov and Iu.A. Petrov, *Istoriia Rossii. XX–nachalo XXI veka* (Moscow: Russkoe slovo, 2007). Novorossiisk is mentioned on page 243.
16. A.V. Veka, *Istoriia Rossii* (Minsk and Moscow: Kharvest, 2003).
17. Ibid., pp. 872 and 890.
18. Ibid., pp. 891–2 and 928.
19. Stephen M. Norris, *Blockbuster History in the New Russia: Movies, Memory and Patriotism* (Bloomington, IN: Indiana University Press, 2012), p. 116.
20. Roland Oliphant, 'Russian Region Bans British Historians' Books on Second World War', *The Telegraph*, 5 August 2015, <http://www.telegraph.co.uk/news/worldnews/europe/russia/11786024/Russian-region-bans-British-historians-books-on-Second-World-War.html> [accessed 11 October 2016].
21. Oksana Mashkarova 'Lentochka Pobedy', *Novorossiiskii rabochii*, 5 May 2011, <www.novorab.ru/ArticleSection/Details/2779> [accessed 9 May 2011].
22. Marina Rybkina, *NR*, 'Novorossiisk nikogda ne snimet beskozyrku', 2 February 2017, <http://www.novorab.ru/ArticleSection/Details/14884> [accessed 7 February 2017].
23. James V. Wertsch, *Voices of Collective Remembering* (Cambridge: Cambridge University Press, 2002).
24. Merridale, 'Amnesiac Nation', pp. 79–81.
25. For an examination of the relationship between myth and history in the Soviet Union and modern Russia, with an analysis of Putin's exploitation of myth for political expediency, see Sherlock, *Historical Narratives in the Soviet Union and Post-Soviet Russia*.
26. For example: *In Memory of the Heroic Landings*; *Novorossiisk: History and Modernity*; *The Strategy for Victory*; and *Georgii Zhukov: Military Leader*.
27. 'Vneklassnoe meropriiatie "V pamiati i serdtse navsegda"', *Munitsipal'naia novostnaia lenta*, 4 February 2011, <http://www.nrnews.ru/news/?id=42580> [accessed 9 February 2011].
28. However, Thomas Wolfe points to 'hypocrisy and bad faith' around the deployment of veterans in schools: Thomas C. Wolfe, 'Past as Present, Myth, or

History? Discourses of Time and the Great Fatherland War', in *The Politics of Memory in Postwar Europe*, eds Richard Ned Lebow, Wulf Kansteiner and Claudio Fogu (Durham, NC and London: Duke University Press, 2006), pp. 249–83, p. 266.

29. For example, Tamara Iurina, *Teleurok grazhdanstvennosti, posviashchennyi 40-letiiu operatsii 'Beskozyrka'* (Russia: Novaia Rossiia, 3 February 2008).

30. Merridale, 'Redesigning History in Contemporary Russia', p. 27.

31. For example, <http://www.pobediteli.ru>; <http://www.battlefield.ru>; and <http://.iremember.ru>. See Stephen M. Norris, 'Memory for Sale: Victory Day 2010 and Russian Remembrance', *Soviet and Post-Soviet Review*/38 (2011), pp. 201–29, pp. 201–21.

32. Tat'iana Staroverova, 'Novorossiiskii kraeved Galina Krympokha: Snova rvu na sebe tel'niashku', *Zhivaia Kuban'*, 1 December 2010, <http://www.livekuban.ru/node/216972> [accessed 28 January 2011].

33. 'Urok muzhestva "Spasibo im, geroiam, v bitvakh pavshim ..."', *MNL*, 7 February 2011, <http://www.nrnews.ru/news/?id=42589> [accessed 4 January 2015]; and 'Bibliotechnye uroki "Vstretimsia u Vechnogo ognia"', *MNL*, 1 February 2011, <http://www.nrnews.ru/news/?id=42540> [accessed 1 February 2012].

34. *Tsentralizovannaia sistema detskikh bibliotek goroda Novorossiiska*, <http://www.bibldetky.ru/vystavka/1801-vystavka.html> [accessed 23 April 2014].

35. On the concept of *kraevedenie*, see S.G. Novikov, 'Istoricheskoe kraevedenie v svete kontseptual'nogo osmysleniia mestnoi istorii', in *Istoricheskie zapiski: Issledovanniia i materialy, vypusk 4*, eds S.G. Novikov and T.V. Raskatova (Krasnodar: Kubanskoe knizhnoe izdatel'stvo, 2003), pp. 300–9; and Emily D. Johnson, *How St. Petersburg Learned to Study Itself: The Russian Idea of Kraevedenie* (University Park, PA: Pennsylvania State University Press, 2006).

36. Nina Tumarkin, *The Living and the Dead: The Rise and Fall of the Cult of World War II in Russia* (New York: BasicBooks, 1994), p. 134; and Elena Trubina, '"You Can See Now Just How Small All of You Are": Rhetorical Spaces of Volgograd', in *Recalling the Past–(Re)constructing the Past: Collective and Individual Memory of World War II in Russia and Germany*, eds Withold Bonner and Arja Rosenholm, Iyvaskyla (Finland: Gummerus, 2008), pp. 21–9.

37. V.D. Starikova, 'Veteranskoe dvizhenie v Novorossiiske', in *Istoricheskie zapiski: Issledovanniia i materialy, vypusk 4*, eds S.G. Novikov and T.V. Raskatova (Krasnodar: Kubanskoe knizhnoe izdatel'stvo, 2003), pp. 261–73, p. 268.

38. *Novorossiiskii iunarmeiskii Post No. 1: 35 let* (Novorossiisk: Munitsipal'noe obrazovanie gorod-geroi Novorossiisk, 2010), p. 1.

39. A. Karavaev, 'Post odin na ploshchadi geroev', in *Iubileinyi sbornik*, ed. Galina V. Utiugina (Novorossiisk: Poeticheskii klub 'Daktil'', 2010), p. 19.

40. J. Lennon and M. Foley, *Dark Tourism: The Attraction of Death and Disaster* (London: Continuum, 2000).

41. Tumarkin, *The Living and The Dead*, pp. 14–5 and 152–3.
42. On patriotic youth clubs in other towns, see Marlene Laruelle, 'Patriotic Youth Clubs in Russia: Professional Niches, Cultural Capital and Narratives of Social Engagement', *Europe-Asia Studies*/67 (2015), pp. 8–27.
43. Andrew Wilson, *Virtual Politics: Faking Democracy in the Post-Soviet World* (New Haven, CT: Yale University Press, 2005).
44. Ivo Mijnssen, *The Quest for an Ideal Youth in Putin's Russia I: Back To Our Future! History, Modernity, and Patriotism According to Nashi, 2005–2013* (Stuttgart: Ibidem, 2014).
45. 'Rosmolodezh' otkazalas' ot Foruma "Seliger"', *Interfax*, 15 March 2015, <http://www.interfax.ru/russia/430983> [accessed 19 February 2017].

Conclusion Looking Back to the Future

1. G.P. Bondar', *Uroki muzhestva* (Krasnodar: Krasnodarskoe knizhnoe izdatel'stvo, 1982), p. 98.
2. Andrei Shal'opa, *28 panfilovtsev* (St Petersburg: Libyan Palette Studios, 2016).
3. Mazhit Begalin, *Za nami Moskva* (USSR: Kazakhfil'm, 1967).
4. Vasilii Koroteev, 'Zaveshchanie 28 pavshikh geroev', *Krasnaia zvezda*, 28 November 1941, p. 1.
5. 'Russian Archives Cast Doubt on Legends of Soviet War Heroes', *The Moscow Times*, 9 July 2015, <https://themoscowtimes.com/news/russian-archives-cast-doubt-on-legends-of-soviet-war-heroes-48026> [accessed 15 November 2016]; Shaun Walker, 'Russian War Film Set to Open amid Controversy over Accuracy of Events', *Guardian*, 23 November 2016, <https://www.theguardian.com/film/2016/nov/23/russian-war-film-set-to-open-against-controversy-over-accuracy-of-events> [accessed 23 November 2016]; and 'Panfilov's 28 Men: Is Russian War Movie the Whole Story?', *BBC*, 24 November 2016, <http://www.bbc.co.uk/news/world-europe-38083603> [accessed 27 November 2016].
6. Andrew Pulver, 'Russian Film about Disputed Wartime Action Wins Putin's Support', 11 October 2016, *Guardian*, <https://www.theguardian.com/film/2016/oct/11/vladimir-putin-panfilovs-28-men-film-screening-astana-kazakhstan> [accessed 11 October 2016].
7. Elena Kostomarova, 'Rezhisser fil'ma "28 panfilovtsev": "otstupat' nekuda"', 16 November 2014, *Argumenty i fakty*, <http://www.aif.ru/culture/movie/1382520> [accessed 11 October 2016].
8. Shal'opa, *28 panfilovtsev*, <http://28panfilovcev.com> [accessed 11 October 2016]; Harry Bone, 'Putin Backs WW2 Myth in New Russian Film', *BBC*, 11 October 2016, <www.bbc.co.uk/news/world-europe-37595972> [accessed 11 October 2106].
9. Shaun Walker, 'From one Vladimir to Another: Putin Unveils Huge Statue in Moscow', *Guardian*, 4 November 2016, <https://www.theguardian.com/

world/2016/nov/04/vladimir-great-statue-unveiled-putin-moscow> [accessed 15 November 2016].

10. See, for example, Putin's state of the nation address to parliament, 'Ezhegodnoe poslanie Prezidenta RF Vladimira Putina Federal'nomu Sobraniiu', *Pervyi kanal*, 4 December 2014, <http://www.1tv.ru/news/polit/273180> [accessed 4 December 2014].
11. Tat'iana Staroverova, 'V Novorossiiske glava gosudarstva skorrektiroval plany portokivov', *Novorossiiskii rabochii*, 26 September 2014, <http://www.novorab.ru/ArticleSection/Details/12606> [accessed 20 October 2014].
12. Bondar', *Uroki muzhestva*, p. 58; and I.S. Shiian, *Novorossiisk – gorod-geroi* (Moscow: Voennoe izdatel'stvo Ministerstva oborony SSSR, 1982), p. 70.

Appendix I Some Comments from Citizens of Novorossiisk

1. 'Mify – ne rify, no v farvatere "Beskozyrki" – ni k chemu!', *Novorossiiskie izvestiia*, 16 February 2011, <http://novodar.ru/index.php/novohistory-punkt/2148-mnrnvfbnkch-02-2011> [accessed 21 December 2011].

SELECT BIBLIOGRAPHY

Archival Source

RGALI (Russian State Archive of Literature and the Arts)

Newspapers and Online Information Sources

These are abbreviated on the second and subsequent mention in each chapter as indicated in brackets.

7 dnei Kubani	
9may.ru	http://9may.ru
Argumenty i fakty (*AIF*)	http://www.aif.ru
Bab'i Iary Rossii	http://www.holomemory.ru
BBC News	http://bbc.co.uk/news
Bessmertnyi polk	http://www.moypolk.ru
Federatsiia evreiskikh obshchin Rossii	http://www.feor.ru
Financial Times	http://www.ft.com
gazeta.ru	http://gazeta.ru
Guardian	http://www.theguardian.co.uk
Interfax	http://www.interfax.ru
ITAR-TASS	http://www.itar-tasskuban.ru
Iunost'	
Izvestiia	http://izvestia.ru
Kommersant'	http://www.kommersant.ru

Kommersant' Vlast'	http://www.kommersant.ru/vlast
Komsomol'skaia Pravda	http://www.kp.ru
Krasnaia zvezda	
Kuban' TV	http://kubantv.ru
Le Monde	http://www.lemonde.fr
Leningradskaia Pravda (LP)	
lenta.ru	http://lenta.ru
Literaturnaia gazeta (LG)	http://www.lgz.ru
Munitsipal'naia novostnaia lenta (MNL)	http://www.nrnews.ru
Nash Novorossiisk (NN)	http://www.nnvrsk.ru
New York Times	http://www.nytimes.com
Newsland	http://newsland.com
Novaia gazeta	http://www.novayagazeta.ru
Novorossiiskie izvestiia	http://novodar.ru
Novorossiiskie vesti (NV)	
Novorossiiskii rabochii (NR)	http://www.novorab.ru
Novyi mir	
Ofitsial'nyi sait administratsii i Dumy munitsipal'nogo obrazovaniia gorod-geroi Novorossiisk (OSA)	http://www.admnvrsk.ru/
Ogonek	
Pepsico	http://www.pepsico.com
Pervyi kanal	http://www.1tv.ru
Pochta Rossii	http://www.russianpost.ru
Pravda	http://www.pravda.ru
Pravda vostoka	
Prezident Rossii	http://www.kremlin.ru
Proza.ru	http://www.proza.ru
RBK Nedvizhimost'	http://realty.rbc.ru
RIA 'Novosti'	http://ria.ru
Rossiiskaia gazeta	http://www.rg.ru
Sem40: Tsentral'nyi evreiskii resurs	http://sem40.ru
Stavropol'skie gubernskie Vedomosti	http://www.guberniya.ru
Telegraph	http://www.telegraph.co.uk
The Moscow Times	http://themoscowtimes.com
The Times	http://www.thetimes.co.uk

Tsentralizovannaia sistema detskikh bibliotek goroda Novorossiiska	http://www.bibldetky.ru
Tsentral'naia gorodskaia biblioteka im. Gor'kogo	http://www.ballion.ru
TVMuseum.ru	http://www.tvmuseum.ru
Ural.ru	http://www.ural.ru
Vesti	http://www.vesti.ru
Volksbund	http://www.volksbund.de
Vol'naia Kuban'	http://gazetavk.ru
VTsIOM	http://wciom.ru
YouTube	http://www.youtube.com
Zerkolo nedeli	http://www.zn.ua
Zhivaia Kuban'	http://www.livekuban.ru
Znamia Rodiny (ZR)	

Films, CDs and Television Documentaries

Aleksandrovich, D., *Malaia zemlia* (USSR: 1979).
Ash, L., *Russia: Digging up the Dead* (United Kingdom: BBC Radio 4, 13 January 2014).
Babak, M., *Shel soldat* (USSR: TsSDF, 1975).
Begalin, M., *Za nami Moskva* (USSR: Kazakhfil'm, 1967).
Bessarabov, I.V., *Povest' o kommuniste* (USSR: 1976).
Brezhnev, L.I.: *'Budet khleb, budet i pesnia'* (Russia: Kapel'meister, 2005).
Chukhrai, G., *Ballada o soldate* (USSR: 1959).
Donskoi, M., *Nepokorennye* (Kiev: Kiev Studios, 1945).
Eizenshtein, S., *Aleksandr Nevskii* (USSR: 1938).
Galakon Studio, *'Malaia zemlia' Leonida Brezhneva* (Russia: Galakon Studio, 2010).
Gold, R., *Du Sollst Nicht Töten!* (Germany: 2010).
Iurina, T.I., *Teleurok grazhdanstvennosti, posviashchennyi 40-letiiu operatsii 'Beskozyrka'* (Russia: Novaia Rossiia, 2008).
Kalatozov, M., *Letiat zhuravli* (USSR: 1957).
Kolosovii, S., *Vyzyvaem ogon' na sebia* (USSR: Mossfil'm, 1964–65).
Maliukov, A., *My iz budushchego* (Russia: 2008).
Nostal'giia, *General'nyi sekretar': Leonid Il'ich Brezhnev* (USSR: Televidenie SSSR, 1976).
Oborne, P., *Unreported World: Vlad's Army* (United Kingdom: Channel 4, 4 November 2011).
Oganesian, K., *Marafon* (Russia: 2013).
Shal'opa, A., *28 panfilovtsev* (St Petersburg: Libyan Palette Studios, 2016).
Spielberg, S., *Saving Private Ryan* (USA: 1998).
SSSR TV, *Leonid Il'ich Brezhnev: Zhiznennyi put'* (USSR: Televidenie SSSR, 1973).

SSSR TV, *Podvig* (USSR: Tsentral'nyi televidenie SSSR, 1965).
Sudilovskii, A., *Zolotoe pero genseka* (Russia: tvkul'tura, 2006).

Books

Primary Sources

Adamovich, A., and Granin, D., *Blokadnaia kniga* (Moscow: Sovetskii pisatel', 1982) (first published in 1979).
Alexeyeva, L., and Goldberg, P., *The Thaw Generation: Coming of Age in the Post-Stalin Era* (Boston, MA: Little, Brown, 1990).
Anonymous, *Rubezhi Velikoi Epokhi: Fotoal'bom po motivam proisvedenii L.I. Brezhneva. Malaia zemlia; Vozrozhdenie; Tselina* (Moscow: Planeta, 1980).
Bankvitser, A.L., *Liudi nashei divizii* (Moscow: Voenizdat, 1962).
Basistyi, N.E., *More i bereg* (Moscow: Voenizdat, 1970).
Baudelaire, C., *Les Fleurs du Mal* (Paris: Pocket, 2006).
Berggol'ts, O., Druzhinin, V.N., Dymshits, A.L., Rosen, A.G., and Tikhonov, N.S., eds, *900 dnei* (Leningrad: Lenizdat, 1957).
Biriuzov, S.S., *Kogda vremeni pushki* (Moscow: Voenizdat, 1961).
Bondar', G.P., *Uroki muzhestva* (Krasnodar: Krasnodarskoe knizhnoe izdatel'stvo, 1982).
Borzenko, S., '225 dnei muzhestva i otvagi', in *Podvig Novorossiiska*, ed. A.I. Makarenko (Krasnodar: Krasnodarskoe knizhnoe izdatel'stvo, 1978), pp. 76–84.
———, 'Malaia zemlia', in *Ot Sovetskogo informbiuro 1943–45*, ed. L. Lazarev (Moscow: Agentstvo pechati Novosti, 1982), pp. 119–27.
———, *Na avanpostakh* (Moscow: Voennoe izdatel'stvo Ministerstva oborony SSSR, 1964).
———, *Ogni Novorossiiska: Podvig, rasskazy, ocherki* (Elitsa: Kalmytskoe knizhnoe izdatel'stvo, 1975).
———, *Piat'desiat ognennykh strok* (Moscow: DOSAAF SSSR, 1982).
———, *Zhizn' na voine: Zapiski voennogo korrespondenta* (Moscow: Voennoe izdatel'stvo Ministerstva oborony Soiuza SSR, 1958).
Brezhnev, L.I., *Malaia zemlia* (Moscow, Politizdat, 1978).
———, *Malaia zemlia* (Moscow and Krasnodar: Politizdat and Krasnodarskoe knizhnoe izdatel'stvo, 1978).
———, 'Malaia zemlia', in *Malaia zemlia. Vozrozhdenie* (Moscow: Prosveshchenie, 1979), pp. 1–45.
———, *Malaia zemlia. Vozrozhdenie* (Moscow: Prosveshchenie, 1979).
———, *The Great Victory of the Soviet People* (Moscow: Novosti Press Agency, 1965).
Buchevskii, B.V., *Gorod-front* (Moscow: Voenizdat, 1967).
Carell, P., *Scorched Earth: Hitler's War on Russia*, trans. E. Osers (London: Harrap, 1970) (first published in 1966).
Derzhavin, G.R., *G.R. Derzhavin: Stikhotvoreniia* (Leningrad: Sovetskii pisatel', 1957).
Efebovskii, I.V., et al., eds, *Velikaia Otechestvennaia voina Sovetskogo Soiuza 1941–1945: Rekomendatel'nyi ukazatel' literatury* (Moscow: Kniga, 1965).
Ehrenburg, I., and Grossman, V., *The Black Book: The Ruthless Murder of Jews by German-Fascist Invaders Throughout the Temporarily-Occupied Regions of the Soviet*

Union and in the Death Camps of Poland During the War of 1941–1945, trans. J. Glad and J.S. Levine (New York: Holocaust Library, 1981).

Eremenko, A., and Podyma, K., *Imenem Rossii narechennyi* (Moscow: Sovetskaia Rossiia, 1988).

Erokhin, M.V., *Novorossiisk*, ed. D.A. Vasil'evich (Krasnodar: RIO, 2012).

Fadeev, A.V., *Geroi Maloi zemli* (Moscow: Gospolitizdat, 1959).

Gaidovskii, G.N., and Uzlian, A.A., *S 'leikoi' i bloknotom: Vospominaniia voennykh let* (Moscow: Voenizdat, 1961).

Galatenko, A.F., *Katera idut k Myskhako* (Krasnodar: Krasnodarskoe knizhnoe izdatel'stvo, 1979).

Golikov, V.A., ed., *Novorossiisk* (Moscow: Planeta, 1978).

Gorbyev, M.I., and Dokuchaev, A.I., *Goroda-geroi i goroda voinskoi slavy Rossii* (Moscow: Armpress, 2010).

Grechko, A.A., *Bitva za Kavkaz* (Moscow: Voenizdat, 1967).

Grezin, V.I., *Narodnye mstiteli* (Krasnodar: Krasnodarskoe knizhnoe izdatel'stvo, 1982).

Grigor'ev, S.T., *Tak srazhalis' kommunisty* (Krasnodar: Krasnodarskoe knizhnoe izdatel'stvo, 1982).

Kaida, V.N., *Atakuet morskaia pekhota* (Krasnodar: Krasnodarskoe knizhnoe izdatel'stvo, 1980).

Kambulov, N., *Gorod-geroi Novorossiisk* (Moscow: Malysh, 1979).

Karasev, A.V., *Leningradtsy v gody blokady 1941–1943* (Moscow, 1959).

Karavaev, A., 'Post odin na ploshchadi geroev', in *Iubileinyi sbornik*, ed. G.V. Utiugina (Novorossiisk: Poeticheskii klub 'Daktil'', 2010), p. 19.

Kholostiakov, G.N., *Vechnyi ogon'* (Moscow: Voenizdat, 1976).

Kirin, I.D., *Chernomorskii flot v bitve za Kavkaz* (Moscow, 1958).

Kirpichev, R.Ia., *225 dnei muzhestva: Novorossiiskii desant 1943* (Krasnodar: Krasnodarskoe knizhnoe izdatel'stvo, 1978).

Kliunenko, A.S., 'Skarbnitsia lenins'kogo stiliu roboti (Do vikhodu knig L.I. Brezhneva 'Mala zemlia' i 'Vidrodzhennia')', *Ukrainskii istorichnii zhurnal*/8 (1978), pp. 5–13.

Kolesov, N.V., *V pamiati i v serdtse – navsegda* (Moscow: Izdatel'stvo politicheskoi literatury, 1975).

Konev, I.S., *Sorok piatyi* (Moscow: Voenizdat, 1970).

———, *Zapiski komanduiushchego frontom* (Moscow: Voenizdat, 1972).

Lermontov, M.Iu., *M.Iu. Lermontov: Stikhotvoreniia*, Vol. 1 (Moscow: Russkaia kniga, 1996).

Marfin, A.P., *Geroicheskii shturm* (Krasnodar: Krasnodarskoe knizhnoe izdatel'stvo, 1985).

McCrae, J., *In Flanders Fields and Other Poems of the First World War* (London: Arcturus, 2009).

Minakov, V.I., *Pod krylom – Tsemesskaia bukhta: Zapiski morskogo letchika* (Krasnodar: Krasnodarskoe knizhnoe izdatel'stvo, 1979).

Ministerstvo prosveshcheniia SSSR, 'Ob izuchenii v obshcheobrazovatel'nykh shkolakh knig general'nogo sekretaria TsK KPSS, predsedatelia prezidiuma verkhovnogo soveta SSSR tovarishcha L.I. Brezhneva "Malaia zemlia" i "Vozrozhdenie"', *Prepodavanie istorii v shkole*/5 (1978), pp. 17–23.

Mol'chenko, V.F., 'Geroinia "Maloi zemli"', *Ukrainskii istorichnii zhurnal*/6 (1980), pp. 118–23.

Monastyrskii, F.V., *Zemlia, omytaia krov'iu* (Moscow: Voenizdat, 1961).
Munitsipal'noe obrazovanie gorod-geroi Novorossiisk, *Novorossiiskii iunarmeiskii Post No. 1: 35 let* (Novorossiisk: Munitsipal'noe obrazovanie gorod-geroi Novorossiisk, 2010).
Murmantseva, V.S., 'Zhenshchiny-voiny Maloi zemli', *Voprosy istorii*/2 (1981), pp. 177–9.
Novikov, A.A., *V nebe Leningrada* (Moscow: Voenizdat, 1970).
Novikov, S., *Novorossiisk: Istoriia dlia vsekh* (Stavropol': Kniga, 2007).
Novorostsement, *Novorostsement: 1882–2012* (Krasnodar: Hyppogrifon, 2012).
Pedenko, M.P., *Frontovoi dnevnik* (Krasnodar: Krasnodarskoe knizhnoe izdatel'stvo, 1981) (first published in 1945).
———, *'Polundra, Krasnoflottsy!': Povest'* (Kiev: Molod', 1980).
Platonov, I., ed., *Novorossiisk: 1838–1998* (Tula: Lev Tolstoi, 1998).
Pliushin, I.I., *U sten Leningrada* (Moscow: Voenizdat, 1965).
Podyma, K., *'Beskozyrka': Cherez gody i stoletiia: Dokumental'naia povest'* (Novorossiisk and Moscow: 2008).
———, *... chtob ikh ne zabyvali my: Dokumental'nye ocherki* (Novorossiisk and Moscow: 2009).
———, *Na volne pamiati* (Moscow and Novorossiisk: Sentiabr', 2008).
———, *Schastlivogo plavaniia, 'Shkhuna Rovesnikov'!* (Moscow: Detskaia literatura, 1975).
———, *Vechnyi ogon': ty gori, ne sgorai ...* (Moscow: Pilotnoe izdanie, 2008).
Pospelov, P.N. et al., eds, *Istoriia Velikoi Otechestvennoi voiny Sovetskogo Soiuza, 1941–1945*, Vol. 3 (Moscow, Voennoe izdatel'stvo Ministerstva oborony Soiuza SSR, 1961).
Privalov, B.A., *Novorossiisk* (Moscow: Planeta, 1978).
Protsenko, V.T., *Ognennye mili* (Krasnodar: Krasnodarskoe knizhnoe izdatel'stvo, 1981).
Pshenianik, G.A., *Novorossiiskii istrebitel'nyi* (Krasnodar: Krasnodarsko knizhnoe isdatel'stvo, 1981).
Pushkin, A.S., *A.S. Pushkin: Sobranie sochinenii v shesti tomakh*, Vol. 1 (Moscow: Pravda, 1969).
———, *The Complete Works of Alexander Pushkin: Lyric poems 1826–1836*, eds I. Sproat, et al. (Downham Market: Milner, 1999).
Raikunov, A.V., *Rota, za mnoi!* (Krasnodar: Krasnodarskoe knizhnoe izdatel'stvo, 1984).
Rokossovskii, K.K., *Soldatskii dolg* (Moscow: Voenizdat, 1968).
Rozhdestvenskii, R., *Robert Rozhdestvenskii: Sobranie sochinenii v trekh tomakh*, Vol. 2 (Moscow: Khudozhestvennaia literatura, 1985).
Sassoon, S., *The Complete War Poems: Siegfried Sassoon* (USA: CreateSpace Independent Publishing Platform, 2013).
Savitskii, E.Ia., *V nebe nad Maloi zemlei* (Krasnodar: Krasnodarskoe knizhnoe izdatel'stvo, 1980).
Scott, W., *Ivanhoe* (published 1820).
Shakespeare, W., *Henry V.*
Shelley, P.B., *Percy Bysshe Shelley: The Major Works*, eds Z. Leader and M. O'Neill (Oxford and New York: Oxford University Press, 2003).
Shiian, I.S., *Na Maloi zemle* (Moscow: Voennoe izdatel'stvo Ministerstva oborony SSSR, 1971).

———, *Novorossiisk – gorod-geroi* (Moscow: Voennoe izdatel'stvo Ministerstva oborony SSSR, 1982) (first published in 1977).
———, *Ratnyi podvig Novorossiiska* (Moscow: Voennoe izdatel'stvo Ministerstva oborony SSSR, 1977).
Shveitser, V.A., ed., *Skvoz' vremia: Stikhi poetov i vospominaniia o nikh* (Moscow: Sovetskii pisatel', 1964).
Simonov, K.M., *The Living and the Dead* (New York: Doubleday, 1962).
———, *Zhivye i mertvye* (Moscow: Sovetskii pisatel', 1960).
Smirnov, S., *Rasskazy o neizvestnykh geroiakh* (Moscow: Molodaia gvardiia, 1963).
Sofronov, A.V., 'Deviatyi val: Geroicheskaia drama v dvukh chastiakh', in *Uragan: P'esy poslednykh let* (Moscow: Sovetskii pisiatel', 1975), pp. 5–62.
Sokolov, G., *Malaia zemlia* (Moscow: Sovetskaia Rossiia, 1971).
———, *Malaia zemlia: Rasskazy i ocherki* (Krasnodar: Krasnodarskoe knizhnoe izdatel'stvo, 1967).
———, *My s Maloi zemli* (Moscow: Sovetskaia Rossiia, 1979).
———, *My s Maloi zemli: Dokumental'nye rasskazy* (Krasnodar: Krasnodarskoe knizhnoe izdatel'stvo, 1985).
Sokolova, R., *Beskozyrka* (Novorossiisk: Departament kul'tury Krasnodarskogo kraia, *c.*2005).
———, *Memorial'nyi kompleks v gorode-geroe Novorossiiske* (Novorossiisk: KADO, 2006).
Teslia, M.E., Semeniuta, N.I., and Malnach, E.V., eds, *Ne pomerknet nikogda* (Rostov-on-Don: Rostovskoe knizhnoe izdatel'stvo, 1978).
Utiugina, G., ed., *Iubileinyi sbornik* (Novorossiisk: Poeticheskii klub 'Daktil'', 2010).
Veka, A.V., *Istoriia Rossii* (Minsk and Moscow: Kharvest, 2003).
Verbilo, O.M., 'Itogi Vtoroi mirovoi voiny i ee uroki v proizvedeniikh L.I. Brezhneva', *Ukrainskii istorichnii zhurnal*/10 (1979), pp. 7–16.
Voronkin, N.M., and Lavrent'ev, K.G., *Artilleristy Maloi zemli* (Krasnodar: Krasnodarskoe knizhnoe izdatel'stvo, 1982).
Vovchik, A.F., and Nemchenko, M.O., 'Vikoristannia prats' tovarisha L.I. Brezhneva 'Mala zemlia', 'Vidrodzhennia' i 'Tselina' u vuzivs'komy kursy istorii KPRS', *Ukrainskii istorichnii zhurnal*/7 (1979), pp. 113–25.
Voznesenskii, A., *Ne otrekus'. Izbrannaia lirika* (Minsk: Beladi, 1996).
Wiesel, E., *The Jews of Silence: A Personal Report on Soviet Jewry*, trans. N. Kozodoy (Philadelphia, PA: Jewish Publication Society of America, 1967).
Zagladin, N.V., Kozlenko, S.I., Minakov, S.T., and Petrov, Iu.A., *Istoriia Rossii. XX–nachalo XXI veka* (Moscow: Russkoe slovo, 2007).
Zhernovoi, I.V., *Dal'she vrag ne proshel* (Krasnodar: Krasnodarskoe knizhnoe izdatel'stvo, 1980).
Zhukov, G.K., *Reminiscences and Reflections*, Vol. 2 (Moscow: Progress, 1985).
———, *Vospominaniia i razmyshleniia*, Vol. 1 (Moscow: Voenizdat, 1969).
———, *Vospominaniia i razmyshleniia*, Vol. 3 (Moscow: Novosti, 1995).
Zhurkin, I., *Gorod-Geroi Novorossiisk: Stranitsy revoliutsionnoi, trudovoi i boevoi slavy* (Moscow: Mysl', 1983).

Secondary Sources

Aleksievich, S., *U voiny – ne zhenskoe litso* (Moscow: Palmira, 1985).
Alexiyevich, S., *War's Unwomanly Face* (Moscow: Progress Publishers, 1988).

Altman, I., *Kholokost na territorii SSSR: Entsiklopediia* (Moscow: Rosspen, 2009).
Anderson, B., *Imagined Communities* (London: Verso, 1983).
Ashplant, T.G., Dawson, G., and Roper, M., 'The Politics of War Memory and Commemoration: Contexts, Structures and Dynamics', in *The Politics of War, Memory and Commemoration*, eds T.G. Ashplant, G. Dawson and M. Roper (London: Routledge, 2000), pp. 3–85.
Assmann, J., 'Collective Memory and Cultural Identity', *New German Critique*/65 (1995), pp. 125–33.
Bacon, E., 'Reconsidering Brezhnev', in *Brezhnev Reconsidered*, eds E. Bacon and M. Sandle (Basingstoke: Palgrave, 2002), pp. 1–21.
Bacon, E., and Sandle, M., 'Brezhnev Reconsidered', in *Brezhnev Reconsidered*, eds E. Bacon and M. Sandle (Basingstoke: Palgrave, 2002), pp. 203–17.
———, eds, *Brezhnev Reconsidered* (Basingstoke: Palgrave, 2002).
Baranova, O., 'Collaboration by the Soviet Citizens with the Nazi Occupation Authorities during the Great Patriotic War: How the Issue was Represented and Treated in Soviet, Western and Post-Soviet Russian and Belarusian Historiography', in *Recalling the Past–(Re)constructing the Past: Collective and Individual Memory of World War II in Russia and Germany*, eds W. Bonner and A. Rosenholm (Iyvaskyla, Finland: Gummerus, 2008), pp. 267–76.
Bellah, R., Madsen, R., Sullivan, W.M., Swidler, A., and Tipton, S.M., *Habits of the Heart: Individualism and Commitment in American Life* (Berkeley, CA: University of California Press, 1985).
Bennett, G., and Smith, P., 'Introduction', in *Contemporary Legend: A Reader*, eds G. Bennett and P. Smith (New York and London: Garland, 1996), pp. xxi–xxxix.
Berkhoff, K.C., *Harvest of Despair: Life and Death in Ukraine under Nazi Rule* (Cambridge, MA and London: Belknap, Harvard University Press, 2004).
———, *Motherland in Danger: Soviet Propaganda during World War II* (Cambridge, MA: Harvard University Press, 2012).
Bialer, S., ed., *Stalin and his Generals: Soviet Military Memoirs of World War II* (London: Souvenir Press, 1970).
Bloch, M., 'Mémoire Collective, Tradition et Coutume: A propos d'un Livre Récent', *Revue de Synthèse Historique*/40 (1925), pp. 73–83.
Bodnar, J., 'Public Memory in an American City: Commemoration in Cleveland', in *Commemorations: The Politics of National Identity*, ed. J.R. Gillis (Princeton, NJ: Princeton University Press, 1994), pp. 74–89.
———, *Remaking America: Public Memory, Commemoration, and Patriotism in the Twentieth Century* (Princeton, NJ: Princeton University Press, 1992).
———, 'Remaking America: Public Memory, Commemoration and Patriotism in the Twentieth Century', in *The Collective Memory Reader*, eds J.K. Olick, V. Vinitzky-Seroussi and D. Levy (Oxford: Oxford University Press, 2011), pp. 265–8.
Boele, O., 'Remembering Brezhnev in the New Millennium: Post-Soviet Nostalgia and Local Identity in the City of Novorossiisk', *The Soviet and Post-Soviet Review*/38 (2011), pp. 3–29.
Bouchard, M., 'Graveyards: Russian Ritual and Belief Pertaining to the Dead', *Religion*/34 (2004), pp. 345–62.
Bourtman, I., '"Blood for Blood, Death for Death": The Soviet Military Tribunal in Krasnodar, 1943', *Holocaust and Genocide Studies*/22 (2008), pp. 246–65.

Boyer, M.C., 'The City of Collective Memory: Its Historical Imagery and Architectural Entertainments', in *The Collective Memory Reader*, eds J.K. Olick, V. Vinitzky-Seroussi and D. Levy (Oxford: Oxford University Press, 2011), pp. 378–81.

Boym, S., 'From the Russian Soul to Post-Communist Nostalgia', *Representations*/49 (1995), pp. 133–66.

———,'Nostalgia and its Discontents', *Hedgehog Review*/9 (2007), pp. 7–18.

———, *The Future of Nostalgia* (New York: BasicBooks, 2001).

Braithwaite, R., *Moscow 1941: A City and its People at War* (New York: Knopf, 2006).

Bramnik, I.I., 'Gorodskoi komitet veteranov navstrechu 60-letiiu pobedu', in *Novorossiisk: Pamiat' i pravda o Velikoi Otechestvennoi voine* (2005), pp. 147–9.

Brandon, R., and Lower, W., eds, *The Shoah in Ukraine: History, Testimony, Memorialisation* (Bloomington, IN: Indiana University Press, 2008).

Brooks, J., *Thank You, Comrade Stalin! Soviet Public Culture from Revolution to Cold War* (Princeton, NJ: Princeton University Press, 2001).

Broughton, B.B., *The Legends of King Richard I, Coeur de Lion* (The Hague and Paris: Mouton, 1966).

Brown, D., *Soviet Russian Literature since Stalin* (Cambridge: Cambridge University Press, 1978).

Bruner, J., and Fleischer Feldman, C., 'Group Narrative as a Cultural Context of Autobiography', in *Remembering Our Past: Studies in Autobiographical Memory*, ed. D.C. Rubin (Cambridge: Cambridge University Press, 2005), pp. 291–317.

Brunstedt, J., 'Building a Pan-Soviet Past: The Soviet War Cult and the Turn Away from Ethnic Particularism', *Soviet and Post-Soviet Review*/38 (2011), pp. 149–71.

Buckler, J., 'Taking and Retaking the Field: Borodino as a Site of Collective Memory', in *Rites of Place: Public Commemoration in Russia and Eastern Europe*, eds J. Buckler and E.D. Johnson (Evanston, IL: Northwestern University Press, 2013), pp. 203–23.

Buckler, J., and Johnson, E.D., 'Introduction', in *Rites of Place: Public Commemoration in Russia and Eastern Europe*, eds J. Buckler and E.D. Johnson (Evanston, IL: Northwestern University Press, 2013), pp. 3–12.

Bucur, M., *Heroes and Victims: Remembering War in Twentieth-Century Romania* (Bloomington, IN: Indiana University Press, 2009).

Bunce, V., 'The Political Economy of the Brezhnev Era: The Rise and Fall of Corporatism', *British Journal of Political Science*/13 (1983), pp. 129–58.

Calder, A., *The Myth of the Blitz* (London: Pimlico, 1992).

Campbell, D., *Methodology and Epistemology for Social Sciences: Selected Papers of Donald T. Campbell*, ed. E.S. Overman (Chicago, IL: University of Chicago Press, 1988).

Carr, G., 'War, History, and the Education of (Canadian) Memory', in *Contested Pasts: The Politics of Memory*, eds K. Hodgkin and S. Radstone (London and New York: Routledge, 2003), pp. 57–78.

Carrier, P., 'Political and Ethical Contexts of Collective Memories of the Second World War', in *Recalling the Past–(Re)constructing the Past: Collective and Individual Memory of World War II in Russia and Germany*, eds W. Bonner and A. Rosenholm (Iyvaskyla, Finland: Gummerus, 2008), pp. 245–55.

Chepurnenko, G.I., 'Poet frontovik Pavel Kogan', in *Novorossiisk: Pamiat' i Pravda o Velikoi Otechestvennoi voine* (2005).

Chiari, B., and Maier, R., 'Volkskrieg und Heldenstätte: Zum Mythos des Großen Vaterländischen Krieges in Weißrußland', in *Mythen der Nationen, Vol. 2. 1945:*

Arena der Erinnerung, ed. M. Flacke (Mainz am Rhein: Philipp von Zabern, 2004), pp. 737–51.

Clark, K., *The Soviet Novel: History as Ritual* (Bloomington and Indianapolis, IN: Indiana University Press, 2000).

Clover, C., *Black Wind, White Snow: The Rise of Russia's New Nationalism* (New Haven, CT: Yale University Press, 2016).

Colin Lebedev, A., *Le Coeur Politique des Mères: Analyse du Mouvement des Mères de Soldats en Russie* (Paris: EHESS, 2013).

Confino, A., *Germany as a Culture of Remembrance: Promises and Limits of Writing History* (Chapel Hill, NC: University of North Carolina Press, 2006).

———, *The Nation as a Local Metaphor: Württemberg, Imperial Germany, and National Memory, 1871–1918* (London and Chapel Hill, NC: University of Carolina Press, 1997).

Connelly, M., *We Can Take It! Britain and the Memory of the Second World War* (Harlow: Pearson Longman, 2004).

———, '"We Can Take It!" Britain and the Memory of the Home Front in the Second World War', in *Experience and Memory: The Second World War in Europe*, eds J. Echternkamp and S. Martens (New York and Oxford: Berghahn, 2010), pp. 53–69.

Connerton, P., *How Modernity Forgets* (Cambridge: Cambridge University Press, 2009).

———, *How Societies Remember* (Cambridge: Cambridge University Press, 1989).

———, 'Seven Types of Forgetting', *Memory Studies*/1 (2008), pp. 59–71.

Conze, S., and Fieseler, B., 'Soviet Women as Comrades-in-Arms: A Blind Spot in the History of the War', in *The People's War: Responses to World War II in the Soviet Union*, eds R.W. Thurston and B. Bonwetsch (Urbana and Chicago, IL: University of Illinois Press, 2000), pp. 211–34.

Corney, F.C., *Telling October: Memory and the Making of the Bolshevik Revolution* (Ithaca, NY, and London: Cornell University Press, 2004).

Crane, S.A., 'Writing the Individual Back into Collective Memory', *The American Historical Review*/102 (1997), pp. 1372–85.

Crossman, R., ed., *The God that Failed* (New York: Harper, 1949).

Danilova, N., 'Veterans' Policy in Russia: A Puzzle of Creation', in *The Journal of Power Institutions in Post-Soviet Societies* (2007).

Davies, R.W., *Soviet History in the Gorbachev Revolution* (London: Macmillan, 1989).

Davis, V., 'Memory for Sale: Local and National Interpretations of Brezhnev's *Malaia zemlia*', in *Twentieth Century Wars in European Memory*, ed. J. Niznik (Frankfurt am Main: Peter Lang, 2013), pp. 135–49.

———, 'Time and tide: The Remembrance Ritual of "Beskozyrka" in Novorossiisk', *Cahiers du Monde Russe*/54 (2013), pp. 103–29.

Dean, M., *Collaboration in the Holocaust: Crimes of the Local Police in Belorussia and Ukraine, 1941–44* (Basingstoke: Macmillan, 2000).

Derluguian, G.M., and Cipko, S., 'The Politics of Identity in a Russian Borderland Province: The Kuban Neo-Cossack Movement, 1989–1996', *Europe-Asia Studies*/49 (1997), pp. 1485–500.

Désert, M., 'Comment sont Regardés les Films sur la Grande Guerre Patriotique dans la Russie Actuelle?', *The Journal of Power Institutions in Post-Soviet Societies*/12 (2011).

Durkheim, E., *Moral Education*, trans. E.K. Wilson (New York: Free Press, 1961) (first published 1925).

———, *The Elementary Forms of Religious Life*, trans. K.E. Fields (New York: Free Press, 1995) (first published 1912).

Edele, M., 'Collective Action in Soviet Society: The Case of War Veterans', in *Writing the Stalin Era: Sheila Fitzpatrick and Soviet Historiography*, eds G. Alexopoulos, J. Hessler and K. Tomoff (New York: Palgrave Macmillan, 2011), pp. 117–32.

Eliade, M., *Le Mythe de l'Eternel Retour: Archétypes et Répétition* (Paris: Gallimard, 1949).

———, *Myth and Reality*, trans. W.R. Trask (Prospect Heights, IL: Waveland Press, 1998).

Etkind, A., 'Mapping Memory Events in the East European Space', *East European Memory Studies* (2010), pp. 4–5.

Fentress, J., and Wickham, C., *Social Memory* (Oxford: Blackwell, 1992).

Figes, O., *Natasha's Dance: A Cultural History of Russia* (London: Allen Lane, 2002).

———, *The Whisperers: Private Life in Stalin's Russia* (London: Allen Lane, 2007).

Fizeler, B., '"Nishchie pobediteli": Invalidy Velikoi Otechestvennoi voiny v Sovetskom Soiuze', *Neprikosovennyi zapas*/40–1 (2005).

Gallagher, M., *The Soviet History of World War II: Myths, Memories and Realities* (New York: Praeger, 1963).

Ganzenmüller, J., *Das belagerte Leningrad 1941–1944: Die Stadt in den Strategien von Angreifern und Verteidigern* (Paderborn: Ferdinand Schöningh, 2005).

Geldern, J. von, 'Radio Moscow: The Voice from the Center', in *Culture and Entertainment in Wartime Russia*, ed. R. Stites (Bloomington and Indianapolis, IN: Indiana University Press), 1995, pp. 44–61.

Gershenson, O., and Shneer, D., 'Soviet Jewishness and Cultural Studies', *Journal of Jewish Identities*/1 (2011).

Gitelman, Z., 'Politics and Historiography of the Holocaust in the Soviet Union', in *Bitter Legacy: Confronting the Holocaust in the USSR*, ed. Z. Gitelman (Bloomington and Indianapolis, IN: Indiana University Press, 1997), pp. 14–42.

———, 'Remembrance of Things Past: Soviet Histories and Jewish Memories', in *Recalling the Past–(Re)constructing the Past: Collective and Individual Memory of World War II in Russia and Germany*, eds W. Bonner and A. Rosenholm (Iyvaskyla, Finland: Gummerus, 2008), pp. 289–302.

Gorlizki, Y., 'Too Much Trust: Regional Party Leaders and Local Political Networks under Brezhnev', *Slavic Review*/69 (2010), pp. 676–700.

Halbwachs, M., *On Collective Memory*, trans. L.A. Coser (Chicago IL and London: University of Chicago Press, 1992) (originally published 1925).

Hemment, J., *Youth Politics in Putin's Russia: Producing Patriots and Entrepreneurs* (Bloomington and Indianapolis, IN: Indiana University Press, 2015).

Hervieu-Leger, D., *Religion as a Chain of Memory* (Piscataway, NJ: Rutgers University Press, 2000).

Hicks, J., 'Confronting the Holocaust: Mark Donskoi's "The Unvanquished"', *Studies in Russian and Soviet Cinema*/3 (2009), pp. 33–51.

Hirsch, M., *Family Frames: Photography, Narrative and Postmemory* (Cambridge, MA and London: Harvard University Press, 1997).

———, 'Projected Memory: Holocaust Photographs in Personal and Public Fantasy', in *Acts of Memory: Cultural Recall in the Present*, eds M. Bal, J. Crewe and

L. Spitzer (Hanover, NH and London: University Press of New England, 1999), pp. 3–23.
———, 'The Generation of Postmemory', *Poetics Today*/29 (2008), pp. 103–28.
Hirsch, M., and Smith, V., 'Gender and Cultural Memory', *Signs*/28 (2002), pp. 1–19.
Hobsbawm, E.J., 'Introduction: Inventing Traditions', in *The Invention of Tradition*, eds E. Hobsbawm and T. Ranger (Cambridge: Cambridge University Press, 2008), pp. 1–14.
———, 'The Social Function of the Past', *Past Present* (1972), pp. 3–17.
Hobsbawm, E., and Ranger, T., eds, *The Invention of Tradition* (Cambridge: Cambridge University Press, 1983).
Hodgkin, K., and Radstone, S., eds, *Contested Pasts: The Politics of Memory* (London: Routledge, 2003).
———, 'Introduction: Contested Pasts', in *Contested Pasts: The Politics of Memory*, eds K. Hodgkin and S. Radstone (London and New York: Routledge, 2003), pp. 1–21.
Hodgson, K., *Written with the Bayonet: Soviet Russian Poetry of World War Two* (Liverpool: Liverpool University Press, 1996).
Hosking, G., *Russia and the Russians: A History from Rus to the Russian Federation* (London: Allen Lane, Penguin, 2001).
———, 'The Second World War and Russian National Consciousness', *Past and Present*/175 (2002), pp. 162–87.
Hutchins, E., *Cognition in the Wild* (Cambridge, MA: MIT Press, 1995).
Huyssen, A., 'Monumental Seduction', in *Acts of Memory: Cultural Recall in the Present*, eds M. Bal, J. Crewe and L. Spitzer (Hanover, NH and London: University Press of New England, 1999), pp. 191–207.
Hynes, S., 'Personal Narratives and Commemoration', in *War and Remembrance in the Twentieth Century*, eds J. Winter and E. Sivan (Cambridge: Cambridge University Press, 2000), pp. 205–20.
———, *The Soldiers' Tale: Bearing Witness to Modern War* (London: Pimlico, 1998).
Iles, J., 'In Remembrance: The Flanders Poppy', *Mortality*/13 (2008), pp. 201–21.
———, 'Recalling the Ghosts of War: Performing Tourism on the Battlefields of the Western Front', *Text and Performance Quarterly*/26 (2006), pp. 162–80.
Ignatieff, M., 'Soviet War Memorials', *History Workshop Journal*/17 (1984), pp. 157–63.
Irwin-Zarecka, I., *Frames of Remembrance: The Dynamics of Collective Memory* (New Brunswick, NJ: Transaction Books, 1994).
Iurina, T.I., *Novorossiiskoe protivostoianie: 1942–1943 gg.* (Krasnodar: Kniga, 2008).
———, 'Novorossiiskoe protivostoianie 1942–1943 gg.: Istoriografiia problemy', in *Istoricheskie zapiski: Issledovaniia i materialy*, Vol. 4, eds S.G. Novikov and T.V. Raskatova (Novorossiisk: Kubanskoe knizhnoe izdalel'stvo, 2003), pp. 214–35.
Ivanova, N.N., 'Obraz zhenshchiny v proizvedeniikh frontovykh khudozhnikov', in *Novorossiisk: Pamiat' i Pravda o Velikoi Otechestvennoi voine* (2005), pp. 91–4.
Jelin, E., and Kaufman, S.G., 'Layers of Memories: Twenty Years After in Argentina', in *The Politics of War, Memory and Commemoration*, eds T.G. Ashplant, G. Dawson and M. Roper (London: Routledge, 2000), pp. 89–110.
Johnson, E.D., *How St. Petersburg Learned to Study Itself: The Russian Idea of Kraevedenie* (University Park, PA: Pennsylvania State University Press, 2006).

Jones, J.W., '"Every Family Has Its Freak": Perceptions of Collaboration in Occupied Soviet Russia, 1943–1948', *Slavic Review*/64 (2005), pp. 747–70.

Jones, P., *Myth, Memory, Trauma: Rethinking the Stalinist Past in the Soviet Union, 1953–70* (New Haven, CT: Yale University Press, 2013).

———, ed., *The Dilemmas of De-Stalinization: Negotiating Cultural and Social Change in the Khrushchev Era* (New York: RoutledgeCurzon, 2005).

———, 'The Fire Burns On? The "Fiery Revolutionaries" Biographical Series and the Rethinking of Propaganda in the Brezhnev Era', *Slavic Review*/74 (2015), pp. 32–56.

Jones, S.F., 'Old Ghosts and New Chains: Ethnicity and Memory in the Georgian Republic', in *Memory, History, and Opposition under State Socialism*, ed. R.S. Watson (Santa Fe, NM: School of American Research, 1994), pp. 149–65.

Kaimowitz, J.H. (trans.), *The Odes of Horace* (Baltimore, MD: The John Hopkins University Press, 2008).

Katzer, N., 'Dans la Matrice Discursive du Socialisme Tardif: Les 'Mémoires' de Leonid Il'ič Brežnev', *Cahiers du Monde Russe*/54 (2013), pp. 73–101.

Khinshtein, A., *Skazka o poteriannom vremeni: Pochemu Brezhnev ne smog stat' Putinym* (Moscow: OLMA, 2011).

Kirschenbaum, L.A., *The Legacy of the Siege of Leningrad, 1941–1995: Myth, Memories and Monuments* (Cambridge and New York: Cambridge University Press, 2006).

———, 'World War II in Soviet and Post-Soviet Memory', *Soviet and Post-Soviet Review*/38 (2011), pp. 97–103.

Kitch, C., 'Placing Journalism inside Memory – and Memory Studies', *Memory Studies*/1 (2008), pp. 311–20.

Kochavi, A.J., *Prelude to Nuremberg: Allied War Crimes Policy and the Question of Punishment* (Chapel Hill, NC and London: University of North Carolina Press, 1998).

Kolbasina, L.A., Novikov, S.G., Stepko, L.A., Trekhbratov, B.A., Shikin, V.S., and Iurina, T.I., eds, *Novorossiisk: Pamiat' i Pravda o Velikoi Otechestvennoi voine* (2005).

Koposov, N.E., *Pamiat' strogogo rezhima: istoriia politika v Rossii* (Moscow: Novoe literaturnoe obozrenie, 2011).

Kozlov, D., 'The Historical Turn in Late Soviet Culture: Retrospectivism, Factography, Doubt, 1953–91', *Kritika: Explorations in Russian and Eurasian History*/2 (2001), pp. 577–600.

Kucherenko, O., 'That'll Teach 'em to Love Their Motherland!: Russian Youth Revisit the Battles of World War II', *The Journal of Power Institutions in Post-Soviet Societies*/12 (2011).

Kudryashov, S., 'Remembering and Researching the War: The Soviet and Russian Experience', in *Experience and Memory: The Second World War in Europe*, eds J. Echternkamp and S. Martens (New York and Oxford: Berghahn, 2010), pp. 86–115.

Kurilla, I., 'The Symbolic Politics of the Putin Administration', in *Identities and Politics during the Putin Presidency*, eds P. Casula and J. Perovic (Stuttgart: Ibidem, 2009), pp. 255–69.

Lahusen, T., *How Life Writes the Book: Real Socialism and Socialist Realism in Stalin's Russia* (Ithaca, NY: Cornell University Press, 1997).

Landsberg, A., *The Transformation of American Remembrance in the Age of Mass Culture* (New York and Chichester: Columbia University Press, 2004).

Laruelle, M., 'Patriotic Youth Clubs in Russia: Professional Niches, Cultural Capital and Narratives of Social Engagement', *Europe-Asia Studies*/67 (2015), pp. 8–27.

Lazarev, L.I., *Konstantin Simonov: Ocherk zhizni i tvorchestva* (Moscow: Khudozhestvennaia literatura, 1985).

———, 'Russian Literature on the War and Historical Truth', in *World War 2 and the Soviet People*, eds J. Garrard and C. Garrard (New York: St Martin's, 1993), pp. 28–37.

Le Huérou, A., 'Where Does the Motherland Begin? Private and Public Dimensions of Contemporary Russian Patriotism in Schools and Youth Organisations: A View from the Field', *Europe-Asia Studies*/67 (2015), pp. 28–48.

Lennon, J., and Foley, M., *Dark Tourism: The Attraction of Death and Disaster* (London: Continuum, 2000).

Levi-Strauss, C., *Myth and Meaning* (New York: Schocken, 1979).

Lovell, S., *The Shadow of War: Russia and the USSR, 1941 to the Present* (Chichester: Wiley-Blackwell, 2010).

Lower, W., *Nazi Empire-Building and the Holocaust in Ukraine* (USA: University of North Carolina Press, 2005).

Lyons, G., ed., *The Russian Version of the Second World War* (London: Leo Cooper, 1976).

Maisurian, A., *Drugoi Brezhnev* (Moscow: Vagrius, 2004).

Markwick, R.D., '"A Sacred Duty": Red Army Women Veterans Remembering the Great Fatherland War, 1941–45', in *Recalling the Past–(Re)constructing the Past: Collective and Individual Memory of World War II in Russia and Germany*, eds W. Bonner and A. Rosenholm (Iyvaskyla, Finland: Gummerus, 2008), pp. 315–26.

———, *Rewriting History in Soviet Russia: The Politics of Revisionist Historiography 1956–1974* (Basingstoke: Palgrave, 2001).

Matveev, E., *Sud'ba po-russki* (Moscow: Vagrius, 2000).

Mavromataki, M., *Greek Mythology and Religion* (Athens: Haitalis, 1997).

McReynolds, L., 'Dateline Stalingrad: Newspaper Correspondents at the Front', in *Culture and Entertainment in Wartime Russia*, ed. R. Stites (Bloomington and Indianapolis, IN: Indiana University Press, 1995), pp. 28–43.

Medvedev, R., *Lichnost' i epokha: Politicheskii portret L.I. Brezhneva (kniga 1)* (Moscow: Novosti, 1991).

———, *Politicheskie portrety* (Moscow: Moskva, 2008).

Medvedev, Z., *Andropov* (Oxford: Blackwell, 1983).

Merridale, C., 'Amnesiac Nation', *Index on Censorship*/34 (2005), pp. 76–82.

———, *Ivan's War: Life and Death in the Red Army, 1939–1945* (New York: Picador, 2006).

———, *Night of Stone: Death and Memory in Russia* (London: Granta Books, 2000).

———, 'Redesigning History in Contemporary Russia', *Journal of Contemporary History*/38 (2003), pp. 13–28.

———, 'Russia', in *Encyclopedia of Death and Dying*, eds G. Howarth and O. Leaman (London: Routledge, 2001), pp. 390–1.

———, 'War, death and remembrance in Soviet Russia', in *War and Remembrance in the Twentieth Century*, eds J. Winter and E. Sivan (Cambridge: Cambridge University Press, 2000), pp. 61–83.

Mijnssen, I., *Memorial Landscapes in the Postwar Generation: The Soviet Hero-Cities of Tula and Novorossiysk in the Brezhnev era*, PhD thesis (University of Basel, Switzerland, 2015).

———, *The Quest for an Ideal Youth in Putin's Russia I: Back To Our Future! History, Modernity, and Patriotism According to Nashi, 2005–2013* (Stuttgart: Ibidem, 2014).

———, 'The Victory Myth and Russia's Identity', *Russian Analytical Digest*/72 (2010), pp. 6–9.

Mikhailov, K., 'Dmitrii Shostakovich v Novorossiiske', in *Istoricheskie zapiski: Issledovaniia i materialy, vypusk 3* (Krasnodar: Severnyi Kavkaz, 1999), pp. 268–78.

Misztal, B., 'Durkheim on Collective Memory', *Journal of Classical Sociology*/3 (2003), pp. 123–43.

———, *Theories of Social Remembering* (Maidenhead: Open University Press, 2003).

Mitrokhin, N., *Russkaia partiia: dvizhenie russkikh natsionalistov v SSSR, 1953–1985 gody* (Moscow: Novoe literaturnoe obozrenie, 2003).

Mlechin, L., *Brezhnev* (Moscow: Molodaia gvardiia, 2011).

Murphy, P.J., *Brezhnev: Soviet Politician* (Jefferson, NC: McFarland, 1981).

Nadkarni, M., 'The Death of Socialism and the Afterlife of its Monuments: Making and Marketing the Past in Budapest's Statue Park Museum', in *Contested Pasts: The Politics of Memory*, eds K. Hodgkin and S. Radstone (London and New York: Routledge, 2003), pp. 193–207.

Nadkarni, M., and Shevchenko, O., 'The Politics of Nostalgia: A Case for Comparative Analysis of Post-Socialist Practices', *Ab Imperio*/2 (2004), pp. 487–51.

Newman, J.K., 'Pushkin and Horace: Remarks on "Exegi monumentum" and "Pamyatnik"', *Neohelicon*/3 (1975).

Norris, S.M., *Blockbuster History in the New Russia: Movies, Memory and Patriotism* (Bloomington, IN: Indiana University Press, 2012).

———, 'Memory for Sale: Victory Day 2010 and Russian Remembrance', *Soviet and Post-Soviet Review*/38 (2011), pp. 201–29.

Novikov, S.G., 'Istoricheskoe kraevedenie v svete kontseptual'nogo osmysleniia mestnoi istorii', in *Istoricheskie zapiski: Issledovanniia i materialy, vypusk 4*, eds S.G. Novikov and T.V. Raskatova (Krasnodar: Kubanskoe knizhnoe izdatel'stvo, 2003), pp. 300–9.

Olick, J., 'Collective Memory. The Two Cultures', *Sociological Theory*/17 (1999), pp. 333–48.

———, 'Introduction', in *The Collective Memory Reader*, eds J.K. Olick, V. Vinitzky-Seroussi and D. Levy (Oxford: Oxford University Press, 2011), pp. 3–62.

———, ed., *States of Memory: Continuities, Conflicts, and Transformations in National Retrospection* (Durham, NC: Duke University Press, 2003).

Olick, J.K., Vinitzky-Seroussi, V., and Levy, D., eds, *The Collective Memory Reader* (Oxford: Oxford University Press, 2011).

Oushakine, S., *The Patriotism of Despair: Nation, War and Loss in Russia* (Ithaca, NY and London: Cornell University Press, 2009).

———, 'We're Nostalgic but We're not Crazy: Retrofitting the Past in Russia', *The Russian Review*/66 (2007), pp. 451–82.

Palmer, S.W., 'How Memory was Made: The Construction of the Memorial to the Heroes of the Battle of Stalingrad', *The Russian Review*/68 (2009), pp. 373–407.

Peri, A., 'Revisiting the Past: History and Historical Memory during the Leningrad Blockade', *Soviet and Post-Soviet Review*/38 (2011), pp. 105–29.

Petersson, B., *National Self-Images and Regional Identities in Russia* (Aldershot: Ashgate, 2001).

Petrone, K., *The Great War in Russian Memory* (Bloomington, IN: Indiana University Press, 2011).

Ponting, C., *1940: Myth and Reality* (London: Hamish Hamilton, 1990).

Prialkina, E.D., 'V zhizni est' minuty, kotorye ne zabyvaiutsia …', in *Istoricheskie zapiski: Issledovaniia i materialy, vypusk 4*, eds S.G. Novikov and T.V. Raskatova (Krasnodar: Kubanskoe knizhnoe izdatel'stvo, 2003), pp. 294–9.

———, 'Novorossiitsy chtiat i pomniat', in *Novorossiisk: Pamiat' i Pravda o Velikoi Otechestvennoi voine* (2005), pp. 150–53.

Priestland, D., *The Red Flag: A History of Communism* (New York: Grove Press, 2009).

Puseva, L.V., 'Frontovye pis'ma kak istoricheskii istochnik', in *Novorossiisk: Pamiat' i Pravda o Velikoi Otechestvennoi voine. K istoricheskoi istine cherez istochnik*, eds L.A. Kolbasina, S.G. Novikov, L.A. Stepko, B.A. Trekhbratov, V.S. Shikin and T.I. Iurina (Novorossiisk: Departament kul'tury Krasnodarskogo kraia, 2005), pp. 99–102.

Qualls, K.D., *From Ruins to Reconstruction: Urban Identity in Soviet Sevastopol after World War II* (Ithaca, NY: Cornell University Press, 2009).

———, 'Who Makes Local Memories?: The Case of Sevastopol after World War II', *Soviet and Post-Soviet Review*/38 (2011), pp. 130–48.

Ramsden, J., 'Myths and Realities of the "People's War" in Britain', in *Experience and Memory: The Second World War in Europe*, eds J. Echternkamp and S. Martens (New York and Oxford: Berghahn, 2010), pp. 40–52.

Renan, E., 'What is a Nation?', in *Nation and Narration*, ed. H.K. Bhabha (London: Routledge, 1990), pp. 8–22 (originally published 1882).

Richmond, S., *Russia* (China: Lonely Planet, 2012).

Robinson, N., 'What was Soviet Ideology? A Comment on Joseph Schull and an Alternative', *Political Studies*/43 (1995), pp. 325–32.

Romanov, A., 'Russian Grandparent–Grandchild Communications: Stories about the Past and Current Events', *Russian Journal of Communication*/5 (2013), pp. 141–60.

Romanov, E.V., 'Krovotochashchie rany voiny', in *Novorossiisk: Pamiat' i Pravda o Velikoi Otechestvennoi voine* (2005), pp. 158–61.

Rosenzweig, R., and Thelen, D., 'The Presence of the Past: Popular Uses of History in American Life', in *The Collective Memory Reader*, eds J.K. Olick, V. Vinitzky-Seroussi and D. Levy (Oxford: Oxford University Press, 2011), pp. 269–70.

Roth-Ey, K., *Moscow Prime Time: How the Soviet Union Built the Media Empire that Lost the Cultural Cold War* (Ithaca, NY and London: Cornell University Press, 2011).

Sakwa, R., *Putin: Russia's Choice* (London and New York: Routledge, 2004).

Saloshenko, V., *Obiazan skazat'* (Krasnodar: Severnyi Kavkaz, 1998).

Samuel, R., and Thompson, P., 'Introduction', in *The Myths We Live By*, eds R. Samuel and P. Thompson (London and New York: Routledge, 1990), pp. 1–22.

Sandle, M., 'A Triumph of Ideological Hairdressing? Intellectual Life in the Brezhnev Era Reconsidered', in *Brezhnev Reconsidered*, eds E. Bacon and M. Sandle (Basingstoke: Palgrave MacMillan, 2002), pp. 135–64.

Schacter, D.L., *How the Mind Forgets and Remembers: The Seven Sins of Memory* (London: Souvenir, 2003).

———, *The Seven Sins of Memory: How the Mind Forgets and Remembers* (Boston, MA: Houghton Mifflin, 2001).

Scherrer, J., 'Sowjetunion/Rußland: Siegesmythos versus Vergangenheitsaufarbeitung', in *Mythen der Nationen, Volume 2. 1945: Arena der Erinnerung*, ed. M. Flacke (Mainz am Rhein: Philipp von Zabern, 2004), pp. 619–57.

Schöpflin, G., 'The Functions of Myth and a Taxonomy of Myths', in *Myths and Nationhood*, eds G. Hosking and G. Schöpflin (London: Hurst, 1997).

Schudson, M., 'Dynamics of Distortion in Collective Memory', in *Memory Distortion: How Minds, Brains, and Societies Reconstruct the Past*, ed. D.L. Schacter (Cambridge, MA and London: Harvard University Press, 1995), pp. 346–64.

———, 'The Past in the Present versus the Present in the Past', in *The Collective Memory Reader*, eds J.K. Olick, V. Vinitzky-Seroussi and D. Levy (Oxford: Oxford University Press, 2011), pp. 287–90.

———, 'The Present in the Past versus the Past in the Present', *Communication*/11 (1989), pp. 105–13.

Schull, J., 'What is Ideology? Theoretical Problems and Lessons from Soviet-type Societies', *Political Studies*/40 (1992), pp. 728–41.

Schwartz, B., 'Social Change and Collective Memory', *American Sociological Review*/56 (1991), pp. 221–36.

Schwartz, B., Zerubavel, Y., and Bartlett, B., 'The Recovery of Masada', *Sociological Quarterly*/27 (1986), pp. 147–64.

Semanov, S., *Dorogoi Leonid Il'ich* (Moscow: Algoritm, 2007).

Sennett, R., 'Disturbing Memories', in *Memory*, eds P. Fara and K. Patterson (Cambridge: Cambridge University Press, 1998), pp. 10–26.

Sherlock, T., *Historical Narratives in the Soviet Union and Post-Soviet Russia: Destroying the Settled Past, Creating an Uncertain Future* (New York and Basingstoke: Palgrave Macmillan, 2007), pp. 168–73.

Shils, E., *Tradition* (Chicago, IL: University of Chicago Press, 1981).

Shneer, D., 'Picturing Grief: Soviet Holocaust Photography at the Intersection of History and Memory', *American Historical Review*/115 (2010), pp. 28–52.

Shubnikova, T.N., 'Partizanskaia gazeta', in *Novorossiisk: Pamiat' i Pravda o Velikoi Otechestvennoi voine* (2005), pp. 117–9.

Simmons, C., and Perlina, N., *Writing the Siege of Leningrad: Women's Diaries, Memoirs, and Documentary Prose* (Pittsburgh, PA: University of Pittsburgh Press, 2002).

Skinner, B., 'Identity Formation in the Russian Cossack Revival', *Europe-Asia Studies*/46 (1994), pp. 1017–37.

Smith, H., *The Russians* (New York: Quadrangle and The New York Times Book Company, 1976).

Smith, K.E., *Mythmaking in the New Russia: Politics and Memory during the Yeltsin Era* (Ithaca, NY and London: Cornell University Press, 2002).

Smith, M., *Britain and 1940: History, Myth, and Popular Memory* (New York: Routledge, 2000).

Sokolova, I., 'Bardic Song: From Exotica to Utopia', *Russian Studies in Literature*/41 (2005), pp. 83–100.

Starikova, V.D., 'Veteranskoe dvizhenie v Novorossiiske', in *Istoricheskie zapiski: Issledovanniia i materialy, vypusk 4*, eds S.G. Novikov and T.V. Raskatova (Krasnodar: Kubanskoe knizhnoe izdatel'stvo, 2003), pp. 261–73.

Steiner, G., *In Bluebeard's Castle: Some Notes towards the Re-definition of Culture* (London: Faber and Faber, 1971).

Stites, R., 'Frontline Entertainment', in *Culture and Entertainment in Wartime Russia*, ed. R. Stites (Bloomington and Indianapolis, IN: Indiana University Press, 1995), pp. 126–40.

Sturken, M., *Tangled Memories: The Vietnam War, the AIDS Epidemic and the Politics of Remembering* (Berkeley, CA: University of California Press, 1997).

Taubman, W., *Khrushchev: The Man, his Era* (London: Simon and Schuster, 2005).

Thatcher, I.D., 'Brezhnev as Leader', in *Brezhnev Reconsidered*, eds E. Bacon and M. Sandle (Basingstoke: Palgrave MacMillan, 2002), pp. 22–37.

Thomson, A., *Anzac Memories: Living with the Legend* (Clayton, Australia: Monash University Publishing, 2013).

Toje, H., 'Cossack Identity in the New Russia: Kuban Cossack Revival and Local Politics', *Europe-Asia Studies*/58 (2006), pp. 1057–77.

Tompson, W., *The Soviet Union under Brezhnev* (Harlow: Pearson Education, 2003).

Trubina, E., '"You Can See Now Just How Small All of You Are": Rhetorical Spaces of Volgograd', in *Recalling the Past–(Re)constructing the Past: Collective and Individual Memory of World War II in Russia and Germany*, eds W. Bonner and A. Rosenholm, Iyvaskyla (Finland: Gummerus, 2008), pp. 21–9.

Tsipursky, G., 'Conformism and Agency: Model Young Communists and the Komsomol Press in the Later Khrushchev Years', *Europe-Asia Studies*/7 (2013), pp. 1396–416.

Tumarkin, N., *Moscow's War Memorial: The Story of a National Symbol* (Wellesley, MA: Wellesley College, 1988).

———, 'Story of a War Memorial', in *World War 2 and the Soviet People*, eds J. Garrard and C. Garrard (New York: St Martin's, 1993), pp. 125–46.

———, *The Living and the Dead: The Rise and Fall of the Cult of World War II in Russia* (New York: BasicBooks, 1994).

Urban, M.E., and McClure, J., 'The Folklore of State Socialism: Semiotics and the Study of the Soviet State', *Soviet Studies*/35 (1983), pp. 471–86.

Vail', P., and Genis, A., *60-e: Mir sovetskogo cheloveka* (Ann Arbor, MI: Ardis, 1988).

Verdery, K., *The Political Lives of Dead Bodies* (Columbia University Press: New York, 1999).

Vinitzky-Seroussi, V., 'Commemorating a Difficult Past: Yitzhak Rabin's Memorials', *American Sociological Review*/67 (2002), pp. 30–51.

Walke, A., *Pioneers and Partisans: An Oral History of Nazi Genocide in Belorussia* (Oxford: Oxford University Press, 2015).

Walker, R., 'Thinking about Ideology and Method: A Comment on Schull', *Political Studies*/43 (1995), pp. 333–42.

Wedgwood Benn, D., 'The Teaching of History in Putin's Russia', *International Affairs*/84 (2008), pp. 365–70.

Weiner, A., 'In the Long Shadow of War: The Second World War and the Soviet and Post-Soviet World', *Diplomatic History*/25 (2001), pp. 443–56.

———, *Making Sense of War: The Second World War and the Fate of the Bolshevik Revolution* (Princeton, NJ: Princeton University Press, 2001).

———, 'The Making of a Dominant Myth: The Second World War and the Construction of Political Identities within the Soviet Polity', *Russian Review*/55 (1996), pp. 638–60.

Welzer, H., 'Re-narrations: How Pasts Change in Conversational Remembering', *Memory Studies*/3 (2010).

Wertsch, J.V., *Voices of Collective Remembering* (Cambridge: Cambridge University Press, 2002).

Wilson, A., *Virtual Politics: Faking Democracy in the Post-Soviet World* (New Haven, CT: Yale University Press, 2005).

Winter, C., 'Tourism, Social Memory and the Great War', *Annals of Tourism Research*/36 (2009), pp. 607–26.

Winter, J.M., *Remembering War: The Great War between Memory and History in the Twentieth Century* (New Haven, CT and London: Yale University Press, 2006).

———, *Sites of Memory, Sites of Mourning: The Great War in European Cultural History* (Cambridge: Cambridge University Press, 1995).

———, 'Thinking about Silence', in *Shadows of War: A Social History of Silence in the Twentieth Century*, eds E. Ben-Ze'ev, R. Ginio and J. Winter (Cambridge: Cambridge University Press, 2010), pp. 3–31.

Winter, J., and Sivan, E., 'Setting the framework', in *War and Remembrance in the Twentieth Century*, eds J. Winter and E. Sivan (Cambridge: Cambridge University Press, 2000), pp. 6–39.

Wolfe, T.C., 'Past as Present, Myth, or History? Discourses of Time and the Great Fatherland War', in *The Politics of Memory in Postwar Europe*, eds R.N. Lebow, W. Kansteiner and C. Fogu (Durham, NC and London: Duke University Press, 2006), pp. 249–83.

Wood, E.A., 'Performing Memory: Vladimir Putin and the Celebration of World War II in Russia', *Soviet and Post-Soviet Review*/38 (2011), pp. 172–200.

Yampolsky, M., 'In the Shadow of Monuments: Notes on Iconoclasm and Time', in *Soviet Hieroglyphics: Visual Culture in Late Twentieth-Century Russia*, ed. N. Condee (Bloomington, IA and London: Indiana University Press and BFI, 1995), pp. 93–112.

Yanov, A., *The Russian New Right: Right-Wing Ideologies in the Contemporary USSR* (Berkeley, CA: Institute of International Studies, University of California, 1978).

Young, J., *The Texture of Memory: Holocaust Memorials and Meaning* (New Haven, CT and London: Yale University Press, 1993).

Yurchak, A., *Everything was Forever Until It Was No More: The Last Soviet Generation* (Princeton, NJ and Oxford: Princeton University Press, 2006).

Zavorotniak, N.F., 'Proizvedeniia literatov vo frontovoi pechati', in *Novorossiisk: Pamiat' i Pravda o Velikoi Otechestvennoi voine* (2005), pp. 95–8.

Zelizer, B., 'Reading the Past against the Grain', *Critical Studies in Mass Communication*/12 (1995), pp. 214–39.

———, 'Why Memory's Work on Journalism does not Reflect Journalism's Work on Memory', *Memory Studies*/1 (2008), pp. 79–87.

Zeltser, A., 'Differing Views among Red Army Personnel about the Nazi Mass Murder of Jews', *Kritika: Explorations in Russian and Eurasian History*/15 (2014), pp. 563–90.

Zerubavel, E., *Hidden Rhythms: Schedules and Calendars in Social Life* (Chicago, IL: University of Chicago Press, 1981).

———, 'Calendars and History: A Comparative Study of the Social Organization of National Memory', in *States of Memory: Continuities, Conflicts, and Transformations in National Retrospection*, ed. J.K. Olick (Durham, NC and London: Duke University Press, 2003), pp. 315–37.

Zhuk, S.I., 'Religion, "Westernization", and Youth in the "Closed City" of Soviet Ukraine, 1964–84', *Russian Review*/67 (2008), pp. 661–79.

Zubkova, E., *Russia after the War: Hopes, Illusions, and Disappointments, 1945–1957*, trans. H. Ragsdale (Armonk, NY and London: Sharpe, 1998).

INDEX

Page numbers in italics refer to illustrations.